Studies in Jewish and Christian Literature

*Messiah and the Throne*, Timo Eskola
*Defilement and Purgation in the Book of Hebrews*, William G. Johnsson
*Father, Son, and Spirit in Romans 8*, Ron C. Fay
*Within the Veil*, Félix H. Cortez
*Jude's Apocalyptic Eschatology as Theological Exclusivism*, William Wilson
*Intertextuality and Prophetic Exegesis in the War Scroll of Qumran*, César Melgar
*The Past Is Yet to Come: Exodus Typology in Revelation*, Barbara A. Isbell

# The Past Is Yet to Come:
# Exodus Typology in Revelation

To my parents, whose challenging questions, encouraging words,
loving nudges, occasional pushes, and constant love
mean more to me than I can ever say.

And to my brother, Ben, who has taught me more
than I could ever hope to learn through academia.

# The Past Is Yet to Come:
# Exodus Typology in Revelation

Barbara A. Isbell

Fontes

*The Past is Yet to Come:*
*Exodus Typology in Revelation*

Copyright © 2022 by Barbara A. Isbell

ISBN-13: 978-1-948048-67-5 (paperback)
ISBN-13: 978-1-948048-68-2 (hardback)

All rights reserved. No part of this publication may be reproduced, stored in a retrieval system, or transmitted in any form or by any means—electronic, mechanical, photocopy, recording, or any other—except for brief quotations in printed reviews, without the prior permission of the publisher. Unless otherwise noted, all Scripture quotations are from the English Standard Version (ESV).

Typeset by Monolateral in Brill.

Fontes Press
Dallas, TX
www.fontespress.com

# Abbreviations

| | |
|---|---|
| AB | The Anchor Bible |
| *ABD* | *Anchor Bible Dictionary* |
| ACCS | Ancient Christian Commentary on Scripture |
| ACW | Ancient Christian Writers |
| ApOTC | Apollos Old Testament Commentary |
| *AUSS* | *Andrews University Seminary Studies* |
| BDAG | F. Danker, W. Bauer, W. Arndt, and F. Gingrich, *Greek-English Lexicon of the NT and Other Early Christian Literature*, 3rd ed. |
| BECNT | Baker Exegetical Commentary on the New Testament |
| *BJRL* | *Bulletin of the John Rylands University Library of Manchester* |
| BNTC | Black's New Testament Commentaries |
| BR | *Biblical Research* |
| *BSac* | *Bibliotheca Sacra* |
| *CBQ* | *Catholic Biblical Quarterly* |
| ConBNT | Coniectanea Biblica New Testament |
| *CTJ* | *Calvin Theological Journal* |
| *CTR* | *Criswell Theological Review* |
| NCBC | The New Cambridge Bible Commentary |
| *DJG* | *Dictionary of Jesus and the Gospels* |
| *DLNT* | *Dictionary of the Later New Testament and Its Developments* |
| *DNTB* | *Dictionary of New Testament Background* |
| *EDNT* | *Exegetical Dictionary of the New Testament* |

| | |
|---|---|
| *EncJud* | *Encyclopedia Judaica* |
| ESV | English Standard Version |
| *EvQ* | *Evangelical Quarterly* |
| FC | The Fathers of the Church |
| *HALOT* | *Hebrew and Aramaic Lexicon of the Old Testament* |
| *HAR* | *Hebrew Annual Review* |
| *HBT* | *Horizons in Biblical Theology* |
| HCSB | Holman Christian Standard Bible |
| HNTC | Harper's New Testament Commentaries |
| ICC | International Critical Commentary |
| *IDB* | *Interpreter's Dictionary of the Bible* |
| *ISBE* | *The International Standard Bible Encyclopedia* |
| *JBL* | *Journal of Biblical Literature* |
| *JETS* | *Journal of the Evangelical Theological Society* |
| *JSNT* | *Journal for the Study of the New Testament* |
| JSNTSup | Journal for the Study of the New Testament Supplement Series |
| *JSOT* | *Journal for the Study of the Old Testament* |
| JSOTSup | Journal for the Study of the Old Testament Supplement Series |
| JSPSup | Journal for the Study of the Pseudepigrapha Supplement Series |
| *JTS* | *Journal of Theological Studies* |
| KJV | King James Version |
| LCL | Loeb Classical Library |
| NAC | New American Commentary |
| NASB | New American Standard Bible |
| NCBC | New Cambridge Bible Commentary |
| *NDBT* | *New Dictionary of Biblical Theology* |
| NICNT | New International Commentary on the New Testament |
| NICOT | New International Commentary on the Old Testament |
| *NIDNTT* | *The New International Dictionary of New Testament Theology* |
| *NIDOTTE* | *New International Dictionary of Old Testament Theology and Exegesis* |
| NIGTC | The New International Greek Testament Commentary |
| NIV | New International Version |
| NKJV | New King James Version |
| *NovT* | *Novum Testamentum* |

| | |
|---|---|
| NTL | New Testament Library |
| *NTS* | *New Testament Studies* |
| OBT | Overtures to Biblical Theology |
| OECT | Oxford Early Christian Texts |
| OTL | Old Testament Library |
| *OTP* | *The Old Testament Pseudepigrapha* |
| *QR* | *Quarterly Review* |
| *RevExp* | *Review and Expositor* |
| *RHPR* | *Revue d'Histoire et de Philosophie Religieuses* |
| SBL | Society of Biblical Literature |
| SBT | Studies in Biblical Theology |
| SC | Sources chrétiennes |
| SJ | Studia Judaica |
| *SJT* | *Scottish Journal of Theology* |
| SSEJC | Studies in Scripture in Early Judaism and Christianity |
| *SwJT* | *Southwestern Journal of Theology* |
| *TDNT* | *Theological Dictionary of the New Testament* |
| *TDOT* | *Theological Dictionary of the Old Testament* |
| TGST | Tesi Gregoriana Serie Teologia |
| *Them* | *Themelios* |
| *TLNT* | *Theological Lexicon of the New Testament* |
| TOTC | Tyndale Old Testament Commentaries |
| *TynBul* | *Tyndale Bulletin* |
| *VT* | *Vetus Testamentum* |
| WBC | Word Biblical Commentary |
| WUNT | Wissenschaftliche Untersuchungen zum Neuen Testament |

# Contents

Abbreviations ................................................................. ix

1. Introduction ............................................................... 1
   Methodology ................................................................ 2

2. The Old Testament Foundation of Revelation ................................. 7
   Centrality of the Old Testament to Revelation .............................. 7
   Definitions and Terminology ................................................ 8
   Typology .................................................................. 15
   Typology and Apocalyptic .................................................. 19
   Summary ................................................................... 21

3. The Delineation of "Exodus Typology" ...................................... 23
   The "Content" of Exodus Typology .......................................... 24
   Connection of "Exodus Proper" and Wilderness .............................. 26
   Distinction of the Conquest ............................................... 36
   Summary ................................................................... 42

4. Expectation of an Eschatological Exodus within Jewish and
   Early Christian Thought ................................................... 45
   The Old Testament and Ancient Judaism ..................................... 46
       The Prophets .............................................................. 48
           *Jeremiah* ............................................................ 49
           *Ezekiel* ............................................................. 50
           *Hosea* ............................................................... 52
           *Micah* ............................................................... 53
           *Zechariah* ........................................................... 54
       The Isaianic New Exodus ................................................... 55
   Apocryphal Literature and the Intertestamental Period ..................... 66
   The New Testament and Early Christianity .................................. 68
       Gospels and Acts .......................................................... 69
       The Epistles .............................................................. 74
   Summary ................................................................... 77

5. Exodus Imagery in Revelation: Plagues as Paradigm for Judgment ............ 79
   The Exodus Plague Judgments ............................................... 80
       Revelation's Trumpet and Bowl Judgments ................................... 82
       Comparison with Wisdom of Solomon ......................................... 88
       Lack of Exodus Plague Imagery in other Apocalyptic Literature ............. 91
   Summary ................................................................... 94

6. Exodus Imagery in Revelation: The Passover and Paschal Lamb ............... 95
   Inaugural Vision of the Lamb (Rev 5) ...................................... 95
       Was the Passover Expiatory? .............................................. 100
   Song of Moses and Song of the Lamb (Rev 15:1–4) .......................... 103
   Sealing of the 144,000 (Rev 7:1–8) ....................................... 110

    An Examination of Σφραγίς Terminology ................................ 110
    The Identity of the 144,000 ............................................... 113
    The OT Background of the Sealing of the 144,000 ....................... 115
    The Background of Revelation's Lamb ..................................... 120

7. EXODUS IMAGERY IN REVELATION: THE WILDERNESS ....................... 125
    The Woman and the Dragon: A Survey of Salvation History (Rev 12) ......... 125
    They Shall Neither Hunger nor Thirst (Rev 7:9–17) ....................... 132
    "The Temple of the Tabernacle of Meeting" ............................... 137
    The Sinai Theophany ..................................................... 141
    "The Face of God" ....................................................... 145
    The Wilderness—A Summary ............................................... 147

8. HERMENEUTICAL SIGNIFICANCE AND ANALYSIS OF REVELATION'S
    EXODUS TYPOLOGY ...................................................... 149
    Theme and Purpose: Allegiance in a Compromising and Persecuted World ... 150
        Motif of Imitation and Fraud ........................................ 152
        The Plagues and Allegiance .......................................... 155
        The Passover and Allegiance ......................................... 158
        The Wilderness and Allegiance ....................................... 159
        "Choose This Day Whom You Will Serve" ............................... 161
    Is Revelation's Exodus Typology Isaianic? ................................ 162
    The Past Is Yet to Come: The Apocalypse as the Culmination of
    Salvation History ....................................................... 169

9. CONCLUSION AND FURTHER REFLECTIONS .................................. 173
    Summary of the Current Project .......................................... 173
    Areas of Further Study .................................................. 174

BIBLIOGRAPHY ................................................................ 177

INDEX ....................................................................... 191

## CHAPTER 1

## INTRODUCTION

THE BOOK OF REVELATION is perhaps the most mystifying and misunderstood text in the Christian canon. Indeed, its history is such that its canonicity was disputed from the beginning, particularly by the Eastern church.[1] The widespread debate and lack of consensus regarding literary, historical, and theological aspects of Revelation has led to both a plethora of interpretations among scholars and a hesitation to approach this text by lay people. Yet Revelation continues to intrigue both the casual reader and the serious scholar alike.

Without question, OT imagery, themes, concepts, types, and allusions are embedded throughout the text of Revelation, but they are often difficult to identify with any modicum of precision. Certainly there are key texts upon which John[2] relied heavily within the Apocalypse; one cannot deny the marked impact of Daniel, Isaiah, Zechariah, and Ezekiel upon John's recorded visions, and scholars have purposefully read Revelation through the lens of these particular OT texts, analyzing their prominence upon this perplexing book. As Spilsbury states in his insightful monograph, "if we are not familiar

---

[1] William C. Weinrich, ed., *Revelation*, ACCS New Testament 12 (InterVarsity, 2005), xvii–xx; Bruce M. Metzger, *The Canon of the New Testament: Its Origin, Significance, and Development* (Oxford University Press, 1987), 16; D. A. Carson and Douglas J. Moo, *An Introduction to the New Testament*, 2nd ed. (Zondervan, 2005), 732–735; etc.

[2] The matter of authorship is just one area of considerable debate surrounding Revelation. The early church seemed almost universally to identify the author as the apostle John. Weinrich, *Revelation*, xvii, xix. While modern scholars assert various proofs against the apostle John, there is little consensus as to another plausible author, and thus it seems "the wisest course of action is ... to accept in a tentative way that the Apocalypse was written by John the apostle, son of Zebedee and disciple of Jesus." Robert H. Mounce, *The Book of Revelation*, NICNT (Eerdmans, 1977), 31. However, authorship will not play a role in the argument or development of this study. The author of Revelation will be referred to as "John" in keeping with the author's self-designation in Rev 1:1, "his servant, John."

with the grand themes of books like Exodus, Isaiah, Jeremiah, Zechariah and Daniel, our ears will be deaf to the subtleties of John's masterful composition, and much of the book's message will be lost to us."[3]

Spilsbury's statement prompts the question, what illumination might be gleaned if one recognized and understood the purpose behind John's prevalent and inventive employment of exodus typology throughout his Apocalypse? Scholars regularly identify the plagues of Egypt as the OT image underlying the trumpet and bowl judgments, suggest the paschal lamb as a possible background for the Lamb, and note various allusions within Revelation to texts or events within the exodus tradition.[4] Yet they seem to take these OT allusions for granted, with little or no inquiry into the purpose behind them, their hermeneutical or theological function, and the cumulative impact when they are seen as a whole. That is precisely the goal of the present study. Through a three-pronged analysis, we will seek to demonstrate the validity of the twofold thesis—namely, that in employing exodus typology as a hermeneutical axiom throughout Revelation, John was acting in harmony with his Jewish eschatological worldview and early Christian interpretation of the Christ event as a new exodus; and that John exceeds other presentations of a new exodus, fleshing out aspects of the Isaianic/prophetic hope of restoration to represent the eschaton as the culmination of salvation history and a re-creation or reinstatement of God's initial purposes and ideals for mankind and the world.

## Methodology

The face of NT studies has experienced significant change in recent decades with the rise of newer critical methodologies such as rhetorical criticism, social-scientific criticism, narrative criticism, and postcolonial and anti-imperialist readings of the texts, many of which have been applied to Revelation.[5] In contrast to these modern methodologies, N. T. Wright has rightly

---

3 Paul Spilsbury, *The Throne, the Lamb & the Dragon: A Reader's Guide to the Book of Revelation* (InterVarsity, 2002), 37.

4 Such scholars and their notice of these issues are discussed further in chapters 5 and 6.

5 Studies of Revelation based on these newer methods include: rhetorical—Loren L. Johns, *The Lamb Christology of the Apocalypse of John: An Investigation into Its Origins and Rhetorical Force*, WUNT 2nd series 167 (Mohr Siebeck, 2003); social-scientific—Ben Witherington, III, *Revelation*, NCBC (Cambridge University Press, 2003); narrative—J. L. Resseguie, *Revelation Unsealed: A Narrative Critical Approach to John's Apocalypse*, BibInt (Brill, 1998); anti-imperial—Steven J. Friesen, *Imperial Cults and the Apocalypse of John: Reading Revelation in the Ruins* (Oxford University Press, 2001); Leonard L. Thompson, *The Book of Revelation: Apocalypse and Empire* (Oxford University Press, 1990).

asserted that the study of the NT involves the integration of three distinct disciplines—literature, history and theology—though he recognizes that at times it will be necessary to privilege one task above the others.[6]

This threefold analysis is the approach of the current project, seeking consistency with the historical, literary, and theological contexts at each stage of the study. Indeed, each of the main chapters corresponds primarily (though in no way exclusively) to one of these disciplines.[7] The study of exodus typology, however, by its very nature highlights the literary and theological disciplines, especially in exegetical discussions. The historical background of Revelation is the source of many debates, and typically raises more questions than it provides answers. Thus, historical issues such as authorship, date, and the situation of the recipients remain untreated as they are not central to the thesis itself. Whether the book was written by the apostle John or another individual, during the reign of Nero or Domitian, to recipients enduring widespread persecution or not,[8] the fact remains that the OT figures prominently as the primary source for Revelation's background imagery, and Exodus in particular functions typologically to illuminate the author's theological purposes and salvation-historical worldview.[9] Additionally, this study seeks to distance itself from debates over typical interpretive approaches (i.e., preterist, historicist, futurist, idealist), following an eclectic approach to the Apocalypse and presupposing benefits to each view.[10]

---

6  N. T. Wright, *The New Testament and the People of God*, vol. 1 of Christian Origins and the Question of God (Fortress, 1992), 11–14, 31. Wright explicates each of these three disciplines in a separate chapter: literature, pp. 47–80; history, pp. 81–120; theology, pp. 121–144.

7  Chapters 2 and 3 attend to the literary issues surrounding the NT use of the OT, typology, and the delineation of exodus typology. Chapter 4 is historical in nature, exploring the development of the eschatological hope for a new exodus within ancient Judaism and early Christianity. Chapters 5 through 7 contain a literary study of the text of Revelation, examining the presence of specific aspects of exodus typology at key points throughout the Apocalypse. Finally, chapter 8 pulls the whole project together, delving into the hermeneutical, rhetorical, and theological implications of the prominence of exodus typology within Revelation.

8  For a brief but helpful overview of these admittedly important historical issues, see the introduction in Grant R. Osborne, *Revelation*, BECNT (Baker, 2002), 1–49.

9  The study of Revelation's exodus typology may actually help to answer some of these difficult historical questions, as will be explained in the conclusion of this study (chapter 9).

10  At first glance, the reader may question whether the present project by its very nature precludes a preterist reading of the Apocalypse—indeed, the title itself states "The Past Is Yet to Come." However, the study of typology in Revelation does not prevent a preterist reading, as it is the type itself which is predictive, not necessarily the antitype. The ancient Jews and early Christians clearly understood the exodus from Egypt to be a pattern for a greater, future deliverance. John picks up on this tradition, casting the events of the end times as the fulfillment of this new-exodus expectation, whether the reader understands these events as having taken place in the first century (preterist), throughout the various ages of church history (historicist), at a distant future time (futurist), or as merely symbolic of the age-long conflict between good and evil.

The methodology for this project is multi-faceted, and includes three phases, each of which naturally builds upon the previous. The first phase involves examination of the intertextual conversation on two fronts. First, it requires interaction with major OT, Jewish, and early Christian texts which demonstrate exodus influence, noting the early Jewish expectation of an eschatological exodus event and the prophetic (particularly Isaianic) development of this hope through exodus typology. From this analysis emerges what may be an ancillary contribution for the project, namely a systematic delineation of what events, traditions, and literature should be included under the category of "the exodus." Secondly, this study necessitates consideration of the use of the OT in the NT in general, and the use of exodus in Revelation in particular. This includes the analysis and categorization of various types of allusions and the identification of background texts based on verbal, thematic, and structural similarities.

The identification of allusions to the exodus event within the Apocalypse reveals clusters of exodus imagery within particular passages (e.g., Rev 1:10–17; 7:1–17; 12:1–17; 21:8—22:5), structural sections within Revelation which seem to be modeled after specific exodus events (e.g., Rev 8:7–9:21; 15:1–8; 16:1–21), and frequent allusions to certain prominent aspects of the exodus event (e.g., the Passover and paschal lamb, the plagues, the Sinai theophany, the wilderness experience, and the Tabernacle). Thus, the second method involved in this project simply involves exegesis of certain significant portions of Revelation, examining in detail John's creative allusion to the most prominent aspects of the historical exodus in his utilization of exodus typology in the Apocalypse. While exegetical analysis of every occurrence of exodus imagery within Revelation is beyond the scope of this project, an overview of Revelation's cumulative employment of exodus allusions reveals a thematic breakdown of these texts into three main categories: the plague judgments, the Passover, and the wilderness experience (including the Sinai theophany and the Tabernacle). Detailed exegesis of major passages within each category reveals how deeply ingrained and pervasive exodus imagery is within Revelation.

The third facet of this project involves what will be referred to as typological interpretation, recognizing within Revelation the author's philosophy of salvation history which enabled him to anticipate the eschatological future in terms of the past, specifically the exodus. Thus, we explore John's hermeneutical presuppositions and theological purposes for employing exodus typology as a unifying feature throughout Revelation. Assessing Revelation's rhetorical and literary portrait and appreciating John's typological perspective not only allows his theological emphases and intentions for the Apocalypse to come to the forefront, but also ties together the various occurrences of exodus imagery into a meaningful and purposeful whole.

What purpose is there in bringing to focus Revelation's prominent use of exodus typology? To a certain extent the Apocalypse has been avoided, neglected, and feared throughout history, both on the popular and scholarly level, due to its visionary nature, perplexing symbolism, and formidable predictions. This study may help to alleviate some of the hesitancy toward Revelation by clarifying its symbolic and allusive nature in terms of the exodus, perhaps the most well-known of OT accounts[11] and the pivotal experience within salvation history prior to the Christ event. Indeed, this seems to have been one of John's goals in his abundant use of OT imagery, recording in literary and symbolic form the visions which he received from the Lord in terms of OT figures, events, and images which would have been readily recognized and interpreted within the Jewish worldview.[12]

Most importantly, this study will reveal how one particular NT author understood the eschaton as the culmination of salvation history, in fulfillment of the OT prophecies and Jewish expectations, in continuity with God's mighty acts of redemption on behalf of his people throughout history, and in keeping with Christ's own messianic self-understanding. In other words, this project may help tie together salvation history from the beginning of the nation of Israel to God's final eschatological acts on behalf of the new Israel as interpreted through the Christ event.[13]

Thus, ultimately and intentionally, the methodology and result of this project will in many ways resemble at least one form of biblical theology. As such, it will take seriously the authority of the whole canon of Scripture and seek to understand the Bible's cumulative witness to salvation history and God's works of creation and redemption. It will recognize the unity of the canon as it seeks to articulate a relationship between the two Testaments that takes seriously their distinct traditions and historical contexts as well as their common witness and divine inspiration. It will endeavor to explore the

---

11 References to the exodus are prominent throughout the Bible; no other book surfaces elsewhere in the OT more often than Exodus, and only the Psalms and Isaiah are more frequent in the NT.

12 John's first-century readers were well acquainted with the teachings and symbolism of the OT, as was John himself. John P. Newport, *The Lion and the Lamb* (Broadman, 1986), 46.

13 Scholarly speculation has resulted in a number of historical and theological debates related to issues both central to and indirectly related to Revelation (e.g., historical background/situation, authorship, date, millennial stance, tribulational position, and methodological approach). Explicating Revelation's use of exodus typology may shed some light on these questions, lending credence to one position over another and allowing scholars to make a more informed decision based on the evidence of the text itself. See chapter 9.

theological conversation between the OT and NT and discover how the two work together to demonstrate the continuity of God's mighty redemptive acts on behalf of his people in the past, present, and future. And it will do all this while attempting to comprehend and illuminate the profound mystery that is the Apocalypse of Jesus Christ according to John.

CHAPTER 2

# THE OLD TESTAMENT FOUNDATION OF REVELATION

## CENTRALITY OF THE OLD TESTAMENT TO REVELATION

THERE IS NO DENYING the complexity involved in interpreting Revelation; it is a carefully woven tapestry of symbolism, themes, and images reflecting masterful sensitivity and subtle detailing, the intricacies of which are still being discovered today. While on the one hand its message of God's sovereignty and call for allegiance are clearly recognizable by the casual reader who sees only the big picture, on the other hand unlocking the rich and sophisticated mysteries of the text requires the same care in interpretation that John exercised in its composition.

Yet the Apocalypse is also one of the most inspiring biblical writings, especially when the reader is constantly aware of and attentive to the OT imagery which saturates the text. Richard Bauckham goes so far as to claim that Revelation is "designed to be read in constant intertextual relationship with the Old Testament."[1] When one begins to listen in on this intertextual conversation,[2] it becomes evident that John purposefully alludes to OT stories and

---

1 Richard Bauckham, *The Climax of Prophecy: Studies in the Book of Revelation* (T&T Clark, 1993), x–xi. Eugene Merrill would apply this principle to the whole of the NT, asserting that "the New Testament is largely meaningless apart from its Old Testament orientation." Eugene H. Merrill, *Everlasting Dominion: A Theology of the Old Testament* (Broadman & Holman, 2006), 650.
2 For the idea of an intertextual conversation, I am indebted to Francis Watson, *Paul and the Hermeneutics of Faith* (T&T Clark, 2004), 3–6. The term "intertextuality" is difficult to define, as Porter demonstrates. Though Porter discusses the lack of conformity among scholars as to the definition of intertextuality, he does not offer a working definition himself. Stanley E. Porter, "The Use of the Old Testament in the New Testament: A Brief Comment on Method and Terminology," in *Early Christian Interpretation of the Scriptures of Israel: Investigations and Proposals*, ed. Craig A. Evans and James A. Sanders, JSNTSup 148, SSEJC 5 (Sheffield, 1997), 84–85. Nor does Watson, though he does describe Pauline theology as "*intertextual* in form,

evokes well-known OT images and events in order to provide a typological foreshadowing of what is to come and to convey the rhetorical purpose of his writing to his audience, both first-century and modern.

It is difficult to overstate the significance of the OT to John's record of his eschatological visions, for the language of Revelation is arguably "more dependent on the Old Testament than any other work of the New."[3] That the analysis of this matter has been rather neglected until recently is somewhat astonishing, but the tide of scholarship has turned and interest in the OT foundation which underlies Revelation is ever increasing. Clearly scholars are intrigued by the potential of unlocking the mystery of Revelation's symbolism and visions by uncovering their underlying background.

### Definitions and Terminology

Revelation is saturated with an astounding array of OT images, allusions, symbols, phrases, names, and titles, such that its OT foundation is inescapable. Jenkins notes that 278 of the more than four hundred verses in Revelation contain references to an estimated 250 different OT passages.[4] Yet analyzing the use of the OT in Revelation and identifying a specific OT origin for a particular image, phrase, or symbol is a daunting task with no easy place to begin. Two primary factors have contributed to this difficulty—one internal to the text itself, the other a deficiency within scholarship. First, the task is hindered by the manner in which John utilized the OT within the Apocalypse. Unlike the pattern seen in the gospels and Pauline epistles, it seems that Revelation does not contain a single formal quotation of the OT, but, rather, is replete with various degrees of allusions and echoes.[5] It is possible that this

---

in the sense that it is constituted by its relation to an earlier corpus of texts that functions as communally normative scripture." Watson, *Hermeneutics of Faith*, 3. According to Koptak, intertextuality is an umbrella term which covers not only inner-biblical exegesis but also literary theory and biblical theology, in which "the two Testaments are seen not as discontinuous, but as part of a story with recurring themes and patterns." Paul E. Koptak, "Intertextuality," *Dictionary for Theological Interpretation of the Bible*, 334. For the purposes of this study, intertextuality will function as an umbrella term indicating the relationship between two texts with regard to word, phrase, passage, or theme, or as Moyise puts it, "the complex interactions that exist between 'texts' (in the broadest sense)." Steve Moyise, "Intertextuality and the Study of the Old Testament in the New Testament," in *The Old Testament in the New Testament: Essays in Honour of J.L. North*, ed. Steve Moyise, JSNTSup 189 (Sheffield, 2000), 41.

3 Ian Paul, "The Use of the Old Testament in Revelation 12," in Moyise, *Old Testament in the New Testament*, 256; L. Paul Trudinger, "Some Observations Concerning the Text of the Old Testament in the Book of Revelation," *JTS* 17 (1966): 82.

4 Ferrell Jenkins, *The Old Testament in the Book of Revelation* (Baker, 1972), 23.

5 Moyise, "Intertextuality," 14; David A. DeSilva, *Seeing Things John's Way: The Rhetoric of the Book of Revelation* (Westminster John Knox, 2009), 147; etc.

allusive nature is simply an indication of its genre; indeed, Paulien states that the profusion of allusive references is "one of the most vexing problems in the study of apocalyptic literature" in general.[6]

Secondly, the problem is compounded by the different criteria, terminology, and definitions employed by scholars in discussing the NT use of the OT in general. To demonstrate the general bedlam that results from attempting to establish a definitive number of OT references within the Apocalypse, Paulien undertook a detailed, systematic study of ten commentators and lists of OT occurrences in the NT.[7] He noted proposed allusions to 288 different OT passages in Revelation, yet the only point of agreement across all ten studies was that Rev 9:5–6 "was written with Job 3:21 in mind."[8]

The majority of the present project will be intensely engaged in the study of John's manner of using the OT in general and Exodus in particular within the Apocalypse. But given scholarly inconsistencies regarding terminology and methodology, it is crucial to establish a set of working definitions for the various forms of the NT use of the OT before delving into a detailed analysis of the text. According to Porter, the range of vocabulary used in discussing the NT use of the OT is astounding:

> citation, direct quotation, formal quotation, indirect quotation, allusive quotation, allusion (whether conscious or unconscious), paraphrase, exegesis (such as inner-biblical exegesis), midrash, typology, reminiscence, echo (whether conscious or unconscious), intertextuality, influence (either direct or indirect), and even tradition, among other terms.[9]

The task of defining and distinguishing between these terms is monumental, and thus will be limited at this time to the four primary forms: citation, quotation, allusion, and echo.

As stated above, scholars tend to agree that Revelation does not contain a single OT quotation. But how do they define quotation? Certainly, Tenney is correct that a quotation at least "involve[s] the selection of significant amounts of wording from a previous passage, sufficient to make it certain that the author had the previous work in mind."[10] Trudinger narrows

---

6 Jon Paulien, "Elusive Allusions: The Problematic Use of the Old Testament in Revelation," *BR* 33 (1988): 37.

7 Jon Paulien, "Allusions, Exegetical Method, and the Interpretation of Rev 8:7–12" (PhD diss., Andrews University, 1987); for a concise summary of his findings see his article, Paulien, "Elusive Allusions: Problematic Use."

8 Paulien, "Elusive Allusions: Problematic Use," 49.

9 Porter, "OT in the NT," 80.

10 Merrill C. Tenney, *Interpreting Revelation: A Reasonable Guide to Understanding the Last*

the definition further, stating that a quotation is always accompanied by an introductory formula (e.g., καθὼς γέγραπται, "as it is written"), though Tenney and others classify such as a "citation."[11] Porter adds to the confusion by using "citation" as an umbrella term which he then breaks into "at least five categories ... on the basis of explicit to non-explicit citation: formulaic quotation, direct quotation, paraphrase, allusion, and echo."[12] For Porter, then, a formulaic quotation is labeled by the author as a quotation using an introductory formula, whereas a direct quotation is not introduced but contains a minimum of three words from an OT text, thereby forming a "unit of determinable syntax and conceptual relation" with its source.[13]

The matter of terminology is muddied further when moving from straightforward quotations and citations to the elusive realm of allusions and echoes. In general, an allusion consists of a word, brief phrase, or idea which can be traced to a known OT text, but in vocabulary or language that is not necessarily uniform with its antecedent.[14] Beale and Fekkes speak of levels of probability when discerning allusions, with Beale identifying the lowest level of probability as echoes.[15] Porter adds a third category, paraphrase, into the mix and distinguishes based on what aspect of the OT is being brought into the NT text—paraphrases appeal to an identifiable passage, allusions to a person, place, or literary work, and echoes to a more general notion or concept.[16]

Most often, however, scholars distinguish between allusion and echo based on the author's intent to draw the reader's mind to a particular OT text. Yet even then the dividing line is still quite obscure. Hollander, a literary critic, distinguishes between allusions as the author's conscious attempt to expand the reader's horizons, and echoes, which require neither cognizant authorial intention nor even awareness of the original source.[17] Echoes, it is often said,

---

*Book in the Bible* (Hendrickson, 2001), 102; cf. Paulien, "Elusive Allusions: Problematic Use," 39.

11  Trudinger, "Observations," 82–83. For Tenney, "a citation is a fairly exact reproduction of the words of the original text, accompanied by a statement of the fact that they are being quoted and by an identification of the source." Tenney, *Interpreting Revelation*, 102.

12  Stanley E. Porter, "Further Comments on the Use of the Old Testament in the New Testament," in *The Intertextuality of the Epistles: Explorations of Theory and Practice*, ed. Thomas L. Brodie, Dennis R. MacDonald, and Stanley E. Porter, New Testament Monographs 16 (Sheffield Phoenix, 2006), 107.

13  Ibid., 107–108.

14  Paulien, "Elusive Allusions: Problematic Use," 39; Tenney, *Interpreting Revelation*, 102.

15  Beale's classifications are clear allusion, probable allusion, and possible allusion (echo), whereas Fekkes breaks them down into certain/virtually certain, probable/possible, and unlikely/doubtful. G. K. Beale, *The Book of Revelation,* NIGTC (Eerdmans, 1999), 77–78; Jan Fekkes, *Isaiah and Prophetic Traditions in the Book of Revelation: Visionary Antecedents and Their Development*, JSNTSup 93 (JSOT, 1994), 280–281.

16  Porter, "Further Comments," 108–109.

17  John Hollander, *The Figure of Echo: A Mode of Allusion in Milton and After* (University

reflect an idea that was part of the "common domain" of the world in which the author lived; in the case of the NT, echoes indicate a mind saturated with the language and ideas of the OT, which spill over into the writer's words with no degree of forethought. Thus, scholars tend to afford echoes minimal interpretive significance in comparison with allusions and quotations.[18] Porter, however, seems unclear where or even *if* the line of intentionality should be drawn, indicating that it is possible for both allusions and echoes to be consciously intentional or unintentional.

It is often difficult to determine whether NT authors were intentionally pointing their readers to a particular OT text or whether their writings simply bear the unconscious mark of the Jewish milieu in which they were situated, and this is particularly true of Revelation. As Hays astutely asserts, "from this distance in time ... it is difficult to distinguish between intentional and unintentional intertextual references.... Because the question of authorial intentionality is a slippery one, we should not place too much weight upon it."[19] Additionally, authorial intent does not necessarily result in intertextual accuracy. The NT authors were highly creative in their use of the OT, often interpreting the OT through a Christological lens,[20] reworking the text to fit their own writing,[21] finding new meaning in the OT texts,[22] or combining

---

of California Press, 1981), 64. Cf. David Mathewson, "Assessing Old Testament Allusions in the Book of Revelation," *EvQ* 75 (2003): 312; Jon Paulien, "Elusive Allusions in the Apocalypse: Two Decades of Research into John's Use of the Old Testament," in Brodie, MacDonald, and Porter, *Intertextuality of the Epistles*, 62.

18  Mathewson refers to Fekkes's threefold classification scheme and asserts that "interpretive significance should only be confidently attached to those instances which fall into the first category." Mathewson, "Assessing OT Allusions," 313.

19  Richard Hays, *The Conversion of the Imagination: Paul as Interpreter of Israel's Scripture* (Eerdmans, 2005), 29. Likewise, Beale allows for "the possibility that later authors (like Paul) may have merely presupposed the Old Testament association in their mind, since they were such deep and long-experienced readers of the Old Testament Scriptures. This would not mean that there is no semantic link with the Old Testament text under discussion, but rather that the author was either unconscious of making the reference or was not necessarily intending his audience to pick up on the allusion or echo. In either case, identification of the reference and enhancement of meaning that comes from the context of the source text may well disclose the author's underlying or implicit presuppositions, which form the bases for his explicit statements in the text." G. K. Beale, *We Become What We Worship: A Biblical Theology of Idolatry* (InterVarsity, 2008), 25.

20  Maurice Casey, "Christology and the Legitimating Use of the Old Testament in the New Testament," in Moyise, *Old Testament in the New Testament*, 42–64; Norman R. Ericson, "The NT Use of the OT: A Kerygmatic Approach," *JETS* 30 (1987): 339.

21  For example, James's flexibility in blending allusions or ideas from multiple OT passages (e.g., Isa 40:6–7 and Ps 103:15–17 in Jas 1:10–11; Gen 15:6 and Gen 22:9–12 in Jas 2:21, 23) highlights the freedom he felt to reformulate the OT texts and make them his own. Richard Bauckham, *James: Wisdom of James, Disciple of Jesus the Sage*, New Testament Readings (Routledge, 1999), 79.

22  Craig A. Evans, "The Old Testament in the New," in *The Face of New Testament Studies: A*

multiple seemingly unrelated OT texts into intertextual clusters to reinforce their point.[23] Yet, despite this creative application, scholars do not deny the intentionality of quotations within the text. The same should be true for allusions and echoes, which incorporate less of the actual OT language but are no less effective in conveying the message of the NT writer. The fact that the traditional means of distinguishing between allusions and echoes has been based on such indeterminate and potentially inaccurate attempts to determine intentionality or motivation gives more impetus for the decision not to distinguish but to associate echoes with allusions, albeit on the lower end of the probability spectrum.

In contrast to scholars who distinguish between types of NT use of the OT based on authorial intentionality, there are those who stress the importance of the audience's recognition, indicating that intertextuality is not present if it is not accepted or identified by the reader. Hays, for example, does not seem to apply the same logic to the issue of audience recognition as he does to authorial intent. While he states that distinguishing between intentional and unintentional intertextuality is difficult from this distance in time, such that attempts should therefore be avoided,[24] he seems to have no problem determining the presence of intertextual references based on the equally subjective standard of isolating what might have been recognizable to an audience just as far removed in time.[25] Porter disagrees, asserting contra Hays that "making the success of citation dependent upon the audience runs the risk of determining literary success on the basis of the level of ignorance or information of the audience, rather than on how the author crafts the work."[26]

---

*Survey of Recent Research*, ed. Scot McKnight and Grant R. Osborne (Baker, 2004), 145.

23   For example, the conflation of LXX Exod 23:20, Mal 3:1, and LXX Isa 40:3 in Mark 1:2–3. Ibid., 137–138.

24   Hays, *Conversion of the Imagination*, 29.

25   He has set forth seven tests for discerning the presence of intertextual echoes—availability, volume, recurrence or clustering, thematic coherence, historical plausibility, history of interpretation, and satisfaction—many of which revolve around determining whether or not the first-century audience would have recognized intertextuality within a given passage. While Hays is focused on the Pauline letters, his principles are applicable throughout the NT. Richard B. Hays, *Echoes of Scripture in the Letters of Paul* (Yale University Press, 1989), 29–33. Hays delineates and elaborates on these seven criteria in his *The Conversion of the Imagination*, and gives the caveat that "no one of these criteria is decisive: they must be employed in conjunction with one another. We should also bear in mind that the use of such criteria will often yield only greater or lesser degrees of probability about any particular reading, especially where echoes are concerned." Hays, *The Conversion of the Imagination*, 34.

26   Porter, "Further Comments," 105–106. In his earlier work, Porter critiques the usefulness of Hays's seven-fold criteria for determining echoes, asking the question, "if one is writing to an uninformed audience who does not know the source text, does that mean that the echoes

*The Old Testament Foundation of Revelation*

It is evident that much of the difficulty in studying biblical intertextuality arises when terms are too narrowly delineated, resulting in a profusion of labels and a lack of consistency among interpreters. Thus, Porter suggests working with two broader definitions which would suitably cover the majority of the NT use of the OT. As such, a quotation would include "formal correspondence with actual words found in antecedent texts ... [with] debate over data, as opposed to hypotheses about reconstructed competencies."[27] The more streamlined definition of allusion would simply cover material not found in quotation, "the nonformal invocation by an author of a text (or person, event, etc.) that the author could reasonably have been expected to know."[28] Neither authorial intentionality nor audience recognition factors into either definition. This is the approach adopted by the present project, wherein a quotation involves the reproduction of a significant portion of an earlier passage, with or without an introductory formula, and "allusion" functions as a summary term incorporating all levels of allusive activity, including echoes.

This more minimalist approach to defining terminology can certainly aid in labeling occurrences of the OT within the NT, but there is still the matter of discerning the antecedent of a particular reference and how it functions within the text, a task more difficult within Revelation than in perhaps any other NT book. Indeed, the narrative of Revelation involves such a masterful interweaving of OT imagery that focusing on an individual passage, paragraph, or even a structural section is not always conclusive. Scholars must also rely on the witness of the book as a whole and the cumulative presence and pattern of specific books or themes to make an informed determination of the precise OT background of a particular allusion.[29]

To minimize the confusion, Paulien has suggested a system of categorizing allusions into three classes: verbal, thematic, and structural. Verbal allusions occur when there are at least two words parallel between a passage in Revelation and a passage in the LXX or other first-century Greek version. Thematic parallels, on the other hand, can allude not only to the LXX but also to the Hebrew and Aramaic OT, and are characterized by similarities in thought,

---

are no longer present? If they are clear to another audience, does that mean that the text itself is now different, or only the audience?" Idem, "OT in the NT," 83.

27  Ibid., 95.
28  Ibid.
29  Fekkes, *Prophetic Traditions*, 62–63; G. B. Caird, *A Commentary on the Revelation of St. John the Divine*, HNTC (Harper & Row, 1966), 319–320. As Beale states, "Some of the evidence will be stronger than others, but when all of the relevant material is viewed as a whole, the less convincing material should become more significant than when seen by itself." Beale, *We Become What We Worship*, 33.

focus, or "contextual mooring," or even deliberate contrast. Unlike verbal parallels, thematic allusions have variations in wording or only a single word in common with the LXX.[30]

Paulien's third classification of allusion, structural parallels, consists of an interconnecting combination of verbal and thematic parallels, and occurs when an entire section of Revelation is framed around the literary or theological structure of a significant passage of OT text, though without any necessary linguistic connection.[31] Structural allusions are not limited to parallel passages but may also refer to larger historical or theological structures that transcend individual passages to be found more broadly throughout the OT. The NT writers were aware of wider OT contexts and did not focus merely on single verses independent of the segments from which they were taken. Rather, "single verses and phrases are merely signposts to the overall Old Testament context from which they were cited."[32] This seems to be especially true within the Apocalypse. For example, John's vision of the New Heaven and New Earth in Rev 21–22 appears to be modeled upon the accounts of creation and the Fall in Gen 1–3, with complete and seemingly intentional reversal such that God's creation is finally how he intended it to be. Table 2.1[33] demonstrates this structural connection:

---

30  Paulien, "Elusive Allusions: Problematic Use," 41–43; David Mathewson, "Assessing OT Allusions," 311. Scholars have struggled with the identity of John's textual source. Verbal differences between the text of Revelation and the LXX led Charles to determine that John drew directly from the Hebrew or Aramaic text, implying that John would have followed the text of the LXX more closely if he had been familiar with it. R. H. Charles, *A Critical and Exegetical Commentary on The Revelation of St. John: With Introduction, Notes, and Indices, also the Greek Text and English Translation*, 2 vols., ICC (T&T Clark, 1920), 1:lxii–lxvii. In contrast, the majority of scholars agree with Swete that John's primary text was the LXX. H. B. Swete, *The Apocalypse of St. John: The Greek Text with Introduction, Notes, and Indices* (Macmillan, 1906), cl–cli. This problem, like many others, is compounded by the highly allusive nature of the Apocalypse. It seems clear that John's purpose was not to quote texts at all, regardless of the source, and differences from the LXX or MT are likely due more to his "particular way of using Scripture" than his dependence upon or lack of knowledge of any one particular source text. Moyise concludes that "John makes use of both Greek and Semitic sources and is not solely dependent on either the Greek (*contra* Swete) or the Hebrew (*contra* Ozanne)." Steve Moyise, *The Old Testament in the Book of Revelation*, JSNTSup 115 (Sheffield, 1995), 17 n.25; for the full argument, see chapter 7 of Steve Moyise, "The Use of the Old Testament in the Book of Revelation," (PhD diss., University of Birmingham, 1994).

31  Paulien, "Elusive Allusions: Problematic Use," 41–43.

32  G. K. Beale, "Positive Answer to the Question: Did Jesus and His Followers Preach the Right Doctrine from the Wrong Texts? An Examination of the Presuppositions of Jesus' and the Apostles' Exegetical Method," in *The Right Doctrine from the Wrong Texts? Essays on the Use of the Old Testament in the New*, ed. G. K. Beale (Baker, 1994), 390; C. H. Dodd, *According to the Scriptures: The Sub-Structure of New Testament Theology* (Nisbet, 1952), 126–127.

33  Modified from Bruce K. Waltke, *An Old Testament Theology: An Exegetical, Canonical, and Thematic Approach* (Zondervan, 2007), 169.

|  | **First Creation**<br>*Gen 1–3*<br>"In the beginning God created the heavens and the earth" (1:1) | **Final Creation**<br>*Rev 21–22*<br>"Then I saw a new heaven and a new earth" (21:1) |
|---|---|---|
| Source of light | Luminaries – sun, etc. (1:16) | God (21:23) |
| Division of light | Day and Night (1:5) | No night (21:25) |
| Creation | Under a curse (3:17) | Curse lifted (22:3) |
| Satan | Appears as deceiver of man (3:1) | Disappears forever (20:10) |
| Human moral state | Capable of sin (3:6–7) | Sinless (21:7, 27) |
| Human physical state | Mortal and painful (2:17, 3:16) | Immortal and painless (21:4) |
| Human political state | Divided in allegiance (3:12–13) | Universal allegiance to God (22:3–4) |
| Human spiritual state | Banished from God (3:8–10; 23) | God with humans (21:3; 22:5) |
| Water | Provides physical life (2:5–6) | Provides spiritual life (21:6; 22:1) |
| Tree of Life | Access lost in Adam (3:24) | Access gained in Christ (22:14) |
| Victory | Initial triumph of the serpent (3:13) | Ultimate triumph of the Lamb (20:10; 22:3) |
| Man's dominion | Broken in Adam (3:19) | Restored in Christ (22:5) |
| God | Invisible, man driven from God's presence (3:24) | Visible, "they will see his face" (22:4) |

Table 2.1: Comparison of Genesis 1–3 and Revelation 21–22

It is not a single verbal or thematic allusion but the cumulative effect of John's vision over these two chapters, replete with verbal hints and thematic imagery, that clearly and conclusively points back to Gen 1–3 as the structural background for Revelation's New Heaven and New Earth. Though verbal allusions are perhaps the easiest parallels to notice and tie to a particular OT text, structural allusions tend to be built into the actual framework of the text and thus carry the most weight theologically and are "the most easily proven to have been in the mind of the writer when he wrote down his visions."[34]

## Typology

In addition to using citations, quotations, and various sorts of allusions, the NT writers employed the OT typologically. Typology, both its definition and its use as a mode of interpretation, is often misunderstood, and is thus

---

34 Paulien, "Elusive Allusions: Problematic Use," 43.

frequently misidentified within Scripture and misused or rejected as a valid manner for modern scholars to read Scripture. To move forward with this project, then, it is necessary to clarify what is meant (and not meant) by the term "typology."

Much of the confusion regarding typology centers on the lack of a consistent definition and approach. Hoskins distinguishes between the "traditional" and the "modern" approaches to typology within scholarship, outlining them in great detail.[35] Certainly there are commonalities between the two approaches. For instance, both camps would affirm I. Howard Marshall's description of typology as "the study which traces parallels or correspondences between incidents recorded in the Old Testament and their counterparts in the New Testament such that the latter can be seen to resemble the former in notable respects and yet to go beyond them."[36] In addition, both identify significant[37] correspondences between persons, institutions, and events within a framework of promise and fulfillment, and acknowledge that such correspondences are not unique to the NT but can be seen within the OT as well, particularly in the prophetic writings. Finally, most scholars understand typology to entail some degree of escalation or progression.[38]

The distinction between the two approaches to typology concerns not what the above definition affirms but what is not explicitly stated within it. Marshall himself seems to recognize that his definition is not entirely

---

35  Paul M. Hoskins, *Jesus as the Fulfillment of the Temple in the Gospel of John*, Paternoster Biblical Monographs (Wipf and Stock, 2006), 18–32. This section is a summary of Hoskins's findings, and as such is heavily indebted to his work and terminology. Hoskins's more popular-level monograph on typology also provides many helpful insights. Idem, *That Scripture Might Be Fulfilled: Typology and the Death of Christ* (Xulon, 2009). Cf. John H. Stek, "Biblical Typology Today and Yesterday," *CTJ* 5 (1970): 133–162; David L. Baker, "Typology and the Christian Use of the Old Testament," in Beale, *Right Doctrine*, 314–315.

36  I. Howard Marshall, "An Assessment of Recent Developments," in *It Is Written: Scripture Citing Scripture; Essays in Honour of Barnabas Lindars*, ed. D. A. Carson and H. G. M. Williamson (Cambridge University Press, 1988), 16.

37  The word "significant" is key for Hoskins, who notes that "typology has often been caricatured as fanciful, because it has been practiced in a haphazard fashion ... failing to establish a significant correspondence between the type and antitype." Hoskins, *Jesus as Fulfillment*, 19. One of the most common examples is the association drawn by some early church fathers between Rahab's scarlet thread and salvation through the blood of Christ. Such an arbitrary approach to typology has resulted in typology being falsely equated with allegory, and as such being rejected alongside allegory as a valid means of interpretation. It is important, however, to recognize that typology is quite distinct from allegory, in which "no real correspondence, historical or theological, between the Old Testament history and the application is required." R. T. France, *Jesus and the Old Testament: His Application of Old Testament Passages to Himself and His Mission* (Tyndale, 1971), 40; cf. Baker, "Typology," 324. For a helpful explanation of the differences between allegory and typology, as well as an explanation of how the two came to be conflated, see Hoskins, *That Scripture Might Be Fulfilled*, 30–33.

38  Hoskins, *Jesus as Fulfillment*, 19–20.

sufficient, for he goes on to ask one of the most pertinent questions in the study of typology, namely, "whether the OT incident was thought to have been deliberately planned as a type for its antitype."[39] This issue, the inherent predictive or prospective nature of types, hits at the crux of the typology debate. The "traditional" view of typology rests squarely upon an understanding of salvation history as the working out of God's teleological plan of redemption throughout the history of his people. By reading the record of salvation history in Scripture, one finds that God's actions of leading and delivering his people reveal certain intentional patterns, such that the type has a distinctly prophetic nature, prefiguring and predicting its goal, which fulfills, surpasses, and ultimately replaces the OT type.[40] In other words, God is active in directing the story of his people; correspondences between events are not coincidental similarities but are part of God's progressive work in history, intended to reveal not only God's promises but also his plan of redemption.[41]

In contrast, the "modern" approach to typology is an attempt to harmonize typology with critical scholarship.[42] As such, this approach denies the predictive element, as the forward reference within the type would go beyond authorial intent to a further meaning hidden to the author.[43] The inherent demythologization within critical scholarship initially categorized traditional typology as "unscientific" and has ultimately yielded an approach to typology that is simply the retrospective recognition that God works in familiar, consistent patterns of promise and fulfillment, and the resultant description of NT events, places, or individuals based on an OT prototype.[44]

---

39  Marshall, "Assessment," 16.
40  Hoskins, *Jesus as Fulfillment*, 22–23; cf. idem, *That Scripture Might Be Fulfilled*, 20–23. According to von Hofmann, the events recorded in the OT are of the same nature as their goal (the full realization of the history of salvation as recorded in the NT), though they are "modified by their respective place in history. Since the course and the events of that history are determined by their goal, this goal will manifest itself in all important stages of its progress in a way which, though preliminary, prefigures it." J. C. K. von Hofmann, *Interpreting the Bible*, trans. Christian Preus (Ausburg, 1959), 135.
41  Hoskins, *That Scripture Might Be Fulfilled*, 22.
42  Hoskins, *Jesus as Fulfillment*, 31.
43  Ibid., 23. See, for example, France, who states that "typology may, indeed must, go beyond mere exegesis. But it may never introduce into the Old Testament text a principle which was not already present and intelligible to its Old Testament readers." France, *Jesus and the Old Testament,* 41. Indeed, France actually distinguishes typology from the appeal to prediction, stating that "a prediction looks forward to, and demands, an event which is to be its fulfilment; typology, however, consists essentially in looking back and discerning previous examples of a pattern now reaching its culmination." Ibid., 40.
44  Friedbert Ninow, *Indicators of Typology within the Old Testament: The Exodus Motif,* Friedensauer Schriftenreihe; Reihe I, Theologie, Bd. 4 (Peter Lang, 2001), 17; cf. Hoskins, *Jesus as Fulfillment,* 20–21; G. W. H. Lampe, "The Reasonableness of Typology," in *Essays on Typology*, ed. G. W. H. Lampe and K. J. Woollcombe, SBT 22 (Allenson, 1957), 29.

It is evident that this distinction between the two approaches to typology has at its very heart several closely intertwined presuppositions—historicity, inspiration, and the unity of Scripture. Proponents of traditional typology take very seriously the historical validity of the salvation-historical events and the record of those events found in Scripture, such that a type had a significant historical purpose at its original occurrence but was also divinely fashioned to fulfill a role within God's redemptive plan.[45] This traditional approach to typology necessitates something more than just human authorial intent, and strongly affirms the divine inspiration of the entire canon. The OT and NT are a unified whole, held together by a single divine author, the same God whose sovereign purposes are worked out through history and in the Scriptures.[46]

On the other hand, the modern approach to typology, guided in large part by the historical-critical tendency to snub "fanciful" ideas such as inspiration, unity, and historicity, refuses to make any claims that must be based on these presuppositions. This is not to suggest that they reject these presuppositions outright. Rather, they approach the study of Scripture from a hermeneutic of suspicion so that their interpretation is in no way dependent upon them. Hence, proponents of modern typology often buy into one or more of the following: a focus on the human author rather than divine inspiration, devaluation of the canon as a cohesive whole,[47] skepticism regarding the historical accuracy of the OT,[48] and speculation that the NT writers advanced their own agenda by modifying the details of the first century events and recording them in the rich significance of OT imagery.[49] In certain cases,

---

45 Stek, "Biblical Typology," 139; cf. 160–161, discussing Fairbairn's understanding of typology (Patrick Fairbairn, *The Typology of Scripture: Two Volumes in One, Complete and Unabridged* [Zondervan, 1967], 67). According to Hoskins, types are by their very nature prophetic, intended to point forward to something greater, the *telos* or goal. The prophetic import of a type is often best recognized by examining the context of OT quotations within the NT, whereas the OT passage itself "will normally appear to have more to do with Israel's history than with prophecy regarding the future of God's people." Hoskins, *That Scripture Might Be Fulfilled*, 24; Hoskins, *Jesus as Fulfillment*, 26–27.

46 Hoskins, *Jesus as Fulfillment*, 23–25.

47 Gerhard von Rad, *The Theology of Israel's Prophetic Traditions*, vol. 2 of *Old Testament Theology*, trans. D. M. G. Stalker (Harper & Row, 1965), 362; cf. Hoskins, *Jesus as Fulfillment*, 27.

48 Rather, one might question whether there is any historical basis for Israel's foundational beliefs as set forth in the OT. Von Rad notes that, in the secular world, by the seventeenth century "classical and historical scholarship had ... begun to undermine the old idea of saving history. Typology began unconsciously to alter completely. It more and more lost its old connexion with historical facts and concerned itself—as for example in Michaelis—with 'the general truths of religion,' which were regarded as 'symbolically set forth for all time' in the Old Testament. Typology thus turned into a general study of symbols and pictures." Von Rad, *Israel's Prophetic Traditions*, 366.

49 "The events came to be clothed, as it were, in Old Testament dress, and thereby came

then, modern typology has become little more than a literary enterprise, utilizing patterns to depict entities within the NT in terms of the OT.[50]

Thus, while on the surface the traditional and modern approaches to typology may appear to agree, their underlying presuppositions seem incongruent, and their resulting conclusions regarding the purpose and theological import of typology cannot be reconciled. For the current project, the traditional, canonical approach to typology (as set forth above) is the starting point—typology is the theological interpretation of God's history among his people, observing correspondences or patterns within Scripture and presupposing the continuity of God's purpose and action throughout history. Typology highlights the prophetic nature of the OT types, the progressive repetition of the acts of God, and the ultimate fulfillment or replacement of OT types within the record of the NT. The NT antitypes are often characterized by intensification or escalation, exceeding the OT type or possessing traits not attributed to the original type.[51]

## Typology and Apocalyptic[52]

Leonhard Goppelt concluded that, due to its frequency and its very nature, typology is the dominant and characteristic manner in which the NT interprets the OT.[53] Certainly, this was the example Jesus set forth, as he taught his disciples to read the OT through a Christological lens and specifically

---

to acquire a richer significance, so that the more closely a narrative could be assimilated to scriptural imagery, the more readily could its full significance be apprehended by men whose ideas found their natural expression in terms of the Hebraic history, prophecies, and liturgy...." Lampe, "Reasonableness of Typology," 19.

50  Von Rad, *Israel's Prophetic Traditions*, 368; K. H. Woollcombe, "The Biblical Origins and Patristic Development of Typology," in Lampe and Woollcombe, *Essays on Typology*, 39–40.

51  Hoskins, *Jesus as Fulfillment*, 21–27.

52  While there remains intense discussion related to the understanding of apocalypse (as well as related concepts such as apocalyptic and apocalypticism), the present study will seek to remain true to the working definition of apocalypse offered by the SBL study group: "a genre of revelatory literature with a narrative framework, in which a revelation is mediated by an otherworldly being to a human recipient, disclosing a transcendent reality which is both temporal, insofar as it envisages eschatological salvation, and spatial insofar as it involves another, supernatural world." John J. Collins, ed., *Apocalypse: The Morphology of a Genre,* Semeia 14 (Scholars, 1979), 9. The majority of the ongoing debate concerns whether apocalypse should be regarded as a genre or simply the literary outgrowth of an ideology. For further discussion on these matters, see John J. Collins, *The Apocalyptic Imagination: An Introduction to Jewish Apocalyptic Literature*, 2nd ed., The Biblical Resource Series (Eerdmans, 1988); Craig R. Koester, *Revelation and the End of All Things* (Eerdmans, 2001); and L. J. Kreitzer, "Apocalyptic, Apocalypticism," *DLNT* 55–68.

53  Leonhard Goppelt, *Typos: The Typological Interpretation of the Old Testament in the New*, trans. Donald H. Madvig (Eerdmans, 1982), 200.

highlighted several types concerning himself.⁵⁴ The earliest Christians understood the history recorded in the OT to contain certain patterns divinely ordained specifically to foreshadow the period of the eschaton, and thus they often employed typology to portray the end times in terms of God's unfailing faithfulness in fulfilling his promises.⁵⁵

Apocalypticism in particular is known for employing historical experiences to portray future events typologically, due in large part to its starting point in the post-exilic era. At a time when God's relative silence was pervasively perceived in the cessation of prophecy, at a time when it seemed the exile had never ended, at a time when the lack of explicit saving activity caused God's people to fear that he had abandoned them, apocalypticism broke forth. So it was that "God's silence was broken by the renewal of his past promises in their relevance to the present. God had not abandoned his people; his promised salvation was coming.... [Apocalyptic] ensured the survival of hope."⁵⁶

While the revelatory form of apocalyptic literature necessarily shifts the reader's attention from earthly history to visions of the eternal heavenly stage, and from this age to the age to come, these works are "often colorfully portrayed by various rehearsals or 'recitals' of Israel's past."⁵⁷ This typological

---

54 E.g., the serpent being lifted up in the wilderness as a type of Christ's crucifixion (John 3:14–15); Jonah's experience and ministry as a type of Jesus' ministry and passion (Matt 12:39–41; Luke 11:29–32); David as a type of Christ (Mark 12:35–37; Matt 12:42). See C. A. Evans, "Typology," *DJG* 863–865; cf. France, *Jesus and the Old Testament*, 75.

55 In fact, in Jewish literature contemporary to the NT, typology is found solely in the development of eschatology. Goppelt, *Typos*, 200; David A. DeSilva, "Final Topics: The Rhetorical Functions of Intertexture in Revelation 14:14–16:21," in *The Intertexture of Apocalyptic Discourse in the New Testament*, ed. Duane F. Watson, SBL Symposium Series 14 (SBL, 2002), 231; Beale, "Positive Answer to the Question," 394; Ninow, *Indicators of Typology*, 100. According to Davidson, "it is not to just any similar realities that the OT τύποι ... are linked. Rather the OT persons/events/institutions find their fulfillment ... in the *eschatological* realities of the NT." Richard M. Davidson, *Typology in Scripture: A Study of Hermeneutical τύπος Structures*, Andrews University Seminary Doctoral Dissertation Series 2 (Andrews University Press, 1981), 398, emphasis original.

56 Richard J. Bauckham, "The Rise of Apocalyptic," *Them* 3.2 (1978): 20–21. Bauckham indicates that there is never an absolute contrast between the two ages; rather, apocalyptic involves a typological view of history in which God's future actions are not divorced from those in the past but are in consonance with and even prefigured by his actions throughout salvation history. Cf. Carol A. Newsom, "The Past as Revelation: History in Apocalyptic Literature," *QR* 4.3 (1984): 42.

57 Mark Adam Elliott, *The Survivors of Israel: A Reconsideration of the Theology of Pre-Christian Judaism* (Eerdmans, 2000), 356. In his chapter entitled "A New Approach to Apocalyptic Forms," Elliott examines the process of historical rehearsal in a number of apocalyptic works, including 1 Enoch, Jubilees, Assumption of Moses, Testaments of the Twelve Patriarchs, 4 Ezra, and 2 Baruch. The historical rehearsals not only contain independent worth, but also provide a helpful framework for interpreting the apocalyptic message. Aristotle spoke to the rhetorical technique of using historical precedents to make a case: "While the lessons conveyed by fables

perspective of history enabled the early apocalypticists to hold fast to their faith in the God who rules history in spite of present feelings of abandonment. In the NT writings, the negative view of the present was replaced by an understanding that God had acted in the present age in a decisively eschatological way through the death and resurrection of Jesus.[58] Thus, given the significance of typology for the NT authors and early Christians, as well as its role in apocalyptic literature in general, it is only natural, even prudent, to approach the book of Revelation with an eye for typology, instances in which John records his visionary experiences of the end times in terms of the historical events which foretold them.

## Summary

This chapter has set forth much of the necessary foundation for the study of exodus typology in the Apocalypse. We have delineated the definitions of key terminology related to the NT use of the OT, determining that Revelation is exclusively allusive and creatively contextual in its use of Scripture. Additionally, we have contrasted the two major approaches to typology—traditional and modern—and concluded that the traditional approach, which takes seriously the divinely intended, prospective nature of types, is most in keeping with the presuppositions of the NT writers and thus is the understanding followed by the current study. Moving forward, we must examine one final background element before delving into the text of Revelation—namely, what exactly is meant by exodus typology and how the expectation of an eschatological exodus developed within Jewish and early Christian thought prior to the Apocalypse.

---

are easier to provide, those derived from facts are more useful for deliberative oratory, because as a rule the future resembles the past" (*Rhet.* 2.20.8). DeSilva, "Final Topics," 233; see also Dan Lioy, *The Book of Revelation in Christological Focus*, SBL 58 (Peter Lang, 2003), 103.

58  Bauckham, "Rise of Apocalyptic," 22. Newsom summarizes well the NT application of apocalypticism: "The authentic appropriation of apocalyptic hope does not consist in attempts to predict the eschaton but in experiencing the events of human history as already participating in the paradigmatic event and anticipating its final resolution." Newsom, "Past as Revelation," 52.

CHAPTER 3

## THE DELINEATION OF "EXODUS TYPOLOGY"

SCRIPTURE IS REPLETE with occurrences of historical rehearsal, occasions when the people of God recount his mighty works as a means of both remembering God's action on their behalf throughout history and expressing their hope for even greater acts in the future.[1] This sense of anticipation for the future is often conveyed through typology. A typological reading of the events, purposes, and circumstances of the exodus from Egypt, God's first great deliverance of his chosen people, is perhaps the most prevailing example.[2] The commemoration and paradigmatic significance of the exodus is evident in the content of Israel's covenant code (see Exod 19:3–8; 24:1–18), Israel's ethical and legal instructions (e.g., Exod 22:21; Deut 10:18–19; 15:15), and especially the liturgy of ancient religious festivals (see Exod 13:8; Deut 5:2–4), in which the exodus was contemporized by celebrators of subsequent generations.[3] Indeed, according to Plastaras, "the first great affirmation of

---

1 According to Foulkes, "For Israel, history was never simply the narration of past events. Throughout the Old Testament history is written theologically; and behind the actual writing of this history lay the practice, its roots far back in the nation's past, of the rehearsal of the former acts of God. The people were held responsible for making these acts known to each succeeding generation.... They were to tell the meaning of the memorials that were set up to commemorate what God had done.... The people are urged to know and to remember history, because history is instruction in the ways of God." Francis Foulkes, "The Acts of God: A Study of the Basis of Typology in the Old Testament," in *The Right Doctrine from the Wrong Texts? Essays on the Use of the Old Testament in the New*, ed. G. K. Beale (Baker, 1994), 353.

2 Jean Daniélou, *From Shadows to Reality: Studies in the Biblical Typology of the Fathers*, trans. Wulstan Hibberd (Burns & Oates, 1960), 153–166; Nahum M. Sarna, *Exploring Exodus: The Origins of Biblical Israel* (1986; repr., Pantheon Books, 1996), 1–2; etc.

3 Friedbert Ninow, *Indicators of Typology within the Old Testament: The Exodus Motif*, Friedensauer Schriftenreihe; Reihe I, Theologie, Bd. 4 (Peter Lang, 2001), 98; cf. J. Muilenburg, *The Way of Israel: Biblical Faith and Ethics* (Harper, 1961), 48–54. Ninow refers to this contemporization as the "You-Were-There" Motif, the Israelites' obedience to the instruction to keep the Passover as a "lasting ordinance for you and your descendants" (Exod 12:24). This is evidenced

Israel's faith always has been: 'Yahweh freed us from the land of Egypt, from the house of bondage' (Ex 20:1; Dt 5:6; 6:21; Ps 81:10)."[4]

Jewish and early Christian eschatology in particular placed profound significance on the exodus, maintaining that in the future God would again reveal his power, justice, and faithfulness in the final deliverance of his people, just as he did in the exodus.[5] References to the book of Exodus and the events recorded in it are prominent throughout the Bible. The biblical writings were recorded over a broad span of time by a variety of human authors[6] for a range of different purposes and audiences. The contexts of the exodus typology within these ancient works differ greatly, and its employment ranges from subtle, implicit imagery (Revelation) to bright, colorful descriptions (Isaiah) to explicit statements of fact (Jeremiah). Yet across this diverse collection of literature there remains surprising agreement in the major elements and theological emphases at work within the framework of exodus typology, and the prevalent use of exodus typology throughout both testaments of Scripture makes it evident that the historical exodus from Egypt provided a well-established pattern and hope for a more dramatic future deliverance which would both fulfill and exceed the historical exodus.

## The "Content" of Exodus Typology

The Old and New Testaments are inseparably connected by a pattern of promise and fulfillment, which is woven throughout the fabric of the canon, beginning with Genesis and ending only with Revelation. This pattern is depicted clearly in God's acts of deliverance throughout the book of Exodus, and so exodus connections are often implicit (if not explicit) when the pattern recurs in later biblical texts.[7] Thus, if typology is, as we defined it in

---

by the later generations' use of first-person pronouns in their explanation of the festival and description of the exodus events (e.g., Deut 6:20–25; 25:5b–9; Josh 24:5–8). Ninow, *Indicators of Typology*, 115–120.

  4 James Plastaras, *Creation and Covenant* (Bruce Publishing, 1968), 5.

  5 According to Dempster, "the account of the liberation of a band of Hebrew slaves from horrific oppression in Egypt is the event that shaped virtually everything in the biblical imagination." Stephen G. Dempster, "Exodus and Biblical Theology: On Moving into the Neighborhood with a New Name," *Southern Baptist Journal of Theology* 12.3 (2008): 4. See also John Goldingay, *Israel's Faith*, vol. 2 of *Old Testament Theology* (InterVarsity, 2006), 423–429; Sarna, *Exploring Exodus*, 1–2; etc.

  6 This is not to discount the key component of divine inspiration but simply to recognize the diversity of the human individuals who received this inspiration and took part in the actual writing of the biblical texts.

  7 John I. Durham, *Exodus*, WBC 3 (Word, 1987), xx–xxiii; Augustine Stock, *The Way in the Wilderness: Exodus, Wilderness, and Moses Themes in Old Testament and New* (Liturgical Press, 1969), 18. This is not to say that promise-fulfillment is the only, or necessarily the central, pat-

the previous chapter, the theological interpretation of God's history among his people, observing correspondences or patterns within Scripture and presupposing the continuity of God's purpose and action throughout history, then exodus typology could be defined as the *theological interpretation of the events of the exodus as the divinely intended model for Yahweh's future acts of deliverance on behalf of his people.* The presence of exodus typology throughout the canon evidences that the historical exodus from Egypt provided both the pattern and hope for a more dramatic final deliverance which would simultaneously fulfill and exceed the historical exodus in the future.[8] Indeed, the present project explicitly recognizes the prophetic character inherent within the historical exodus which is developed within other OT, NT, and extracanonical writings, and which culminates in the eschatological fulfillment of the exodus, as presented in John's Apocalypse.

In order to understand and recognize exodus typology within the biblical narratives, it is important to identify exactly which events are covered by the word "exodus." Does exodus typology take into account only the exodus proper—namely, the events immediately leading up to and including the departure from Egypt (Exod 1–14)? Is it broader, including the entire history of Israel contained in the book of Exodus—namely, the exodus proper as well as the wilderness wanderings to Sinai and the establishment of the tabernacle? Is it advisable to extend the umbrella even further to incorporate the laws associated with the covenant and tabernacle and Israel's continued journey from Sinai to and encampment by the bank of the Jordan River, as recorded in Leviticus, Numbers, and Deuteronomy? Does exodus typology go so far as to encompass the crossing of the Jordan River and conquest of Canaan, the Promised Land—that is, the events described in the first twelve chapters of Joshua? How narrowly or broadly should the term "exodus typology" be defined?[9]

---

tern of continuity between the Testaments (cf., Gerhard Hasel, *Old Testament Theology: Basic Issues in the Current Debate*, 3rd rev. ed. [Eerdmans, 1972], 145–167, esp. 155–157). However, this pattern is clearly a crucial aspect of both canonical continuity and, as will be shown below, John's Apocalypse.

8 Sarna, *Exploring Exodus*, 2–3.

9 The interpretation of the boundaries of exodus typology varies from scholar to scholar, yet rarely do they provide a detailed, comprehensive analysis to support their approach. For example, Ninow simply states outright, with no explanation, that "the Exodus event that was to be remembered encompassed the ritual of the Passover, the deliverance, the going out from Egypt, the crossing of the Red Sea with the destruction of the Egyptian army, the giving of the law at Mt. Sinai, the instruction of the people before they entered the land, and their discipline in the wilderness." Ninow, *Indicators of Typology*, 98. Casey, on the other hand, builds his argument around four "tradition clusters" which he claims make up the exodus tradition—events in Egypt, the wilderness, Sinai, and the conquest—yet acknowledges that tradition does not

## Connection of "Exodus Proper" and Wilderness

From a historical, theological, and literary perspective, it is possible to see that the exodus and wilderness wanderings are two parts of a whole, with the story flowing seamlessly from the departure from Egypt to the Israelites' trek through the desert. The one naturally results in the other—the exodus leads directly to the wilderness sojourn; geographically the people move out of Egypt and into the wilderness. Historically, Yahweh's act of deliverance in the exodus "was not, by its nature, an isolated occurrence, giving rise to nebulous hopes for similar good luck in the future: it had its root in, and set the seal on, a permanent institution—hence it was something on which absolute reliance might be placed."[10] This was not a random event, disconnected from the history preceding it and having no sense of purpose for the future. Rather, from the time of Abram, all of Israel's history led up to the exodus.[11] God's covenant with Abram involved the twin themes of geography and genealogy, land and posterity—God called Abram to "go ... to the land that I will show you" and promised to make of him "a great nation" (Gen 12:1–3). This twofold promise "runs through the whole [of the patriarchal narrative] like a *cantus firmus*,"[12] a constant melody upon which all else is built.

Yet Genesis ends with Abram's descendants sojourning in Egypt, neither established as a nation nor inhabiting the land of promise. Thus, "the book of Genesis requires a sequel ... the book of Exodus picks up four hundred years after the end of Genesis, continuing the story of the sons of Israel and their march toward nationhood."[13] God had promised Abram that his offspring

---

give equal stress to each of the four elements, as "shown already in the separation of the Conquest tradition from the other traditions" within the Canon. Jay Casey, "Exodus Typology in the Book of Revelation," (PhD diss., The Southern Baptist Theological Seminary, 1981), 4–5. Thus, the present chapter is intended to provide a historical, literary, and theological rationale for the delineation of exodus typology.

10  David Daube, *The Exodus Pattern in the Bible* (Faber and Faber, 1963), 14.

11  Stephen G. Dempster, *Dominion and Dynasty: A Theology of the Hebrew Bible*, New Studies in Biblical Theology (InterVarsity, 2003), 93–94; idem, "Exodus and Biblical Theology," 6.

12  Gerhard von Rad, "Typological Interpretation of the Old Testament," trans. John Bright, *Interpretation* 15 (1961): 185. Ninow goes into great detail to demonstrate how the two aspects of God's promise to Abraham—"seed" and "land"—are both the beginning of Jewish eschatology and the precursors to the exodus event. See Ninow, *Indicators of Typology*, 100–111. Kaiser claims the promise was made up of three elements: seed, land, and "the climactic element." Walter C. Kaiser, Jr., "The Promise Theme and the Theology of Rest," *BSac* 130 (1973): 136.

13  Bruce K. Waltke, *An Old Testament Theology: An Exegetical, Canonical, and Thematic Approach* (Zondervan, 2007), 56; Terence E. Fretheim, "'Because the Whole Earth is Mine': Theme and Narrative in Exodus," *Interpretation* 50 (1996): 229. Compare Merrill, who states, "to [the Exodus] the Book of Genesis provides an introduction and justification, and from it flows all subsequent Old Testament revelation." Eugene H. Merrill, *Kingdom of Priests: A History of Old Testament Israel* (Baker, 1996), 57.

would be innumerable as the dust of the earth (Gen 13:16) and the stars of the sky (Gen 15:5), and Exodus begins with the declaration that the Israelites had multiplied greatly (Exod 1:7–8). Yet this vast group of individuals was more than simply the descendants of Abram; rather, central to the exodus narratives is the idea that Israel is the Lord's firstborn son, that the Israelites are his children (e.g., Exod 4:22–23).[14] Throughout the first twelve chapters of Exodus the elite identity of the Israelites as God's people is impossible to miss—from the survival of the people in spite of Pharaoh's determination to kill the Hebrew boys (Exod 1:15–22) to the assertion that God remembered his covenant (Exod 2:24) to Yahweh's repetition of the phrase "my people" (Exod 3:7, 10; 5:1; 6:7; 7:4, 16; 8:1, 20–23; 9:1, 13–17; 10:3). Yahweh intentionally and explicitly distinguishes the Israelites from other peoples, protecting them from many of the plagues with which he punished the Egyptians (Exod 8:22–23; 9:4, 6–7, 26; 10:23) and culminating in the preservation of the Hebrew firstborn by means of the Passover (Exod 12:12–13, 29). The distinction between Yahweh's firstborn and the firstborn in Egypt could not be clearer.

God formally secured and ratified this relationship with his chosen people in the wilderness through the covenant at Mount Sinai. According to Anderson, from the earliest days "Exodus and Sinai, redemption and covenant belonged essentially together. Sinai was regarded as the place from which Yahweh came to deliver his people (Judg. 5:4–5), just as it was the place where he established his covenant with Israel on the basis of his commandments (Exod. 24:3–8)."[15] It was through the exodus that Israel came to know Yahweh as the God who is truly present.

The presence of God in and among the Israelites was a unique privilege; no other nation had the living God abiding within their midst.[16] There is a

---

14 Dempster, *Dominion and Dynasty*, 97; cf. Eugene H. Merrill, *Everlasting Dominion: A Theology of the Old Testament* (Broadman & Holman, 2006), 253. This designation of Israel as God's firstborn (cf. Jer 31:9; Hos 11:1) is not without significance. In most ancient cultures, firstborn sons were considered special, but in Egypt they were sacred, rightfully belonging to god in gratitude for his copious gifts to mankind. The firstborn son took priority in both inheritance and succession. Sarna, *Exploring Exodus*, 94; Merrill, *Everlasting Dominion*, 256–257.

15 Bernhard A. Anderson, "Exodus and Covenant in Second Isaiah and Prophetic Tradition," in *Magnalia Dei: The Mighty Acts of God: Essays on the Bible and Archaeology in Memory of G. Ernest Wright*, ed. Frank Moore Cross, Werner E. Lemke, and Patrick D. Miller, Jr. (Doubleday, 1976), 344. According to Daube, the expectation of a new exodus-type deliverance "always included Sinai." Daube, *Exodus Pattern*, 45.

16 Sarna, *Exploring Exodus*, 207. For Fretheim, the tabernacle initiates a "change of address [for God]. Rather than being associated with a fixed place, God will now reside in—and not just appear at (as in 33:7–11)—a portable Sinai, a dwelling place in the midst of an on-the-move people.... No more trips up the mountain for Moses! God here begins a 'descent' that will climax in the incarnational move God makes in Jesus (see John 1:14)." Fretheim, "Because the Whole Earth is Mine," 232.

poignant correlation between divine presence and national identity; without Yahweh's presence the Israelites would no longer be set apart from other nations. It is God's presence that created the Israelites, and without him the chosen people of God would cease to exist.[17] As Merrill states it, through the exodus Yahweh "brought them from slavery to freedom, from fragmentation to solidarity, from a people of promise—the Hebrews—to a nation of fulfillment—Israel."[18] God's presence was displayed through his power in delivering the Israelites out of bondage, manifested in his provision in the wilderness, and confirmed through the privilege of the Sinai theophany, covenant and tabernacle.[19] God's presence among his people was the goal of the entire exodus story, as expressed in Exod 29:45–46—"I will dwell among the people of Israel and will be their God. And they shall know that I am the Lord their God, who brought them out of the land of Egypt that I might dwell among them. I am the Lord their God."[20]

Yet God's concern in bringing about the exodus is not only genealogical. In his burning bush encounter with Moses, Yahweh connects the coming events with the geographical element of his promise as well—"I have come down to deliver them out of the hand of the Egyptians and to bring them up out of that land to a good and broad land, a land flowing with milk

---

17  Thomas W. Mann, *Divine Presence and Guidance in Israelite Traditions: The Typology of Exaltation* (Johns Hopkins University Press, 1977), 157–158; Samuel Terrien, *The Elusive Presence: The Heart of Biblical Theology* (Harper & Row, 1978), 124. According to Merrill, "the exodus did not make Israel the people of the Lord; rather, it delivered them because they were his people (Exod. 4:22–23)." Merrill, *Everlasting Dominion*, 122. While this is true, it was the covenant at Sinai that solidified the Hebrew people into God's holy nation and delineated both the privilege (Exod 19:5–6) and responsibility (Exod 20:1–17) of this elite status (see 2 Sam 7:23–24; 1 Chr 17:21–22). As Merrill himself asserts, "The Abrahamic covenant consistently describes the descendants of the patriarch as a nation (*gôy*) rather than a people (*'am*) (Gen. 12:2; 17:4–6, 16; 18:18; 25:23; 35:11; 46:3) whereas Israel in Exodus is called a people scores of times and a nation only three times and then never prior to the establishment of Israel as the covenant nation (Exod. 19:6; 32:10; 33:13).... Israel as a people was a temporary phase on the way to nationhood." Ibid., 254–255 (see also pp. 269–272)..

18  He goes on to suggest that "in the final analysis, the exodus served to typify that exodus achieved by Jesus Christ for people of faith." Merrill, *Kingdom of Priests*, 57–58.

19  John I. Durham, *Understanding the Basic Themes of Exodus*, Quick-Reference Bible Topics (Word, 1990), 5.

20  Antonius Gerardus Weiler and Marcus Lefébure, eds., *Exodus—A Lasting Paradigm* (T&T Clark, 1987), 20; cf. Merrill, *Everlasting Dominion*, 255; Kaiser, "Promise Theme," 136. Compare the words of the Lord regarding the promised return from exile in Jeremiah—"Behold, I will gather them from all the countries to which I drove them in my anger and my wrath and in great indignation. I will bring them back to this place, and I will make them dwell in safety. And they shall be my people, and I will be their God" (Jer 32:37–38). Indeed, God's dwelling among his people could be said to be a goal of salvation history as a whole, beginning with man's dismissal from the Garden, where God walked among them (Gen 3:8) and culminating in the last days when "the dwelling place of God is with man. He will dwell with them, and they will be his people, and God himself will be with them as their God" (Rev 21:3).

and honey" (Exod 3:8; cf. 3:17; 6:4, 8; 13:3–5, 11; 33:1–3; Lev 20:24; Num 13:27; 14:8; 16:13–14; Deut 6:3; 11:9; 26:9, 15; 27:3; 31:20; Josh 5:6). While the goal of the exodus was to solidify the nation of Israel as God's chosen people, the destination of the exodus and the Israelites' wandering in the wilderness was the land of promise.[21] Indeed, even Moses reminds Yahweh of this fact when pleading with him on behalf of the Hebrew people (Exod 32:10–13). Yet, just as Genesis ends without God's promises to Abram being fulfilled, so too the Pentateuch closes without God's people inhabiting the Promised Land. As Waltke puts it, "the Pentateuch (the Jewish Torah, Genesis—Deuteronomy) traces the history of Israel from the creation of the cosmos to Israel's being perched on the threshold of the Sworn Land (the Promised Land), and the Former Prophets (Joshua–2 Kings, apart from Ruth) continues that history from Israel's conquest of the land to their exile from the land."[22]

The history of Israel is clearly a story that progresses without ceasing throughout the OT. Yet certain events stand out as high points within the overall historical narrative—creation, the Fall, the flood, the Abrahamic covenant, the exodus, the conquest, the Davidic kingship, the exile, and the return from Babylon. Likewise, with regard to the literary record of Israel's history, Waltke states,

> A careful reader of the Old Testament immediately notices that although the Old Testament is a collection of books of different kinds and periods, certain books share commonalities with others: vocabulary, literary genre, thematic continuities, and other intertextual evidences. These natural boundaries, not imposed by a scholar seeking to systematize, but present in the text as a reflection of the authors' intentions, allow us to organize the Old Testament books into blocks of writing and in turn to track the themes of the books both within and among the blocks. By taking these natural boundaries seriously, we begin the process of building a coherent theology that is based on the shape of the canon and/or on the thrust of the texts themselves. This a posteriori approach to the shape of the canon finds some confirmation by its shape in the Talmud: Torah

---

[21] Dempster connects the ideas of genealogy and geography when he states that the goal of the exodus is "the building of the Edenic sanctuary so that the Lord can dwell with his people" as anticipated in Exod 15:16–17. Dempster, *Dominion and Dynasty*, 100.

[22] He goes on to say that "the linchpin of the Primary History, binding together these two great histories, is the book of Deuteronomy … both the capstone of the Pentateuch and the foundation stone of the Deuteronomistic History." Waltke, *Old Testament Theology*, 57. Cf. Walter C. Kaiser, Jr., "The Promised Land: A Biblical-Historical View," *BSac* 138 (1981): 305–306.

(Genesis – Deuteronomy), Prophets—former (Joshua – Kings) and later (Isaiah – Malachi), and Writings (the rest of the corpus).[23]

Because of this historical continuity, it is possible to trace several common theological aims through the exodus and wilderness narratives, themes which are developed in later texts through exodus typology. First, by showing his authority over nature, Yahweh affirms his absolute sovereignty over all creation, including human rulers. The entire account of the exodus involves a contest of power and supremacy between Pharaoh, the self-appointed deity, and Yahweh, the God of the Israelites.[24] The Egyptians considered Pharaoh to be "lord of diadems," possessing universal dominion over nature and politics, authority over life and death, immeasurable power, and unending knowledge. So the plagues against Egypt not only proved Yahweh's sovereignty over creation by touching every area of the natural world, but also demonstrated his sovereignty over earthly rulers and the inferiority of Pharaoh's dominion, as evidenced by his magicians' failure in stopping the plagues.[25] Yahweh announced his authority over nature with climactic finality to Pharaoh and his army by supernaturally parting, and restoring the flow of, the Red Sea (Exod 14:15–28). For the Israelites, Yahweh's absolute sovereignty was further proven in the wilderness through the pillar of cloud and fire with which God led them (Exod 13:21–22; cf. 14:19–20; Num 9:15–22; 14:14; Deut 1:33), his provision of water from the rock (Exod 17:6; Num 20:8–11) and fresh water from bitter (Exod 15:23–25), as well as manna and quail for sustenance (Exod 16:4–35; Num 11:1–32), their victory over the Amalekites as long as Moses' arms were raised (Exod 17:8–16), and Yahweh's undeniable presence in the Sinai theophany (Exod 19:16–20; 20:18–21).

Second, the judgment meted out upon the Egyptians conveys the impossibility of successfully defying God's will. During the period of the plagues, Pharaoh was given multiple opportunities to acknowledge the superiority

---

23  Waltke, *Old Testament Theology*, 55; R. E. Nixon, *The Exodus in the New Testament*, Tyndale New Testament Lecture 1962 (Tyndale, 1963), 6. Jensen divides the OT into three eras: "to the land" (Pentateuch), "in the land" (Former Prophets), and "from the land" (Latter Prophets). In Genesis the land is first promised to Abraham, and throughout the rest of the Pentateuch God leads his people on a journey to the banks of Canaan. In Joshua, the story picks up with the people entering and conquering the land and dividing the inheritance among the tribes of Israel. "In a real sense Joshua is the *climax* of a progressive history as well as the *commencement* of a new experience for Israel." Irving L. Jensen, *Joshua: Rest-Land Won*, Everyman's Bible Commentary (Moody, 1966), 13–14.

24  Edward R. Dalglish, *The Great Deliverance: A Concise Exposition of the Book of Exodus* (Broadman, 1977), 41.

25  Lester Meyer, *The Message of Exodus: A Theological Commentary* (Augsburg, 1983), 73. According to Merrill, "even Pharaoh's magicians were forced to concede, in light of the evidence, that 'this is the finger of God' (Exod 8:19)." Merrill, *Everlasting Dominion*, 111.

of Yahweh and release the Israelites from bondage. Yet Pharaoh's repeatedly hardened heart depicts his "willful suppression of the capacity for reflection, self-examination, unbiased judgments about good and evil."[26] The longer he resisted Yahweh's authority, the more serious the judgments became, ultimately resulting in the death of the firstborn throughout Egypt and the destruction of the Egyptian army in the Red Sea. Through it all, God warned Pharaoh that he and the Egyptian people would come to know his absolute power and bow before his authority (Exod 7:5; 9:14).[27] But in the wilderness, the Israelites also came to know the judgment of God and the folly of defying him. Even after witnessing God's immense wrath poured out upon the Egyptians and experiencing his palpable presence and seemingly endless patience, the Hebrew people still fashioned an idol in the form of a golden calf (Exod 32:1–5), an action which resulted in Yahweh destroying three thousand of his own people (Exod 32:27–28), setting a plague upon the camp (Exod 32:35), and threatening to remove his presence from among them (Exod 33:1–5).

Third, the deliverance of the Israelites out of Egypt illustrates that God alone is the Great Redeemer, responsible for the Israelites' release.[28] In the burning bush episode, Yahweh declared to Moses, "I have surely seen the affliction of my people … I know their sufferings, and I have come down to deliver them out of the hand of the Egyptians and to bring them up out of that land to … a land flowing with milk and honey" (Exod 3:7–8). This announcement had been anticipated since the story began. Not only did God hear the cries of his people, he remembered his covenant promise and was preparing to set in motion its fulfillment.[29] God's response to Moses' claims of inadequacy was not a denial of his unworthiness, but instead a promise, "Certainly I will be with you" (Exod 3:12, NASB). Moses knew that Yahweh alone delivered them from Egypt—as evidenced by the oft-repeated refrain, "the Lord who brought you out of the land of Egypt"[30]—and sustained them in the wilderness. When the people grumbled in the wilderness about a lack of food or water, God himself provided for his people; when Yahweh threatened to remove his presence from the Israelites, Moses pleaded with him, saying "If

---

26 Sarna, *Exploring Exodus*, 64; cf. Robert B. Chisholm, Jr., "Divine Hardening in the Old Testament," *BSac* 153 (1996): 428–429.

27 Roger Dalman, *A People Come Out of Egypt: Studies in the Books of Exodus, Deuteronomy and Judges* (Send the Light Press, 2002), 43.

28 Sarna, *Exploring Exodus*, 2–3.

29 Meyer, *Message of Exodus*, 47; Durham, *Basic Themes of Exodus*, 21.

30 Exod 16:6; 20:2; Lev 11:45; 19:36; 22:32–33; 25:38; 26:13; Num 15:41; Deut 5:6; 6:12; 8:14; 13:5, 10; 20:1; cf. Josh 24:6, 17; Judg 6:8; 1 Sam 12:6; 1 Kgs 8:51–53; 2 Kgs 17:7; 2 Chr 7:22; Ps 81:10; Amos 2:10; 3:1; 9:7; Hos 12:9; 13:4; Mic 6:4; Jer 7:22; 11:4, 7; 31:31–32; 32:21. Casey refers to this as a stock formula "reminding Israel that their God is Yahweh, the God of the Exodus." Casey, "Exodus Typology in Revelation," 6.

your Presence does not go with us, do not send us up from here ... What else will distinguish me and your people from all the other people on the face of the earth?" (Exod 33:15–16, NIV). Even at the end of his life, as the Israelites were on the verge of entering the Promised Land, Moses reminded them that God himself goes before them where Moses cannot (Deut 31:1–8). Scripture makes it very plain—everything that took place, both in Egypt and beyond, was accomplished by the presence and power of God alone.[31]

Finally, and in summary, "the Exodus is the moment at which the Lord ceased to be Israel's God in potential alone and became her God in actual fact."[32] God is mentioned only twice within the first two chapters of Exodus (Exod 1:17–21; 2:23–25), though the promise and activity of Yahweh are implicit in every detail of these verses, driving toward the sole purpose of establishing that God is present among his people. When the Israelites groaned in anguish (Exod 2:23), they did not cry out to anyone in particular, for during the long sojourn in Egypt they seem to have forgotten about the God of their Fathers and did not know where to turn for help.[33] Yahweh, however, heard their cries, not because of any initiative by the Israelites, but because he is true to his promises. And "the intensity with which God now turns to Israel is underscored by the repeated use of the noun where a simple pronoun would have been adequate: 'God heard ... God remembered ... God saw ... God knew...'" (Exod 2:24–25).[34] Once Yahweh revealed himself to the Israelites in the events of the exodus, it was possible for them to look back and understand that God's deliverance had been in motion all along. His hand had been actively working behind the scenes throughout the Egyptian bondage in the multiplication of the Hebrews (Exod 1:12), the rescue of Moses by Pharaoh's daughter (Exod 2:5), and Moses' flight from Egypt (Exod 2:15).[35] Though

---

31 "The whole enterprise from beginning to end—from Egypt to Canaan—was an unending series of miraculous acts whereby God redeemed, sustained, and delivered his people." Merrill, *Kingdom of Priests*, 82. See also Douglas M. White, *Holy Ground: Expositions from Exodus* (Baker, 1962), 21.

32 Samuel E. Loewenstamm, *The Evolution of the Exodus Tradition*, trans. Baruch J. Schwartz, Publication of the Perry Foundation for Biblical Research in the Hebrew University of Jerusalem (Magnes Press, Hebrew University, 1992), 24.

33 According to Stalker, "the effective knowledge of God had apparently been forgotten in Egypt." D. M. G. Stalker, "Exodus," in *Peake's Commentary on the Bible*, ed. Matthew Black and H. H. Rowley (Thomas Nelson, 1962), 208.

34 Meyer, *Message of Exodus*, 42; C. Marvin Pate et al., *The Story of Israel: A Biblical Theology* (InterVarsity, 2004), 38.

35 Plastaras, *Creation and Covenant*, 5; Nixon, *Exodus in the NT*, 5. As Dempster states, "by repeating the noun 'God' as the main actor in this brief paragraph, the narrator indicates that the One who has been lurking in the background during the events of the opening chapters of Exodus is about to take center stage. The covenant has not been forgotten." Dempster, "Exodus and Biblical Theology," 10.

God's providence is hidden up to this point in the exodus story, in the deliverance from Egypt and subsequent wilderness wanderings he bursts onto the forefront of history in an amazing display of sovereign power, righteous judgment, and constant presence.[36]

The exodus and the journey in the wilderness are not merely tied together by these common theological foci. As a unified whole, the exodus and the experiences connected with it (e.g., bondage, liberation, presence, covenant, wilderness, redemption, and journey to the Promised Land) form one of the most dominant and repeated themes throughout Scripture, and function typologically to represent the anticipation that God will act in an even greater way in the future. This pivotal act of deliverance in the history of Israel and the unique relationship between God and his people that emerged from it serve as the preeminent model for another salvation event, one that would surpass the first exodus in authority and finality. As Stalker so eloquently affirms, the exodus is "the great constitutive action of God by which he not only brought the nation of Israel into being, but also gave his plan for the salvation of mankind its final shape.... The Exodus is for the OT and Judaism what the life, death and resurrection of Christ are for the NT and Christianity. And for Christians, what Jesus brought to fulfilment was the purpose of the Exodus."[37]

When examined from a literary perspective, the irrevocable bond between the exodus and wilderness can be seen in various ways, not the least of which is the inclusion of both within the book of Exodus and the fact that the Pentateuch draws to a close with the anticipation of the next step in the Israelites' journey, the conquest of Canaan. Elsewhere in Scripture, the two elements are linked as well. Perhaps the earliest instance is the Song of Moses (Exod 15), sung by the Israelites on the bank of the Red Sea as they witnessed their deliverance and the Egyptians' destruction. Structurally, this ancient hymn is divided into two main parts—the first two strophes (vv.1b–5 and 6–10) praise Yahweh's power and victory over the Egyptian army at the Red Sea, while the final two strophes (vv.11–16a and 16b–18) describe his loving protection during the subsequent wilderness wanderings, events which,

---

36 James Plastaras, *The God of Exodus: The Theology of the Exodus Narratives* (Bruce Publishing, 1966), 26–27; White, *Holy Ground*, 17. As Plastaras asserts elsewhere, "Israel's faith in Yahweh was born from the events of the exodus. It was only in light of that fact that Israel was able to look back into her past and piece together the story of the patriarchs." Plastaras, *Creation and Covenant*, 4–5.

37 Stalker, "Exodus," 208; Sarna, *Exploring Exodus*, 1–2. Cf. Stock, who states, "The Exodus was the decisive historical experience that formed the Hebrews into something they had not been before – a self-conscious historical community, a people, the People of God.... The Exodus therefore represents the starting point of that plan of salvation which finds its realization in Jesus of Nazareth. And as the first decisive saving act, the Exodus established the pattern, as it were, for all future saving acts." Stock, *Way in the Wilderness*, viii.

literarily[38] at least, happen in the future.[39] Ninow actually sees within this song the first occasion of exodus typology. By shifting the perspective to a "prophecy" in Exod 15:13, the song takes on both a retrospective and prospective dimension; "by virtue of this transfer of a future redemptive act into the historical narrative of the original Exodus, the way seems open for fitting later saving acts of YHWH into the same structure."[40] Thus the drowning of the Egyptian army (and in reality, the whole of the exodus experience) becomes a type for another deliverance from danger.[41]

As has already been stated, the exodus is referred to frequently throughout the OT, NT, and extracanonical texts, often in a way which typologically points toward an even greater, future deliverance. What is significant regarding this intertextual witness to the expectation of an eschatological exodus is the propensity to refer to both the "exodus proper" and the wilderness experience in close proximity, many times within the same verse, suggesting that the ancient writers understood the two aspects to be united as one event. One such indication of this concomitant relationship is found within the context of God's purpose for the command to set aside an omer of manna—

> Moses said, "This is what the Lord has commanded: 'Let an omer of it be kept throughout your generations, so that they may see the bread with which I fed you in the wilderness, when I brought you out of the land of Egypt'" (Exod 16:32).

Within this single verse there is a reference to the exodus proper immediately preceded by an explicit mention of the wilderness experience and the explanation that all of this is so that future generations will see, know, and remember God's mighty acts on behalf of his people. Throughout Scripture,

---

38 This is not a statement regarding the song's composition, as there is little scholarly consensus regarding the date, source(s), and genre. However, given the song's location within the OT, there can be no disagreement that the encounters described in vv.14–15 occur during the Israelites' subsequent journey to the Promised Land. Ninow, *Indicators of Typology*, 124–126, 128.

39 In other words, in commemorating the present Red Sea experience, the Israelites also celebrate both the past and the future. Ibid., 127–130. Cf. W. J. Dumbrell, *Covenant and Creation: A Theology of the Old Testament Covenants*, Biblical and Theological Classics Library 12 (Paternoster, 1984), 101.

40 Ninow, *Indicators of Typology*, 132. Merrill suggests that this poetic account of the deliverance at the Red Sea makes the point that "the conquest of Egypt was to be viewed proleptically as the conquest of all opposition to him both historically and eschatologically. What he did for his people in redeeming them from bondage to a competing sovereign he will do over and over again until all evil dominions are overthrown and the kingdom of God remains alone and supreme." Merrill, *Everlasting Dominion*, 264–265.

41 Ninow, *Indicators of Typology*, 134.

the exodus and wilderness are characteristically intertwined[42] to indicate a single epic experience.[43]

The most common way in which Scripture refers to the "exodus proper" involves some form of the stock phrase "I brought you out of the land of Egypt."[44] God's plagues, signs, and wonders in Egypt,[45] the parting of the Red Sea,[46] and the destruction of Pharaoh and his army at the Red Sea[47] also feature prominently as indicators of the exodus.[48] The most frequent markers of the wilderness experience are references to being guided in and through the wilderness and the pillar of cloud and fire,[49] the provision of water, quail, and manna or bread in the wilderness,[50] Israel's grumbling and rebellion and God's judgment of the Israelites in the wilderness,[51] and the Sinai covenant.[52] Amos 2:10 is perhaps the most concise statement in which wilderness and

---

42  Exod 16:32; Lev 23:42–43; Deut 1:30–31; 8:1–20; 9:7; 11:2–6; 29:2–6; Josh 24:5–8; 24:17–18; Neh 9:9–21; Pss 78:12–20, 23–29, 40–54; 105:26–45; 106:7–27; 136:10–16; Jer 2:6; 31:31–33; Ezek 20:10–26; 20:34–44; Hos 13:4–5; Amos 2:10; Acts 7:34–43; 1 Cor 10:1–11; Heb 3:16–18. This list is by no means exhaustive of every occasion the exodus or wilderness occurs within Scripture. Rather, in each passage listed, exodus and wilderness are combined in close proximity, and the cumulative effect of these passages demonstrates that the ancient Jews (and the early church) understood them to be two parts of a single whole rather than two distinct events.

43  The incomparability of this epic exodus event is reinforced by its close association with knowing God (Lev 23:42–43; Deut 8:1–20; 29:2–6; Ps 106:7–27; Ezek 20:10–14; Hos 13:4–5), remembering his mighty acts (Deut 8:1–20; 9:7; Pss 78:40–54; 106:7–27), and preserving the story for future generations (Exod 16:32; Lev 23:42–43; Deut 11:2–6), as well as its preeminence within occasions of historical rehearsal (Deut 1:30–31; 8:1–20; 9:7; 11:2–6; 29:2–6; Josh 24:5–8, 17; Neh 9:9–21; Pss 78:12–20, 40–54; 105:26–45; 106:7–27; 136:10–16; Ezek 20:10–14; Acts 7:36) and prophecy (Jer 2:6; 31:32; Ezek 20:34–36; Hos 13:4–5; Amos 2:10).

44  Exod 16:32; Lev 23:43; Deut 8:14; 9:7; Josh 24:5, 6, 17; Pss 105:37, 43; 136:11; Jer 2:6; 31:32; Ezek 20: 6, 9, 10; Amos 2:10; Acts 7:36, 40; Heb 3:16.

45  Deut 11:3; 29:2–3; Josh 24:5, 17; Neh 9:10; Pss 78:12, 43–51; 105:27–36; 106:7; Acts 7:36.

46  Neh 9:11; Pss 78:13; 106:9; 136:13–14; Acts 7:36; 1 Cor 10:2.

47  Deut 11:4; Josh 24:7; Neh 9:11; Pss 78:53; 106:11; 136:15.

48  In addition, hints of the exodus are found in references to slavery, affliction, and oppression in Egypt (Josh 24:17; Neh 9:9; Acts 7:34), the Passover (Ps 105:36), the judgment of Pharaoh and his servants (Deut 29:2), Moses and/or Aaron (Josh 24:5; Ps 105:26; 1 Cor 10:2; Acts 7:35, 37, 40; Heb 3:16), and simply the word "Egypt" (Deut 1:30; Hos 13:4).

49  Deut 8:15; 29:5; Neh 9:12, 19; Pss 78:14, 52–53; 105:39; 106:9; 136:16; Jer 2:6; Acts 7:36; 1 Cor 10:1–2.

50  Exod 16:32; Deut 8:15–16; Neh 9:15, 20; Pss 78:15–16, 20, 24–29; 105:40–41; 1 Cor 10:3–4.

51  Deut 11:5; Neh 9:16–17; Pss 78:18, 40–41; 106:13–27; Ezek 20:13–16, 21–26, 35–38; Acts 7:39–42; 1 Cor 10:5–10; Heb 3:17–18.

52  Neh 9:13; Jer 31:32; Ezek 20:11–12, 37; Acts 7:38. Other indicators of the wilderness experience include a mention of protection on the journey (Josh 24:17–18), being carried in the wilderness (Deut 1:31, an allusion to Exod 19:4, "You yourselves have seen what I did to the Egyptians, and how I bore you on eagles' wings and brought you to myself"), dwelling in the wilderness for forty years (Deut 29:5; Neh 9:21; Acts 7:36, 42; Heb 3:17; "a long time", Josh 24:7), dwelling in booths (Lev 23:42–43), the Israelites' clothing and sandals not wearing out during the wilderness wanderings (Deut 29:5; Neh 9:21), and simply the word "wilderness" (Deut 9:7; Hos 13:5).

exodus imagery are united: "Also it was I who brought you up out of the land of Egypt and led you forty years in the wilderness, to possess the land of the Amorite." Yet even such a terse recollection of this epic deliverance carries much weight, for just as the NT writers employed single verses and phrases as "signposts to the overall Old Testament context from which they were cited,"[53] so throughout the whole of Scripture references to a single detail call to mind the broader historical event or context.

### Distinction of the Conquest

The combined historical, theological, and literary witness of the Scriptures has given validity to the inclusion of wilderness imagery within exodus typology. Yet the question remains, does exodus typology extend so far as to include allusions to the conquest of Canaan (Josh 1–12)? There is no doubt that the exodus/wilderness experience and the conquest are closely related. While the genealogical aspect of the Abrahamic covenant is realized in the establishment of his offspring as a holy nation at Sinai (Exod 19:6), the conquest is the initial fulfillment of the geographical promise of a land which his descendants would inhabit forever (Gen 12:1; 13:14–17). Throughout their journey in the wilderness, the Israelites moved progressively closer to this promised land, until they set up camp in the plains of Moab by the Jordan (see Num 26:3). For forty years they waited in the wilderness, longing for the opportunity to possess the land yet suffering the consequences of God's wrath for their grumbling and lack of belief (Num 14:34), unable to establish a permanent home in the land God had promised yet protected from the elements and provided for by his hand alone (Exod 16:35; Deut 2:7; 8:4; 29:5).

Yet in other ways, the conquest is set apart from and distinct from the events of the exodus and wilderness wanderings. God himself established one such distinction when he decreed that "none of the men who have seen my glory and my signs that I did in Egypt and in the wilderness ... shall see the land that I swore to give to their fathers. And none of those who despised me shall see it" (Num 14:22–23; cf. Josh 5:6). Because of their willful lack of obedience and disbelief, the exodus generation was forced to die in the wilderness without experiencing the fulfillment of the land of promise. It was only after

---

53 G. K. Beale, "Positive Answer to the Question: Did Jesus and His Followers Preach the Right Doctrine from the Wrong Texts? An Examination of the Presuppositions of Jesus' and the Apostles' Exegetical Method," in Beale, *Right Doctrine*, 390; C. H. Dodd, *According to the Scriptures: The Sub-Structure of New Testament Theology* (Nisbet, 1952), 126–127. Accordingly, Nixon states that the observance of the Passover and the Feast of Unleavened Bread would "recall not simply the passing over of the houses of the Israelites but also the whole complex of events which went to make up the Exodus." Nixon, *Exodus in the NT*, 7–8.

Moses' death (Deut 34:4–12) that the new generation received a new leader and instructions to prepare to enter the land (Josh 1:3–9).

This new generation followed a new leader, Joshua,[54] and faced their own miraculous "crossing." Like those who experienced the departure from Egypt firsthand, the Israelites camped (Exod 14:2, 9; Josh 3:1) at the bank of a great body of water, on the brink of entering a new land and a new phase of their journey.[55] As Moses told the exodus generation to watch and see the deliverance the Lord would accomplish for them (Exod 14:13–14), so Joshua instructed the Israelites to prepare themselves for the amazing things the Lord will do among them (Josh 3:5). Just as Yahweh parted the waters of the Red Sea to allow the Hebrew people to cross on dry land (Exod 14:21–22, 29), so he also stopped the flow of the flooded Jordan River so the people could cross over on dry ground (Josh 3:14–17). As the exodus generation celebrated the crossing of the Red Sea with a song extolling God's praise (Exod 15:1–21), the new generation commemorated their crossing by erecting a stone memorial (Josh 4:1–9).[56]

In a sense, the crossing of the Jordan River is a recapitulation of the deliverance at the Red Sea, a new demonstration of Yahweh's constant character. The entry into Canaan follows the paradigm of God's greatest act of salvation on behalf of his people. Yet while the crossing of the Jordan and the conquest of Canaan clearly appears to be modeled after the crossing of the Red Sea, the event is less dramatic than the exodus, lacking the sense of escalation and eschatological fulfillment that characterizes an antitype.[57] The conquest (like the exile) thus becomes further proof, reinforcing the expectation that God

---

54 While Joshua is the new leader of the Israelites, Deut 34:10–12 makes it clear that he does not fulfill the expectation of another prophet like Moses (see Deut 18:15–20). James Hamilton, *God's Glory in Salvation through Judgment: A Biblical Theology* (Crossway, 2010), 132; Ninow, *Indicators of Typology*, 146.

55 "Israel's crossing of the Jordan symbolically marks their transition out of the hostile, precarious, and chaotic wilderness." Waltke, *Old Testament Theology*, 517.

56 Dempster notes further comparisons between the exodus/wilderness and the conquest: 1) the original Passover occurred before the exodus from Egypt "and the conquest of Egypt's army," and the Israelites likewise celebrated the Passover feast before the conquest of Canaan; 2) the manna stopped after the Israelites crossed the Jordan into Canaan—"the people need no more miraculous provision: the food of Canaan is miracle itself (Jos. 5:11–12)"; and 3) like Moses, Joshua is confronted by an angel of the Lord and instructed to remove his shoes for he was only holy ground (Exod 3:1–5; Josh 5:13–15). Dempster, *Dominion and Dynasty*, 128. As Daube states, the crossing of the Jordan in Josh 3–4 "is full of elements designed to recall the crossing of the Red Sea under Moses." Daube, *Exodus Pattern*, 11. See also Waltke, *Old Testament Theology*, 517; Merrill, *Everlasting Dominion*, 417; etc.

57 Typology is not simply about repetition and common patterns throughout history. Rather, typology involves a single horizon of fulfillment, with the eschaton as its goal. It is a melding of correspondence and increase; the element of escalation is crucial, for "Israel hoped not simply for a repetition of God's acts but for a repetition of an unprecedented nature." David L. Baker, "Typology and the Christian Use of the Old Testament," in Beale, *Right Doctrine*, 316–317.

will continue to act in the same way, and even greater, in the future. Joshua himself demonstrates an expectation of a future exodus-type event when he calls the people to renewed commitment and rehearses God's acts on their behalf, in particular the deliverance at the Red Sea and protection in the wilderness (Josh 24:2–13).[58]

Theologically, the conquest involves possession and dominion. While the exodus was concerned with the creation of a people, the nation of Israel, the conquest was centered on the possession of a land, the land promised to Abraham.[59] Joshua's objective from the outset of the conquest was clearly military. Relying on God's power and direction, the Israelites conquered city after city and battled with fierce armies, systematically taking control of the land of Canaan through a "divide and conquer" tactic beginning with the destruction of Jericho.[60] The significance of the land is reinforced by the summary of the Conquest in Josh 11:16–23:

> So Joshua took all that land, the hill country and all the Negeb and all the land of Goshen and the lowland and the Arabah and the hill country of Israel and its lowland from Mount Halak, which rises toward Seir, as far as Baal-gad in the Valley of Lebanon below Mount Hermon. And he captured all their kings and struck them and put them to death. Joshua made war a long time with all those kings. There was not a city that made peace with the people of Israel except the Hivites, the inhabitants of Gibeon. They took them all in battle. For it was the Lord's doing to harden their hearts that they should come against Israel in battle, in order that they should be devoted to destruction and should receive no mercy but be destroyed, just as the Lord commanded Moses. And Joshua came at that time and cut off the Anakim from the hill country, from Hebron, from Debir, from Anab, and from all the hill country of Judah, and from all the hill country of Israel. Joshua devoted them to destruction with their cities. There was none of the Anakim left in the land of the people of Israel. Only in Gaza, in Gath, and in Ashdod did some remain. So Joshua took the whole land, according to all that the Lord had spoken to Moses. And Joshua gave it for an inheritance to Israel according to their tribal allotments. And the land had rest from war.

---

58  Dempster, *Dominion and Dynasty*, 130.

59  David M. Howard, Jr., *Joshua*, NAC 5 (Broadman & Holman, 2000), 56. Each of the four sections of the book of Joshua revolves in some way around the land—entry into the land (Josh 1–5), fighting for the land (Josh 6–12), dividing the land (Josh 13–21), and living in the land (Josh 22–23). Jensen, *Joshua*, 16.

60  Merrill, *Kingdom of Priests*, 108; Antony F. Campbell, *Joshua to Chronicles: An Introduction* (Westminster John Knox, 2004), 17.

Joshua portrays the importance of the land and Israel's possession of it utilizing terminology hearkening back to Genesis.[61] According to Dempster, "the land itself is viewed as a new Eden, the place from which a new restoration of the pristine conditions of the entire creation can commence."[62] Hamilton draws a connection between the angel holding a drawn sword whom Joshua encounters at Jericho, the first city conquered by the Israelites (Josh 5:13), and the cherubim guarding the way to Eden with a flaming sword after man's removal from the Garden (Gen 3:24). Yahweh's presence in the midst of the Israelites seems to have "recaptured something of the Edenic experience. As they cross into the land, Israel moves in the direction of the reversal of the curse."[63] Yet, as was the case in the Garden, residence in the Promised Land requires obedience to Yahweh, and disobedience results in expulsion or exile.[64] Life in the Promised Land was not as Edenic as the Israelites must have hoped.

As noted previously, the OT is organized into literary blocks which share common vocabulary, genre, thematic continuities, and other intertextual connections.[65] Literarily, the conquest introduces the second major section of the Old Testament, the Former Prophets (Joshua to Kings), which recounts the history of Israel from their entry into Canaan to the exile in Babylon. Brueggemann describes the crossing of the Jordan as "the juncture between two histories"—that is, between "landlessness on the way to the land" and "landed Israel in the process of losing the land."[66] While the story of salvation history is clearly continuing, there is a natural break between the Pentateuch and the Former Prophets, between Deuteronomy and Joshua.[67]

We have already noted the abundance of intertextual references in which the Exodus and wilderness wanderings are united in statements of typological expectation. If the conquest was thought by the ancient Jews to be inseparably linked with these events, and thus included within the anticipation of a

---

61 Within Joshua all else is superseded by a focus on the land as fulfillment of God's promises. According to Kaiser, land "is the fourth most frequent substantive in the Hebrew Bible." Kaiser, "Promised Land," 302. He goes on to say that the Bible insists that the land was a gift where God's chosen people would both dwell and rule as a nation. The idea of the land as God's gift to Israel is repeated throughout the Pentateuch, but in Joshua it dominates, occurring over fifty times. Howard, *Joshua*, 57.

62 Dempster, *Dominion and Dynasty*, 127–128.

63 Hamilton, *God's Glory*, 148. See also Dempster, *Dominion and Dynasty*, 128.

64 Dempster, *Dominion and Dynasty*, 129; Ninow, *Indicators of Typology*, 148–149; Howard, *Joshua*, 59–60.

65 Waltke, *Old Testament Theology*, 55.

66 Walter Brueggemann, *The Land* (Fortress, 1977), 71–72. According to Dempster, "in recent times, the Former Prophets have been viewed as one historical work, the Deuteronomistic History—the working out in history of the blessings and curses of Deuteronomy in the life of the Israelite nation." Dempster, *Dominion and Dynasty*, 125; Merrill, *Everlasting Dominion*, 413.

67 Howard, *Joshua*, 54–56.

new exodus event, one would expect to see references to the conquest within these same passages, or at least within close proximity. Yet this is not typically the case. Within the Pentateuch there are several statements which seemingly unite the entry into Canaan with what came before, yet these passages are actually anticipatory of the conquest itself, not a typological repetition of the event.[68] For example, Casey draws upon what he calls "Israel's primary confession of faith" (Deut 26:8–9) to validate the inclusion of the conquest under the umbrella of "exodus."[69] Yet, while this passage clearly connects the deliverance from Egypt and the journey to the Promised Land, Casey does not seem to recognize that at this time the nation of Israel is still outside the land, having not yet crossed over the Jordan and settled in Canaan. This may be a subtle distinction, but it is a distinction nonetheless.

Certainly, instances of historical rehearsal move quite quickly from recollection of the exodus to statements regarding "the land" and possession of it (Neh 9:9–21; Pss 78:40–54; 105:26–45; 106:7–27; 136:10–22; Jer 2:6–7; Ezek 20:10–16). Yet these passages are not explicitly typological in emphasis;[70] they are instead reminiscences of Israel's history for later generations. References to the land of the Amorites occasionally appear within close proximity to exodus/wilderness language (Josh 24:5–8; Ps 136:10–22; Amos 2:10), but do not

---

68  E.g., Deut 1:30–31, "The Lord your God who goes before you will himself fight for you, just as he did for you in Egypt before your eyes, and in the wilderness, where you have seen how the Lord your God carried you, as a man carries his son, all the way that you went until you came to this place." See also Exod 16:32–35; Deut 8:1–20; 9:7; 11:2–6. Hamilton indicates that Moses' historical review in Deut 1–3 is intended to motivate Israel to obedience as they move forward in the next step of their journey by reminding them of Yahweh's acts of salvation on their behalf and of the judgment God sent on the sinful wilderness generation. Hamilton, *God's Glory*, 120–121.

69  He designates the term "exodus" as "the collection of traditions about Israel's experiences from the time of the Egyptian captivity until its settlement in Canaan." Casey, "Exodus Typology in Revelation," ix–x.

70  According to Casey, "the linkage of Exodus and typology ... limits what may be labeled 'Exodus typology.' Exodus traditions are cited in the Bible in remembrances of the past, as clues to the identity of God, and as the basis for social and cultic legislation. Such uses are to be distinguished, however, from the typological understanding of Exodus in which the constitutive traditions are used analogically to provide a silhouette of the continuing redemptive activity of God." Casey, "Exodus Typology in Revelation," xi. This distinction may be a bit forced, however, particularly with regard to what Casey calls "remembrances of the past." These often-lengthy historical rehearsals recall Israel's past with the purpose (whether implicit or explicit) of making sure the later generations do not forget the ways God has acted on their behalf or brought judgment upon the nations in the past, so that they do not repeat the mistakes of their ancestors or the pagan nations, and that they might believe and not lose hope, even in their trials. The basis of this is clearly an understanding that Yahweh does not change, that he is faithful to keep his promises, and that he will act in the future in ways that are consistent with his name, character, and the past. In short, even Israel's historical rehearsals have a typological undercurrent. Yet within the historical rehearsal, the conquest is typically excluded from explicit typological emphasis.

refer to the Promised Land itself.[71] In other such passages (Lev 23:42–43; Deut 29:2–6; Josh 24:17; Ps 78:12–20) there is no mention of the land or the conquest of it.

One cannot deny the presence of Conquest language within the prophets (e.g., Jer 11:3–8; Ezek 20:34–38), most explicitly in Jeremiah 16:14–15 (cf. Jer 23:7–8),

> Therefore, behold, the days are coming, declares the Lord, when it shall no longer be said, "As the Lord lives who brought up the people of Israel out of the land of Egypt," but "As the Lord lives who brought up the people of Israel out of the north country and out of all the countries where he had driven them." For I will bring them back to their own land that I gave to their fathers.

However, this passage seems to be the exception rather than the norm in its incorporation of the conquest into a passage of typological import.[72] More often, the prophets used conquest language to remind the people of God's judgment on the exodus generation for their violation of the covenant. For example, when Ezekiel mentions "the land of Israel" in 20:38, he is recalling the Israelites' rebellion in the wilderness and Yahweh's subsequent prohibition of the exodus generation from entering the land (cf. Ezek 20:6–10; Jer 11:3–8). Thus, mentioning "the land" in these instances is not a case of typological expectation of a future conquest, but rather a warning that God will act likewise to judge future rebellion. Even the very hopeful Jer 16:14–15 occurs within the context of a prophecy about the coming exile as a means of judgment.

The same is true in the NT. Stephen's rehearsal of Israel's history before Caiaphas in Acts 7 proceeds naturally from discussion of the exodus and wilderness wanderings (7:30–44) to the entry into Canaan (7:45). However, Stephen's sermon did not have an explicitly typological purpose, but was instead

---

71 According to Waltke, "Israel's original land grant, and their heartland, is Canaan ... (Gen. 11:31; 12:5; 17:8; Exod. 6:4; Lev. 14:34; 25:38; Num. 13:2, 17; Deut. 32:49; Josh. 14:1–19:51). This is the land Israel is instructed to dispossess. But the first land they occupy, because the Amorites attack the pilgrim nation on their way to their inheritance, is the land of the Amorites in Transjordan (Num. 21:24, 35; 32:29; Jos. 22:9, 13, 15, 32)." Waltke, *Old Testament Theology*, 538.

72 Compare the pledge of a future covenant in Jer 31:31–32, "Behold, the days are coming, declares the Lord, when I will make a new covenant with the house of Israel and the house of Judah, not like the covenant that I made with their fathers on the day when I took them by the hand to bring them out of the land of Egypt, my covenant that they broke, though I was their husband, declares the Lord." In this and other such passages which anticipate a future exodus (e.g., Isa 10:26; 11:16; Hos 2:16–17 MT; 12:10 MT; 13:4–5; Joel 1–2), the emphasis is on God's action in bringing his people out of bondage in Egypt and protecting them in the wilderness, with little or no mention of the conquest.

intended to identify the Jewish leaders with the unbelieving and rebellious Jews of ancient history (7:51–53).[73] In 1 Cor 10, Paul exemplifies the Israelites' deliverance at the Red Sea (10:1–2) and protection in the wilderness (10:4), as well as God's judgment on them for their acts of disobedience (10:5–11) in order to demonstrate the folly of participating in idolatry, sexual immorality, grumbling, and testing God. He does so with no conquest language whatsoever. The typologically rich letter to the Hebrews urges Christians to be cautious of unbelief (Heb 4:1), lest they meet the same fate as the exodus generation, who "were unable to enter because of unbelief" (Heb 3:19). There is no explicit mention of "the land," and like in the prophets, the implicit reference relates their lack of entry, not the conquest itself.

## Summary

So we return to the question with which this section commenced. What exactly is entailed within exodus typology? From our analysis, we can conclude that historically, exodus typology covers the period immediately leading up to the Israelites' deliverance from Egypt up to their arrival and encampment at the bank of the Jordan River. This includes the plagues, the Passover, the Red Sea crossing, the wilderness wanderings, God's provision of water and food, the Sinai theophany and covenant, the Ten Commandments, the golden calf episode, the instructions for and assembly of the tabernacle, and the journey itself.[74] Theologically, one can recognize within exodus typology the key themes which characterize these events—Yahweh as sovereign ruler, righteous judge, and ever-present redeemer of his chosen people. Literarily, one cannot limit exodus typology to simply the exodus proper, as the exodus and wilderness wanderings have been bound together both historically and theologically. Likewise, it is not possible to focus solely on the book of Exodus, since these same historical events are narrated and expounded upon throughout the remainder of the Pentateuch.

---

73 This is not to say that there is no typological significance to the identification of the Jewish leaders with the unbelieving Jews of the wilderness generation, for Yahweh's future acts of judgment are modeled after the past in the same way as his works of salvation. But the emphasis on Canaan is not typological in nature.

74 Ninow, *Indicators of Typology*, 20. Clifford makes the case that "the Exodus in the Book of Exodus is a comprehensive event, embracing the defeat of Pharaoh, the leading out of the people from Egypt, the journey in the wilderness, the giving of the Law, and the taking of Canaan (symbolized by Sinai). And it was so read by readers in early Judaism and Christianity and beyond." Richard J. Clifford, "The Exodus in the Christian Bible: The Case for 'Figural' Reading," *Theological Studies* 63 (2002): 347–348. It is not clear from this statement, however, whether Clifford would include the conquest itself within exodus typology, for he is referring specifically to Exodus as a distinct literary unit.

Yet the conquest must be considered a separate, though closely related, event which falls outside the umbrella of exodus typology, for it involves a new generation, a new leader, a second "crossing," and is recorded in the OT in terms of distinct theological emphases. Additionally, while the later OT and NT writers do make reference to the conquest on occasions of historical rehearsal, "the land" is typically given explicit typological import only in negative terms, relating Yahweh's judgment upon the unbelieving Israelites and refusal to allow the exodus generation to enter the Promised Land. Thus, exodus typology incorporates the events immediately leading up to and including the departure from Egypt, as well as the wilderness wanderings from Egypt to the bank of the Jordan River. It includes not only the book of Exodus itself, but also elements from Leviticus, Numbers, and Deuteronomy as they pertain to this particular period of time and amplify the exodus and wilderness accounts. Essentially, exodus typology begins and ends with Moses. With his death (Deut 34:7), a new chapter of history could commence; with the end of the exodus generation, the new generation could finally begin their conquest of the land of promise.

CHAPTER 4

# EXPECTATION OF AN ESCHATOLOGICAL EXODUS WITHIN JEWISH AND EARLY CHRISTIAN THOUGHT

HAVING DELINEATED the boundaries of exodus typology to include the wilderness wanderings but exclude the conquest,[1] we now turn to an analysis of this exodus tradition within ancient literature. There was indeed a prevailing expectation within Judaism and early Christianity that in the future God would redeem his people in a deliverance even greater than the historical exodus from Egypt, and exodus typology was the means by which they espoused this expectation. As Eslinger so eloquently stated,

> To have read much of the Bible is to have read something about the exodus. Where it isn't lying on the surface, as in the argument for establishing the law (Exod. 20.2), the exodus is often an assumption without knowledge of which a reader will go astray. It becomes a leitmotif whose theological-political significance echoes through the pages of the Bible.[2]

A comprehensive analysis of exodus typology within ancient literature is well beyond the scope of this project. Yet even a brief overview is helpful for realizing the breadth of exodus imagery throughout the canon as well as for identifying patterns of occurrence.[3] This chapter will review the presence of

---

[1] Evidence in the form of numerous examples from the OT and NT was used to determine the content of exodus typology as the events contained in the books of Exodus, Numbers, Leviticus, and Deuteronomy, from the bondage of the Hebrew people in Egypt to the encampment of the young nation of Israel on the bank of the Jordan River.

[2] Lyle Eslinger, "Freedom or Knowledge? Perspective and Purpose in the Exodus Narrative (Exodus 1–15)," *JSOT* 52 (1991): 43.

[3] For a more extensive and inclusive discussion of the Exodus tradition in ancient literature, see Jay Casey, "Exodus Typology in the Book of Revelation" (PhD diss., The Southern Baptist Theological Seminary, 1981). Casey devotes a chapter each to the OT, the writings of

exodus imagery within OT, NT, apocryphal, and Qumran writings, with special attention given to the so-called "Isaianic new exodus." [4]

## The Old Testament and Ancient Judaism

The typological interpretation or rehearsal of key elements of the exodus is not limited to any one section of the OT, but occurs widely across historical, poetic, and prophetic literature. According to Watts, "there are over 120 explicit Old Testament references to the Exodus in law, narrative, prophecy, and psalm, and it is difficult to exaggerate its importance."[5] The usage and prominence of exodus imagery varies greatly from writing to writing, and even from verse to verse within a particular text. Yet every occasion of exodus imagery serves to recall God's great deliverance of his people, to reinforce the reader's relationship to the covenant generation, and to remind the reader of the responsibilities inherent in being God's chosen people and the judgment that falls on those who reject Yahweh and his commandments.

Even while the events of the larger exodus experience were still unfolding, the Scriptural accounts demonstrate an expectation of a new exodus. As discussed in the previous chapter, the structure, content, and context of the Song of Moses in Exod 15 portray the events at the Red Sea as a type for future deliverance, including God's protection of the Israelites in the wilderness. Another example is found in the Balaam oracles of Num 23–24. Balaam recounts God's deliverance of the Israelites out of Egypt in Num 23:22, saying "God brings them out of Egypt and is for them like the horns of the wild ox." In the next chapter, Balaam quotes this same verse but converts the plural personal pronoun ("them") to singular ("him") and changes the focus from the Israelites of old to a future king of Israel (see Num 24:8a). Context makes it clear that "the experience of this future king of Israel is described in the same terms as the exodus experience of the Israelites."[6] Elsewhere, near the conclusion of the exodus account, Moses describes Israel's future in terms of their recent history—disobedience will result in curses such as their bondage in Egypt and the plagues they witnessed there (Deut 28:15–68), while God will ultimately reward obedience by gathering his people

---

Judaism, and the NT, describing his study not as "a detailed investigation, but only a descriptive analysis of the relevant texts" (Ibid., xi). Casey's coverage of intertextual references to the exodus period in ancient literature is the most exhaustive I have found.

    4  Perhaps no other prophet draws upon the exodus as frequently or as fully as Isaiah. For this reason, Isaiah will be discussed separately and in great detail.

    5  Rikki E. Watts, "Exodus," in *NDBT*, 478.

    6  Friedbert Ninow, *Indicators of Typology within the Old Testament: The Exodus Motif*, Friedensauer Schriftenreihe; Reihe I, Theologie, Bd. 4 (Peter Lang, 2001), 139–140.

from their lands of captivity and restoring to them the land of promise (Deut 30:1–10).[7]

Among the widely varied themes and tenors of the Psalms, the reader again finds an emphasis on the continuity of God's activity and the constancy of his character throughout history. While Casey may be correct that "the Exodus rarely has a typological significance in the Psalms comparable to that seen among the prophets,"[8] it should come as no surprise to find within Israel's worship liturgy numerous recollections of the most defining moment in Israel's history, for "if the Psalmists wish to sing of God as Redeemer, they naturally take the Exodus as their theme."[9] There is a sense in which, for the psalmist, remembering God's actions in the past, particularly in the exodus, functions as a source of comfort and expectation that Yahweh will once again act on behalf of his people in the future.[10] For example, Ps 106 recounts their miraculous deliverance from Egypt at the Red Sea (Ps 106:8–12) to typify God's gathering of his people from among the nations ("Save us, O Lord our God, and gather us from among the nations, that we may give thanks to your holy name and glory in your praise," Ps 106:47).[11] Hyde sums up the use of the exodus in the Psalter in the following way:

> First, when there is any appeal to history in the psalms, the Exodus is overwhelmingly the choice for the appeal. Second, although we are handicapped by not knowing exactly when and how the psalms were used, the ones containing Exodus material cover every type and appear to be among the most important. Third, the Exodus is used in a way that is often

---

7 Ibid., 148–149.

8 Casey, "Exodus Typology in Revelation," 40.

9 R. E. Nixon, *The Exodus in the New Testament*, Tyndale New Testament Lecture 1962 (Tyndale, 1963), 8; Clark Hyde, "The Remembrance of the Exodus in the Psalms," *Worship* 62 (1988): 409–410.

10 In concert with the rest of Scripture, the Psalms employ some reference to the creedal formula, "brought you out of the land of Egypt" (Pss 105:37, 43; 136:11) and contain references to the most characteristic elements of the exodus event—the plagues, signs and wonders in Egypt (Pss 78:12, 43–51; 105:27–36; 106:7), the crossing of the Red Sea and destruction of Pharaoh's army (Pss 78:13, 53; 106:9, 11; 136:13–15), the Passover (Ps 105:36), guidance in the wilderness by the pillar of cloud and fire (Pss 78:14, 52–53; 105:39; 106:9; 136:16), the provision of water, manna, and quail (Pss 78:15–16, 20, 24–29; 105:40–41), and Israel's rebellion and subsequent judgment (Pss 78:18, 40–41; 106:13–27).

11 Psalms of communal lament tend to remember the glorious past, particularly the exodus, as a prayer for God to "renew the exodus" in the not-so-glorious present (e.g., Pss 44:7–14; 74:12–17; 77:12–20; 80:8–11). In addition, the exodus features prominently within psalms associated with covenant renewal, reminding the reader of God's faithfulness during the exodus, despite the deceitfulness of the Hebrew people (Pss. 78, 81, 105, 106, 135, 136). Hyde, "Remembrance of the Exodus," 405, 407–408; Richard J. Clifford, "The Exodus in the Christian Bible: The Case for 'Figural' Reading," *Theological Studies* 63 (2002): 349–350.

crucial within the psalms that refer to it. Finally, there is so much parallelism between the use of the Exodus in the psalms and its use in the 'historical credos' of the Pentateuch, the Deuteronomic history and the prophets, that we can make the same sort of assertions which are often made about the credos. In general, we can see that the Exodus is remembered when the psalmists wish to make a basic statement about identity—both that of Israel and that of God.[12]

THE PROPHETS

The typological interpretation of the exodus is most prevalent in the prophetic literature—"it is the key by which the prophets understand her past and explain the hope of her future."[13] The attentive reader finds exodus connotations in Jeremiah, Ezekiel, Daniel, Hosea, Joel, Amos, Micah, Nahum, Haggai, Zechariah, Malachi, and of course, Isaiah. Often, prophetic references to the exodus are contained within the formulaic expression, "brought you up out of the land of Egypt," that also recurs throughout the Pentateuch, historical writings, and the psalter. This confession functions as a call to covenant obedience by reminding Israel that their God is Yahweh, the God of the exodus.[14] In other instances, the imagery is more subtle, veiled in allusions to the key themes and events of the exodus and often intertwined with other OT

---

12  Hyde, "Remembrance of the Exodus," 411–412. Hyde determines that sixteen psalms "either obviously or apparently mention the principal events of the Exodus" (which he takes to be everything from the departure from Egypt to the entry into the Promised Land. He admits that, "measured against 150, this is not a large proportion of the Psalter. Nonetheless, it is clear that the Exodus is by far the most common historical event referred to in the psalms." Ibid., 404–405.

13  Philip S. Haugen, "The Consummation of the Exodus: A Study of the Exodus Motif in the Revelation" (S.T.M. thesis, Concordia Seminary, 1985), 4; James Plastaras, *The God of Exodus: The Theology of the Exodus Narratives* (Bruce Publishing, 1966), 7. According to Clifford, "the prophets, of course, are not modern historians recounting an event 'as it actually happened,' but preachers confronting their hearers with the claims the Exodus makes upon them." Clifford, "Exodus in the Christian Bible," 350.

14  Pentateuch (Exod 4:8; 6:6; 13:3; 20:2; Num 15:41; Deut 13:5, 10; 20:1), Historical (Josh 24:6; Judg 6:8; 1 Kgs 8:51–53; 2 Kgs 17:7; 2 Chr 7:22), Psalter (Pss 81:10; 136:11), Prophets (Jer 2:6; 7:22; 11:4, 7; 31; 32:21; 34:13; Dan 9:15; Amos 2:10; 3:1; 9:7; Hos 12:9; 13:4; Mic 6:4). According to Casey, these statements do not contain typological significance, but are simply references to the God of the exodus within remembrances of Israel's past. Casey, "Exodus Typology in Revelation," 6–7. Yet, as we have asserted previously, the use of a stock formula or historical rehearsal does not negate the typological emphasis within a passage. Rather, the overall witness of Scripture demonstrates that the biblical writers understood the exodus period typologically, and so one cannot dismiss at least the possibility of typological import within intertextual references to these events. Even Casey admits that the stock phrases can occur "in contexts that sometimes give them a typological meaning." Ibid., 9.

imagery.[15] As within the rest of the later OT writings, the prophetic literature spans the gamut of the broader exodus experience—from the departure from Egypt to the forty years in the wilderness, from the Sinai covenant to the Israelites' rebellion against Yahweh.

### Jeremiah

At various points in his prophecy, Jeremiah employs exodus imagery to establish a typology of disobedience—"Israel/Judah is identified as the disobedient and rebellious people, and the reminiscences of the whole story of the Exodus provide a history of their disobedience."[16] Jeremiah portrays the coming judgment in terms reminiscent of the trials endured by the Israelites in the wilderness. For instance, the "poisoned water" (Jer 8:14; 9:15) with which Yahweh nourishes his people signifies a reversal of Yahweh's provision of water from the rock (Exod 17:1–6), and even the turning of bitter water to sweet at Marah (Exod 15:23–25). Jeremiah frequently depicts Israel as unfaithful and disobedient, in contrast to God's gracious faithfulness.[17]

However, Jeremiah's prophecy is not only characterized by judgment and doom. His new exodus expectations portray a time when the messianic Davidic king would reign in righteous justice. Jeremiah 23:1–8 makes it evident that he anticipated not only a return from bondage, but an eschatological event in which the people would return to an Edenic state and experience the fulfillment of the Abrahamic promises. The concepts of land and posterity are both present in Jer 23:3—"Then I will gather the remnant of my flock out of all the countries where I have driven them, and I will bring them back to their fold, and they shall be fruitful and multiply"—uniting the new exodus expectation with God's charge to Adam and Eve in the garden (Gen. 1:28).[18] Twice in this passage (Jer 23:5, 7) Jeremiah states, "behold, the days are coming" before recalling the messianic prophecy of an eternal Davidic king and

---

15  For example, see Nah 1:1–8. The prophet portrays God as exercising his wrath upon his enemies (1:2) and drying up the sea (1:4), destroying his foes with a flood (1:8), and caring for those who believe in him (1:7). While implicit, these images combine to draw the reader's mind back to a time when God rained judgment on the Egyptians, parted the Red Sea, destroyed Pharaoh and his army by causing the water to rush back over them, and provided for his people in a multitude of ways in the wilderness. With this context in mind, Nahum's description of the mountains quaking and the earth trembling at Yahweh's presence (1:5) likewise calls to mind the natural phenomena that took place when the Lord's presence descended on Mount Sinai (Exod 19:16–20).

16  Ibid., 12.

17  For more of how this "typology of disobedience" is fleshed out in Jeremiah, see ibid., 12–15.

18  Ninow, *Indicators of Typology*, 196–198.

the eschatological era of redemption.[19] Jeremiah expects this new exodus to exceed even the most significant event in Israel's history, anticipating a day when the Israelites no longer say

> "As the LORD lives who brought up the people of Israel out of the land of Egypt," but "As the LORD lives who brought up and led the offspring of the house of Israel out of the north country and out of all the countries where he had driven them." Then they shall dwell in their own land (Jer 23:7–8; cf. 16:14–15).

Jeremiah's hope for a new exodus culminates in the inauguration of a new covenant (Jer 30–31), unlike the one Yahweh made with Israel after bringing them out of Egypt, a covenant which the Israelites soon broke. This new covenant will not be written on stone like the Ten Commandments, but on the hearts of the people (Jer 31:32–33).[20] Jeremiah again uses the words "behold, days are coming" (Jer 30:3; 31:31), this time to introduce their restoration to the land of their fathers, as well as the eschatological new covenant. References to the coming Davidic king (Jer 30:9, 21), images of a fruitful vineyard and garden (Jer 31:5, 12), and the depiction of God turning sorrow and mourning into celebration and joy (Jer 31:4, 7, 9, 12–13) highlight the eschatological nature of these events.[21] The couching of this future day in terms of a new exodus is further evident in Jeremiah's recollection of the ultimate goal of the exodus itself, "And you shall be my people, and I will be your God" (Jer 30:22; see also 31:1; 32:38; cf. Exod 29:45–46). Jeremiah envisions God once again leading his people, this time in an even greater exodus that would not only result in liberation from exile throughout the "ends of the earth" (Jer 31:8, NIV), but also in a special relationship with him, one that involves salvation from sin.[22] For as Yahweh promises, "I will forgive their iniquity, and I will remember their sin no more" (Jer 31:34).

### Ezekiel

Like his contemporaries, Ezekiel couches his prophetic oracle of the coming judgment of Israel (Ezek 20:5–26) within a rehearsal of Israel's rebellion

---

19 Ibid., 199; Casey, "Exodus Typology in Revelation," 14.

20 Jeremiah's "statement of the new Exodus will later be borrowed by New Testament passages (Matthew 26:28; Mark 14:24; Luke 22:20; 1 Corinthians 11:25; 2 Corinthians 3:6)." Clifford, "Exodus in the Christian Bible," 351–352.

21 Ninow, *Indicators of Typology*, 202; Gary Yates, "New Exodus and No Exodus in Jeremiah 26–45: Promise and Warning to the Exiles in Babylon," *TynBul* 57 (2006): 4–5.

22 Ninow, *Indicators of Typology*, 203; Yates, "New Exodus and No Exodus," 4.

in the wilderness through "a threefold charge of idolatry, profanation of the Sabbaths, and rejection of the Covenant statutes and ordinances."[23] He then promises a deliverance from exile that is patterned after the original exodus (Ezek 20:32–44) and will result in Israel acknowledging Yahweh's sovereignty (Ezek 20:38, 42, 44) and meeting him "face to face" (Ezek 20:35).[24] This eschatological exodus is portrayed in terms of a new "covenant of peace" (Ezek 34:25) and a period of protection and provision in a restored wilderness (Ezek 34:11–16, 25–29). Ezekiel prophesies of a time when Yahweh will rescue his people from their plight and gather them from all the corners of the earth (Ezek 34:6, 10–13, 27), a day when "they shall know that I am the Lord their God with them, and that they, the house of Israel, are my people" (Ezek 34:30; cf. 37:25–28).[25]

While the content of Ezekiel's new exodus expectation is consistent with the other prophetic texts, at times the form of the exodus imagery within Ezekiel differs, perhaps due in part to its more apocalyptic[26] features. At least two sections of Ezekiel are built on structural allusions pointing back to major sections of the exodus narrative. For example, Ezek 9 portrays the slaying of the rebellious inhabitants of Jerusalem in a manner similar to the tenth plague of the Passover—those who receive a mark on their foreheads are spared death by the six messengers who are sent through the city to "kill, without showing pity or compassion" but are instructed "not [to] touch anyone who has the mark" (Ezek 9:5–6, NIV; cf. Exod 12:12–13, 22–23). Perhaps a more obvious structural allusion to the exodus is Ezekiel's prophecy of the rebuilding of the Temple and its furnishings (Ezek 40–42; cf. Exod 25–31, 35–40) and the glory of the Lord indwelling the Temple (Ezek 43:1–5; cf. Exod 40:34–35).[27]

---

23  Casey, "Exodus Typology in Revelation," 220. Casey asserts that Ezek 20 "is unmatched in all of scripture in terms of its comprehensive use of the Exodus tradition." Ibid., 221.

24  Clifford, "Exodus in the Christian Bible," 352; Casey, "Exodus Typology in Revelation," 22.

25  Bernhard A. Anderson, "Exodus and Covenant in Second Isaiah and Prophetic Tradition," in *Magnalia Dei: The Mighty Acts of God: Essays on the Bible and Archaeology in Memory of G. Ernest Wright*, ed. Frank Moore Cross, Werner E. Lemke, and Patrick D. Miller, Jr. (Doubleday, 1976), 354.

26  Although Ezekiel does not entirely fit the accepted description of apocalyptic as "a genre of revelatory literature with a narrative framework, in which a revelation is mediated by an otherworldly being to a human recipient, disclosing a transcendent reality which is both temporal, insofar as it envisages eschatological salvation, and spatial insofar as it involves another, supernatural world" (John J. Collins, *Apocalypse: The Morphology of a Genre*, Semeia 14 [Scholars, 1979], 9), it does employ literary devices typically associated with apocalyptic literature in general, such as the use of dream visions, symbolic language, and themes of divine judgment, victory, and intervention in history. Lamar Eugene Cooper, *Ezekiel*, NAC 17 (Broadman & Holman, 1994), 37–38.

27  Interestingly, both of these structural allusions recur in the Apocalypse. Compare Ezek 9 with the sealing of believers on the foreheads in Rev 7, and the temple imagery with John's

## Hosea

In Hosea, God's promise of future deliverance is played out through the actions of the author, Hosea, whose name means "salvation."[28] Hosea describes Israel's attempts to gain power through their own strength and alliances with foreign nations, their lust for success, and their repeated refusal to honor the covenant and return to Yahweh.[29] Throughout his oracle, Hosea likens the political, spiritual, and moral state of the Israelites to an adulterous wife bearing the consequences for her indiscretions (e.g., Hos 2:1–12).[30] Yahweh had delivered them, calling them out of the land of Egypt (see Hos 11:1, "out of Egypt I called my son," which hearkens back to the reference to Israel as God's "firstborn" in Exod 4:22–23). As Gomer returns to her former lifestyle (Hos 1:7), so Israel returns to a state of captivity much greater than that in Egypt (see Hos 8:13; 9:3; 11:5). Yet Hosea's loving act of buying back his wife out of the bonds of prostitution illustrates God's faithfulness not to leave his people in exile, but to redeem them out of their bondage to sin.[31]

Hosea clearly sets this coming deliverance within the context of a new exodus event, a connection immediately evident from the close proximity of the word "wilderness" with a reference to coming up from the land of Egypt:

> Therefore, behold, I will allure her, and bring her into the wilderness, and speak tenderly to her. And there I will give her her vineyards and make the Valley of Achor a door of hope. And there she shall answer as in the days of her youth, as at the time when she came out of the land of Egypt (Hos 2:14–15).

---

description of the New Jerusalem in Rev 21.

28  The name "Hosea" derives from the same Hebrew verb as the names Joshua, Isaiah, and Jesus, all of which have connotations of help, deliverance, or salvation. The name was quite appropriate for a messenger of God. Paul A. Kruger, "Hosea," *NIDOTTE* 4:707. Whether one considers Gomer's adultery, first mentioned in Hos 1:2, as a literal indication of a lifestyle of prostitution, as a proleptic statement of adulterous events occurring later in their marriage, or as a figurative reference to her spiritual idolatry, it appears that the marriage between Hosea and Gomer was a literal relationship in which Hosea was "'acting out' God's message for his people." Ninow, *Indicators of Typology*, 207–209; Eugene H. Merrill, *Kingdom of Priests: A History of Old Testament Israel* (Baker, 1996), 421–422. For discussion of the various views, see C. Hassell Bullock, *An Introduction to the Old Testament Prophetic Books* (Moody, 1986), 88–92.

29  Ninow, *Indicators of Typology*, 213–214; Steve McKenzie, "Exodus Typology in Hosea," *Restoration Quarterly* 22 (1979): 103.

30  As Anderson so eloquently states, from the time they entered Canaan, there was a "'harlotrous spirit' which gripped the people with such power that they were held helplessly in bondage to their false style of life." Anderson, "Exodus and Covenant," 350.

31  Ninow, *Indicators of Typology*, 206, 213, 215; Merrill, *Kingdom of Priests*, 423.

This theme continues in Hos 12:9—"I am the LORD your God from the land of Egypt; I will again make you dwell in tents, as in the days of the appointed feast." This most likely refers to the Feast of Booths, a time of joyful remembrance of Yahweh's provision for both their spiritual and physical needs in the wilderness (cf. Lev 23:40, 43).[32] For Hosea, the wilderness represents a state a dependency on Yahweh, a time when Israel learned to rely on him for every need, great or small, and a period of intimate fellowship between God and his people.[33] While the Israelites are condemned to exile because of their sins, Hosea foretells a new exodus in which God will lead his people back to the wilderness and establish with them an even greater covenant.

Hosea's language reveals his understanding that this coming redemption is not immediate but eschatological in nature.[34] He recalls Yahweh's covenantal vow to Abraham that his descendants would be as vast as "the sand of the sea" (Hos 1:10; cf. Gen 22:17; 32:12), and suggests that the Israelites will once again inherit the land of promise ("her vineyards," Hos 2:15). Yet the new, future exodus will surpass the original in significance, as suggested by the transformation of Achor from a hallmark of Israel's disobedience (see Josh 7) to "a door of hope" (Hos 2:15).[35] Israel will turn from her idolatrous ways once and for all (Hos 2:17), and righteousness, justice, and mercy will replace war and violence (Hos 2:18–19). "In that day" (Hos 2:16; 2:18; 2:21), the goal of the exodus will be fulfilled in its entirety, when Yahweh "will say to Not My People, 'You are my people'; and he shall say, 'You are my God'" (Hos 2:23).[36]

### Micah

The book of Micah is a series of three cycles of oracles, each of which progresses from doom to hope, from judgment to salvation, in a pattern that is evident in the very basis of Israel's history, the exodus tradition.[37] Micah looks forward to that day when God will again redeem his people from their present exile and establish his messianic kingdom (Mic 4:1–10).[38] The prophet uses a

---

32 Ninow, *Indicators of Typology*, 216.

33 Ibid., 217; Plastaras, *Creation and Covenant*, 6. Casey refers to this as Hosea's "idealized understanding of the wilderness era." Casey, "Exodus Typology in Revelation," 10.

34 McKenzie, "Exodus Typology in Hosea," 107–108.

35 Ninow, *Indicators of Typology*, 211–212.

36 God commanded that Gomer's third child be named Lo-Ammi (meaning "Not My People"), "for you are not my people, and I am not your God" (Hos 1:9). The reversal of this designation in Hos 2:23 draws to mind Exod 6:7, "I will take you as my own people, and I will be your God" (cf. Jer 30:22). Clifford, "Exodus in the Christian Bible," 350.

37 R. L. Smith, *Micah–Malachi*, WBC 32 (Word, 1984), 11.

38 Merrill, *Kingdom of Priests*, 430; Ninow, *Indicators of Typology*, 220–221. That Micah was envisioning an eschatological kingdom is suggested by the phrase "in the last days" (Mic

verbal allusion to the exodus in Mic 4:10 by linking the words "to snatch away" or "to deliver" (נצל) and "to redeem" (גאל), a combination which appears elsewhere only within the context of the historical exodus (Exod 6:6; Num 35:25).[39] Later, Micah makes the connection even more explicit, reminding the Israelites of their deliverance "from the land of Egypt … from the house of slavery" (Mic 6:4) and condemning their rebellion against the covenant (Mic 6:9–16). Yet his prophecy ends with words of hope—a promise of restoration for Jerusalem and redemption for Israel, a time of wondrous deeds "as in the days when you came out of the land of Egypt" (Mic 7:15).[40]

*Zechariah*

Zechariah has been called "the most Messianic, the most truly apocalyptic and eschatological, of all writings of the OT,"[41] so its typological development of exodus themes is especially significant. In the first of two prophetic oracles, within a pronouncement of Zion's coming king, Zechariah describes Yahweh's mighty acts on behalf of Israel and his care for his flock in terms of the exodus from Egypt and God's protection of his people in the wilderness. As he foretells the coming deliverance and restoration of Israel, he announces for Yahweh,

> I will whistle for them and gather them in, for I have redeemed them, and they shall be as many as they were before. Though I scattered them among the nations, yet in far countries they shall remember me, and with their children they shall live and return. I will bring them home from the land of Egypt, and gather them from Assyria, and I will bring them to the land of Gilead and to Lebanon, till there is no room for them. He shall pass through the sea of troubles and strike down the waves of the sea, and all the depths of the Nile shall be dried up. The pride of Assyria shall be laid low, and the scepter of Egypt shall depart (Zech 10:8–11).[42]

Zechariah closely connects the concepts of restoration (שוב) and deliverance (ישע), and couches their purpose in terms of the goal of the Sinai

---

4:1) and the expression "for ever and ever" (Mic 4:5).

39 Ninow, *Indicators of Typology*, 224.

40 Ibid., 225; Clifford, "Exodus in the Christian Bible," 351. Note also the allusion to the Red Sea deliverance in Mic 7:19. Contra Casey, who claims Micah's exodus typology is "underdeveloped and is not thematic for the salvation promised in the larger context." Casey, "Exodus Typology in Revelation," 11.

41 G. L. Robinson, "Zechariah, Book of," *ISBE* 5:3136.

42 Ninow, *Indicators of Typology*, 231–232.

covenant—"for I am the Lord their God" (Zech 10:6; cf. Exod 20:2; 29:45–46). His reference in Zech 10:8 to the Hebrew people multiplying (רבה) as a result of being redeemed recalls God's promise to Abraham (Gen 22:17; 32:12; 47:27) and draws the reader's mind back to Exod 1:7, the only other context within the Scriptures in which the reader is told that the Hebrew people increased abundantly.[43] The imagery of passing through the sea of distress, the depths of the water becoming dry, and the authority of Egypt being overthrown clearly recalls the crossing of the Red Sea. Whether through explicit phrases such as "I will bring them home from the land of Egypt" (Zech 10:10) or implicit images from the exodus, Red Sea, wilderness, and covenant, Zechariah chooses to describe the scattering of the nation of Israel in terms of ancient history rather than more recent events such as the Babylonian exile.[44] He prophesies of a future messianic king who will end the judgment and dispersion of God's people by bringing them out of exile and into a close covenant relationship with Yahweh in a manner similar to, but far greater than, their long-remembered deliverance from Egypt.

THE ISAIANIC NEW EXODUS

Scholars have coined the phrase "Isaianic new exodus" to refer to the portrayal of a second exodus in Isaiah (particularly Isa 40–55[45]). Yet the witness of Scripture makes it clear that Isaiah certainly was not alone in his expectation of a coming new exodus. Truly, nowhere in Isaiah is this expectation as blatantly clear as the statement in Jer 16:14–15:

---

43 Ninow, *Indicators of Typology*, 233. Exodus 1:7 reads "But the people of Israel were fruitful and increased greatly; they multiplied and grew exceedingly strong, so that the land was filled with them."

44 Ibid., 234–235.

45 Scholars have long questioned the unity of the book of Isaiah. Drawing on perceived differences in theme, focus, and timing, OT scholars often distinguish between Isaiah (Isa 1–39) and Deutero-Isaiah (Isa 40–66), while some further divide the text into Deutero-Isaiah (Isa 40–55) and Trito-Isaiah (Isa 56–66). For a helpful overview, see Linzy H. Hill, Jr., "Reading Isaiah as a Theological Unity Based on an Exegetical Investigation of the Exodus Motif" (PhD diss., Southwestern Baptist Theological Seminary, 1993), 10–18. While such matters cannot be ignored, the present project focuses on inter*text*uality and will thus recognize the book of Isaiah as a unified whole. Exodus typology is clearly more abundant in the chapters referred to as Deutero-Isaiah (Isa 40–55), but is certainly not exclusive to those chapters (see Isa 10:24–27; 11:12–16; 12:1–3; 35:1–10). Indeed, Hill investigates the "possibility of continuity in the book of Isaiah based upon the placement throughout the book of the Exodus motif," and ultimately concludes that the intentional use of the exodus motif throughout Isaiah is evidence for the single-authorship view. Hill, "Reading Isaiah," abstract, 185; Ninow, *Indicators of Typology*, 166–168.

> Therefore, behold, the days are coming, declares the Lord, when it shall no longer be said, "As the Lord lives who brought up the people of Israel out of the land of Egypt," but "As the Lord lives who brought up the people of Israel out of the north country and out of all the countries where he had driven them." For I will bring them back to their own land that I gave to their fathers.

Indeed, it is important to acknowledge that even scholars question the paradigmatic role of Isaiah's use of exodus typology on his theology. Merrill, for instance, seems to suggest that Isaiah represented the return from exile in terms of creation typology rather than the exodus. While he certainly recognizes the prominence of exodus imagery within Isa 40–66 (see specifically Isa 43:14; 51:9–10), he focuses more on the creation imagery which is woven throughout the whole of Isaiah. According to Merrill,

> Two major passages in the Old Testament focus on God's work of creation, namely, Genesis 1–2 and Isaiah 40–55…. These occur where they do (1) in order to instruct Israel as to her origins as a nation among nations and as to her role in the kingdom purposes of God that precipitated his work of creation; and (2) to enable exilic Israel to understand that a re-creation is about to take place, one with both historical (return from exile) and eschatological (restoration and reconstitution of the nation to its intended perfection) dimensions. Thus, in a sense history begins and ends with creation.[46]

While Merrill interprets the coming judgment in Isaiah as a return to the state of chaos which existed before Yahweh brought about order in creation (Isa 24:1; cf. 18b–19),[47] Hamilton understands Isaiah's metaphorical description of Israel as a vineyard (Isa 5) to call to mind God's initial purposes for man in the Garden. Instead of a reversal of creation, he sees God's judgment on Israel as exile "from Yahweh's vineyard just as Adam was exiled from Eden."[48] Merrill and Hamilton agree, however, that Isaiah contrasts this judgment by portraying the return from exile and the restoration of Judah in terms of a new creation—he emphasizes Yahweh as the Creator who cares for Israel as a mother tends her newborn child (Isa 49:15), who restores to her the land

---

[46] Eugene H. Merrill, *Everlasting Dominion: A Theology of the Old Testament* (Broadman & Holman, 2006), 102.

[47] Ibid., 504.

[48] James M. Hamilton, Jr. *God's Glory in Salvation through Judgment: A Biblical Theology* (Crossway, 2010), 193.

which he promised to Abraham (Isa 51:2), and who redeems the land to its Edenic state (Isa 51:3). Isaiah provides "a glimpse into a future day when the Lord would destroy the old foundations and create a new heaven and earth (Isa. 65:17–66:24) ... and [Israel] would share with all creation the universal peace of such a new environment (Isa 65:18–25)."[49]

It is important to recognize, however, that the themes of new creation and new exodus are not mutually exclusive. Rather the traditions often meld together in the prophetic writings. According to Anderson, Isaiah "is a debtor to the Israelite sacred story (*Heilsgeschichte*) found classically in the Pentateuch, to the prophets who preceded him, to wisdom circles, to the liturgical traditions of the Psalter, and to the royal theology of Zion. In his prophecy all of the traditions of Israel came together and, under the alchemy of his poetic and theological insight, were given a new synthesis."[50] Indeed, throughout Isaiah in particular, the eschatological era is depicted as a new exodus out of physical and spiritual captivity into a period of abundant provision and transformation such that the earth experiences a new creation. Some scholars go so far as to attempt to characterize eschatology entirely as "new creation." In this way, Israel's history "points beyond itself and bears witness to the Creator whose faithfulness embraces the whole sweep of history, from creation to consummation."[51]

To a certain extent, the hesitation to accept the concept of an "Isaianic new exodus" hinges not on the presence of exodus imagery within the text but rather on whether Isaiah intended to portray this deliverance in terms of the immediate sense—the literal return from Babylonian exile—or an eschatological sense—the future, final salvation and restoration of the people of God. On the surface, it may appear that Isaiah identifies the return of the Israelites from Babylon as an event parallel to the exodus from Egypt, and thus a new exodus. Indeed, Dale Patrick asserts this to be true—"the coming liberation of Israel from Babylonian exile is depicted by Second Isaiah as a recapitulation of the exodus from Egypt."[52]

---

49  Merrill, *Everlasting Dominion*, 518, see also 506–508; Hamilton, *God's Glory*, 197.
50  Anderson, "Exodus and Covenant," 340.
51  Ibid., 356; see also G. K. Beale "The Eschatological Conception of New Testament Theology," in *"The Reader Must Understand": Eschatology in Bible and Theology*, ed. K. E. Brower and M. W. Elliott (Apollos, 1997), 11.
52  Dale A. Patrick, "Epiphanic Imagery in Second Isaiah's Portrayal of a New Exodus," *HAR* 8 (1984): 125. Isaiah is not alone in such interpretation. Thomas claims that "Ezekiel does not appear to envisage all this in the far-off distant future, but as following Israel's return from exile in Babylon.... Entire sanctification, the making of a holy people in a holy land fit for a holy God to live among, is portrayed by the prophets as the action of God, if not in the here and now, at least in the near future. Such bright prospects are viewed as imminent because the recent cataclysmic judgement is interpreted as an effective instrument of catharsis, where the

However, the sense of escalation in Isaiah, such that the new exodus surpasses the old, suggests that the historical return from exile may not be all that the prophet had in mind.[53] According to Merrill, Isaiah's reference to "the exile locates this oracle solidly in an Old Testament historical context, but it does not remain there. The thrust is forward looking, including in its scope the age of the church, in which all may come to the Lord on an equal footing, as well as a more distant future as the larger context makes plain (cf. Isa. 55:6–13)."[54] Indeed, there is a sense in which the coming return from exile and the anticipated eschatological salvation were fused in the minds of the ancient prophets—from their standpoint looking forward, they saw no distinction between the two.[55] Thus, perhaps the most convincing evidence for the eschatological nature of the Isaianic new exodus comes from a retrospective analysis of history, recognizing that, in their journey out of exile in Babylon, the Israelites did not experience all that Isaiah prophesied—"the concrete occurrences announced by him materialized more or less as he foretold, but the eschatological 'overplus' did not."[56] Surely the error lies in a woodenly literal reading of the thrust of Isaiah's exodus imagery by modern scholars, rather than in an invalidated and therefore false prophecy by this "prince of prophets."[57]

---

nation's defilement is concerned." Gordon J. Thomas, "A Holy God among a Holy People in a Holy Place: The Enduring Eschatological Hope," in Brower and Elliott, "*The Reader Must Understand*," 62–63.

53 Ninow, *Indicators of Typology*, 171–172.

54 Merrill, *Everlasting Dominion*, 517. Patrick asserts that the vivid creation imagery within many of Isaiah's new exodus passages "transform[s] the prospective return into an event of eschatological dimensions.... Isaiah drew upon traditions already in existence, which (1) depicted the exodus as an epiphany of Yahweh and (2) portrayed Yahweh's future intervention in history as epiphanic, and combined them to render the prospective return from exile as a new—'eschatological'—exodus." Patrick, "Epiphanic Imagery," 125–126.

55 As Merrill states, "eschatological salvation, at least from the Old Testament viewpoint, is tantamount to Israel's return from exilic bondage and restoration to covenant service in the kingdom of the Lord." Merrill, *Everlasting Dominion*, 121.

56 Patrick, "Epiphanic Imagery," 139. Patrick continues, "His disciples were forced to live in that ambiguity that inheres in eschatological theologies, viz., between the present and the yet to be" (p. 139). Later, he concludes, "though he was confirmed in concrete details of his message, his portrayal of the return as a new exodus, as an epiphany of God recognized by the whole world, was by any reasonable assessment disconfirmed" (p. 140). Cf. Moo, who asserts that "Israel did, of course, return from exile, but it quickly became clear that this return fell far short of what the prophets had claimed. And so a new deliverance was still anticipated." Douglas J. Moo, "Nature in the New Creation: New Testament Eschatology and the Environment," *JETS* 49 (2006): 457.

57 Merrill, *Kingdom of Priests*, 424. Indeed, "the postexilic prophets clarify that the postexilic situation is *not* the glorious restoration. Disobedience continues, and hope still looks to the future for the fulfillment of the promised restoration." C. Marvin Pate et al., *The Story of Israel: A Biblical Theology* (InterVarsity, 2004), 24; cf. Walter C. Kaiser, "The Promised Land: A Biblical-Historical View," *BSac* 138 (1981): 309.

This question, namely the historical or eschatological nature of the Isaianic new exodus, is highlighted in Barstad's small volume, *A Way in the Wilderness: The "Second Exodus" in the Message of Second Isaiah*. Barstad does not deny that certain images connected with the historical exodus can be found within the metaphorical language of Isa 40–55,[58] nor that the cumulative witness of these images tends to draw the exodus to mind as one reads this text. He does go to great lengths to prove his assertion that there is very little within Isa 40–55 that specifically connects a return from Babylonian exile to the historical exodus from Egypt.[59] Indeed, Barstad asserts that this is the beauty of Deutero-Isaiah. Rather than giving particular comments about a specific event in the immediate history of Israel, the prophet provides words of comfort that the people of Israel will one day experience lasting salvation and encouragement that the nation will ultimately be restored, and he does so using pictures of deliverance from Israel's past. Isaiah's words of hope and salvation concern the general restoration of the Judean people and Yahweh's providence in general (not in any specific event). Though he does not say so in such explicit terms, it seems Barstad is rejecting the idea of the Isaianic new exodus as the historical return from Babylonian exile in favor of a greater, anticipated, eschatological deliverance such as his fellow prophets described.[60]

Why, then, is the anticipated new exodus so commonly linked with Isaiah, if it is prominent in other OT literature as well, and there is no consensus in the interpretation of Isaiah's use of exodus imagery? While Isaiah was by no means alone in his promotion of the new exodus expectation, the phrase "Isaianic new exodus" acknowledges that Isaiah utilized exodus typology more abundantly and programmatically than his contemporaries, explicitly imbedding within his oracles a salvific and intentionally eschatological

---

58  He admits that one cannot help but recall the exodus when confronted with such images as wandering in the wilderness, hunger and thirst, water in the desert, and even a rare reference to the Red Sea (Isa 48:20–21). Hans M. Barstad, *A Way in the Wilderness: The "Second Exodus" in the Message of Second Isaiah*, Journal of Semitic Studies Monograph 12 (University of Manchester Press, 1989), 61, 63, 70.

59  After examining in detail the major passages in Deutero-Isaiah which commentators regard as "exodus texts" referring to the exiles' return from Babylon through the desert to Judah as a "new exodus" modeled on the exodus from Egypt and subsequent wilderness wanderings, Barstad concludes that not a single text meets this designation. Rather, he asserts that the language of Isa 40–55 is highly poetic, drawing heavily on the Psalms, and not marked by concrete historical indicators, thus requiring the historical situation to be reconstructed—"it is for the same reason, of course, that poetry can be interpreted and reused again and again to suit any historical situation." Ibid., 108–109.

60  This is in harmony with Ninow, who states that "the historical event of the Exodus serves as the *Vorlage* [type, model] for an eschatological *Nachbild* [antitype] and not for multiple redemptions in the near future." Ninow, *Indicators of Typology*, 162.

expectation of a new exodus. As Westermann asserts, the exodus tradition is so deeply rooted within Isaiah "that all the other events in Israel's history recede into the background."[61] Likewise, Watts states that in Isaiah the new exodus is "elevated to its most prominent status as a hermeneutic, and according to some commentators, shapes the heart of 40–55 even replacing the first Exodus as *the* saving event."[62] Like his contemporaries, Isaiah's prophecies represent a tension between the inevitable judgment and exile experienced by God's people and the promise of eventual hope, cast in the mold of the most significant act of deliverance in Jewish history, the exodus from Egypt. Yet Isaiah calls to mind the redemption *par excellence* through single words, phrases, or images scattered throughout his writing in a poetical and metaphorical manner, drawing a picture "that allows the larger event of the new Exodus to shine with inaudible distinctiveness."[63]

Within Isaiah, one is confronted with the fact that the Israelites retained hope for a dramatic rescue of God's people in the pattern of the original exodus, as they would depart from bondage and suffering (Isa 52:11–12) and enter the restored Jerusalem/Zion (Isa 52:1–2). This hopeful anticipation is not exclusive to the so-called Deutero-Isaiah. Indeed, Isaiah proclaimed the coming of this day early on in his prophecy:

> In that day the Lord will extend his hand yet a second time to recover the remnant that remains of his people, from Assyria, from Egypt, from Pathros, from Cush, from Elam, from Shinar, from Hamath, and from the coastlands of the sea. He will raise a signal for the nations and will assemble the banished of Israel, and gather the dispersed of Judah from the four corners of the earth … And the Lord will utterly destroy the tongue of the Sea of Egypt, and will wave his hand over the River with his scorching breath, and strike it into seven channels, and he will lead people across in sandals. And there will be a highway from Assyria for the remnant that

---

61 Claus Westermann, *Isaiah 40–66: A Commentary*, trans. David M. G. Stalker, OTL (Westminster, 1969), 22.

62 Rikki E. Watts, *Isaiah's New Exodus and Mark*, WUNT 2nd series 88 (Mohr Siebeck, 1997), 79–80.

63 Casey, "Exodus Typology in Revelation," 26. Here Casey is translating Zimmerli, who writes, "Immer wieder überflutet die Bildrede die eigentliche Rede. Dabei verrät die Vielzahl von einzelnen Worten, die je eine Episode, ein Bild, eine Hindeutung auf das große Geschehen des neuen Exodus aufleuchten lassen, mit unüberhörbarer Deutlichkeit, wie zentral diese Ankündigung für die Predigt Deuterojesajas ist." Walther Zimmerli, "Der 'Neue Exodus' in der Verkündigung der Beiden Grossen Exilspropheten," in *Gottes Offenbarung: Gesammelte Aufsatze zum Alten Testament*, ed. Walther Zimmerli, Theologische Bücherei; Neudrucke und Berichte aus dem 20. Jahrhundert, Bd. 19. Altes Testament (Kaiser, 1963), 198.

remains of his people, as there was for Israel when they came up from the land of Egypt (Isa 11:11–12, 15–16).

The references to "a second time" (Isa 11:11) and "as ... when they came up from the land of Egypt" (Isa 11:16) disclose the expectation that the judgment of Israel's enemies and the assembly and reunification of God's people will take the form of a second exodus.[64] Verses 11–12 reveal that Isaiah is not speaking solely of a return from Babylon, but instead a gathering of the Israelites from "the four corners of the earth" (Isa 11:12). This congregation will not be limited to the Jewish nation; rather Jews and Gentiles alike will experience a deliverance and restoration which by far exceeds the historical exodus.[65]

This passage likewise reveals the eschatological nature of the deliverance, highlighting the description of the one who brings it about as both "a shoot from the stump of Jesse" in Isa 11:1 and "the root of Jesse" in Isa 11:10—namely, the Messiah himself.[66] This word of salvation is located within the broader context of impending divine judgment on Israel (Isa 2–12), suggesting that its fulfillment will occur in the more remote future when the messianic branch of the Lord (Isa 4:2) will rule on David's throne and reign over the whole earth (Isa 9:1–7).[67] Isaiah 4:2–6 describes that far-off day in terms of three promises related to the period of the exodus—"in that day" God will make the land fruitful (Isa 4:2), call his people holy (Isa 4:3–4), and create over them "a cloud by day, and smoke and the shining of a flaming fire by night" (Isa 4:5).

Chapter 40 begins what many believe to be Deutero-Isaiah with a shift from oracles of judgment over Israel to God's promises of comfort and forgiveness for his people.[68] The passage across the desert wastelands (Isa 40:3–4) and the presence of God's glory (Isa 40:5) recall the time in which God led his people out of Egypt and through the wilderness toward the Promised Land.[69] As Anderson states, Isaiah "employs effectively the symbolization of Israel's *Heilsgeschichte* in his portrayal of the new exodus of salvation," yet he does so not with the formulaic language characteristic of ancient Israel's re-

---

64  Ninow, *Indicators of Typology*, 158–159.
65  Ibid., 161.
66  According to Motyer, "the reference to *Jesse* indicates that the *shoot* is not just another king in David's line but rather another David." At the same time, referring to the expected king as the Root of Jesse indicates that he is the source and origin of Jesse, and thus the messianic family. J. A. Motyer, *The Prophecy of Isaiah: An Introduction and Commentary* (InterVarsity, 1993), 121 (italics original).
67  J. G. Baldwin, "*SEMAH* as a Technical Term in the Prophets," *VT* 14 (1964): 94; Ninow, *Indicators of Typology*, 161.
68  Ninow, *Indicators of Typology*, 169; Anderson, "Exodus and Covenant," 354.
69  Hill, "Reading Isaiah," 105–106; Ninow, *Indicators of Typology*, 170.

membrance of the exodus, but instead through "hymnic forms which ascribe praise to the God who created the heavens and the earth, who formed Israel as a people, and who declares the end from the beginning (42:5, 44:2, 45:18, 51:15f.)."[70]

The victory song in Isa 42:10–17 also has exodus connotations. While Barstad suggested that the shepherding motif in these verses simply reflects Yahweh's care for his people in general,[71] the immediate context may suggest otherwise. This passage closely follows God's promise to provide abundant water in the wilderness for his people (Isa 41:17–20)[72], and is itself followed by a reminiscence of the Red Sea and God's pledge to deliver his people in the same way again (Isa 43:2). The order of the events is reversed (Exodus=Red Sea, Song of Moses, water in the wilderness; Isaiah=water in the desert, victory song, passing through the waters), but the overall effect serves to anchor this shepherding passage securely within the bounds of exodus typology. The similarities between the victory song (Isa 42:10–17) and the Song of Moses (Exod 15) reinforce this point.[73] Both songs praise Yahweh as a warrior who

---

[70] Anderson, "Exodus and Covenant," 356.

[71] Barstad examines the shepherd motif, which he determines to be one of the most prevalent motifs in Deutero-Isaiah. He notes that this motif is most commonly found in the Psalms (eg. Pss 27:11; 142:10), yet of all the instances of the shepherd motif in the Psalms, only in Ps 78 does it occur in an exodus context. In other words, "the picture of Yahweh shepherding his people is most frequently found *outside* of this [Exodus] tradition!" In Ps 23, likely the most well-known of all shepherd texts, the idea of Yahweh leading his people is very similar to that in Deutero-Isaiah. Yet this is not a statement about the exiles' return from Babylonian captivity, but rather an expression of the general conviction that Yahweh is taking care of his people. Certainly, Yahweh led his people through the wilderness—Exodus makes frequent reference to the pillar of cloud by day and fire by night, and the fact that the Lord went before them. However, that alone is not reason enough to classify any use of the shepherding motif as an exodus text. According to Barstad, there is nothing wrong with connecting the shepherd motif with the new exodus; "this, however, is *not done* by the texts themselves." Barstad, *Way in the Wilderness*, 50–51. Likewise, Casey asserts, "the shepherd motif is not common in the pentateuchal Exodus tradition (cf. Num. 27:17), and though given greater emphasis in Deutero-Isaiah's typology, it still does not occupy a predominant place in his reinterpretation of the Exodus." Casey, "Exodus Typology in Revelation," 31–32.

[72] Isaiah refers to God's provision of water in the wilderness on several occasions. He mentions the water from the rock (Isa 48:20–21; cf. Exod 17:1–6) and promises to "open rivers on the bare heights" and to "make the wilderness a pool of water" for the oppressed (Isa 41:18). Indeed, in the new exodus God will provide water to such a great extent that the desert will become a paradise with abundant rivers and lush trees. This act of re-creation by Yahweh reinforces the eschatological emphasis of the Isaianic new exodus. Ninow, *Indicators of Typology*, 173–175; Patrick, "Epiphanic Imagery," 133–134.

[73] Casey goes so far as to assert that "the evidence indicates ... that Deutero-Isaiah's references to the Red Sea deliverance are drawn almost entirely from the song in Exodus 15:1–18, in terms of conceptions, style, and language." Casey, "Exodus Typology in Revelation," 29. Cf. Brevard Childs, *The Book of Exodus: A Critical, Theological Commentary*, OTL (Westminster, 1974), 243–253.

overthrows his enemies (Exod 15:1, 3–6, 10; Isa 42:13), exalt his power over nature (Exod 15:8, 10, 19; Isa 42:15–16), worship him for shepherding his people (Exod 15:13, 17; Isa 42:16), and recognize him as incomparably sovereign over all gods (Exod 15:11; Isa 42:17).

Isaiah 43 connects God's future acts of deliverance with the crossing of the Red Sea. As God provided a way for his people to pass through the Red Sea on dry land, he says "When you pass through the waters, I will be with you; and through the rivers, they shall not overwhelm you" (Isa 43:2). The link to the Red Sea is made more explicit in Isa 43:16–17 when Yahweh is described as one who makes a path in the waters and the sea, and defeats armies and warriors with their chariots and horses. The expression, "I am the Lord your God," in Isa 43:3 further highlights the exodus connection (Exod 20:2).[74] However, here the Lord instructs the reader not to dwell on the past or things of old, for he is "doing a new thing" (Isa 43:19). While the deliverance from Egypt was certainly the most significant act of salvation in Israel's history, it pales in comparison to what Yahweh will accomplish in the future.[75] Looking back, the return from Babylon is inadequate as the final fulfillment of this expectation, as it did not exceed or even equal the exodus (the exodus took place through Yahweh's superior power over Pharaoh and the Egyptian gods; the return from exile occurred at the permission of the Persian king). The return from Babylon was only the beginning, a brief glimpse of the day when God will redeem the whole world and restore all of creation to its former Edenic glory.[76]

Isaiah's new exodus anticipation continues within the servant song of Isa 49, in which the servant is commissioned for the mission of reuniting Israel (Isa 49:5–6a) and spreading salvation to the ends of the earth (Isa 49:6b).[77] The prophet portrays the execution of this task as a joyful homecoming described through exodus imagery. To the desolate, imprisoned people, Yahweh promises a day when they will neither hunger nor thirst, when he will guide them out of their captivity, through the desert, and beside springs of water, restoring their land (Isa 49:8–11). Most significantly, this servant will be "a covenant to the people" (Isa 49:8). All of the divine blessings that the Hebrew people enjoyed in the wilderness (food, water, guidance, protection) will be

---

74 Ninow, *Indicators of Typology*, 178–179; Patrick, "Epiphanic Imagery," 125.
75 Plastaras, *Creation and Covenant*, 6–7; Moo, "Nature in the New Creation," 475–476.
76 Ninow, *Indicators of Typology*, 179–181. As Patrick states, "The return home, especially, will be so spectacular that no human can miss the hand of Yahweh in it (Isa 41:20). All those who survive the catastrophic events of the time will recognize that here is the true God (Isa 45:20–25)." Patrick, "Epiphanic Imagery," 137.
77 Hill, "Reading Isaiah," 142–143.

revisited upon the nations[78] to an even greater extent "in a time of favor ... a day of salvation" (Isa 49:8).[79]

Within his description of the future redemption of Israel (Isa 51–52), Isaiah sets his words in an eschatological context by prophesying of the long-awaited day when the Lord will restore the world to its original state, making "her wilderness like Eden, her desert like the garden of the Lord" (Isa 51:3).[80] He then specifically recalls events of the original exodus in which God manifested his glory and power in order to provide for his people. The Lord is praised as the one who dried up the sea in order to provide his people safe passage across (Isa 51:9–11). Isaiah expects nothing less for the future, a time when the people will respond with singing, everlasting joy, and gladness (51:11), perhaps recalling the Israelites' song of praise on the other side of the Sea (Exod 15).[81]

Continuing along this theme, Isa 52 recalls the Israelites' bondage in Egypt, reminding them that they were "sold for nothing" into captivity when they "went down at the first into Egypt to sojourn there" (Isa 52:3–4). Yet Yahweh promises to redeem them once again, so that "my people shall know my name ... they shall know that it is I who speak" (Isa 52:6, seemingly reminiscent of Yahweh's revelation of his divine name and promise to speak through Moses, Exod 3:13–15; 4:10–12). Even the call to depart has new exodus connotations. This deliverance, not from Babylonian captivity but from something far greater, will not involve the haste (cf. Exod 12:11, 33) and flight (cf. Exod 12:39; 14:5) characteristic of the departure from Egypt.[82] Yet God's redeemed

---

78  The land of Syene (Isa 49:12) is difficult to identify. However, if it is correctly associated with Aswan in the south, then Isaiah portrays God's people coming from the north, west, and the south. Motyer argues that Isaiah intentionally left out any mention of the east in order to eliminate confusion of this journey with the return from Babylon. Motyer, *Prophecy of Isaiah*, 392.

79  Ninow, *Indicators of Typology*, 184–185. Interestingly, John draws upon this particular passage in his vision of the multitude from every nation worshiping the Lamb in Rev 7:9–17. Is it significant that the text John comes closest to quoting has such strong new exodus connotations? See chapter 7 below for a discussion on Rev 7:9–17.

80  Ibid., 186; Edward J. Young, *The Book of Isaiah: The English Text, with Introduction, Exposition, and Notes*, NICOT (Eerdmans, 1972), 3:308–309; Moo, "Nature in the New Creation," 475.

81  Continuing in his vision of the redeemed people, Isaiah instructs Zion to clothe herself with garments of splendor (Isa 52:1). While this particular expression is exclusive to this passage, it hearkens back to the high priest's garments, which were made for glory and for splendor (Exod 28:2). In "that day," the people of God will truly fulfill the priestly role which God intended for them (Exod 19:6). Motyer, *Prophecy of Isaiah*, 416; Ninow, *Indicators of Typology*, 189.

82  Ninow, *Indicators of Typology*, 191–192; see also Casey, "Exodus Typology in Revelation," 27–28. Motyer states, "There will be no unwelcome pressure in the situation and nothing to distract the mind from calm commitment to walk with God in holiness. They will experience neither the panic flight of sinners under condemnation nor the opportunist escape of those

will enjoy God's protection on every front, just as the miraculous pillar of cloud and fire went before them in the exodus of old (Isa 52:12).[83]

Isaiah portrays the accomplishment of this new exodus and reemphasizes its eschatological timeframe in the following chapter by highlighting the messianic identity of the servant. For the first time, we see a human rather than an animal sacrificed for the sins of mankind, and not just any human but God's servant! This individual, though "despised and rejected by men" (Isa 53:3), will receive the wounds for our sins (Isa 53:4–5) and bear "the iniquity of us all" (Isa 53:6). Through this punishment, his wounds will bring peace and healing (Isa 53:5), and ultimately his death (Isa 53:12) will accomplish redemption.[84] Just as in the original exodus, Isaiah connects this coming deliverance of God's people with "a lamb led to the slaughter" (Isa 53:7, NIV; cf. the Passover lamb in Exodus), a figurative foreshadowing of Christ (cf. John 1:29; Gal 1:3–4; Rom 4:24–25).[85]

There is no escaping the overwhelming anticipation of a new, greater exodus event in the writings of Isaiah. While there may be certain similarities between the return from Babylon and the historical exodus, the eschatological and messianic overtones within the book of Isaiah, as well as the course of history, make it clear that this new exodus event is yet to take place. Like his fellow prophets, Isaiah was aware that God's actions in the past form a pattern for his vision of the future. However, the poetic and metaphorical character of Isaiah "transposes the whole sacred story into a higher key as he announces the good tidings of salvation. The new exodus will be a radically new event"[86] involving God's people from every nation, spiritual deliverance

---

whose master might change his mind, but rather every favourable circumstance." Motyer, *Prophecy of Isaiah*, 422.

83 Patrick, "Epiphanic Imagery," 133–134. Casey claims this as another example of the "heightened character of the new exodus as compared to the original, in which Yahweh's presence with the people, symbolized by the matinal pillar of cloud and nocturnal pillar of fire, is either ahead of Israel (Exod. 13:21–22) or behind it (Exod. 14:19–20), but never in both places." Casey, "Exodus Typology in Revelation," 28.

84 Paul M. Hoskins, *That Scripture Might Be Fulfilled: Typology and the Death of Christ* (Xulon, 2009), 62.

85 Paul Spilsbury, *The Throne, the Lamb & the Dragon: A Reader's Guide to the Book of Revelation* (InterVarsity, 2002), 70–71; Kirsten Nielsen, "Shepherd, Lamb, and Blood: Imagery in the Old Testament—Use and Reuse," *Studia Theologica* 46 (1992): 130–131. Isaiah's connection of the coming new exodus with the figure of a lamb proves quite helpful in understanding John's mention of the Lamb standing "as though it had been slain" (Rev 5:6).

86 Bernhard A. Anderson, "Exodus Typology in Second Isaiah," in *Israel's Prophetic Heritage: Essays in Honor of James Muilenburg*, ed. Bernard A. Anderson and Walter Harrelson (Harper, 1962), 190–191. Elsewhere, he emphasizes the connection between new exodus and new creation: "By placing the Exodus—the crucial event of Israel's history—in this new theological context, the prophet transposed the meaning of the event into the higher key of the announcement of a new creation into which Israel and all the people are summoned to enter at

from a tyrant much more tenacious than Egypt, and a state of virtual re-creation on the earth. This new exodus remained a hope, a messianic expectation which would carry them past the return from Babylon and into the day of Christ.[87]

Like Isaiah, the OT prophets as a whole have a unique position as the bridge between the exodus of history and the eschatological redemption of the future. Their hope for a coming deliverance was tied up in the historicity and majesty of their past; their messianic expectations were formed around the traditions of God leading his people from bondage, protecting and providing for them in the wilderness, and establishing a covenant with them as their God. Yet the prophets fully expected the eschatological event to be something new and greater than the exodus of old, to the extent that it would overshadow the original exodus as the defining moment in the history of God's people. A new covenant would be written on the hearts instead of stone, and the restored covenant people will consist of believers from every nation, Jews and Gentiles, gathered from every corner of the world. The prophets portrayed this coming exodus in such dramatic terms that it is clearly "not just any positive turn of Israel's history,"[88] but a paradigm for eschatological, final, complete redemption which involves both a new deliverance and a new creation.

## Apocryphal Literature and the Intertestamental Period

Exodus typology is also present to varying degrees in a number of other ancient Jewish writings, mostly notably in the Apocrypha and Qumran texts.[89] The Apocrypha's use of the exodus tradition is rather minimal, apart from its inventive development within Wisdom of Solomon. Certainly, the exodus is cited within recitations of Israel's history (e.g., Sir 45), and as in the prophets such historical rehearsal serves both to identify Yahweh (Bar 2:11; 2 Esd 1:7) and to remind Israel of her disobedience in spite of God's mighty acts (2 Esd 1:10, 12–23; 2:1; 14:28–30; Bar 1:19–20).[90] In other passages, Yahweh's acts of deliverance in the exodus function typologically as beacons of hope for future salvation. For example, Judas Maccabeus reminds his men of the Red

---

the gracious invitation of Yahweh, the Holy One of Israel." Idem, "Exodus and Covenant," 357.
  87  Ninow, *Indicators of Typology*, 194–195; Plastaras, *Creation and Covenant*, 7.
  88  Ninow, *Indicators of Typology*, 238.
  89  Casey ("Exodus Typology in Revelation") devotes a fifteen-page chapter to the "writings of Judaism," in which he surveys the exodus typology in these bodies of literature, as well as the Pseudepigrapha and rabbinic writings. In the present project, space does not allow for such an extensive analysis of extracanonical literature, so the current section is largely a summary of Casey's work.
  90  Ibid., 41–42.

Sea deliverance and calls on them to petition Yahweh for a similar deliverance from their present situation (1 Macc 4:9–10, RSV; cf. 2 Macc 2:8, 18; 3 Macc 2:6ff). Perhaps the most explicit example of exodus typology within the Apocrypha can be found in 2 Esdras, which states,

> See, my people are being led like a flock to the slaughter; I will not allow them to live any longer in the land of Egypt, but I will bring them out with a mighty hand and with an uplifted arm, and will strike Egypt with plagues, as before, and will destroy all its land. Let Egypt mourn, and its foundations, because of the plague of chastisement and castigation that the Lord will bring upon it (2 Esd 15:10–12 NRSV). [91]

The exodus features clearly in the third and most lengthy division (chapters 11–19) of Wisdom of Solomon, exemplifying God's care for and presence with the Israelites throughout history and demonstrating the folly of falling into idolatry. In a midrash on the major patriarchal stories, the author creatively adapts and reshapes the exodus account [92] into a series of seven antithetical events which function typologically to reinforce his point—that God punishes the ungodly but blesses the righteous. Thus, the plagues smiting the Egyptians serve as a type for God's judgment and are contrasted with God's provision and protection of the Israelites during the exodus events, which likewise typify his blessings. [93]

The Qumran writings provide a picture of the character of the community out of which they arose. They were a people devoted to strict observance of the Mosaic law (1QS VIII, 22; CD VII, 5) and the study of the history of Israel. [94]

---

91  Ibid., 43.

92  Cheon distinguishes Wisdom of Solomon's interpretive method from "forms of Palestinian biblical interpretation such as midrash, targum, pesher or rewritten Bible," preferring to refer to it as a "reshaping of the biblical story." Samuel Cheon, *The Exodus Story in the Wisdom of Solomon: A Study in Biblical Interpretation* (Sheffield, 1997), 150–151. Kee points out that the author of Wisdom of Solomon leaves out personal names and many historical details from the exodus account, since his emphasis was the "wisdom principle" and not the specifics. Howard Clark Kee, "Appropriating the History of God's People: A Survey of Interpretations of the History of Israel in the Pseudepigrapha, Apocrypha and the New Testament," in *The Pseudepigrapha and Early Biblical Interpretation*, ed. James H. Charlesworth and Craig A. Evans, JSPSup 14, SSEJC 2 (Sheffield, 1993), 52–53.

93  David A. DeSilva, *Introducing the Apocrypha: Message, Context, and Significance* (Baker, 2002), 139–140; Kee, "Appropriating the History," 52–53. Casey states that Wisdom of Solomon's use of the exodus tradition "is not typological, but only illustrative of what the writer believes to be the universal principles associated with Wisdom." Casey, "Exodus Typology in Revelation," 45. A discussion of exodus plague imagery within this third section of Wisdom of Solomon will figure prominently in our treatment of Revelation's use of the exodus plagues as the pattern for the trumpet and bowl judgments in the following chapter.

94  Todd S. Beall, "Essenes," *DNTB*, 344, 346; Casey, "Exodus Typology in Revelation," 47.

They saw their community as the "remnant" or true Israel (1QS II, 9, 11–12; IV, 23; V, 1–3, 8, 21–22; 1QM XIII, 7–9) living in the last days, and held the Sinai tradition and the commandments therein with the utmost regard. By consecrating themselves at the foot of Mount Sinai, they believed themselves to be reliving Israel's wilderness experience, "in exile and yet in the process of exodus," a mindset which permeates the Qumran interpretation of Israel's history and literature.[95]

The Qumran War Scroll is an excellent example of exodus typology. The War Scroll is apocalyptic in its emphasis on the supernatural world and the coming judgment, framed around the theme of eschatological warfare and the ultimate conquest of good over evil. The author anticipates God's intervention on behalf of his people, the Sons of Light, and destruction of his enemies, the Sons of Darkness, in a manner consistent with the deliverance from Egypt—"You shall act against them as against the Pharaoh and the officers of his chariots in the Re[d] Sea" (1QM XI, 9–10).[96] Likewise, praise for Yahweh's mighty acts takes the form of an allusion to the Song of Moses—"Who is like you according to power, O God of Israel!" (1QM XIII 13; cf. Exod 15:11, "Who is like you, O Lord, among the gods? Who is like you, majestic in holiness, awesome in glorious deeds, doing wonders?").[97]

The use of exodus typology within intertestamental literature is not extensive. Nevertheless, what is significant is that where the expectation of an eschatological exodus extends to the apocryphal and Qumran writings, it seems to be in harmony with the theology of the OT. Yahweh's sovereign power and righteous judgment in the first great deliverance of his people becomes the paradigm and hope for a greater redemption yet to come.

## The New Testament and Early Christianity

It is clear that, from the earliest days, the ancient Jews based their identity as the people of God on the exodus, the foundation of Israel's history and faith.

---

95 Thomas R. Hatina, "Exile," *DNTB*, 349; Otto Betz, "The Eschatological Interpretation of the Sinai-Tradition in Qumran and in the New Testament," *Revue de Qumran* 6 (1967), 89, 93–94; Casey, "Exodus Typology in Revelation," 47.

96 Compare 1QM XV, 1–2, "for this shall be a time of tribulation for Isr[ael...]dt of war against all the nations. The lot of God [shall be] in everlasting redemption but a destruction [is] for all the wicked nations." James H. Charlesworth, ed., *Damascus Document, War Scroll, and Related Documents*, vol. 2 of *The Dead Sea Scrolls: Hebrew, Aramaic, and Greek Texts with English Translations* (J. C. B. Mohr, 1995), 80, 88.

97 Charlesworth, *Dead Sea Scrolls* 119, 123, 129; Robert Kirk Kilpatrick, "Against the Gods of Egypt: An Examination of the Narrative of the Ten Plagues in the Light of Exodus 12:12" (ThD diss., Mid-America Baptist Theological Seminary, 1995), 75. This same textual pattern shows up as an element of imitation and fraud in the worship of the beast in Rev 13:4.

The early Christians were familiar with the Jewish anticipation of a new exodus, in particular the expectation of escalation surrounding this event, the sense that the exile was continuing, and the conviction that the return from Babylon, while reminiscent of the historical exodus, was not the fulfillment they awaited. Thus, the NT writers maintained this eschatological expectation of a new exodus that was a hallmark of their Jewish heritage,[98] employing exodus imagery in their own writings and interpreting the Christ event within the context of a new exodus. As the exodus and covenant at Sinai form the pivotal event in the life of ancient Israel, so "the whole Gospel tradition ... is cast into a Pentateuchal shape, because the Exodus-deliverance of Israel from Egypt was the only pattern of redemption which the NT writers knew."[99]

There is no doubt that the new exodus anticipation features prominently in the NT. As in the OT, exodus imagery cannot be isolated to one particular author or text but spans the gamut of NT genres. More significantly, the awareness that Christ has inaugurated a new and greater exodus pervades every NT writer with the exception of James and Jude.[100] What follows is simply a survey of the major ways in which exodus typology features within the NT.

GOSPELS AND ACTS

The gospels portray various key aspects of Jesus' life within the context of the exodus. Given the Jewish character of Matthew's Gospel, it should come as no surprise that the birth narratives in the first Gospel reveal striking similarities between the infancies of Moses and Jesus.[101] For example, the mass killing of male Hebrew babies by Pharaoh (Exod 1:9–12, 15–16; 2:1–10) is echoed in

---

98  Ninow, *Indicators of Typology*, 153; Jindřich Mánek, "New Exodus in the Books of Luke," *NovT* 2 (1958): 13. According to Clifford, "the widespread view at least in Palestinian Judaism in the first century B.C.E. that Jews were still in exile meant that early Jewish-Christians would use the Exodus as a paradigm for explaining the significance of Jesus as liberator and founder." Clifford, "Exodus in the Christian Bible," 353–354. Clifford further asserts that the NT writers held to the Jewish belief of the continuing exile and understood that the restoration was inaugurated in Jesus ("Exodus in the Christian Bible," 355).

99  Alan Richardson, *An Introduction to the Theology of the New Testament* (SCM, 1958), 167; Plastaras, *God of Exodus*, 313.

100  Plastaras, *God of Exodus*, 313.

101  In intertestamental Judaism, Moses came to be seen in a messianic light. Indeed, the phrase "As the first deliverer (i.e., Moses), so the last deliverer" (i.e., the Messiah) was common during this time. Thus it is only natural that the NT Scriptures reveal Jesus as the fulfillment of the Hebrew expectation of a prophet like Moses (Deut 18:15–20; 34:10; cf. Acts 3:19–22; John 1:21, 45; 7:40). Harold Sahlin, "The New Exodus of Salvation According to Paul," in *The Root of the Vine: Essays in Biblical Theology*, ed. Anton Fridrichsen (Dacre, 1953), 82; Fred L. Fisher, "The New and Greater Exodus: The Exodus Pattern in the New Testament," *SwJT* 20 (1997): 70, 75.

the holy family's flight to Egypt to escape the hand of Herod (Matt 2:13–16). Reinforcing this exodus imagery, Matthew applies to Jesus the words which the prophet Hosea spoke concerning Israel—"Out of Egypt I called my son" (Matt 2:15, quoting Hos 11:1)—recalling the designation of the Hebrew people as Yahweh's "firstborn" in Exod 4.[102] In the Sermon on the Mount, Matthew records Jesus' delivery of the law of the new covenant with the oft-repeating expression, "You have heard that it was said ... But I say to you ..." (Matt 5:21–22, 27–28, 31–32, 33–34, 38–39, 43–44), causing many scholars to suggest that throughout his Gospel, Matthew portrays Jesus as "the New Moses, the giver of the perfect Law."[103] It has even been argued that Jesus' five discourses in Matthew parallel the Pentateuch, the five books of the Torah traditionally attributed to Moses.[104]

Exodus imagery permeates the accounts of Jesus' temptation. Occurring soon after his baptism, Jesus' forty days of temptation parallel the forty years of wandering and testing in the wilderness which Israel entered after the crossing of the Red Sea (Matt 4:1–2; Mark 1:12–13; Luke 4:1–2).[105] The trials Jesus endured during that time resemble the temptations to which Israel succumbed in the desert, with Jesus responding to the temptations in the way the Israelites were expected to do so. As Nixon writes,

> Where they had been dissatisfied with Yahweh's provision of manna, He is tempted to turn stones into bread. Where they put God to the test at Massah demanding proof of His presence and power, He is tempted to jump from the Temple pinnacle to force God to honour His promises. Where they forgot the Lord who had brought them out of Egypt and substituted a molten calf for Him, He is tempted to fall down and worship Satan.[106]

Not only did Jesus resist the temptations to which the Israelites succumbed, he responded to each with a quotation from Deuteronomy, emphasizing what Israel should have done in the wilderness, but failed to do.[107] Matthew

---

102 Plastaras, *God of Exodus*, 319–320; Fisher, "New and Greater Exodus," 76.

103 Plastaras, *God of Exodus*, 319; Jean Daniélou, *From Shadows to Reality: Studies in the Biblical Typology of the Fathers*, trans. Wulstan Hibberd (Burns & Oates, 1960), 159–160.

104 Benjamin W. Bacon, *Studies in Matthew* (Constable & Company, 1930), 81–82; Richardson, *Theology of the NT*, 167; Nixon, *Exodus in the New Testament*, 19.

105 Haugen, "Consummation of the Exodus," 8. Notice also the words which Yahweh spoke about Jesus upon his baptism, "This is my beloved Son" (Οὗτός ἐστιν ὁ υἱός μου ὁ ἀγαπητός, Matt 3:17; cf. Mark 1:11; Luke 3:22). While the immediate referent is Gen 22:2, "your son ... whom you love" (τὸν υἱόν σου τὸν ἀγαπητόν LXX), one also finds similarities to Yahweh's description of Israel to Pharaoh as "my firstborn son" (υἱὸς πρωτότοκός μου, Exod 4:22, LXX).

106 Nixon, *Exodus in the New Testament*, 13–14.

107 Beale, "Eschatological Conception," 29; Clifford, "Exodus in the Christian Bible," 355.

includes the additional detail of Jesus's hunger after fasting for forty days and nights in the wilderness (Matt 4:2), recalling Moses fasting on the mountain for the same length of time (Deut 9:9).[108]

Likewise, the gospels depict the transfiguration as having characteristics of a new Sinai theophany, prepared for over a period of six days (Mark 9:2; cf. Exod 24:16). High upon the mountain, Jesus was transfigured before his inner circle, much as Moses's face shown with the shekhinah glory when he returned from Mount Sinai (Mark 9:2–3; cf. Exod 34:29–31), and the voice of the Lord entreats the disciples to "listen to him" (Mark 9:7), alluding to the description of the prophet like Moses as one to whom the people will listen (Deut 18:15).[109] Within the context of the transfiguration, Luke actually refers to Jesus' coming passion as his departure, or more literally, his "exodus" (ἔξοδον) "which he was about to accomplish at Jerusalem" (Luke 9:31). According to Nixon, "for the instructed Christian reader of the Gospel that could mean nothing less than the repetition of God's mighty acts of redemption in His death and resurrection at Jerusalem."[110] Elsewhere, Luke refers to Jesus' coming ascension as his "assumption" (ἀνάλημψις, Luke 9:51). This is significant because according to Jewish tradition the only OT figures "taken up" to heaven were Elijah (2 Kgs 2) and Moses (Assumption of Moses; cf. Jude 9). This resemblance in the end of their public, prophetic ministries is just one parallel between Jesus, Moses, and Elijah, and serves as an explanation for why Moses and Elijah in particular appeared to Jesus on the mount of transfiguration.[111] When one recognizes there are three primary eras characterized by miraculous displays in the Bible—namely the time of Moses and the exodus, the age of Elisha and Elijah, and the earthly ministries of Jesus and the apostles—the connection is highlighted further.[112]

The Lukan writings repeatedly present Jesus as the long–awaited prophet like Moses, most explicitly in Peter's casting of Deut 18:15 as a messianic prophecy in his sermon at Solomon's portico: "... that he may send the Christ appointed for you, Jesus ... about which God spoke by the mouth of his holy

---

108 With this representation of Jesus as the new Moses, Matthew sets the stage for the giving of a new law through the Sermon on the Mount (Matt 5–7), which he seems to intend as a new Sinai event. Plastaras, *God of Exodus*, 321.

109 Ibid., 316–317; Nixon, *Exodus in the New Testament*, 16.

110 Nixon, *Exodus in the New Testament*, 16–17; F. F. Bruce, *The New Testament Development of Old Testament Themes* (Eerdmans, 1968), 34; George L. Balentine, "Death of Jesus as a New Exodus," *RevExp* 59 (1962): 38.

111 Mánek, "New Exodus," 8–9; Plastaras, *God of Exodus*, 323.

112 "In each case [the miracles] marked the introduction of a new direction in God's redemptive program. They were never ends in themselves but were used to authenticate the speakers as spokesmen of God." Fisher, "New and Greater Exodus," 76; Ferrell Jenkins, *The Old Testament in the Book of Revelation* (Baker, 1972), 49–51.

prophets long ago. Moses said, 'The Lord God will raise up for you a prophet like me from your brothers. You shall listen to him in whatever he tells you'" (Acts 3:20–22; cf. 7:37). Luke likewise portrays the first Pentecost as a new Sinai experience. In Acts 2, the outward manifestations of the Spirit—a sound from heaven (cf. Exod 19:16, 19), tongues of fire (cf. Exod 19:18; 24:17), and a mighty wind (cf. 1 Kgs 19:11)—parallel elements associated with a theophanic encounter with God. However, rather than giving the law as at Sinai, at Pentecost God gave the Spirit, "the distinctive feature of the new covenant" according to the OT prophets and the NT apostles (cf. Jer 31:31–33; Ezek 16:59–62; 34:25–26; 2 Cor 3:3–6; Heb 9:14–15; 10:15–16).[113] The sermons in Acts are consistently shaped by the recognition that Jesus Christ is the eschatological fulfillment of the promises of God expressed by the prophets and imbedded throughout Jewish history.[114]

Within the Gospel of John, Jesus' ministry, passion, and glorification resound with overtones of the exodus. As Plastaras writes, "there is hardly a page of this Gospel which does not contain at least one allusion to the exodus story."[115] By imbedding his Gospel with the imagery of this most profound event in the history of the Jews, John makes it clear that in Jesus Christ all the promises and expectations from the first exodus have been fulfilled. Jesus is the embodiment of the Great I AM, revealed to Moses in the burning bush (Exod 3) but now fully manifest to mankind in human form (John 4:26; 8:24, 28, 58; 13:19; 18:5). Like Moses before Pharaoh, Jesus performs "signs and wonders" (or simply "signs;" John 2:11; 4:48, 54; 6:14; 9:16; 11:47; cf. Exod 3:12; 4:8–9; 7:3; 8:23; 10:1–2) in order to bring about a recognition of the power of God in his observers.[116] Jesus Christ fulfills all of the supernatural miracles by which the Israelites recognized God's presence throughout the exodus—he is the light of the world (John 8:12; 12:46; cf. the pillar of fire providing light in Exod 13:21–22), the living water (John 7:37–40; 19:32–35; cf. God providing water from the rock in Exod 17:3–7), the "Way" leading to salvation (John 14:6; cf. God leading them out of Egypt along a specific way in Exod 13:17–21), and the

---

113 Plastaras, *God of Exodus*, 325; Watts, "Exodus," 485.
114 Kee, "Appropriating the History," 64.
115 Plastaras, *God of Exodus*, 325.
116 According to Smith, the phrase "signs and wonders" (σημεῖα καὶ τέρατα) in the OT "almost always refers to Moses' miraculous deeds, either as they were originally performed (e.g., Deut 4:34; Ps 78:43–51) or as God will perform them in an eschatological repetition of the exodus experience…. It is evident that the tradition of Moses' signs and wonders lies in the background" of Jesus' miracles in the Gospel of John. Robert Houston Smith, "Exodus Typology in the Fourth Gospel," *JBL* 81 (1962): 334. Smith draws interesting, though perhaps exaggerated, parallels between what he calls the "signs of Moses" (the plagues in Egypt) and seven miracles highlighted by John's Gospel, noting that "whereas Moses demonstrated divine power by works of destruction, Jesus demonstrated that same power by beneficial acts." Ibid., 335.

*Expectation of an Eschatological Exodus within Jewish and Early Christian Thought*        73

bread from heaven (John 6:32, 41; cf. God providing manna in Exod 16).[117] Indeed, John even presents Jesus as the fulfillment of the tabernacle ordained at Sinai: "the Word became flesh and dwelt among us, and we have seen his glory" (John 1:14).[118]

Jesus himself understood his life as the fulfillment of the exodus, as seen most clearly at the Last Supper and his institution of the Eucharist (Matt 26:17–30; Mark 14:12–25; Luke 22:1–23). In the observance of the annual Passover festival, the Jews not only commemorated their rescue from Egypt but also anticipated the future messianic deliverance and restoration of Israel. As the Passover itself was a defining moment in the exodus from Egypt, the paschal meal reflected the most fervent hope for the coming of the Messiah. Thus, as Jesus broke the bread and offered the cup at his last Passover, he related his impending sacrificial death to the history of the deliverance from Egypt, emphasizing "that his death is the new saving event that believers are supposed to celebrate until he comes."[119] The expression "my blood of the covenant" (Mark 14:24) echoes Moses's words in the covenant ceremony at Sinai ("Behold the blood of the covenant," Exod 24:8), and the nature of the meal itself recalls the original Passover lambs.[120] Jesus seems to reinforce his death as the fulfillment of the Passover promises when he states, "I have earnestly desired to eat this Passover with you before I suffer. For I tell you I will not eat it until it is fulfilled in the kingdom of God" (Luke 22:15–16).

All four gospel writers connected Jesus' death in some way with the Passover.[121] For John, however, Jesus' entire life centered around the Passover. From the very first introduction, Jesus is identified as "the Lamb of God, who

---

117 Plastaras, *God of Exodus*, 326–27; Smith, "Exodus Typology," 329–330; Daniélou, *From Shadow to Reality*, 161. As Nixon states, "the 'I AMs' may be derived from the Passover Haggadah and therefore have Exodus significance, indicating that God Himself has intervened in His own Person to redeem His people." The fact that Jesus's self-designation as "the bread from heaven" takes place within the context of the feeding of the five thousand, an event which John places at Passover time (John 6:4), reinforces the manna comparison and Jesus' fulfillment of the exodus. Nixon, *Exodus in the New Testament*, 20.

118 Stephen G. Dempster, "Exodus and Biblical Theology: On Moving into the Neighborhood with a New Name," *Southern Baptist Journal of Theology* 12.3 (2008): 5; Thomas, "Holy God," 64.

119 Hoskins, *That Scripture Might Be Fulfilled*, 74; C. K. Barrett, "The Lamb of God," *NTS* 1 (1954–1955): 218. Cf. John D'Souza, *The Lamb of God in the Johannine Writings* (St. Paul, 1968), 165; etc. Just as the Passover and Feast of Unleavened Bread were a yearly feast celebrating the exodus from Egypt, the Last Supper becomes a "lasting ordinance" (Exod 12:14, NIV) celebrated repeatedly "in remembrance" (Luke 22:19; 1 Cor 11:24–25) of the greater deliverance accomplished in Christ's sacrificial death. Hoskins, *That Scripture Might Be Fulfilled*, 77–80.

120 Nixon, *Exodus in the New Testament*, 19. According to Hoskins, Jesus is likely alluding to both Exod 24:8 and Jer 31, a "direct prophecy that contributes to the Old Testament's covenant typology." Hoskins, *That Scripture Might Be Fulfilled*, 65.

121 Robert J. Daly, *The Origins of the Christian Doctrine of Sacrifice* (Fortress, 1978), 38–41.

takes away the sin of the world" (John 1:29).[122] Within John's passion narrative (and the events immediately leading to the passion), the word πάσχα ("Passover") occurs seven times (John 11:55 twice; 12:1; 13:1; 18:28, 39; 19:14), reinforcing the significance of the festival to his understanding of the crucifixion. John explicitly states that the soldiers did not break Jesus' legs in order "that the scripture might be fulfilled" (John 19:33, 36), referring to the instructions concerning the Passover lamb (Exod 12:46; Num 9:12) and the expectations for the righteous one (Ps 34:20). Melito of Sardis summarizes John's paschal imagery well, stating that Jesus "ransomed us from the world's service as from the land of Egypt and freed us from the devil's slavery as from the hand of Pharaoh."[123]

THE EPISTLES

It seems evident that Paul expected his readers to be familiar with the Passover traditions and the interpretation of Jesus' death and resurrection in light of the exodus – as he states, "for Christ our Passover also has been sacrificed" (1 Cor 5:7, NASB). While explicit references are infrequent within the Pauline corpus, there is no doubt that exodus ideas undergird much of his theological vocabulary. For instance, the word redemption had a single meaning in the Jewish mindset, namely "the act whereby God went down to the slave market called Egypt and bought there his enslaved people in order to set them free."[124] Paul often used exodus imagery within certain antitheses to contrast the former existence with life in Christ.[125] He sets the judgment the Israelites experienced in the wilderness against the miraculous acts of God in delivering them at the Red Sea and providing water and manna, which he

---

122  Though "sin" is not a common word in John, the Gospel does teach that sin results in death (John 8:21–24) and describes sin as slavery (John 8:34). This highlights the paschal background of John 1:29, for as Hoskins states, "Compared to the Passover sacrifice, is any other Old Testament sacrifice more closely related to deliverance from death?" Hoskins, *That Scripture Might Be Fulfilled*, 111; T. C. Smith, *Jesus in the Gospel of John* (Broadman, 1959), 80–81.

123  Melito of Sardis, *On Pascha and Fragments*, trans. and ed. Stuart Hall, OECT (Clarendon, 1979), 35, 37 (section 67). Hoskins (*That Scripture Might Be Fulfilled*, 107) provides an interesting chart illustrating correspondences between the death of Jesus and the Passover in John's Gospel.

124  N. T. Wright, "New Exodus, New Inheritance: The Narrative Structure of Romans 3–8," in *Romans and the People of God: Essays in Honor of Gordon D. Fee,* ed. Sven Soderlund and N. T. Wright (Eerdmans, 1999), 32–33; Hermann Martin Friedrich Büchsel, "λύω," *TDNT* 4:349. Similarly, other NT terms such as "deliver, deliverance, ransom, purchase, slavery, and freedom entered the religious vocabulary of Israel through the Exodus event." Fisher, "New and Greater Exodus," 71.

125  Sylvia C. Keesmaat, "Paul and His Story: Exodus and Tradition in Galatians," *HBT* 18 (1996): 302.

understands to be "types" (τύποι, 1 Cor 10:6) for the Christian sacraments of baptism and the Eucharist inaugurated through Christ's death on the cross (1 Cor 10:5–11; cf. Rom 6).[126] Elsewhere Paul contrasts the imparting of the Law at Sinai, which was imperfect and recorded on stone, with the revelation of the new, greater covenant through the Spirit—perfect, written on the hearts of believers, transforming them to the likeness of God's glory (2 Cor 3:3–18).[127]

The exodus is the basis of the transition from slavery to freedom which recurs throughout the Pauline epistles, a paradigm for redemption from sin in Christ. According to Wright, "there is no question that in Judaism in general any story about slaves and how they come to be free must be seen at once as an allusion to the events of the Exodus" (e.g., Gal 3:23–26; 4:1–7).[128] In Galatians, Paul takes an unusual stance which would naturally be offensive to the Jews—rather than focusing on the exodus as a release from bondage in Egypt, he reverses the story and identifies Hagar with Mount Sinai, which "bears children into slavery" (Gal 4:24, HCSB); thus the Jews are presently enslaved to the law (Gal 4:25). In contrast, the covenant through the son of promise, "born according to the Spirit," results in freedom, sonship, and inheritance (Gal 4:28–31; cf. Col 1:13–14).[129] The exodus context makes it clear that believers are heirs to the impenetrable presence of God through the love of Christ (Rom 8:31–39), as well as the eschatological realization of the glory of God in all creation, which "will be set free from its bondage to corruption and obtain the freedom of the glory of the children of God" (Rom 8:21).[130]

---

126 Plastaras, *God of Exodus*, 329; N. T. Wright, *The New Testament and the People of God*, vol. 1 of Christian Origins and the Question of God (Fortress, 1992), 447; etc. Wright understands the exodus to be the underlying narrative substructure for Rom 6–8 as a whole—"those who were enslaved in the 'Egypt' of sin, an enslavement the law only exacerbated, have been set free by the 'Red Sea' event of baptism.... They are now given as their guide, not indeed the law, which, although given by God, is unable to do more than condemn them for their sin, but the Spirit, so that the Mosaic covenant is replaced, as Jeremiah and Ezekiel said it would be, with the covenant written on the hearts of God's people by God's own Spirit." Wright, "New Exodus," 29.

127 According to Nixon, "the thought is most obviously drawn from Jeremiah 31:31ff., but while the Exodus and the blood are not mentioned they could not have been far from his mind." Nixon, *Exodus in the New Testament*, 24.

128 Wright, "New Exodus," 29. Cf. J. M. Scott, *Adoption as Sons of God: An Exegetical Investigation into the Background of UIOTHESIA in the Pauline Corpus* (Mohr Siebeck, 1992), 155–157. According to Keesmaat, because the vocabulary of slavery and sonship "can all plausibly be rooted in Israel's time of bondage in Egypt and the exodus, it is likely that the language of slavery in these verses refers to the same events.... [T]he language of sonship was associated with God's restoration of the people in a number of new exodus contexts in Jewish tradition." Keesmaat, "Paul and his Story," 302–303.

129 Keesmaat, "Paul and his Story," 309–310. According to Keesmaat, Paul's warning to the believers against reverting back to bondage under the law (Gal 5:1) should be understood in terms of the Israelites' grumbling desire to return to Egypt. Cf. Wright, "New Exodus," 29–30.

130 Wright, "New Exodus," 35.

In the Epistle to the Hebrews, the exodus takes center stage in the author's presentation of an "eschatological view that contrasts historical past and present with future fulfilment of the divine purpose."[131] Accordingly, Christ is depicted as greater than both Moses (Heb 3:1–6) and Joshua (Heb 4:6–9), as well as superior to the Levitical priesthood (Heb 7:1–28), the high priest (Heb 4:14–5:11), the sacrificial system (Heb 9:25–10:12), and the old covenant (Heb 9:1–22; 10:16–23), all of which were established within the context of the original exodus. Hebrews portrays the people of God as continuing on the journey to the promised rest that the Israelites began in the wilderness (Heb 3:16–4:11). Just as the Hebrew people traveled to Mount Sinai, and ultimately the Promised Land, with the goal of God's presence dwelling among them, so too Christians press on to the heavenly Zion and the city of the living God (Heb 12:18–24).[132]

Likewise in 1 Peter, believers are addressed as "sojourners and exiles" (1 Pet 2:11), recipients of the calling given to the Israelites at Mount Sinai—" you are a chosen race, a royal priesthood, a holy nation, a people for his own possession ..." (1 Pet 2:9; cf. Exod 19:5–6).[133] Like John, Peter presents the salvation of believers in terms of the paschal sacrifice; Christ is a perfect, spotless lamb whose blood has ransomed his people and delivered them from their exile in sin and death (1 Pet 1:17–19). As Smith states,

> while the blood of the Paschal lamb in itself did not effect deliverance but was a sign of deliverance (Ex. 12:13), the thought prevailed among the Jews that the deliverance from Egypt came about through the blood of the Paschal lamb. For Peter release from Egyptian bondage by the blood of the Paschal lamb was a type of deliverance from the bondage of sin through Christ, the new Paschal lamb of the new Exodus.[134]

Within the NT, the exodus maintains its original significance as a means of both liberation and formation; thus, it is not surprising to find allusions to the exodus permeating the NT writings, both implicitly and explicitly, ranging from isolated phrases to the typological foundation for larger passages or even complete texts.[135] Yet, the NT authors did not limit their understanding of the

---

131  Kee, "Appropriating the History," 61; Nixon, *Exodus in the New Testament*, 25.
132  Plastaras, *God of Exodus*, 330–32; Thomas, "Holy God," 66; etc.
133  Terence E. Fretheim, "'Because the Whole Earth is Mine': Theme and Narrative in Exodus," *Interpretation* 50 (1996): 236; Daniélou, *From Shadow to Reality*, 162–163; etc.
134  Smith, *Jesus in John,* 80–81. The verb λυτρόω ("ransom, redeem") in 1 Pet 1:18 is also used to describe the deliverance from Egypt (ἐλυτρώσω, Exod 15:13 LXX). Haugen, "Consummation of the Exodus," 9–10; Balentine, "Death of Jesus," 34.
135  For instance, Piper asserts that "we do not contend that everything in Mark's Gospel

exodus to the original departure from Egypt and wilderness wanderings. They also built upon the prophetic development of the new exodus expectation. For example, the NT concept of covenant (Luke 22:20; 1 Cor 11:25) relies more on Jeremiah's new covenant (Jer 31:31) than the Sinai tradition itself. Likewise, the Gospels quote from Isaiah to introduce John the Baptist in terms of the anticipated final return from exile—" Behold, I send my messenger before your face, who will prepare your way, the voice of one crying in the wilderness: 'Prepare the way of the Lord, make his paths straight'" (Mark 1:2–3; cf. Isa 40:3).[136] Indeed, Pao claims that "the scriptural story which provides the hermeneutical framework for Acts is none other than the foundation story of Exodus as developed and transformed through the Isaianic corpus."[137] Yet, both in passages that are clearly based on the historical exodus and in those which take their cue from the prophetic development of the tradition, the NT writings demonstrate that they are in harmony with the Jewish expectation of a new, greater eschatological deliverance, and highlight the early Christian belief that the Christ event inaugurated just that. Indeed, that is the primary distinction between the new exodus anticipation in the OT and in the NT—in the OT the deliverance is prophesied; in the NT redemption is consummated in Christ.[138]

## Summary

From the earliest OT traditions—even within the Pentateuch's record of the historical exodus traditions—there is evidence that the ancient Jews held the

---

can be explained from Exodus but rather that the framework within which the material was arranged was based upon a typological use of Exodus." Otto A. Piper, "Unchanging Promises: Exodus in the New Testament," *Interpretation* 11 (1957): 19. Similarly, Watts determines that throughout his Gospel, beginning with his opening quotation of Isa 40:3, Mark reveals "his fundamental hermeneutic for interpreting and presenting Jesus" as a "dual perspective of salvation and judgment," both of which derive from the Isaianic new exodus. Watts, *Isaiah's New Exodus in Mark*, 4.

136 Clifford, "Exodus in the Christian Bible," 358; Watts, "Exodus," 484. Both Pao and Watts place great stress on "way" (ὁδός) terminology, both in Isaiah's portrayal of the new exodus and in the NT books which they analyze (Acts and Mark, respectively). The prominence of the summons to prepare a way for Yahweh (Isa 40:3) suggests that the emphasis of the new exodus concerned the return of Yahweh's actual presence—to deliver his people out of bondage, to lead and shepherd them, to provide food and water, and most importantly, to reveal to them his glory. Thus the prologue to Deutero-Isaiah (Isa 40:1–11), most especially Isa 40:3, "came to be understood as encapsulating the critical event upon which the whole of the [new Exodus] depends: the call made by an unidentified 'messenger' to prepare the way in the desert for the coming of Yahweh whose advent as warrior and shepherd presages the redemption of his people." Watts, *Isaiah's New Exodus in Mark*, 82; cf. David W. Pao, *Acts and the Isaianic New Exodus*, WUNT 2nd series 130 (Mohr Siebeck, 2000).

137 Pao, *Acts and the Isaianic New Exodus*, 5.

138 Daniélou, *From Shadow to Reality*, 157.

events of the exodus in highest esteem, and that they firmly believed that in the future God would once again act in the lives of his people to bring about a deliverance even greater than this pinnacle event in the history of Israel. This anticipation is especially prominent in the prophetic writings, particularly Isaiah, in which it becomes clear that the return from Babylonian captivity, while certainly similar to the exodus in many respects, did not fulfill the many eschatological expectations wrapped up within the new exodus hope.[139] There was an even more significant redemption still to come.

The final, eschatological new exodus was inaugurated in the Christ event. As we have seen, Jesus himself linked the defining event of the new covenant—namely, his passion, death, and resurrection—with the central experience in Jewish history, the exodus from slavery in Egypt. Throughout the NT, we find the early Christians "unfold[ing] the implications of the typology which Jesus Himself had taught the Church."[140] Whether Jesus is the new Israel awaiting a future deliverance from exile, the true prophet like Moses who will lead his people out of bondage and inaugurate the new covenant through the Spirit, the true Passover lamb sent as the perfect redemptive sacrifice, or the true tabernacle in fleshly form who goes before his people to prepare the way for a new, final exodus from slavery to freedom, it is clear that all of the eschatological hopes for salvation culminate in him.

---

139 "It is true that there was a return from the Babylonian captivity. But this event did not mark the fulfillment of the expectations of the new Exodus as foretold by the prophets. *Relative Eschatology* let the people expect the *eschaton* after the captivity. They had the hope that similar to the inheritance of the Promised Land after the first Exodus from Egypt the return from the Babylonian exile was the fulfillment of the proclaimed 'new Exodus.' Yet, this fulfillment of the *eschaton* remained preliminary. With the progress of history God revealed more detail to the eschatological picture which made clear that the return of the Israelites from the Babylonian captivity was not *the* eschatological fulfillment that they expected." Ninow, *Indicators of Typology*, 238 (italics original).

140 Plastaras, *God of Exodus*, 333–334.

CHAPTER 5

## Exodus Imagery in Revelation: Plagues as Paradigm for Judgment

We now turn our attention to how exodus typology features within Revelation. John's readers were already aware of God's reputation of judgment and redemption, as presented in the exodus account as well as throughout Scripture. Hence by typologically employing the exodus model in his vision of eschatological salvation, John lent increased validity to his vision of the future and created a link between the believers' anticipation of a future deliverance and God's past work of redemption.[1]

The most obvious facet of Revelation's broad use of exodus typology is the adaptation of the exodus plagues for the trumpet and bowl judgments (Rev 8:7–9:21; 11:15–19; 16:1–21). Another prominent aspect of Revelation's use of exodus typology is the Passover imagery dominating the character of the Lamb (especially in Rev 5:6–10), God's sealing his people for protection and deliverance (Rev 7:1–8), and the context of the Song of Moses and the Song of the Lamb (Rev 15:1–8). Additionally, as exodus typology involves the entire exodus event from bondage to wilderness, one must consider aspects of wilderness imagery such as the woman's flight from the dragon in Rev 12, theophanic elements (compare the Sinai experience) and allusions to the tabernacle (particularly in Rev 21–22), the eschatological reworking of divine provision (Rev 7:9–17), and the identification of God's people as a kingdom of priests (Rev 1:6; 5:10). These three sets of images—the plagues, the Passover, and the wilderness—represent three major facets of the original historical exodus, and function as the three primary aspects of John's employment of exodus

---

[1] Jay Casey, "The Exodus Theme in the Book of Revelation against the Background of the New Testament," in *Exodus: A Lasting Paradigm*, ed. Antonius G. Weiler, Marcus Lefébure, and Bastiaan Martinus Franciscus van Iersel (T&T Clark, 1987), 34.

typology in his Apocalypse. Thus, the next three chapters will proceed in examining each of these elements in turn.

## The Exodus Plague Judgments

The plagues which Yahweh sent upon the land of Egypt (Exod 7–12) are one of the most familiar aspects of the exodus story. When Pharaoh refused to heed Yahweh's command to allow the Hebrews to hold a festival to him in the wilderness (Exod 5:1–2), God promised his people that he would bring them out from the yoke of the Egyptians and deliver them to the land which he promised to Abraham (Exod 6:6–8). He smote Egypt with a series of ten mighty acts of judgment (Exod 7:4)—the Nile turning to blood; frogs, gnats, and then flies teeming throughout the land; disease killing the livestock; boils festering upon man and animal; a massive hailstorm pounding the earth; swarms of locusts devouring the fields; an oppressive darkness paralyzing the nation; and finally, the death of the firstborn. To compound the suffering, Yahweh drew an intentional distinction between the Hebrews and the Egyptians, setting apart the land of Goshen where the Hebrew people dwelt and shielding them from his wrath. Exodus explicitly records that God's judgments did not affect the Israelites in five of the ten plagues.[2]

There is widespread agreement that the plagues of Egypt serve as John's underlying paradigm for the trumpet (Rev 8:6–9:21) and bowl judgments (Rev 16:1–21), though John does not allude to each of the ten plagues and not all of the judgments contain clear exodus imagery. Yet John makes it clear that he has the exodus plagues in mind by his repeated use of the word πληγή ("plague") to describe the judgments, both individually and as a collective whole (Rev 11:6; 15:1, 6, 8; 16:9, 21; 18:4, 8; 21:9; 22:18). The word itself indicates intense trouble, severe distress, or widespread suffering.

The specific connection with the plagues of Egypt is reinforced in Revelation 11, in which the judgments the two witnesses bring down on their

---

2 Scripture does not mention this distinction until the fourth plague (Exod 8:22–23). At the very least, the Hebrew people were protected from the plagues of flies, livestock disease, hail, darkness, and the death of the firstborn. However, Loewenstamm asserts that "there can be no doubt that the Mishnaic statement 'Ten miracles were wrought for our ancestors in Egypt' ('Abot 5:5) ... means that they were delivered from ten plagues, as Scripture states explicitly in some of the plagues and as may be deduced concerning all the others." Samuel E. Loewenstamm, *The Evolution of the Exodus Tradition*, trans. Baruch J. Schwartz, Publication of the Perry Foundation for Biblical Research in the Hebrew University of Jerusalem (Magnes Press, Hebrew University, 1992), 165–166. Whether the Israelites were indeed protected from the effects of all ten plagues or only those explicitly stated in Scripture, the principle of God's supernatural protection of his people during the judgment of his enemies remains a signature element of the exodus, one that is picked up and developed in both Judaism and Christianity.

oppressors are parallel to the trumpet and bowl judgments. John describes these witnesses as having "power over the waters to turn them into blood and to strike the earth with every kind of plague (ἐν πάσῃ πληγῇ), as often as they desire" (Rev 11:6), a verbal allusion to the Philistines' summary of Egyptian plagues in 1 Sam 4:8, "These are the gods who struck the Egyptians with every sort of plague (ἐν πάσῃ πληγῇ) in the wilderness."[3] Two verses later, John refers to "the great city that symbolically is called Sodom and Egypt" (Rev 11:8). The word "symbolically" (πνευματικῶς, "allegorically, spiritually") suggests that the mention of Sodom and Egypt is intended to remind the reader of the historical events associated with those locations. While Sodom was a city of widespread depravity and rebellion against Yahweh (see Gen 18–19), Egypt was the source of extensive oppression against God's people during the time of the exodus (e.g., Exod 1:8–22; 2:23–24).[4] In both cases, God rained down righteous judgment upon the land—in Sodom and Gomorrah in the form of sulfur and fire (Gen 19:24), in Egypt in the form of ten plagues. The fact that the beast is able to conquer and kill the witnesses in Rev 11:7 may be an element of escalation; though the Lord rescued Lot's family from Sodom and Gomorrah and the Hebrew people from Egypt, the two witnesses in Revelation fall victim to the tyrannical power of the beast. Like Egypt of old, this eschatological city and the forces of evil with which it is associated have caused extensive suffering for God's people, but she will soon experience the incomparable plagues of God's just and holy wrath.

Any doubt as to the background of the trumpets and bowls as a whole is eliminated when one reads the accounts and recognizes the similarities between the plagues of Egypt and the wrath of God's judgment, both in content and purpose. Both the historical and eschatological plagues emphasize God's judgment on idolaters and their gods, protection of his chosen people, divine wrath against those who persecute his children, and absolute sovereignty over nature, mankind, and false deities.[5]

---

3 G. K. Beale and Sean M. McDonough, "Revelation," in *Commentary on the New Testament Use of the Old Testament*, ed. G. K. Beale and D. A. Carson (Baker, 2007), 1120; Brian K. Blount, *Revelation: A Commentary*, NTL (Westminster John Knox, 2009), 211.

4 Gordon D. Fee, *Revelation*, New Covenant Commentary Series (Wipf and Stock, 2010), 152. There is debate over the identity of this "great city." Some claim that the phrase "where their Lord was crucified" identifies the city as Jerusalem. E.g., Paige Patterson, *Revelation*, NAC 39 (Broadman & Holman, 2012), 248–249. Others recognize the city as Rome. E.g., Robert H. Mounce, *The Book of Revelation*, NICNT (Eerdmans, 1977), 226, for whom Rome epitomizes the Antichrist. Another option is that the city symbolizes unbelieving humanity or the unbelieving world as a whole. E.g., G. K. Beale, *The Book of Revelation*, NIGTC (Eerdmans, 1999), 591. In any case, however, the point stands that this great city which has persecuted God's people will soon experience God's judgment in the form of "every kind of plague."

5 Pablo Richard, "Plagues in the Bible: Exodus and Apocalypse," in *The Return of the*

## Revelation's Trumpet and Bowl Judgments

Within Revelation, John records three series of judgments—seven seals, seven trumpets, and seven bowls. Many questions surround these judgments, such as whether or not they should be understood chronologically, whether they are actually just one set of seven judgments restated for effect or viewed from three different perspectives, and whether or not they should be understood in a literal or symbolic sense. Given the close parallels between the trumpets and bowls, it is unlikely that the visions beginning in chapter six are chronological; John recorded them in the fashion in which he experienced them, but they will not actually occur in this sequence.[6] There is, rather, a telescoping effect, in which the judgments are interrelated through the process of recapitulation. This recapitulation, accompanied by an increase in intensity and scope of the judgments as they move from seals to trumpets to bowls, serves to overwhelm the reader with the force of God's persistent anger on a sinful world.[7] The function of the judgments in Revelation is to relate something of God's nature and to symbolize the authority and severity of God's righteous anger.[8] The three sets of judgments are neither simultaneous nor consecutive but interrelated. While the seals contain very little in the way of exodus imagery, the trumpet and bowl judgments share a common dependence on the plagues of Egypt. The many similarities between the two therefore warrant a concurrent discussion.

The portrayal of hail (χάλαζα) and fire (πῦρ; Exodus = literally "fire flashing", πῦρ φλογίζον) as instruments of destruction in the first trumpet (Rev 8:7) clearly alludes to the seventh plague (Exod 9:13–35). In both cases, hail and

---

*Plague*, ed. José Oscar Beozzo and Virgil Elizondo, Concilium 5 (SCM, 1997), 45–51; Lester Meyer, *The Message of Exodus: A Theological Commentary* (Augsburg, 1983), 73; David A. DeSilva, *Introducing the Apocrypha: Message, Context, and Significance* (Baker, 2002), 139–140; etc.

6 Ted Grimsrud, *Triumph of the Lamb: A Self-Study Guide to the Book of Revelation* (Herald, 1987), 66.

7 J. Ramsey Michaels, *Interpreting the Book of Revelation* (Baker, 1992), 64; Paul Spilsbury, *The Throne, the Lamb & the Dragon: A Reader's Guide to the Book of Revelation* (InterVarsity, 2002), 116. Note the escalation in the scope of the judgments—while the seals affect only one fourth of the earth (Rev 6:8), the impact of the trumpets increases to one third of creation and mankind (Rev 8:7–12, 15, 18). With the bowls, God's wrath is no longer limited to a fourth or a third; the judgments have power over the entire earth (Rev 16:17–21), all creatures (e.g., "every living thing died that was in the sea," Rev 16:3), all mankind who worship the beast (Rev 16:2), and the entire kingdom of the beast (Rev 16:10). Notice also the increase in intensity—the seventh seal brings about "peals of thunder, rumblings, flashes of lightning, and an earthquake" (Rev 8:5). In the seventh trumpet, these theophanic elements escalate to include "heavy hail" (Rev 11:19), while the seventh bowl again amplifies the description to a "a great earthquake such as there had never been since man was on the earth" (Rev 16:18) and "great hailstones, about one hundred pounds each" (Rev 16:21).

8 Spilsbury, *Throne, the Lamb & the Dragon*, 114.

fire are sent from heaven against trees, earth (land), and grass/vegetation. Although Revelation and the LXX text of Exodus contain differences in vocabulary for the affected elements of creation (δένδρων vs. ξύλα, χόρτος χλωρός vs. βοτάνην), verbal similarities in the means of judgment present an overall picture of devastation by hail and fire. Interestingly, Beale notes that "one Greek ms. [75] of Exodus 9 even adds καὶ σάλπιγγας ('and trumpets') to the description of the storm plague in Ex. 9:23."[9] Revelation's addition of blood mixed with fire probably stems from Joel 2:30–31 and attests to the force of God's judgment on this world.[10] The events of trumpet one, both in Revelation and in the exodus paradigm, demonstrate Yahweh's sovereignty over nature, combining hail, fire, and blood with devastating consequences.

The first bowl has little parallel with trumpet one; its effect relates to the sixth Egyptian plague of "boils breaking out in sores on man and beast throughout all the land of Egypt" (Exod 9:9). According to Revelation, "harmful and painful sores came upon the people who bore the mark of the beast and worshiped its image" (Rev 16:2).[11] Both Revelation and Exodus make the point that only the enemies of God experienced the effects of this judgment. While the exodus distinction between the Egyptians and the Hebrew people is not as explicit as in other plagues, this first bowl is one of the most overt statements in Revelation of God's divine wrath being focused specifically on the idolaters. With one action, Yahweh judges his enemies and protects his chosen people.

Trumpet two, as well as the second and third bowls, describe the sea turning to blood, using the same terminology found in Exod 7:19 (ἐγένετο ... αἷμα, Rev 8:8; 16:3,4) in a clear verbal allusion to the water of the Nile turned to blood in the first plague. To the Egyptians, the Nile was considered the bloodstream of Osiris, who was worshiped as the symbol of eternal life,[12] and was thought to flow from the place where the world began.[13] Through this first plague, God struck a blow directly at the heartbeat of Egyptian life, impeding the "entire hydrography of Egypt and pollut[ing] the existing sources of water

---

9 Beale claims this addition to Exod 9:23 likely reflects the influence of the Sinai tradition (Exod 19:16–19), in which "the Lord sent thunderings and hail *and trumpets.*" Beale, *Revelation*, 473, italics original.

10 Ibid., 473–475; Grant R. Osborne, *Revelation*, BECNT (Baker, 2002), 350.

11 Both Exodus (LXX) and Revelation use forms of the Greek word ἕλκος to refer to the sores.

12 Barbara Watterson, *The Gods of Ancient Egypt* (Facts on File Publications, 1984), 72–80. It is said that Osiris's death and resurrection are repeated annually in the receding and flooding of the River Nile. Alan W. Shorter, *The Egyptian Gods: A Handbook* (Kegan Paul, Trench, Trubner, 1937), 37.

13 Watterson, *Gods of Ancient Egypt*, 30.

supply."[14] Just as the plague caused the fish in the Nile to die (Exod 7:21), so too in Revelation a third of the creatures living in the sea died (Rev 8:9). The third trumpet (Rev 8:10–11) is also connected with the plague of blood. The star that fell into the rivers and other waters in trumpet three is named Ἄψινθος ("Wormwood"), a bitter plant which is used figuratively in the Scriptures to indicate sorrow, distress, and catastrophe.[15] The demise of those who drank from the water in Rev 8:11 parallels the fact that the exodus plagues, including the plague of blood, resulted in the loss of much life.[16] Interestingly, bowl three states outright that God's wrath is being poured out to avenge the persecution of his children—"for you brought these judgments … they have shed the blood of saints and prophets, and you have given them blood to drink. It is what they deserve!" (Rev 16:5–6).

The fourth trumpet is the last of the trumpet judgments demonstrating God's sovereignty through the destruction of nature, and is identified with the penultimate plague of Egypt, the plague of darkness. Revelation 8:12 records that "a third of the sun was struck, and a third of the moon, and a third of the stars, so that a third of their light might be darkened, and a third of the day might be kept from shining, and likewise a third of the night." Similarly, the fifth bowl (Rev 16:10–11) fills the kingdom of the beast with darkness, affecting his ability to rule. In the Exodus account (Exod 10:21), Yahweh caused a permeating darkness to reign over the entire land of Egypt, with the exception of the Israelites' dwelling, for three days and three nights. God's dominance over the sun was an offense against Pharaoh, humiliating him by striking at his own divine claim as the incarnation of the sun god, Amun-Re, considered the source of light and worshiped as the King of the Gods.[17] In the Hebrew Bible, darkness represents destruction; in early Christian and Qumran literature (1QM I, 9–11), it symbolizes the force that is opposed to God. In the apocalyptic judgments, however, this darkness was actually brought about by the hand of Yahweh, simultaneously degrading the sun god while decisively confirming the supreme authority of the God who caused it.[18]

---

14 Nahum M. Sarna, *Exploring Exodus: The Origins of Biblical Israel* (Schocken Books, 1986; repr., Pantheon Books, 1996), 78–79.

15 "Ἀψίνθιον," BDAG, 161. The water being made bitter in the third trumpet may also be a creative reversal of the bitter water being made sweet at Marah (Exod 15:22–27).

16 Beale, *Revelation*, 479, citing Philo, *Mos.* 1.100. According to Blount, citing Jer 9:15 and Jer 23:15, wormwood was an appropriate punishment for idolatry—"the angelic 'poisoning' of the waters is a deliciously ironic way of punishing a people who have so poisoned their faith." Blount, *Revelation*, 170.

17 Watterson, *Gods of Ancient Egypt*, 144; Shorter, *Egyptian Gods*, 4–18.

18 Jonathan Knight, *Revelation* (Sheffield, 1999), 76; Sarna, *Exploring Exodus*, 79.

The fifth trumpet depicts an abundance of locusts coming up from the abyss and tormenting man for five months (Rev 9:2–5), recalling the eighth plague of exodus, in which "locusts came up over all the land of Egypt and settled on the whole country of Egypt, such a dense swarm of locusts as had never been before, nor ever will be again" (Exod 10:14). The prophet Joel also spoke of God sending a plague of locusts against the unrepentant nation of Israel (Joel 1:4; 2:25).[19] In the sixth bowl (Rev 16:13–14), John describes the dragon, beast, and false prophet spewing out evil spirits that appear as frogs, somewhat paralleling trumpet five in that both the locusts and frogs symbolize demonic forces. While in isolation the images portrayed in bowl six would not necessarily call to mind the events of the plagues, the exodus context of the surrounding judgments may suggest connotations of the Egyptian plague of frogs (Exod 8:2–6). This background is reinforced when one recognizes that the frogs actually come forth from the dragon, beast, and false prophet, recalling that the second Egyptian plague was one of only two that Pharaoh's magicians were able to reproduce through their "secret arts" (Exod 7:22; 8:7).[20] Pharaoh's minions were unsuccessful in stopping or reversing the plagues; rather, they also "made frogs come up on the land of Egypt" (Exod 8:7). Through their manipulations, the number of frogs swelled and the nuisance upon the Egyptian people was magnified.[21]

The sixth trumpet (Rev 9:13–21) contains minor parallels with the fourth bowl (Rev 16:8–9, 12–16), in that the imagery of men "scorched by the fierce heat" (Rev 16:9) and fire is suggestive of the "fire and smoke and sulfur" (Rev 9:17) from the mouths of the horses. Notice also the response of the survivors of these two judgments, who "did not repent and give him glory" (Rev 16:9; cf. 9:20–21). However, the more striking similarities are between the sixth trumpet and the sixth bowl, as they share a common mention of the Euphrates (Rev 9:14; 16:12). Revelation 9 refers to a vast apocalyptic army with the power to kill a third of mankind (Rev 9:15–19), awaiting the release of the four angels at the Euphrates, while in the sixth bowl, the Euphrates "was dried up, to prepare the way for the kings from the East" (Rev 16:12),[22] and the frogs which

---

19 Osborne, *Revelation*, 364. In all three cases, the Greek word for locusts is a form of ἀκρίς.

20 This is one aspect of the theme of imitation and fraud found throughout the Apocalypse—for further explanation, see chapter 8, "Motif of Imitation and Fraud."

21 Meyer, *Message of Exodus*, 73. The magicians also mimicked the transformation of Aaron's staff into a snake, doing "the same by their secret arts" (Exod 7:11). Yet Yahweh proved superior, and Pharaoh's heart was hardened as the magicians' staffs were consumed by Aaron's (Exod 7:12).

22 Fee, *Revelation*, 134–135; Craig R. Koester, *Revelation and the End of All Things* (Eerdmans, 2001), 151. There is within the sixth bowl a sense of reversal of Israelite history, in which the Red Sea parted to allow the people to flee their oppressors, the Egyptians (Exod 14:21–22),

issued from the mouth of the false trinity "go abroad to the kings of the whole world, to assemble them for battle on the great day of God the Almighty" (Rev 16:14). In both cases, the barrier which was preventing the advancement of an immense army is removed.[23]

The similarities between the sixth trumpet and sixth bowl extend to include an intriguing exodus connection, for both contain subtle imagery from the plague of the firstborn, the Passover. In bowl six, believers receive the message, "Behold, I am coming like a thief! Blessed is the one who stays awake, keeping his garments on, that he may not go about naked and be seen exposed!" (Rev 16:15). This is reminiscent of God's command to the Israelites to eat the first Passover meal in haste, fully dressed and prepared for the flight from Egypt (Exod 12:11).[24] In both instances, the people of God are to wait in readiness, for the moment of deliverance is soon at hand. The Passover imagery in trumpet six (Rev 9:13–21) relates not to the meal itself but the preparation. Though not stated overtly, the overall context indicates that this judgment is directed only against those not having the seal of God, while believers are protected. Whereas four angels held the winds at bay until God's people were protected by the seal of God in Rev 7:1, the release of four angels in Rev 9:14–15 allows the wrath of God to fall upon his enemies.[25] In the same manner, God prevented "the destroyer" (Exod 12:23) from striking the firstborn of Egypt until the Israelites had marked their doorposts with the blood of the Passover lamb.[26] So it is in Revelation that the judgment which most

---

and swept away the Egyptians when the Lord caused the water to return to its natural state. In Revelation, however, the drying up of the Euphrates enables the invasion by an assembly of God's enemies (Rev 16:12). Blount, *Revelation*, 302; Stephen S. Smalley, *The Revelation to John: A Commentary on the Greek Text of the Apocalypse* (InterVarsity, 2005), 407.

23 Some scholars suggest that trumpet six and bowl six are describing the same event—the preparation of armies for battle—from different perspectives. Michaels, *Interpreting Revelation*, 64; Blount, *Revelation*, 302; Smalley, *Revelation*, 407. As Beale explains, if trumpet six "covers the whole inter-advent period … then the sixth trumpet contains a punitive pattern that finds consummation in the sixth bowl. On the other hand, the sixth trumpet could be temporally parallel with the sixth bowl." Beale, *Revelation*, 829.

24 Sarna, *Exploring Exodus*, 85. Compare Yahweh's warning to the church at Sardis in Rev 3:3—"Remember, then, what you received and heard. Keep it, and repent. If you will not wake up, I will come like a thief, and you will not know at what hour I will come against you."

25 Osborne, *Revelation*, 381. Fee questions whether the four angels in Rev 7:1 and Rev 9:14–15 are the same, determining that John is following his own pattern of introducing a character or prop in one setting which he then develops at a later point—"just as the altar was introduced in 6:9, and later plays a considerable role in the introductory vision of 8:1–5, so the angels introduced in that vision now play a larger role in the present one." Fee, *Revelation*, 134–135.

26 While later tradition held that an "angel of death" ("destroyer," NKJV, NASB, NIV, etc.) actually brought about this plague, the Lord is mentioned at least seventeen times in Exod 12 alone, emphasizing that the Passover was nothing less than the mighty act of God himself. He set his wrath upon his enemies, but not before he protected those who were faithful to his commands. Richard Elliott Friedman, *The Hidden Face of God* (HarperCollins, 1996), 14.

directly brings death to the idolaters and persecutors of the church (trumpet six) is that which shares the strongest association with the Passover event itself.

The final judgment in Revelation, the culmination of the whole of God's wrath upon the beast and his followers, is presented in both trumpet seven and bowl seven. There is no mention of repentance, for the opportunity for repentance has passed. Though the language of lightning, rumblings, thunder, and great hail from heaven (Rev 11:19; 16:18, 21) suggests an allusion to the theophanic elements at Mount Sinai (Exod 19:16–18),[27] there is also a contextual intimation to the destruction of Pharaoh's army in the Red Sea. God demonstrates his undeniable power over the forces of nature in these two judgments, just as he revealed his authority over nature by driving the Red Sea back "by a strong east wind" (Exod 14:21). In the same way that Yahweh expelled all doubt as to his incontestable sovereignty by overthrowing "the Egyptians in the midst of the sea" (Exod 14:27–29, NASB), the function of the seventh trumpet and bowl is to declare God's absolute preeminence through the eradication of the entire corrupt and rebellious world.

The accounts of the trumpet and bowl judgments contain perhaps the most striking occurrences of exodus typology in Revelation. Within these passages the reader is repeatedly confronted with verbal and thematic parallels to seven of the ten Egyptian plagues, as well as the deliverance at the Red Sea and the Mount Sinai theophany.[28] The purpose of these eschatological judgments is also consistent with that of the plagues of exodus, emphasizing God's judgment on idolaters and their gods, his protection of his chosen people, and his absolute sovereignty over nature, mankind, and false deities. Given this analysis, there is no question that the exodus plague narrative forms the paradigm for John's apocalyptic presentation of God's final judgments.

---

27  Beale, *Revelation*, 841–845; Ian Boxall, *The Revelation of Saint John*, BNTC 19 (Hendrickson, 2009), 177; Andrew of Caesarea, *Commentary on the Apocalypse*, vol. 1 of *Studien zur Geschichte des griechischen Apokalypse-Testes,* ed. Josef Schmid (K. Zink, 1955–56), 16.17–18, translated in William C. Weinrich, ed., *Revelation*, ACCS New Testament 12 (InterVarsity, 2005), 262. See chapter 7, "The Sinai Theophany."

28  One will quickly note that John manipulated the order of the plagues from the traditional exodus account, and that he incorporated only seven of the ten original plagues. This interesting observance should be considered further in light of the fact that Wisdom of Solomon, Ps 78:44–51, and Ps 105:27–36 likewise each list only seven of the ten Egyptian plagues, with variation in both order and the plagues mentioned. It is significant, however, that "seven" and "ten" are both numbers that signify completion. According to Loewenstamm, "the seven-plague tradition is on a par with the ten-plague tradition; both express the desired idea, that the Egyptians were smitten with a *complete* series of plagues." Loewenstamm, *Evolution of the Exodus Tradition*, 83.

## Comparison with Wisdom of Solomon

Revelation is not alone in its adaptation of the plagues of Egypt. A precedent was already set forth in Wisdom of Solomon, sometime between 220 BC and AD 50.[29] The purpose here is not to suggest Revelation's dependence upon Wisdom of Solomon, but simply to demonstrate the adaptation of the exodus plagues as an established technique.[30] Certainly, intriguing similarities are revealed when one compares Revelation's trumpet and bowl judgments with the reshaping of these same traditions in the apocryphal Wis 10–19, in which the author recounts instances of divine deliverance throughout the history of Israel, illustrating God's concern for and plan to bring about justice and encouraging readers facing persecution or death with the fact of God's continuing active presence among his people.[31]

Wisdom of Solomon's stylistic recasting of the Egyptian plague tradition into a series of seven antithetical events[32] results in a theological assertion of the principle of *lex talionis*, in which "one is punished by the very things by which he sins" (Wis 11:16).[33] In deliberate contrast, the Israelites benefited "through the very things by which their enemies were punished" (Wis 11:5). For example, the Egyptians' water supply was turned to blood as judgment for drowning the Hebrew infants in the Nile (Wis 11:6), while the Israelites in

---

29 Samuel Cheon, *The Exodus Story in the Wisdom of Solomon: A Study in Biblical Interpretation* (Sheffield, 1997), 12; W. O. E. Oesterley, *An Introduction to the Books of the Apocrypha* (MacMillan, 1935), 207–209; Daniel J. Harrington, *Invitation to the Apocrypha* (Eerdmans, 1999), 55.

30 Nor is this an attempt to suggest that the background of the apocalyptic genre is found in Wisdom literature as opposed to the prophetic. For a summary and critique of this argument, see Michael E. Stone, "Apocalyptic Literature," in *Jewish Writings of the Second Temple Period*, ed. Michael E. Stone (Fortress, 1984), 388–389.

31 Peter Enns, "Wisdom of Solomon and Biblical Interpretation in the Second Temple Period," in *The Way of Wisdom: Essays in Honor of Bruce K. Waltke*, ed. J. I. Packer and Sven K. Soderlund (Zondervan, 2000), 215–216; David A. DeSilva, *Seeing Things John's Way: The Rhetoric of the Book of Revelation* (Westminster John Knox, 2009), 162–164. This is a significant connection between Wisdom of Solomon and apocalyptic literature, which in general was produced by the oppressed and persecuted, those who had experienced a crisis of faith and whose hope was located in future divine intervention. James H. Charlesworth and James R. Mueller, *The New Testament Apocrypha and Pseudepigrapha: A Guide to Publications, with Excursuses on Apocalypses*, ATLA Bibliography Series 17 (American Theological Library Association, 1987), 20–21; D. S. Russell, *The Method & Message of Jewish Apocalyptic, 200 BC–AD 100* (SCM, 1964), 16–18; etc.

32 Cheon, *Exodus Story*, 150–151. According to Cheon, the author "freely handles the biblical material and produces a creative composition to fit the purposes of his arguments," supplementing the biblical accounts with additional materials and rearranging the biblical sequence into a series of seven antithetical events in Wis 11:1–14 and 16:1–19:17 (thirst vs. water, hunger vs. satisfaction, dying vs. healing, hail vs. manna, darkness vs. light, death vs. salvation, and drowning vs. crossing). Ibid., 109–110.

33 Osborne, *Revelation*, 40.

the wilderness received abundant water out of the rock (Wis 11:7). In this way, Wisdom of Solomon stresses God's judgment of his enemies and his protection and blessing of the righteous.

Though the principle of *lex talionis* does not drive the theological agenda of the Apocalypse to the same extent, it is stated outright in the letter to the church in Thyatira—"I will repay [or punish] each of you according to your deeds" (Rev 2:23, NIV). More significantly, this principle also occurs twice within the context of the bowl judgments, both within allusions to the exodus plagues. In the first bowl (Rev 16:2), those who sinned by taking the mark of the beast were likewise marked by God with painful and visible boils.[34] Additionally, the extended account of bowl three, in which the rivers and springs turn to blood (Rev 16:3–7), significantly parallels Wisdom of Solomon's treatment of the first plague (Exod 7:14–24). In both Wisdom of Solomon and Revelation, God's enemies receive blood to drink as punishment for slaying his people. As the angel states, "they have shed the blood of saints and prophets, and you have given them blood to drink. It is what they deserve!" (Rev 16:6; cf. Wis 11:6–7).[35]

A greater comparison between Wisdom of Solomon and Revelation is the tendency to elaborate on the exodus plague accounts in order to amplify the point, using dramatic vocabulary and intensifying the elements and effects of the judgments (e.g., Wis 16:9–10, 16–17; 17:3–10, 14–19; Rev 8:7, 11; 16:4–6, 10–11).[36] In the first trumpet (hail and fire, Rev 8:7), for example, Revelation enhances the plague by adding the element of blood (μεμιγμένα ἐν αἵματι).[37] Revelation augments the effect of the first Egyptian plague of water turning to blood (cf. Exod 7:21) by splitting its impact into two separate accounts over four judgments, two highlighting the results of the plague on creation, focusing on the death of the sea creatures (Rev 8:8–9; 16:3),[38] and two intensifying

---

34 John Sweet, *Revelation*, SCM Pelican Commentaries (SCM, 1979), 244; Casey, "Exodus Theme," 37; G. B. Caird, *The Revelation of St. John the Divine*, 2nd ed., BNTC (Black, 1984), 202.

35 This seems to suggest that God's judgments upon his enemies are a direct response to the cry of the martyrs under the altar crying out, "O Sovereign Lord, holy and true, how long before you will judge and avenge our blood on those who dwell on the earth?" (Rev 6:10). This calls to mind the children of Israel crying out to God because of their bondage in Egypt (Exod 2:23–25). Just as in Revelation, God heard their cries and soon sent forth the plagues to bring about their deliverance.

36 Cheon, *Exodus Story*, 111–114.

37 Interestingly, while Exodus emphasizes the damage caused by the hail, both Revelation and Wisdom of Solomon stress the effect of the fire. In addition to seven occurrences of the noun "hail," the exodus account of the seventh plague employs the verbs "to strike down" and "to crush, break,", whereas Rev 8:7 utilizes the verb "to burn up, consume." The impact of the fire is explicit in Wis 16:17, which states "the fire had a greater effect."

38 The inclusion of the sea in this judgment (unlike its prototype) may have to do with the idea that the sea in Revelation may symbolize satanic evil or chaos. Beale, *Revelation*, 327–328.

the plague by stressing the physical impact upon mankind (Rev 8:11; 16:4–6). Both Wisdom of Solomon and Revelation also significantly heighten the Egyptian plague of darkness.[39] While in Exodus the darkness that could be felt simply forced the Egyptians to closet themselves in their homes for three days (Exod 10:21–23), Revelation amplifies the pain and anguish endured as a result of the darkness (Rev 16:10–11), and Wisdom of Solomon's lengthy account magnifies the bondage and hallucinatory terror that the prisoners of darkness experienced (Wis 17:1–20).

Perhaps the most compelling example of Revelation augmenting the exodus plagues is found in the fifth trumpet (Rev 9:1–11), paralleling the plague of locusts (Exod 10:13–15). Revelation's description of the locusts through horrific and demonic language is reminiscent of Wisdom of Solomon's bent toward dramatic vocabulary. In addition, Revelation and Wis 16:8–10 contain a substantial connection regarding the impact of this judgment. In Exodus the locusts affect only the trees and vegetation. In Revelation, however, the locusts are explicitly prohibited from harming the grass, plants, or trees; the focus shifts to mankind and the torture of those bearing the mark of the beast (Rev 9:4). Wisdom of Solomon heightens the power of the locusts over man even further, not only to bite but also to kill (Wis 16:9).[40] Moreover, while Exodus contains no explicit statement that God protected his people from this plague, both Revelation and Wisdom of Solomon stress this point.

The amplification of the exodus plague paradigm in Revelation's trumpet and bowl judgments is characteristic of the typological feature of escalation; as in the prophets, Revelation presents the eschatological deliverance as a new exodus more spectacular than the first.[41] Revelation's augmentation of the plagues is not limited to the techniques found in Wisdom of Solomon described above. Within the Apocalypse, the scope of the judgments' effect is also escalated. According to Irenaeus (*Haer 4.30.4*),

> The whole Exodus from Egypt ... was a type and image of the Exodus of the church from the nations ... and if anyone pays careful attention to the

---

However, it may just be another example of amplification of the exodus plagues. See Blount, *Revelation*, 168, 294–295.

39  The focus on heavenly bodies growing dark in trumpet four (Rev 8:12) has little in common with the ninth plague other than the effect of darkness. However, the plague imagery in the preceding trumpets, as well as in the parallel bowl five, suggests that trumpet four follows the same pattern of exodus influence. Osborne, *Revelation*, 356–357.

40  Wisdom of Solomon contrasts this with the Israelites experiencing divine healing from the bites of venomous serpents (Wis 16:5, 10, an allusion to the bronze serpent episode in Num 21:4–9).

41  J. Comblin, *Le Christ dans l'Apocalypse*, Théologie Biblique (Desclée, 1965), 29.

things being stated by the prophets about the [time of the] end and to those which John, the witness of the Lord, saw in the Apocalypse, he will find the nations universally receiving those plagues which at that time Egypt received particularly.[42]

No longer is judgment focused upon the Egyptians and salvation for the Hebrew people alone. Revelation makes it plain that all who worship the beast will face God's righteous and eternal judgment, but salvation and everlasting life in God's presence are offered to anyone who places his trust in the sacrificial blood of the Lamb.

LACK OF EXODUS PLAGUE IMAGERY IN OTHER APOCALYPTIC LITERATURE

Yet one may question whether the use of exodus plague imagery as a model for eschatological judgments is typical among Jewish and early Christian apocalyptic literature in general. An examination of select apocalyptic literature[43] reveals a common tradition regarding the end-time judgments, describing these catastrophes in terms of birth pains, famine, pestilence, tribulation, war, wild beasts, fire from heaven, earthquakes, and other natural elements acting in an atypical manner.[44] Yet very little exodus plague material can be found within their accounts of these judgments.

The OT writings of Daniel and Ezekiel share apocalyptic tendencies and significant influence on Revelation. Daniel contains very little description of specific eschatological judgments, but those described in Dan 9:26 (flood,

---

42  Irenaeus, *Adversus haereses 4*, vol. 2 of *Irénée de Lyon: Contre les heresies*, trans. and ed. A. Rousseau et al., SC 100 (Cerf, 1965), 785–787.

43  In order to narrow the investigation, we will analyze judgment passages only in select texts which are apocalyptic either in genre or language and thought—namely, Daniel, Ezekiel, 1 Enoch, 2 Esdras, Apocalypse of Abraham, 2 Baruch, and the Sibylline Oracles. According to Swete, other Jewish literature of an apocalyptic nature, including Jubilees, Assumption of Moses, Psalms of Solomon, and Testaments of the Twelve Patriarchs are quite removed from Revelation "either in literary form or in their general purpose." H. B. Swete, *The Apocalypse of St. John: The Greek Text with Introduction, Notes, and Indices* (Macmillan, 1906), xxii. Thus, they do not warrant as detailed of an analysis as those included here. Also, for the purposes of this project, matters of dating or background are less crucial. Whether the texts preceded Revelation and drew upon OT or Jewish ideas, or originated after Revelation and reflect a Christian influence, is peripheral to this discussion. The intention is solely to examine the text of these ancient works and determine whether they employ exodus plague imagery in their presentation of eschatological catastrophes. Indeed, interesting questions may arise about their *lack* of exodus imagery if the literature comes from Christian circles and shows dependence upon Revelation elsewhere.

44  Cf. Sib. Or. 3.330–336; 530–44; 672–701; 4.173–178; Apoc. Ab. 30:4–31:1; Jub 23:13ff.; 2 Esdr 16:18–22; Matt 24:6–8; Zech 14:13; Dan 12:1; 1 Enoch 80:2–7; 99:4, 5, 8; As. Mos. 10:4–6. Russell, Jewish Apocalyptic, 272–281.

war, and desolation) have no exodus connection.[45] Ezekiel draws frequently upon the exodus in its description of the marking of the faithful, the new covenant with Israel resulting in the rebirth of the nation, and the detailed blueprint of the temple; yet again the exodus plagues have no influence on its proclamations of judgment. Rather, the judgments in Ezekiel come in the standard apocalyptic form, both in God's chastisement of the Israelites and his judgment on the nations. Outside the OT, it is especially significant that 1 Enoch shows no use of exodus plague imagery in its judgment passages, given its influence in Jewish and early Christian circles and impact on apocalyptic and NT literature.[46] Additionally, the various sections of 2 Esdras demonstrate clear familiarity with the exodus story (2 Esdras 1:7, 10, 13–23; 2:1; 3:17; 14:3–6), yet its eschatological judgments have more in common with the synoptic mini-apocalypses (Matt 24; Mark 13; Luke 21) and the typical pattern of apocalyptic judgments than with the exodus plagues.[47]

The idea of devastation by hail or fire as an eschatological judgment can be seen in 2 Esdras (15:40–42), 2 Baruch (27:10), Sibylline Oracles (5:377–378), and Apocalypse of Abraham (30:6). It is important to realize, however, that an allusion to the exodus plague specifically requires the co-mingling of hail and fire. The lack of fire in Apocalypse of Abraham and the absence of hail in 2 Baruch and Sibylline Oracles removes the likelihood of an exodus allusion in all three accounts. Only 2 Esd 15:40–42 contains both elements and therefore a potential allusion to the seventh plague.

None of the literature surveyed presents a broad picture of exodus-type judgment. Second Esdras, with the allusion to the plague of hail and fire combined with the reference to having only blood to drink (2 Esd 15:58), shows the most potential for such a pattern, yet the plague connections are minimal. While the judgments in Apocalypse of Abraham do take the form of ten plagues (29:14–16; 30:2–31:1), which one might expect to have similarities

---

45 Daniel 9:26b reads, "Its end shall come with a flood, and to the end there shall be war. Desolations are decreed."

46 According to Isaac, the list of writings influenced (whether directly or indirectly) by the language and thought of 1 Enoch includes Jubilees, Testaments of the Twelve Patriarchs, Assumption of Moses, 2 Baruch, 4 Ezra, Matthew, Luke, John, Acts, Romans, 1 and 2 Corinthians, Ephesians, Colossians, 1 and 2 Thessalonians, 1 Timothy, Hebrews, 1 John, Revelation, and especially Jude. E. Isaac, "1 (Ethiopic Apocalypse of) Enoch: A New Translation and Introduction," in *Apocalyptic Literature and Testaments*, vol. 1 of *OTP*, ed. James H. Charlesworth (Doubleday, 1983), 8, 10. See also George W. E. Nickelsburg, *Jewish Literature between the Bible and the Mishnah* (SCM, 1981), 223.

47 Commonalities between 2 Esdras and Revelation either occur where there is no exodus imagery in Revelation, or the exodus imagery found in Revelation does not carry over to 2 Esdras. Compare 2 Esd 2:38–41 with Rev 7:2–8; 2 Esd 2:42–48 with Rev 7:9, 13–14; 19:1; 2 Esdr 3:7 with Rev 5:9; 7:9; 11:9; 13:7; 14:6; 2 Esd 4:35–37 with Rev 6:9–11; 2 Esd 6:17 with Rev 1:15; 2 Esd 7:39–42 with Rev 21:23–25.

with those in Egypt, only the livestock disease contains even a vague hint of exodus imagery. Interestingly, Revelation never alludes to this fifth exodus plague on the livestock. Finally, in Sibylline Oracles (5:454), swarms of locusts as agents of judgment do not necessarily imply an exodus allusion, as locusts are used in this same way elsewhere (most notably in Joel 1–2).[48] It is Revelation's cumulative witness throughout the trumpets and bowls to the exodus plagues as a model for eschatological judgment that causes the reader to immediately recall the exodus plague when faced with the demonic locusts in trumpet five.[49]

One final text has immediate relevance for this study. It has already been demonstrated that, though not apocalyptic, Isaiah is the OT text most commonly associated with the idea of a second exodus[50], yet the plague tradition is absent from Isaiah, even within judgment passages. The closest possible plague imagery in Isaiah is Isa 19:5–8, within the context of the oracle against Egypt. The statement that the sea and river will dry up, the canals will emit a stench, and those who fish in the Nile will mourn is perhaps a vague allusion to the first plague (Exod 7:15–25). Yet one ambiguous, potential allusion to a single plague does not begin to approach the cumulative effect of continuous allusions to seven of the ten exodus plagues in Revelation.

For a conclusive determination regarding exodus influence on eschatological judgments in general to be made, it would be necessary to delve into additional literature of apocalyptic genre or thought. Yet based on the above analysis, we can assert with a guarded sense of confidence that Revelation is unique among apocalyptic literature in using the exodus plagues to depict its end-time catastrophes. It must be noted, however, that Revelation does not break entirely from the typical apocalyptic paradigm for judgment. The seal judgments in Rev 6:1–17 seem to fit this mold quite effectively, having many parallels with both Ezekiel and the synoptic mini-apocalypses.[51]

---

48  Cf. Amos 4:9; Jer 46:23; 51:14; Nah 3:15–17.

49  There is also the possibility of exodus imagery within Joel's account of the locusts, and obvious allusions to Joel throughout trumpet five. Osborne, *Revelation*, 364; Beale, *Revelation*, 499–501; G. B. Caird, *A Commentary on the Revelation of St. John the Divine*, HNTC (Harper & Row, 1966), 119–120.

50  See Nickelsburg, *Jewish Literature*, 11–13.

51  Beale, *Revelation*, 372–373. Apocalyptic judgment elements found in the seven seals include war (seal 1), sword (seals 2 and 4), famine (seal 3), wild beasts (seal 4), and an earthquake, fire from heaven, and other unusual natural phenomena (seal 6). Fee asserts that the first four seals "are not 'plagues' at all, nor are they eschatological. Thus they are almost certainly not intended to relate to the final, eschatological conclusion of all things; rather they have all the markings of a prophetic word regarding the *near future* for John and his readers." Fee, *Revelation*, 91, emphasis original. Compare Matt 24:6–7, in which these same phenomena are described as "but the beginning of the birth pains" (Matt 24:8).

## Summary

What implication can be drawn, then, from Revelation's unusual use of the plague tradition as a paradigm for the end-time judgments? The adaptation of the plagues as a reminder of God's unfailing mercy in the past and continuing presence in the present was firmly established in Wisdom of Solomon. Like Wisdom of Solomon, Revelation's consistent use of the plague imagery affirms that, just as God delivered the Israelites out of Egypt by judging their enemies and supernaturally protecting the faithful, he still works on behalf of his people to deliver them from inevitable trials and persecutions.[52]

Yet unlike Wisdom of Solomon, Revelation extends its use of the exodus plagues to serve as both a literary and theological model for Revelation's eschatological judgments. Revelation's uniqueness among apocalyptic literature in utilizing the plague imagery suggests that this tradition has a more significant function within the work as a whole than might be previously recognized. Pattemore's suggestion that the trumpets and bowls are a direct response to the plea of the saints for vindication (Rev 6:10)[53] perhaps highlights a parallel to God's response to the Israelites' groaning in slavery (Exod 2:23–25, immediately preceding God's explicit interactions with Moses and the Israelites). The fact that, as in Exodus, the judgments in Revelation affect only those not covered by God's protection displays God's unique omnipotence as compared to idols or other so-called gods. The plague-like trumpet and bowl judgments function as a substantial, but by no means the only, facet of Revelation's broader portrayal of the nature and manner of the final eschatological deliverance through the paradigm of the historical exodus.

---

52 Enns, "Wisdom of Solomon," 215–217; Oesterley, *Books of the Apocrypha*, 197.

53 Stephen Pattemore, *The People of God in the Apocalypse* (Cambridge University Press, 2004), 90, 99; cf. Fee, *Revelation*, 121.

## Chapter 6

## Exodus Imagery in Revelation: The Passover and Paschal Lamb

If the plagues are one of the most recognizable features of the exodus tradition, the tenth plague is easily the most famous and is in some ways synonymous with the exodus itself. This final plague, the death of the firstborn, is the culmination and climax of Yahweh's judgment upon Egypt. It serves not only to demonstrate to the Egyptians with absolute finality the unqualified authority and sovereignty of Yahweh, but also to achieve his purpose of setting his people apart and delivering them from bondage to their Egyptian oppressors. Yahweh accomplished all this through the blood of an unblemished lamb and his people's willful obedience to his commands.

The story is time-honored and familiar. Yahweh determined that the tenth plague would do what the previous nine had not accomplished—Pharaoh would drive the people out of Egypt (Exod 11:1). The Lord commanded each Hebrew household to sacrifice a spotless lamb and paint the doorframes of their homes with the blood of the animal (Exod 12:3–7). The blood on the doorposts would serve as a sign—when Yahweh passed through Egypt striking the firstborn from every household, he would pass over the houses marked with the blood, and they would be shielded from the calamity (Exod 12:13). The events played out just as Yahweh said they would, and as a result, the distraught Pharaoh urged the Israelites to leave Egypt with haste. In a sense, the Passover lamb brought about their deliverance.

### Inaugural Vision of the Lamb (Rev 5)

Within the highly imaginative and symbolic language of the Apocalypse, the most frequent and significant Christological image is τὸ ἀρνίον, "the Lamb," first introduced in Rev 5:6.¹ Though scholars have sought the background of Revelation's portrayal of Christ as a Lamb within various milieus, including intertestamental Judaism, the ancient Near East, first-century Greco-Roman society, and of course, the OT,² most determine that the source of the Christological Lamb imagery is in some way connected with the paschal lamb. Using the song of praise (Rev 5:9–10) in the inaugural vision of the Lamb (Rev 5:6–14) as a primary point of reference, this chapter will demonstrate how the abundant exodus imagery throughout Revelation, in combination with the sacrificial and redemptive language in the context of "the Lamb," results in powerful paschal overtones which illuminate the significance of the title "the Lamb" for the theology of the Apocalypse. In light of the Apocalypse's pervasive employment of exodus typology, it seems "almost certain that John wants his readers to recognize in the Messiah-Lamb God's Passover Lamb.... The warrior Lamb thus has 'conquered' through his accepting the role of the sacrificed Passover Lamb, and so made possible a second Exodus."³

The figure of the Lamb is first introduced in Rev 5, though hints at his identity and sacrificial nature occur as early as Rev 1:5–6. From this point on, the Lamb is at least implicitly at the heart of the action and progression of events.⁴ The links between the throne-room visions of God and the Lamb (Rev 4–5), and the worship that occurs within them highlight the praiseworthiness of the Lamb (Rev 5:4, 9). Revelation 5 specifically presents the worship of the Lamb in a manner that underscores his sacrificial role in salvation, the cumulative effect of which is a clear allusion to the paschal lamb.⁵

After the Lamb takes the scroll from the One seated on the throne (Rev 5:8), the four living creatures and twenty-four elders fall down before him and sing a new song regarding the Lamb's worthiness to receive this scroll. In this song (Rev 5:9–10), the ὅτι clause introduces three progressive causal clauses linked with the conjunction καί which follow the basic succession of the events of the original exodus:

---

1 The word ἀρνίον occurs 29 times in the Apocalypse: Rev 5:6, 8, 12, 13; 6:1, 16; 7:9, 10, 14, 17; 12:11; 13:8, 11; 14:1, 4 (2x), 10; 15:3; 17:14 (2x); 19:7, 9; 21:9, 14, 22, 23, 27; 22:1, 3. In every case it is employed as a Christological title, except in Rev 13:11 ("it had two horns like a lamb"), where it is used in reference to the beast rising out of the earth, and is an example of the motif of fraud or imitation used throughout the text with regard to the Antichrist.

2 See Loren L. Johns, *The Lamb Christology of the Apocalypse of John: An Investigation into Its Origins and Rhetorical Force*, WUNT 2nd series 167 (Mohr Siebeck, 2003).

3 G. R. Beasley-Murray, "How Christian Is the Book of Revelation?," in *Reconciliation and Hope: New Testament Essays on Atonement and Eschatology, Presented to L. L. Morris on his 60th Birthday*, ed. Robert Banks (Paternoster, 1974), 279.

4 Maurice Carrez, "Le Déploiement de la Christologie de l'Agneau dans l'Apocalypse," *RHPR* 79 (1999): 7; Donald Guthrie, "The Lamb in the Structure of the Book of Revelation," *Vox Evangelica* 12 (1981): 65.

5 J. Daryl Charles, "An Apocalyptic Tribute to the Lamb (Rev 5:1–14)," *JETS* 34 (1991): 462.

> Worthy are you to take the scroll and to open its seals,
> > for (ὅτι) you were slain,
> > and (καί) by your blood you ransomed people for God
> > > from every tribe and language and people and nation,
> > and (καί) you have made them a kingdom and priests to our God,
> > > and (καί) they shall reign on the earth.

In Egypt, the divinely-initiated sacrifice of the paschal victim was the commencement of the tenth and final plague (Exod 12:3–11, 21), in which the sacrificial blood on the doorposts of the homes protected the Hebrews from the wrath and judgment of Yahweh and functioned as their deliverance from Egyptian slavery (Exod 12:12–13, 22–28). As a result, the Hebrews entered into a covenant with God and were created by him to be a treasured possession, a kingdom of priests (Exod 19:3–6). Likewise in Revelation, the Lamb is praised because he bears the marks of slaughter or sacrifice. As a result of his sacrifice, the Lamb has purchased with his blood a chosen people out of all the nations, transforming these redeemed into a kingdom of priests who will reign on earth.[6] This progression seems to indicate a structural allusion to the exodus from Egypt, and is a central facet of Revelation's overarching exodus typology.

The Lamb is first celebrated as having been slain (ἐσφάγης, Rev 5:9). This initial picture in itself contains no explicit reference to the Passover or redemption. From this verse alone it is not clear which sacrifice is in view, only that John plainly had the OT sacrificial system in mind.[7] Outside of Revelation the verb σφάζω ("to slay") is not used in the NT to refer to the sacrificial death of Christ, yet here it serves as the basis for the Lamb's worthiness to open the seven-sealed scroll.[8] Earlier in the noteworthy first mention of the Lamb (Rev 5:6), the simple phrase "standing, as though it had been slain" (ἑστηκὸς ὡς ἐσφαγμένον) becomes an allusion both to Christ's sacrificial death and his resurrection. Though one might expect the Messianic Lamb to be seated on the throne, as the Father is portrayed in Rev 4:9–10 and Rev 5:7,

---

6  David Aune, *Revelation 1–5*, WBC 52a (Word, 1997), 361; John D'Souza, *The Lamb of God in the Johannine Writings* (St. Paul, 1968), 26–27.

7  Aune, *Revelation 1–5*, 372; Roland Bergmeier, "Die Buchrolle und das Lamm (Apk 5 und 10)," *Zeitschrift* für die *neutestamentliche Wissenschaft und die Kunde der* älteren *Kirche* 76 (1985): 233–234. Due to the importance of blood sacrifice in the Judaism, the basic OT term for animal slaughter (זָבַח) assumed the technical meaning of sacrifice. Gary A. Anderson, "Sacrifice and Sacrificial Offerings (OT)," *ABD* 5:870–886.

8  The verb σφάζω ("to slay") in Rev 5:9 conveys the sense of slaughtering animals in the Jewish sacrificial system. Otto Michel, "Σφάζω, σφαγή," *TDNT* 7:925–938; Aune, *Revelation 1–5*, 353, 361; etc. The language of slaughter is also found on the tongues of the multitude of angels in Rev 5:12, and in connection with the Lamb's book of life in Rev 13:8.

here John depicts the slain Lamb as standing (ἑστηκὸς) in the midst of the throne.[9]

The second causal clause of Rev 5:9, "by your blood you ransomed people for God," carries much weight theologically. In a technical or commercial sense, ἀγοράζω conveys the idea of buying back, or ransoming (Exod 15:13, 16; Ps 74:1–2), as in the manumission of slaves. In a religious sense, however, this verb should be interpreted more broadly as the redemption of men.[10] Within the framework of a Jewish worldview, the concept of redemption would immediately evoke exodus connotations, for Yahweh had redeemed Israel out of Egypt (Lev 25:37, 55).[11] It was the blood of the Passover lamb which marked the homes of the Israelites and allowed them to experience the deliverance of the Lord and not the wrath of his judgment. The fact that the OT prophets used ransom/redemption language in their anticipation of a future deliverance modeled after the exodus (e.g., Isa 43:1–3; 52:3) helps to solidify the place of redemptive language within John's exodus typology.[12] The eschatological redemption of men is accomplished through the blood of "the true Lamb who is Christ Jesus, of whom the lamb slaughtered in Egypt was the true type, when he delivered the Hebrews of that time from the power of the one governing Egypt."[13]

This ransom is not merely deliverance from the oppressive bonds of slavery, as in Egypt. Rather, the fact that the freedom is accomplished by his blood (ἐν τῷ αἵματί) contextually associates this ransom/redemption with the forgiveness of sins, atonement, and purification received through Christ's death (cf. Mark 10:45; Heb 9:15; 1 Pet 1:18–19).[14] Indeed, the statement in Rev 1:5 that Christ has "freed us from our sins by his blood" appears to be a parallel assertion to Rev 5:9—the first indicates forgiveness or atonement, while the second

---

9 Aune, *Revelation 1–5*, 353; Oecumenius, *Commentary on the Apocalypse*, trans. John N. Suggit, FC 112 (Catholic University of America Press, 2006), 62. Elsewhere in the NT (John 20:19, 26; Luke 24:36) the same verb is used of Christ's post-resurrection appearances to the disciples. Grundmann suggests that references to Jesus as standing are theologically significant, presenting him as the Risen Lord. "Through His coming to them He becomes and is the centre around which everything is grouped." Walter Grundmann, "Στήκω, ἵστημι," *TDNT* vol 5:636–653.

10 D'Souza, *Lamb of God*, 16; Vincent Taylor, *The Atonement in New Testament Teaching*, 2nd ed. (Epworth, 1945), 37.

11 J. Schneider and C. Brown, "Redemption," *NIDNTT* 3:190–193.

12 M.-E. Boismard, "Christ the Lamb, Redeemer of Men," in *Theology of the Atonement: Readings in Soteriology*, ed. John R. Sheets (Prentice-Hall, 1967), 159; D'Souza, *Lamb of God*, 13.

13 Origen, *Treatise on the Passover and Dialogue of Origen with Heraclides and His Fellow Bishops on the Father, the Son, and the Soul*, trans. and annotated by Robert J. Daly, ACW 54 (Paulist, 1992), 56.

14 A number of Greek words, including λύω, ἀγοράζω, λυτρόομαι, σῴζω, and ῥύομαι, bring out the various facets of these intricately connected themes within the NT. Schneider and Brown, *NIDNTT* 3:177–223). Leon Morris, *The Cross in the New Testament* (Eerdmans, 1965), 322.

focuses on redemption.[15] References to the blood of the Lamb elsewhere connote the concept of atonement, drawing to mind the mercy seat and the Day of Atonement, when blood sprinkled around the altar was thought to remove or cover one's sin and consecrate or purify the sinner (Exod 29:11–37; Lev 16:14–19).[16] Revelation brings out the cleansing quality of the blood (e.g., Lev 16:18–19, 30; Ezek 43:19–27; cf. Heb 9:13–14) through the idea of being washed in the blood of the Lamb (Rev 7:14; 22:14), the metaphorical equivalent to the purification of sins (cf. Isa 1:18; 1 Cor 6:11; Eph 5:25–27; 1 John 1:7).[17] Thus in Revelation, as in the rest of the NT, "the phrase 'the blood of the Lamb' or 'the blood of Christ' ... is a metonymy for the death of Christ or more particularly the atoning death of Christ."[18] The cumulative occurrences of Lamb and blood imagery throughout Revelation come together with this introductory vision of the Lamb to present a broader picture of the sacrificial nature of the Lamb's salvific death and the transformational effect for those who align themselves with the Lamb through his blood.

The third causal clause in the song of praise to the Lamb is a declaration of effective re-creation for the redeemed. John states that through his blood the Lamb has "made them a kingdom and priests to our God, and they shall reign on the earth" (Rev 5:10). The phrase "a kingdom and priests" (βασιλείαν καὶ ἱερεῖς) is one of the strongest verbal allusions in the entire Apocalypse, recalling God's promise to create out of the nation of Israel "a kingdom of priests" in Exod 19:6 (βασίλειον ἱεράτευμα, LXX).[19] Thus John reworks the regal, priestly promise that God gave to the Israelites and applies it to believers in Christ by alluding to Yahweh's words at the beginning of the covenant ceremony at Mount Sinai.[20] The verbal correspondence with Exod 19:6 is

---

15 In this sense λύω (Rev 1:5; cf. Acts 2:24) and ἀγοράζω (Rev 5:9) are to a certain extent synonymous. Schneider and Brown, *NIDNTT* 3:180; Friedrich Büchsel, "ἀγοράζω, ἐξαγοράζω," *TDNT* 1:125–126; C. K. Barrett, "The Lamb of God," *NTS* 1 (1954–55): 217. The expression "to free someone from sin" (Rev 1:5) conveys the idea of forgiveness of sins, which in the Levitical system was accomplished through animal sacrifice (e.g., Lev 4:26). Revelation 1:5 is the only NT occurrence of the phrase "to free someone from sin," though NT connections between the death of Christ and the removal of guilt are abundant (e.g., Rom 3:25; 1 Cor 15:3; 1 John 1:7; 2:2; 3:5; cf. Ps 130:8). Perhaps the most explicit statement regarding the role of blood in the forgiveness of sins is found in Heb 9:22—"without the shedding of blood there is no forgiveness of sins."

16 Aune, *Revelation 1–5*, 353; D'Souza, *Lamb of God*, 18–19, 21; Anderson, "Sacrifice," 879.

17 D'Souza, *Lamb of God*, 25; David E. Aune, *Revelation 6–16*, WBC 52b (Thomas Nelson, 1998), 475. Note the less accepted textual variant in Rev 1:5—"washed (λουσαντι) us from our sins."

18 Aune, *Revelation 6–16*, 475.

19 Aune, *Revelation 1–5*, 48.

20 1 Peter 2:9 also draws upon the promise in Exod 19:5–6, though emphasizing believers as a "holy nation" (cf. Exod 19:6, ἔθνος ἅγιον) and Yahweh's own "possession" (cf. Exod 19:5, λαὸς περιούσιος) rather than a kingdom. John is in good company in his transferal of the identifying characteristics and calling of the people of God from Israel to believers.

strengthened by the context. In the preceding verse, the combination of purchasing language with the phrase "from every tribe and language and people and nation" is conceptually parallel to Exod 19:5, "you shall be my treasured possession among all peoples." It is the people who have associated themselves with the blood and been redeemed from bondage (to Egypt in Exodus, to sin in Revelation) who become a chosen people of God, a priestly kingdom.[21]

## Was the Passover Expiatory?

Contextually and structurally, then, Passover allusions clearly exist within the song of praise in Rev 5:9–10. This heightens the likelihood that John imbedded paschal overtones within this inaugural vision and throughout the Apocalypse. However, two major objections to the paschal nature of Revelation's Lamb must be countered. First, some scholars immediately reject a Passover background by claiming that the original Passover victim was not necessarily a lamb at all. It is true that Exod 12:5 allows the sacrifice to be taken from either the sheep or the goats;[22] yet the OT sacrificial animal *par excellence* was a lamb, and "to the readers of the Apocalypse the most obvious of all slain lambs was the Passover lamb.... It is surely the obvious, the well-known, the easily understood that counts, not the ingenious, the torturous, the remote."[23]

The weightier argument against a paschal background is the idea that the Passover, as a form of peace offering, did not have redemptive or atoning significance but was observed simply as a memorial of the deliverance from

---

21  Grant R. Osborne, *Revelation,* BECNT (Baker, 2002), 261. Cf. D'Souza, *Lamb of God*, 18; G. K. Beale, *The Book of Revelation*, NIGTC (Eerdmans, 1999), 352. This is not the only allusion to Exod 19:6 in the Apocalypse. In Rev 1:6 the formation of a kingdom of priests (βασιλείαν, ἱερεῖς τῷ θεῷ) is applied to those who are freed from their sins by Christ's blood. A final allusion to this regal, priestly promise occurs in Rev 20:6—"they will be priests of God and of Christ, and they will reign with him for a thousand years." Admittedly this last allusion is the least solid verbally, for the kingship element is only conveyed through the idea of reigning (βασιλεύω), and the distance between the priestly and regal words is much greater than in Rev 1:6 or Rev 5:10. However, the language of reigning is identical in both Rev 5:10 and Rev 20:6, thus strengthening the possibility of an allusion to Exod 19:6 in Rev 20:6. Consider the similar concept in Rev 22:5, "and they will reign forever and ever" (καὶ βασιλεύσουσιν εἰς τοὺς αἰῶνας τῶν αἰώνων), in what appears to be a verbal allusion to Exod 15:18, the only other NT or LXX occurrence of a verbal form of βασιλεύω with the idiom ὁ αἰών τῶν αἰώνων (cf. Rev 1:6 for the noun βασιλεία + the idiom).

22  Indeed, the Hebrew word for lamb (שֶׂה) found in Exod 12:5 is indiscriminate. J. Jeremias, "ἀμνός, ἀρήν, ἀρνίον," *TDNT* vol 1:339; George Buchanan Gray, *Sacrifice in the Old Testament: Its Theory & Practice* (Clarendon, 1925), 345–346; Leon Morris, *The Apostolic Preaching of the Cross*, 3rd rev. ed. (Eerdmans, 1994), 132.

23  Godfrey Ashby, *Sacrifice: Its Nature and Purpose* (SCM, 1988), 87; Morris, *Cross in the NT*, 355.

Egyptian bondage (cf. Jub. 49:7–8).[24] However, it is possible that the Jews understood the original Passover event to have an atoning significance, even if the annual killing of the paschal lambs at the Jerusalem Temple was not.[25] The blood of the lamb on the doorposts was the method of Israel's redemption—it was a sign of protection for the Hebrew people to shield them from the judgment of God manifested in the tenth plague (Exod 12:12–13).[26] Similarly in sacrifices specifically offered for atonement, the people are protected from God's judgment as he passes over their sins (cf. Ps 88:16; Rom 3:25). Pirqe Rabbi Elieser 29 explicitly attributes redemptive value to the original Passover event, and applies this connotation to the expected eschatological deliverance as well.[27]

Other scholars claim that, though in the exodus account there is no indication that the Israelites were redeemed, ransomed, or delivered by the blood of the lamb, by NT times the Jews "gave to the blood of the paschal lamb a redemptive value that it did not have in Exodus."[28] Thus, even if the original Passover sacrifice was not considered to be expiatory at that time, this does not exclude a paschal background for Revelation's Lamb. The ancient Jewish historian Josephus clearly understood the Passover as removing sin,

---

24 Anderson, "Sacrifice," 878–879; C. H. Dodd, *Interpretation of the Fourth Gospel* (Cambridge University Press, 1960), 234; Gray, *Sacrifice*, 364.

25 I. Howard Marshall, "The Development of the Concept of Redemption in the New Testament," in *Reconciliation and Hope: New Testament Essays on Atonement and Eschatology, Presented to L. L. Morris on his 60th Birthday*, ed. Robert Banks (Paternoster, 1974), 160; Rudolf Schnackenburg, *The Gospel According to St. John*, trans. Kevin Smyth, 3 vols. (Herder and Herder, 1968), 1:299; Heinrich Ewald, *The Antiquities of Israel*, trans. Henry Shaen Solly (Lockwood, Brooks, & Co., 1876), 353; etc.

26 "C'est l'agnea pascal qui justifie le sang et l'insistance sur le sang de l'Agneau dans l'Apocalypse. Dans l'Exode, en effet, c'est le sang de l'agneau qui est le moyen du salut d'Israël et le signe de la préservation (Ex., XII, 13, 22–23). Il en est de même dans saint Jean (V, 9)." J. Comblin, *Le Christ dans l'Apocalypse*, Théologie Biblique (Desclée, 1965), 26. Consider the sealing of the 144,000 in Rev 7, which parallels the Passover and which serves to protect the servants of God from the trumpet and bowl judgments which God is preparing to send on the earth. The paschal background of the sealing of believers is further supported by the fact that John identifies this same group with the blood of the Lamb in Rev 7:14. Cf. Beale, *Revelation*, 409; William H. C. Propp, *Exodus 1–18: A New Translation with Introduction and Commentary*, AB 2 (Doubleday, 1999), 460.

27 "Wegen ... des Blutes des Pesachlammes habe ich euch aus Ägypten erlöst, und um ihretwillen werdet ihr einst zum Ende des vierten Königreiches erlöst warden." *Pirke de-Rabbi Elieser*, trans. and ed. Dagmar Börner-Klein, SJ 26 (Walter de Gruyter, 2004), 326–327. This Jewish text "probably stems from Islamicate Palestine during the eighth or ninth centuries CE." John C. Reeves, *Trajectories in Near Eastern Apocalyptic: A Postrabbinic Jewish Apocalypse Reader*, SBL Resources for Biblical Study 45 (SBL, 2005), 67. Likewise, Comblin states "Jésus est donc l'Agneau pascal eschatologique dont le sang a une vertu propitiatoire et expie les péchés." Comblin, *Christ dans l'Apocalypse*, 27.

28 Boismard, "Christ the Lamb," 160; Norman Hillyer, "'The Lamb' in the Apocalypse," *EvQ* 39 (1967): 230; Gray, *Sacrifice*, 24.

referring to the Israelites purifying their houses with blood (*Antiquities* 2.312).[29] Prosic refers to both Josephus and Philo (*De specialibus legibus* 2.148) to assert that the paschal blood smeared on the doorposts was not "an apotropaic rite intended to protect the family members" but a "cleansing, purifying agent, whose application on the entrance temporarily transforms the inside of the house into a hallowed ground, a temple."[30]

There is no consensus as to whether the original Passover sacrifice or its repeated practice throughout antiquity contained expiatory value. In either case, the combination of atonement and paschal imagery in the single figure of the Lamb could be an example of typological escalation, attributing a greater significance and power to the antitype, the true Lamb of God, than the type itself, such that the ultimate Passover Lamb extinguishes the sins of the world where the original and annual paschal lambs could not.[31] In this sense, the expiatory nature of Revelation's Lamb is theologically parallel to the typology of the book of Hebrews, in which the entire sacrificial system was a type or foreshadowing of Christ's sacrificial death. Though "it is impossible for the blood of bulls and goats to take away sins" (Heb 10:4), the blood of Christ was effective as an offering for sin once for all. The author of Hebrews associated the blood of the covenant with the expiatory blood of various sacrifices, without distinguishing the different types. Even Lev 17:11 connects atonement not with any particular sacrifice, but with the blood of sacrifice in general.[32] Thus there is no need to distinguish between the efficaciousness of the paschal lamb and the animal victims of atoning sacrifices. Melito very clearly identifies the atoning sacrifice of Christ as the fulfillment of the Passover:

> Come then, all you families of men who are compounded with sins, and get forgiveness of sins. For I am your forgiveness, I am the Pascha of salvation, I am the lamb slain for you; I am your ransom, I am your life, I am your light, I am your salvation, I am your resurrection, I am your king.[33]

---

29  Flavius Josephus, *Judean Antiquities 1–4*, trans. Louis H. Feldman, vol. 3 of *Flavius Josephus: Translation and Commentary* (Brill, 2000), 222.

30  Tamara Prosic, *The Development and Symbolism of Passover until 70 CE* (T&T Clark, 2004), 49–50.

31  Baruch M. Bokser, "Unleavened Bread and Passover, Feasts of," *ABD* 6:755–765; Schnackenburg, *Gospel According to St. John*, 1:300.

32  Frances M. Young, *The Use of Sacrificial Ideas in Greek Christian Writers from the New Testament to John Chrysostom*, Patristic Monograph Series 5 (Philadelphia Patristic Foundation, 1979), 150–151; Morris, *Apostolic Preaching*, 131.

33  Melito of Sardis, *On Pascha and Fragments*, trans. and ed. Stuart George Hall, OECT (Clarendon, 1979), 103.

## Song of Moses and Song of the Lamb (Rev 15:1–4)

If there was any remaining doubt as to the paschal background of Revelation's ἀρνίον, it should be dispelled by the juxtaposition of the Lamb with multiple allusions to the exodus within Rev 15. While verbal connections are admittedly minimal, the many thematic allusions to the exodus suggest that the overarching theme of Rev 15, which directly precedes the final series of seven judgments, appears to be the enactment of a new exodus. This is manifest in the seven plagues, a sea of glass that the faithful seem to cross, and the song of Moses and of the Lamb, all of which introduce the culmination of the great conflict as displayed in the bowl judgments (Rev 16).[34]

With his opening statement, "then I saw another sign in heaven," John connects this vision with the only two other occurrences of σημεῖον in the Apocalypse—the woman in childbirth in Rev 12:1–2, and the dragon in Rev 12:3.[35] In this instance, the sign consists of "seven angels with seven plagues (πληγὰς), which are the last," an introductory prologue for all that is to come in Rev 15:1–16:21.[36] John expounds upon this third sign with the description "great and amazing" (μέγα καὶ θαυμαστόν, cf. Rev 15:3 recounting the deeds of the Lord). The use of θαυμαστός is rare in the NT; as in the LXX, the word depicts God's marvelous deeds, often in allusions to or quotations of the Psalms.[37] Perhaps here it is a verbal allusion to Deut 28:59 LXX, where the two words are similarly combined with reference to plagues of judgment (πληγὰς μεγάλας καὶ θαυμαστάς) which the Lord will cast on those who do not obey his

---

34 Jay Casey, "The Exodus Theme in the Book of Revelation against the Background of the New Testament," in *Exodus: A Lasting Paradigm*, ed. Antonius G. Weiler, Marcus Lefébure, & Bastiaan Martinus Franciscus van Iersel (T&T Clark, 1987), 39; Stephen S. Smalley, *The Revelation to John: A Commentary on the Greek Text of the Apocalypse* (InterVarsity, 2005), 383. As in the parallel trumpet account, John's initial glimpse of the seven angels (Rev 15:1; cf. Rev 8:2) is followed by a scene of heavenly worship (Rev 15:2–4; cf. Rev 8:3–4), theophanic elements (Rev 15:8; cf. Rev 8:5), a restatement of the angelic presence (Rev 15:5–7; cf. Rev 8:6), and ultimately, God's judgment upon the earth (Rev 16:1ff.; cf. Rev 8:7ff.). Just as the bowl judgments in Rev 16 have increased in scope and intensity from the trumpets, so too John has expanded the liturgical and theophanic elements with which they are introduced. Other exodus elements in Rev 15 include smoke reminiscent of a theophany and the tent of testimony, both of which are discussed in chapter 7, "The Temple of the Tabernacle of Meeting."

35 The word σημεῖον in this context can refer to a miraculous event outside the normal course of nature, or an appearance in the heavens as a portent of the last days. "σημεῖον," BDAG, 921.

36 Although the angels are introduced in Rev 15:1, the action begins in Rev 15:5 when John's eyes are drawn to the heavenly temple, and escalates quickly with no extended interruptions or expanded narrations to break up the flow of the bowl judgments. Dennis E. Johnson, *Triumph of the Lamb: A Commentary on Revelation* (P & R, 2001), 214; etc.

37 Franz Annen, "θαυμαστός," *EDNT* 2:135–136. In the NT, θαυμαστός occurs only in Mark 12:11; Matt 21:15, 42; John 9:30; 1 Pet 2:9; Rev 15:1, 3.

law.[38] In both cases, the expression refers to plagues and is followed with a reference to or imagery from the judgments in Egypt.[39]

With a second "and I saw," John introduces his vision of the saints worshiping in heaven beside "something like a sea (θάλασσαν) of glass mingled with fire" (Rev 15:2, NASB).[40] Caird draws upon the apocalyptic notion of water as destructive and chaotic[41] to say that the sea here stands for everything contrary to the will of God, a "barrier which the redeemed must pass in a new Exodus, if they are to win access to the promised land."[42] Yet in Revelation, nineteen of the twenty-six occurrences of θάλασσα are neutral, portraying the sea as a part of God's creation (e.g., Rev 14:7), no more subject to God's judgments than the rest of the created world.[43] Rather, the key to the θάλασσα in Rev 15:2 is found in its two descriptors—"of/like glass" (cf. Rev 4:6) and "mingled with fire." The description "a sea of glass" may derive from Moses's vision of Yahweh's throne or footstool while on Mount Sinai—"a pavement of sapphire stone, like the very heaven for clearness" (Exod 24:10).[44] Elsewhere, Jewish exegetical tradition depicts the Red Sea in the exodus as a sea of glass

---

38  Smalley, *Revelation*, 382; Aune, *Revelation 6–16*, 869; etc.

39  The word πληγή is the first and perhaps most obvious occurrence of exodus imagery in Rev 15. As has already been demonstrated, John clearly modeled his description of the trumpet and bowl judgments after the plagues which God sent upon Egypt during the exodus account. The combination of the word πληγή in relation to the bowl judgments in Rev 15:1 and the subsequent description of the judgments themselves using exodus imagery immediately connects them with the Egyptian plagues in content and purpose. Prigent traces the tradition of the seven angels with seven plagues back to Lev 26, especially verses 21 and 24. Pierre Prigent, *Commentary on the Apocalypse of St. John*, trans. Wendy Pradels, rev. ed. (Mohr Siebeck, 2001), 459. However, given the wide use of exodus imagery in this short passage, as well as throughout the Apocalypse, it seems more likely that John is drawing upon his reader's knowledge of the historical exodus and expectation of eschatological deliverance.

40  The comparative phrase recalls earlier throne-room visions where the crystal sea stretched before God's throne (Rev 4:6) and the heavenly chorus sang a new song with harps (Rev 5:8–9; cf. Rev 14:2–3). Craig R. Koester, *Revelation and the End of All Things* (Eerdmans, 2001), 141. The use of the particle ὡς ("like") in apocalyptic visions draws the reader's attention to the mysterious content (e.g., Rev 5:6; 6:6; 8:8; cf. Dan 7:4; Ezek 1:26–28; 4 Ezra 11:37). The emphasis is not on a literal sea but on "God's awesome vastness, his transcendence and his holiness." Osborne, *Revelation*, 231; etc.

41  The Psalms portray the Red Sea as the abode of the evil sea monster (Ps 74:12–14), a view which seems to carry over into John's depiction of the sea as the realm of the beast and demons (Rev 11:7; 12:12, 18; 13:1; 21:1; 20:13). Reinhard Kratz, "θάλασσα," *EDNT* 2:127–128; Beale, *Revelation*, 789.

42  G. B. Caird, *A Commentary on the Revelation of St. John the Divine*, HNTC (Harper & Row, 1966), 65.

43  J. Ramsey Michaels, *Interpreting the Book of Revelation* (Baker, 1992), 115–116.

44  Johnson links this imagery of the crystalline base of God's throne (cf. Exod 24:10; Ezek 1:22) with the river of water "bright as crystal" flowing from the throne in Revelation's picture of the New Jerusalem (Rev 22:1; cf. Rev 21:11, 18, 21). Johnson, *Triumph of the Lamb*, 216; cf. William H. Shea, "Literary and Theological Parallels between Revelation 14–15 and Exodus 19–24," *Journal of the Adventist Theological Society* 12 (2001): 174.

(Exod 15:8; Midr. Ps 136:7).[45] But the sea in Rev 15:2 is not just glassy but also "mingled with fire," a symbol of God's holiness and divine judgment (e.g., Rev 1:14; 2:18; 4:5; 8:5–8; 10:1; 11:5). Thus, the "sea of glass mingled with fire" combines the idea of a celestial sea as the floor of heaven (God's throne room) and "the place where the Lamb has judged the beast."[46] The sea in Rev 4:6 and 15:2 is far from evil; rather, like everything else in the throne room and heavenly city, it radiates the glory of God.[47]

Standing on this sea of glass John sees "those who had conquered the beast and its image and the number of its name" (Rev 15:2). Judging by the subsequent hymn, these victors are the saints of God (cf. Rev 14:1–5). Their location, "standing on the sea of glass" (Rev 15:2, NASB), recalls the Israelites singing the song of Moses beside the Red Sea (Exod 15),[48] yet with a sense of escalation—unlike the Israelites, who stood *beside* the Red Sea as God won the victory on their behalf (Exod 14:15–31), these saints have actively participated in the conquering of the beast "*through* the fiery floods of opposition and strife"[49] by being washed in the blood of the Lamb (Rev 7:14). Their

---

45 The allusion to the Red Sea as a "sea of glass" finds support "where the sea is integrally linked with 'fire,' as in 4:5–6…. The two passages are also linked by the fact that in both the notion of 'overcoming' is applied to people who 'stand' either on or by the 'sea'…. Strikingly similar to Rev. 4:6 is *Mekilta Rabbi Ishmael* (Beshallah 5.13–15, on Exod. 14:16), which says, probably on the basis of Exod. 15:8 ('the deeps were congealed'), that one of the miracles at the Red Sea episode was that the sea became congealed and became like glass vessels." Beale, *Revelation*, 327.

46 Smalley, *Revelation*, 384; Beale, *Revelation*, 789. Witherington claims that the fire in Rev 15:2 is God's wrath, hovering and about to be cast down. It is also possible that John was alluding to the brazen basin in Solomon's Temple, which was known as the "molten sea" (1 Kgs 7:23, KJV; 2 Chr 4:2, KJV). Ben Witherington, III, *Revelation*, NCBC (Cambridge University Press, 2003), 205.

47 Michaels, *Interpreting Revelation*, 116; John Guimond, *The Silencing of Babylon: A Spiritual Commentary on the Revelation of John* (Paulist, 1991), 73; etc. The picture in Rev 13:1 of a beast rising from the sea may at first glance seem to challenge this interpretation. However, in the same passage we read of another beast rising out of the earth (Rev 13:11). It is possible that neither the sea nor the earth in this context represents evil or destruction; rather, the combination of the two signifies the widespread influence of the beast. It is equally possible that there is a distinction in Revelation between the sea from which the beast emerges in Rev 13 and the sea of glass in heaven's throne room.

48 The spatial use of the preposition ἐπὶ can be translated "on, upon," or "beside, near." However, with an accusative (as here) the translation of "on, upon" is preferred. This best fits the current context, and is consistent with other uses of the verb "to stand" with ἐπὶ in the Apocalypse (Rev 3:20; 7:1; 11:11; 12:18; 14:1; cf. 10:5, 8). Daniel B. Wallace, *Greek Grammar Beyond the Basics: An Exegetical Syntax of the New Testament* (Zondervan, 1996), 376–377. The NRSV and ESV prefer "beside" (cf. NIV, RSV). The KJV, NKJV, and NASB all translate this preposition "on."

49 Smalley, *Revelation*, 385; Beale, *Revelation*, 791. Oecumenius understands John to be drawing upon the idea of being tested or purified by fire (e.g., 1 Cor 3:12–13), suggesting that "those who have in every way defeated the beast stand on the sea of glass mixed with fire. For [the sea] is glass because of the brightness and purity of the righteous in it. However, it is

conquest is brought about "by the blood of the Lamb and by the word of their testimony" (Rev 12:11), as they endured faithfully, refusing to compromise with the world, even unto death (Rev 2:7; 3:21; 5:5–6; 12:11, 17; 14:12–13).[50] They themselves have battled with the Lamb against the beast and the unbelieving world in the waters of conflict.

John then removes any doubt that the Red Sea victory is the background of the conquerors as well as reinforces the paschal nature of Revelation's Lamb by describing the saints as "sing[ing] the song of Moses, the servant of God, and the song of the Lamb" (Rev 15:3).[51] This is an obvious allusion to the song of praise to the Lord which Moses led the Israelites in singing after crossing the Red Sea (Exod 15:1–18; cf. the later song attributed to Moses, Deut 31:30–32:44).[52] While this Song of the Lamb contains no formal quotation of the OT song of Moses on the bank of the Red Sea, they exhibit theological continuity through the shared themes of redemptive judgment and God's faithfulness to his people—indeed, this scene directly precedes the final series of judgments upon the beast and his domain. In Rev 15:3–4, John has woven together a glorious symphony of OT allusions extolling the perfect character of God (e.g., Deut 32:4; Pss 86:8–10; 111:2; 139:14; 145:17; Jer 10:6–7).[53] Though the particular melody of the original Song of Moses is not immediately evident, its theme forms an ongoing counterpoint continuously underlying the harmonic phrases of the conquerors' new song.

The hymn begins by praising the saving works of God through two lines of synonymous parallelism, a feature characteristic of the Hebrew psalms

---

mixed with fire because of the cleansing and purification from all filth." Oecumenius, *Oecumenii Commentarius in Apocalypsin*, ed. Marc de Groote (Peters, 1999), 205, translated in William C. Weinrich, ed., *Revelation*, ACCS New Testament 12 (InterVarsity, 2005), 239.

50  Koester, *Revelation*, 141; Guimond, *Silencing of Babylon*, 73; Dan Lioy, *The Book of Revelation in Christological Focus*, SBL 58 (Peter Lang, 2003), 144; etc.

51  Smalley, *Revelation*, 386; David A. DeSilva, *Seeing Things John's Way: The Rhetoric of the Book of Revelation* (Westminster John Knox, 2009), 163. The genitives in the phrase "the song of Moses ... and the song of the Lamb" are somewhat problematic, as they cannot be functionally parallel. "The song of Moses" is best understood with a subjective intent (a song *by* Moses), while the genitive in "the song of the Lamb" is more likely objective, (a song *to* or *about* the Lamb). Beale suggests that τοῦ ἀρνίου may also have a subjective function (a song sung by the Lamb), but it is best to leave both genitives ambiguous. The epexegetical καὶ ("that is") and the content of Rev 15:3–4 reinforce the understanding that this phrase introduces one unified song. Beale, *Revelation*, 793.

52  G. K. Beale and Sean M. McDonough, "Revelation," in *Commentary on the New Testament Use of the Old Testament*, ed. G. K. Beale and D. A. Carson (Baker, 2007), 1133; etc.

53  George A. F. Knight, *The Song of Moses: A Theological Quarry* (Eerdmans, 1995), 139–141. Bauckham suggests that "like the version of the song of Moses which Isaiah 12 predicts that Israel will sing at the new exodus, Revelation's version is an *interpretation* of the song of Moses, which John has produced by typically skillful use of current Jewish exegetical methods." Richard Bauckham, *The Theology of the Book of Revelation*, New Testament Theology (Cambridge University Press, 1993), 99.

and songs of the OT.[54] The parallelism of the elements in Rev 15:3 (NASB) can be seen as follows:

| Great and marvelous are | your works, | Lord God, the Almighty |
|---|---|---|
| a | b | c |
| Righteous and true are | your ways, | King of the Nations |
| a | b | c |

As in Rev 15:1, the expression "great and marvelous" links the coming bowl judgments with the wondrous works of God throughout salvation history (cf. Ps 110:2–4; Deut 28:59–60; Job 42:3). In the second line, God is righteous and just in punishing his enemies and vindicating his people, both in the historical exodus and the end times.[55] This appears to be a verbal allusion to Moses's song in Deuteronomy, "... his work is perfect, for all his ways are justice. A God of faithfulness and without iniquity, just and upright is he" (Deut 32:4; cf. Ps 145:17).[56] These themes are also found in the Song of Moses in Exodus 15 where, rather than providing a concise summary of God's saving work and righteous judgment, the Israelites proclaim the details of his acts of deliverance by shattering the enemy (Exod 15:6) and redeeming his people (Exod 15:13) and praise him for being "majestic in holiness, awesome in glorious deeds, doing wonders" (Exod 15:11).

The designation "the Almighty" (ὁ παντοκράτωρ; Rev 15:3), a title bestowed only upon God, has the connotation of "almighty, all-powerful, omnipotent." Its use in the LXX (e.g., 2 Sam 5:10; Jer 5:14; Amos 3:13 translating אֱלֹהֵי צְבָאוֹת "Lord of Hosts"; Job 11:7; 22:17 translating the title שַׁדַּי, "the Almighty") as well as throughout Revelation (Rev 1:8; 4:8; 11:17; 15:3; 16:7, 14; 19:6, 15; 21:22) stresses

---

54 Ian Boxall, *The Revelation of Saint John*, BNTC 19 (Hendrickson, 2009), 219. Synonymous parallelism states complementary thoughts or ideas in successive phrases, with no significant addition or subtraction. For a detailed treatment of parallelism and other features of Hebrew poetry see Wilfred G. E. Watson, *Classical Hebrew Poetry: A Guide to Its Techniques*, JSOTSS 26 (JSOT, 1984).

55 The word "righteous" (δίκαιος) is used here of God's special activity as judge, as well as his holy righteousness in contrast to the evil character of his enemies (cf. Rev 16:5; 16:7; 19:2). The quality of truth (ἀλήθεια) is ascribed to both God and Jesus in the Apocalypse (Rev 3:7, 14; 6:10, 17; 19:2, 11). The adjectival form used here can mean "dependable, constant, genuine, faithful, upright, or true." Gerhard Schneider, "δίκαιος," *EDNT* 1:324–325; Hans Hübner, "ἀλήθεια," *EDNT* 1:58; Johnson, *Triumph of the Lamb*, 216; etc. The theme of God's righteous judgment of his enemies and salvation of his people within Revelation is not limited to this particular song, however. Later, in a scene that may also hearken back to the Israelites' celebration at the Red Sea, a great multitude in heaven praises God's destruction of Babylon as "true and just; for he has judged the great prostitute who corrupted the earth with her immorality, and has avenged on her the blood of his servants" (Rev 19:2).

56 Osborne, *Revelation*, 565.

God's omnipotence and sovereign control over all earthly and cosmic forces.[57] Here the hymn of victory appropriately incorporates the full and majestic title, "Lord God, the Almighty." The Almighty God is all-powerful, and has enabled his faithful followers to conquer the evil of the beast through his unparalleled dominion over nature in the three series of judgments.[58] Likewise, the Israelites sang of Yahweh as "a man of war" (Exod 15:3), "glorious in power" (Exod 15:6), and great in majesty (Exod 15:7), who was able to control the winds (Exod 15:10), pile up the waters and congeal the seas (Exod 15:8).

In Rev 15:3, the parallel title "King (βασιλεὺς) of the Nations" appears to be a direct allusion to Jer 10:7 (cf. Ps 46:3 LXX; 47:8; 96:10 LXX; 1 Chr 16:31). Although βασιλεὺς was a common translation of the Latin *imperator*, early Christianity reserved this term for the Lord, in contrast to earthly kings.[59] The reference to the nations (ἔθνος) in Revelation is ultimately inclusive, referring to the unbelieving world rather than Gentiles in general.[60] The Apocalypse presents God as sovereign over the entire universe, including the hostile forces within it. Throughout Scripture there are statements that the entire world will one day bow before the one true God and recognize Christ as Lord, even if they refuse to worship him as such (e.g., Ps 86:9; Mal 1:11; Phil 2:9–11). While the Song of Moses does not contain the phrase "King of the Nations," it does acknowledge the reaction of the nations to Yahweh's mighty acts (Exod 15:14–16), and concludes with the assertion that "The Lord will reign forever and ever" (Exod 15:18), an idea which prevails throughout Revelation.[61]

The second section of this hymn (Rev 15:4) demonstrates the proper human response to the attributes and actions of God set forth in Rev 15:3.[62] The singers first raise the rhetorical question, "Who will not fear, O Lord, and glorify your name?" This appears to be a melding together of allusions to Jer 10:6–7 and Ps 86:8–10, both of which stress the incomparability of Yahweh with other gods.[63] Yet there is also an inherent similarity to the Song of Mo-

---

57 "παντοκράτωρ," BDAG, 755; Osborne, *Revelation*, 72; etc.

58 Smalley, *Revelation*, 386.

59 "βασιλεὺς," BDAG, 169–170; B. Klappert, "βασιλεία," *NIDNTT* 2:378; Aune, *Revelation 6–16*, 875.

60 Cf. Rev 10:11; 11:2, 9, 18; 14:8; 15:4; 16:19; 18:3; 19:15. Certainly John envisions a great harvest of souls from "every tribe and language and people and nation" (Rev 5:9; 7:9; 14:6) at the end of the ages. This "does not of course mean that Revelation expects the salvation of each and every human being. From 21.8, 27; 22.15 it is quite clear that unrepentant sinners have no place in the new Jerusalem." Richard Bauckham, *The Climax of Prophecy: Studies on the Book of Revelation* (T&T Clark, 1993), 313; Witherington, *Revelation*, 206; etc.

61 Osborne, *Revelation*, 566.

62 Johnson, *Triumph of the Lamb*, 217; Smalley, *Revelation*, 383.

63 Jeremiah 10:7 asks the question, "Who would not fear you, O King of the nations?" while Ps 86:9 declares, "All the nations ... shall glorify your name." Both of these statements

ses in Exodus, as the Israelites question, "Who is like you, O Lord, among the gods? Who is like you, majestic in holiness, awesome in glorious deeds, doing wonders?" (Exod 15:11). Indeed, for Bauckham, this concept of the incomparability of Yahweh, which is also the theme of Exod 15:11–18, functions as the uniting factor for the remainder of Revelation's Song of the Lamb.[64]

The matter of God's superiority is expounded throughout the remainder of the hymn by means of three causal clauses introduced by the conjunction ὅτι.[65] The Lord is first praised for his perfect holiness ("for you alone are holy [ὅσιος];" cf. Exod 15:11). The use of ὅσιος[66] rather than the more common ἅγιος here may indicate an allusion to Ps 145:17 LXX ("The Lord is righteous in all his ways and ὅσιος in all his works") or the celebration that God is "just and upright" (δίκαιος καὶ ὅσιος, Deut 32:4 LXX; cf. Rev 16:5) in the other Song of Moses. The holiness of God denotes not his sinlessness but the distinction between God's sovereign and upright nature and the unrighteousness and depravity of his creation.[67] With a second ὅτι clause, the saints continue their anthem by proclaiming, "all the nations will come and worship you."[68] This phrase recalls the theological implications of the title "King of the Nations" (Rev 15:3), and is a second allusion to Ps 86:9 in as many verses. The confidence that all nations will worship God in the messianic age is transformed here into an assertion of God's total dominion over the beast and his followers in the end times (Rev 12:5).[69] The final ὅτι clause, "for your righteous acts have been revealed" (cf. Ps 98:2), refers back to the portrait of God's works as righteous and true (Rev 15:3), as well as forward to the imminent bowl judgments (Rev 15:5–16:21).

It is evident that, while verbal allusions are sparse, Rev 15:1–4 contains a number of thematic allusions to the events surrounding the crossing of the Red Sea (Exod 14–15)—from the description of the "glassy sea" to the location

---

are preceded by the assertion, "There is none like you, O Lord" (Jer 10:6; Ps 86:8 adds the words "among the gods"). Osborne, *Revelation*, 566.

64  Bauckham, *Climax of Prophecy*, 305.

65  Wallace, *Greek Grammar*, 460. Rhetorical questions are characteristic of biblical hymns (cf. Exod 15:11; Pss 6:3; 15:1; Isa 40:25; Mic 7:18). Smalley, *Revelation*, 388.

66  The word ὅσιος occurs only eight times in the NT, five times within OT quotations. Both Peter (Acts 2:27) and Paul (Acts 13:35) use this word in quoting Ps 16:10 (LXX) to refer to Jesus as "the Holy One." It is significant that John uses the Greek term ὅσιος, which is rarely used in discussions of God's holiness, rather than the more common ἅγιος. The word ὅσιος is used frequently in the Psalms (e.g., Pss 11:2 LXX; 31:6 LXX; 85:2 LXX; 144:17 LXX) to translate חָסִיד, a word denoting the upright man who accepts the obligations that God prescribes for his people. Horst Seebass, "ὅσιος," *NIDNTT* 2:237.

67  Lioy, *Revelation in Christological Focus*, 144–145; Smalley, *Revelation*, 388.

68  This second ὅτι is consecutive—because of God's holiness, all the nations will come and worship (cf. Ps 86:9).

69  Johnson, *Triumph of the Lamb*, 217; Smalley, *Revelation*, 388.

of the choir of victors; from the theological connections between the contents of the songs of praise in Revelation and Exodus to the fact that Revelation's song is titled "the Song of Moses ... and the Song of the Lamb;" from the fact that the song is in reference to God's judgment in sending the final plagues upon unbelieving mankind to the description of the bowl judgments through the paradigm of the exodus plagues in Rev 16. While certain allusions are much less obvious than others, the cumulative force of exodus typology within this brief vision of the eschatological conquerors is clear. By imbedding within this passage a reference to the Lamb, specifically in connection with the explicit allusion to the Song of Moses, John reinforces the paschal identity of Revelation's most central character and affirms that the messianic Lamb has achieved a new exodus through his cross and resurrection (cf. John 16:33; Rev 5:5–10; 7:14; 12:11).

### Sealing of the 144,000 (Rev 7:1–8)

In addition to the Christological figure of the Lamb, we find another allusion to the Passover tradition within the context of the sealing of the 144,000 (Rev 7:1–8). This passage is an example of John's masterful interweaving of traditions and texts, to the extent that the background of an image or symbol becomes difficult to ascertain apart from an understanding of the Apocalypse as a whole and the creative way John employed the OT themes and stories. Scholars consistently attribute the imagery of the sealing of the 144,000 to the marking of the faithful Israelites in Ezek 9. While there is no question that Ezekiel imagery figures notably throughout the Apocalypse, and perhaps to a certain degree within this particular passage, given the prominence of exodus imagery and the typological anticipation of a new exodus, it is also possible that the primary context of the sealing of the 144,000 is the blood of the Passover lamb.

### An Examination of Σφραγισ Terminology[70]

In Rev 7:1–4, John sees four angels holding back the four winds of the earth, keeping them from releasing their judgment until another angel has "sealed (σφραγίσωμεν) the servants of our God on their foreheads" (Rev 7:3). The use of seals was a common custom in the ancient world and had both legal and religious significance. The primary connotation involved ownership,

---

70 Throughout this section, lexical details regarding Σφραγίς ("seal") terminology in the ancient world and within Scripture are drawn from R. Schippers, "Seal," *NIDNTT* 3:497–501 and Gottfried Fitzer, "σφραγίς," *TDNT* 8:939–953.

protection, authority, and accreditation. Literally, sealing something meant to shut it tight, to prevent entry or escape (for example, sealing a door closed). The seal was also used for legally validating documents or preventing them from premature disclosure (Neh 10:1; Isa 29:11; metaphorically in Job 14:17). When used on documents in this way, the seal served as a signature and indicated the authority of the possessor of the seal (especially with kings and rulers). In the case of property, an owner would guard his possessions, livestock, and slaves from theft by marking them with his seal. In religious life men identified themselves as the property of their deity by the mark of their seal (cf. 3 Maccabees 2:29).[71] It is significant that Judaism often referred to circumcision as a seal—"The idea of the seal offers many themes in interpretation of circumcision: that of the sign ... of designation; it also points to membership, it is a sign of ownership, and finally the idea of power and protection."[72]

In the NT only ten of the thirty-two occurrences of the σφραγίς word-group occur outside the Apocalypse. Most notably, Paul uses this terminology to assert that God is at work not only in justifying but also in sealing believers with the mark of genuine membership in the community of the redeemed (Rom 4:11; 2 Cor 1:22; Eph 1:13–14; 4:30).[73] Revelation employs the concept of sealing in three images. First, the literal sense is present in the command not to keep secret or conceal the words of the prophecy[74] and in the sealing of the abyss for a thousand years.[75] Second, the seven-sealed scroll (Rev 5:1–4) carries the legal connotation of validating a document or endowing it with the authority of the sealer. The significance of the number seven may recall the Roman custom of sealing wills with seven seals, but in this case ought to be

---

71 In the LXX, the noun σφραγίς and its verbal counterparts occur in both royal (Gen 41:42; Esth 3:10; 8:8–10; 1 Kgs 21:8; 2 Kgs 25:23; Dan 6:18) and cultic settings (Exod 28:15, 36; 36:13, 21; 39:14).

72 Fitzer, *TDNT* 8:947–948.

73 Some suggest that Paul connects this "sealing" with baptism, which he refers to as the gift of the Spirit (1 Cor 6:11; 12:13; cf. Acts 2:38; 10:47). Prigent holds that σφραγίς has a precise, almost technical meaning synonymous to baptism (cf. 2 Cor 1:21)—"Used in this way, it denotes the proprietary mark placed by God on an individual who becomes his own at baptism, or else the saving sign which will protect the baptized one during the eschatological judgment. These are not, incidentally, mutually exclusive nuances: God keeps those who are his own." Prigent, *Apocalypse of St. John*, 283–284. Hoehner, however, asserts that this reading confuses the ministries of the Spirit—baptism of the Spirit locates the believer within the body of Christ (1 Cor 12:13), "whereas the sealing of the Spirit indicates God's ownership of the believer." Harold W. Hoehner, *Ephesians: An Exegetical Commentary* (Baker, 2002), 238–239.

74 "And he said to me, 'Do not *seal* up the words of the prophecy of this book, for the time is near'" (Rev 22:10; cf. Matt 27:66; Dan 6:18).

75 "And he seized the dragon, that ancient serpent, who is the devil and Satan, and bound him for a thousand years, and threw him into the pit, and shut it and *sealed* it over him, so that he might not deceive the nations any longer, until the thousand years were ended. After that he must be released for a little while" (Rev 20:2–3).

determined by the repetition of this number throughout Revelation as a symbol of completeness. Finally, the metaphorical sealing of the 144,000 denotes membership in the people of God; those who bear the seal belong to God and benefit from his divine protection.[76]

The angel in Rev 7:2 holds the "seal of the living God" for the purpose of sealing individuals described as "the servants (δούλους) of our God" (Rev 7:3), an image that calls to mind the practice of branding slaves on the forehead as a mark of possession and suggests that this seal is a sign of ownership to both the wearer and the observer.[77] That the seal is a guarantee of spiritual protection is confirmed by the proleptic visions of the sealed community worshiping around the throne and in the heavenly city (Rev 14, 22). It is related to belief, and possibly associated with the seal of the Spirit for the believer in Paul, though Rev 7 contains no mention of the Holy Spirit. The primary purpose of this seal appears to be insuring that those who are already God's people are protected from the coming judgments—"ownership entails protection" (cf. 2 Tim 2:19).[78]

It is significant that the seal does not safeguard the 144,000 from persecution from the beast, martyrdom, physical suffering, or death. Rather, it protects solely against the wrath which God is preparing to send upon the earth.[79] The judgments in Revelation are not indiscriminate; they are directed only at those who do not have the seal of God. Revelation 7:1 states that the sealed believers are protected from the harm aimed at the earth, the sea, and the trees (τῆς γῆς ... τῆς θαλάσσης ... πᾶν δένδρον). The fact that the first three trumpets (Rev 8:7–11) are directed at these same three objects (τὴν γῆν, 8:7; τῆς θαλάσσης, 8:8; τῶν δένδρων, 8:7) confirms that only those who remain unsealed are affected by the judgments.[80] This is made explicit in trumpet five,

---

76 Ford lists six potential connotations of the seal on the foreheads of believers: 1) branding cattle and tattooing slaves; 2) marking soldiers as members of a sacred militia (common in the pagan cults); 3) the mark prophets wore on their forehead or hand (1 Kgs 20:41; Zech 13:6; Isa 44:5); 4) the phylactery (Exod 13:9; 28:36–38; Deut 6:8; 11:19); 5) circumcision (cf. Jubilees 15:26); and 6) Philo's man formed after the image of God (*Opif.* 134). J. Massyngberde Ford, *Revelation*, AB 38 (Doubleday, 1975), 116–117.

77 Smalley, *Revelation*, 183.

78 Robert H. Mounce, *The Book of Revelation*, NICNT (Eerdmans, 1977), 167. See also Witherington, *Revelation*, 136–137; George Eldon Ladd, *A Commentary on the Revelation of John* (Eerdmans, 1972), 110–112; etc.

79 Paul Spilsbury, *The Throne, the Lamb & the Dragon: A Reader's Guide to the Book of Revelation* (InterVarsity, 2002), 74; T. C. Smith, *Reading the Signs: A Sensible Approach to Revelation and Other Apocalyptic Writings* (Smyth & Helwys, 1977), 104. Johnson finds a link between the seal and Jewish phylacteries—"Just as the binding of God's law on the Israelites' foreheads and hands symbolized his sovereignty over their thoughts and actions (Deut. 6:8), so the Lamb's seal shows that he protects his servants from being deceived by the Serpent and the beasts (Rev. 12:15–17; 13:11–18; 16:13–14)." Johnson, *Triumph of the Lamb*, 130.

80 Beale, *Revelation*, 485.

in which the locusts are commanded to harm "only those people who do not have the seal of God on their foreheads" (Rev 9:4).[81] Those who bear the seal must still endure tribulation, but are filled with the assurance of God's eternal protection and the hope of a new experience with Jesus Christ at the end.[82]

THE IDENTITY OF THE 144,000

Who, then, are these 144,000 who have been sealed with the name of God on their foreheads in Rev 7:1–8? Their identity has been the subject of many speculations and theories, especially considering the unusual list of tribes and their close literary proximity to the vast multitude of Rev 7:9–17. The idea that the 144,000 comprises either the faithful remnant of Israel or Jewish Christians is based largely on the roll call of tribes in Rev 7:5–8.[83] While some scholars cling to the idea that by breaking down the 144,000 into 12,000 from each tribe, John must have meant literal Israel, this opinion is not widely held today.[84] Feuillet rightly points out that Revelation never distinguishes between Jewish and Gentile Christians,[85] while Witherington notes that these

---

[81] Spilsbury, *Throne, the Lamb & the Dragon*, 117. Lawrence interprets Rev 9:4 to say that the sealing was to secure them from the demoniac agencies in the coming reign of the Antichrist. However, this reading fails to recognize that the plague of locusts was one of the trumpet judgments sent by God on the unbelieving earthdwellers. John Benjamin Lawrence, *New Heaven and a New Earth: A Contemporary Interpretation of the Book of Revelation* (American, 1960), 79.

[82] Osborne states, "God protects the vital part, the soul, but allows intense suffering in this world. A great deal of space in the NT is given over to this problem (e.g., Rom. 5:3–5; 8:12–39; 1 Cor. 4:8–13; 1 Thess. 1:4–7; Heb. 12:4–11; James 1:2–4; 1 Pet. 1:6–7; 3:13–4:19)." Osborne, *Revelation*, 302. Perhaps Paul stated this concept best in Rom 5:3–5, "Not only that, but we rejoice in our sufferings, knowing that suffering produces endurance, and endurance produces character, and character produces hope, and hope does not put us to shame, because God's love has been poured into our hearts through the Holy Spirit who has been given to us."

[83] The list of tribes does not figure into Draper's argument for this interpretation. He insists that the 144,000 must refer to Jews or at least Jewish Christians as "the 'fulness of Israel', the reunited tribes who had been dispersed by the destruction of Israel and Jerusalem," based on his reading of this passage through the influence of Zech 14. For him, the description of the 144,000 in Rev 14:4 as having not defiled themselves with women indicates Levitical purity; therefore the 144,000 fill the role of the Levites in the temple service. The multitude in Rev 7:9–17 represents the 'survivors' of the Gentiles celebrating the Feast of Tabernacles in the heavenly Jerusalem. J. A. Draper, "The Heavenly Feast of Tabernacles: Revelation 7.1–17," *JSNT* 19 (1983): 136–137.

[84] Steve Moyise, *The Old Testament in the Book of Revelation*, JSNTSup 115 (Sheffield, 1995), 71. One exception is Paige Patterson, *Revelation*, NAC 39 (Broadman & Holman, 2012), 193. For more who hold this view, see R. H. Charles, *A Critical and Exegetical Commentary on The Revelation of St. John: With Introduction, Notes, and Indices, also The Greek Text and English Translation*, 2 vols., ICC (T&T Clark, 1920), 1:193; Richard Shalom Yates, "The Identity of the Tribulation Saints," *BSac* 163 (2006): 79–93.

[85] However, he ultimately concludes that the 144,000 are a Christian remnant of 1st century ethnic Jews, contrasting with the unbelieving Jews of that time. A. Feuillet, "Les 144,000

144,000 are called "servants" (Rev 7:3), which elsewhere in Revelation refers to all believers.[86] Beale argues that "if Satan puts a seal on *all* his followers (13:16–17; 14:9–11), God presumably does likewise for *all* his followers, not just some of them."[87] Smalley suggests that the twelve tribes did not exist as such in the first century AD,[88] and Ladd observes that the tribes named in Revelation, "when interpreted literally, ... *do not represent actual Israel.*"[89] Scholars are quick to speculate on the fact that the order of the tribes in Rev 7:5–8 does not parallel any other biblical or non-biblical list of tribes. Morris, however, wisely asserts that the order should not be a fundamental concern since, in the approximately twenty OT lists of tribes, there are eighteen different orders. For him, the only theologically weighty aspect of this list is the fact that it begins with Judah, the royal tribe from which the Messiah was expected.[90]

There seems to be no satisfactory explanation for the irregular list other than that John intended to identify the tribes as the true, spiritual Israel—the church. There is good reason to understand the number "144,000" (the square of the number "twelve" increased one thousand fold) in a figurative sense. The number "one thousand" is used throughout Scripture to refer generally to a very large quantity (e.g., Exod 20:6; Num 10:36; Deut 7:9; 1 Sam 18:7; Ps 84:10; Dan 7:10), while the number "twelve" indicates completion, particularly in connection with the people of God. Therefore, just as the twelve tribes equaled all of Israel and the twelve disciples equaled the sum of the first disciples, so here the number 144,000 is equivalent to the total number of believers, the whole people of God.[91] This identification of the 144,000 with the church as a whole coheres with the NT conviction that the Christian community is the continuation of and the true Israel (cf. Matt 10:5–6; 19:28; Luke 1:68–79; John 1:47; 5:43–47; Acts 26:14–23; Rom 9–11; Jas 1:1; 1 Pet 2:9–20). The

---

Israelites marques d'un sceau," *NovT* 9 (1967): 191–224.

86 See Rev 1:1; 2:20; 6:11; 10:7; 11:8; 19:2, 5, 10; 22:3, 6, 9. Witherington, *Revelation*, 137.

87 Beale, *Revelation*, 413.

88 Smalley, *Revelation*, 185.

89 Ladd, *Revelation*, 114–115.

90 Leon Morris, *The Revelation of St. John* (Eerdmans, 1980), 113. While the novelties in the list of tribes ought not be discounted too quickly, a detailed analysis of this issue is beyond the scope of the current project. For further reading see Ross E. Winkle, "Another Look at the List of Tribes in Revelation 7," *AUSS* 27 (1989): 53 and Christopher R. Smith, "The Portrayal of the Church as the New Israel in the Names and Order of the Tribes in Revelation 7.5–8," *JSNT* 39 (1990): 111–112. Smith's intriguing explanation of the irregularities in this list has been the subject of much discussion (see, for example, Richard Bauckham, "The List of the Tribes in Revelation 7 Again," *JSNT* 42 (1991): 99–115; Christopher R. Smith, "The Tribes of Revelation 7 and the Literary Competence of John the Seer," *JETS* 38 (1995): 213–218.

91 Witherington, *Revelation*, 137; Osborne, *Revelation*, 312; etc. For a treatment of the number "twelve" in Revelation, see Albert Geyser, "The Twelve Tribes in Revelation: Judean and Judeo Christian Apocalypticism," *NTS* 28 (1982): 388–399.

Apocalypse demonstrates the fact that John "is aware of the Judaic roots of the Christian Church, and affirms them. But he also knows that, since the coming of Christ, 'Israel' embodies an idea which is deeper than the national associations of the word, and embraces the totality of the redeemed."[92]

John's vision of the 144,000 is immediately followed by a second vision of the redeemed in Rev 7:9–17. These two groups are presented through a series of contrasts—the initial group is numbered, while the second is unable to be counted (Rev 7:9); the first is listed in a breakdown of the twelve tribes, while the second is a universal assembly of every nation, tribe, people and language; the 144,000 are on earth, while the multitude is in the heavenly throne room.[93] Yet there is validity to the explanation that the 144,000 and the vast multitude are different images of the same group. Bauckham sees a clear literary link in which this twofold vision deliberately parallels the introductory vision of the Lamb in Rev 5:5–14. John hearing the angel proclaim the triumph of the Lion of Judah in Rev 5:5 corresponds to John hearing the number of the sealed, 144,000 from the tribes of Israel, with Judah leading the list. Likewise, John raising his eyes to see the Lamb standing as if slain in Rev 5:6 parallels his vision of the multitude from every tribe, tongue, people, and nation, identified with the blood of the Lamb (Rev 7:14) and standing before the throne.[94] Just as the Lion and the Lamb are contrasting depictions of the same being, so the two groups in Rev 7 are both images of the true Israel, the church, simply portrayed from different perspectives. The 144,000 are the *ecclesia militans*, the army of God preparing for the tribulation (cf. Rev 14:3–4); the multitude is the *ecclesia triumphans*, having persevered through the tribulation and been found faithful (cf. Rev 12:11).[95]

THE OT BACKGROUND OF THE SEALING OF THE 144,000

The 144,000 are sealed on the foreheads by God's angel as a means of denoting both their membership in the true people of God, the church, and as a way of protecting them from Yahweh's impending judgment upon the earth.

---

92 Smalley, *Revelation*, 187. See also Prigent, *Apocalypse of St. John*, 284; Bruce M. Metzger, *Breaking the Code: Understanding the Book of Revelation* (Abingdon, 1993), 60–61; etc.

93 Yates, "Tribulation Saints," 81; Bauckham, *Climax of Prophecy*, 224; Balmer H. Kelly, "Revelation 7:9–17," *Interpretation* 40 (1986): 290; etc.

94 Bauckham, *Climax of Prophecy*, 213, 215–216.

95 Håkan Ulfgard, *Feast and Future: Revelation 7:9–17 and the Feast of Tabernacles*, ConBNT 22 (Almqvist & Wiksell, 1989), 72–73; etc. For Metzger, the visions are "correlative and refer to the same people distinguished only by their location. The 144,000 on earth are about to enter a period of secular opposition. The purpose of the second vision is to bring encouragement to believers by revealing what awaits them in heaven." Metzger, *Breaking the Code*, 61; cf. Johnson, *Triumph of the Lamb*, 131.

The majority of scholars claim that the most immediate and suitable background for the sealing of the 144,000 is found in Ezek 9.[96] Ezekiel's vision is focused on the impending judgment of the Judean community (Ezek 8:17) in the city of Jerusalem. A loud voice summons forth a squad of supernatural destroyers (Ezek 9:1–2) who are charged to carry out a sentence of execution upon the people of the city (Ezek 8:5–6). This is in effect an intriguing "example of prophetic reversal of an otherwise positive motif for Israel"—whereas in the exodus account the destroying angel smites the *enemies* of Israel (Exod 12:23; cf. 2 Kgs 19:35), *now* God's judgment is sent against his own people.[97]

God does not destroy all of his people, however. He allows for the salvation of those who "grieve and lament over all the detestable things that are done" in Jerusalem (Ezek 9:4, NIV; the sins are revealed in Ezek 8). This deliverance comes in the form of a seventh angel carrying a writing kit (Ezek 9:2) who is instructed to "put a mark" (Ezek 9:4) on the foreheads of those who exhibit signs of repentance for the sins of Jerusalem—"people who will look upon these evils from God's perspective, recognizing the incongruity between prevailing practices and the standards of the covenant Lord."[98] Placed on the most visible part of the body, the mark had protective significance and served to separate God's righteous from the wicked. The destroyers would pass over and not harm those who bore the mark.[99]

While there are certainly similarities between Ezekiel's vision and the sealing of the 144,000 in the Apocalypse, a close analysis reveals contrasts which are as noteworthy as the parallels. John hears the number sealed as 144,000, indicating that the angel found many who qualified as "the servants of our God" (Rev 7:3). In Ezekiel, however, there is no note that any were found worthy of the mark—rather, the narrative simply continues, "so they went out and struck the city" (Ezek 9:7), with no indication that any were actually marked. The primary focus of the events in Ezek 9 is the punishment of the wicked, specifically for "the great abominations that the house of Israel" had committed (Ezek 8:6); God's chosen people faced his wrath. In Revelation however, the judgment falls on the persecutors of God's people.

---

96  For example, see Ulfgard, *Feast and Future*, 71; Jenkins, *OT in Revelation*, 44–45; Moyise, *OT in Revelation*, 71; etc.

97  Leslie C. Allen, *Ezekiel 1–19*, WBC 28 (Word, 1994), 146; Daniel I. Block, *The Book of Ezekiel. Chapters 1–24*, NICOT (Eerdmans, 1997), 303.

98  Block, *Ezekiel*, 307. According to Allen, "the small number of the survivors may be gauged from the proportion of one angel devoted to exemption and six to destruction." Allen, *Ezekiel 1–19*, 148.

99  Block, *Ezekiel*, 307, 310–311; Allen, *Ezekiel 1–19*, 148. Beale and Smalley suggest that the purpose of the mark in Ezekiel 9 is to protect the righteous of Israel from acts of judgment carried out by the Babylonians in Ezek 14:12–23. Beale, *Revelation*, 410; Smalley, *Revelation*, 182.

Revelation 7 actually functions as a pause or intercalation in the narrative of the seal judgments—there is no mention here of those who face God's wrath; rather, the focus is solely on the action of sealing and protecting those who belong to God.[100]

These contrasts allow for the possibility of another OT background for the sealing of the 144,000, one which may be found within the context of the exodus typology that pervades the Apocalypse. During the tenth plague (Exod 12:21–27), the blood of the Passover lamb on the doorposts formed a protective sign, designating the Israelites as God's chosen people and preserving them from the judgment of death which was inflicted on all of Egypt. Only those who were set apart by the blood escaped unscathed.[101] Indeed, this may be where an allusion to Ezekiel fails the most. Where in Ezekiel the subject of God's wrath is the wicked and sinful *from among his own people*, in both Exodus and Revelation, the judgment falls on those who reject God, the Egyptians and the kingdom of the beast. In both, God's chosen people are protected.

It is indeed possible that the Passover tradition should be understood as the background of *both* Ezek 9 and Rev 7.[102] According to Block, "in view of the extensive links between Exod. 12 and Ezek. 9, especially the identification of those to be spared by means of a sign, early Jewish commentators on Ezek. 9 quite naturally referred to the blood of the paschal lamb as a mark of salvation."[103] These links include the advance warning of judgment by Yahweh, the use of similar vocabulary to describe the destruction and the passing over, and the use of a sign to distinguish the righteous so that the destroyer might pass over them.[104]

We have already established that for John, the image of the Lamb "standing, as though it had been slain" (Rev 5:6) is an allusion to the Passover.[105] The

---

100  Block, *Ezekiel*, 310, 313; Bauckham, *Climax of Prophecy*, 216–217.

101  Ulfgard, *Feast and Future*, 39–40. While the protection of the Israelites during the first nine plagues is not actually the result of a seal, this action directly precedes the Passover, the preeminent seal account in the exodus tradition. The parallel of the entire exodus plague sequence with the seal motif in Revelation is relevant, however, to show the consistency of God's action on behalf of his people throughout Scripture.

102  Beale, *Revelation*, 409; Jonathan Knight, *Revelation* (Sheffield, 1999), 71; Witherington, *Revelation*, 136; etc.

103  He continues, "However, when the church fathers began to link the mark of Ezekiel and the blood of the Passover lamb to the cross and blood of Christ, the Jews reversed their position. The blood became a sign of doom instead of life." Block, *Ezekiel*, 312.

104  Ibid. Both Ezek 9:6 and Exod 12:13 use לְמַשְׁחִית to denote the destructive intent of the destroyer, and the word עָבַר "to pass over" is found in both Ezek 9:4 and Exod 12:23.

105  Revelation presents the Lamb as both sacrifice and conqueror. Within the majestic throne room scenes, Christ is the victorious Lamb. In typical apocalyptic fashion, John uses the image of a horned lamb to symbolize a leader and triumphant conqueror (Rev 5:6, 13). Jen-

idea that John also had the Passover in mind in his record of the sealing of the 144,000 is supported by his identification of this same group with the blood of the Lamb in Rev 7:14. The reference to washing their robes in blood does not connote martyrdom or the spilling of their own blood; rather "their robes are white by virtue of the redemptive death of the Lamb."[106] Given the exodus typology permeating Revelation and the paschal background of the Lamb imagery, this evokes the idea of God's delivering the Israelites from Egypt, as believers have deliberately chosen to align themselves with the Lamb through the experience of his blood. Just as the Hebrew people were redeemed from slavery in Egypt (Exod 20:2; Deut 5:6) by means of the sign of blood on the doorposts, so Christ's disciples, sealed with the blood of the Lamb (Rev 14:1), are redeemed from the earth (Rev 14:3) and bondage to sin or rebellion against God.[107]

There are certainly resemblances in Rev 7 to Ezek 9, and the influence of Ezekiel throughout the Apocalypse must not be ignored.[108] Allusions to Ezekiel are at least evident in the sealing of God's faithful (Rev 7), the description of the Lord and the throne of God (Rev 1; 4; cf. Ezek 1; 10), and the measuring of the temple of God (Rev 11:1–11; cf. Ezek 37:1–14).[109] Indeed, Moyise suggests

---

kins, *OT in Revelation*, 100; Morris, *Apostolic Preaching*, 136. Bauckham recognizes John's juxtaposition of the contrasting images of Lion of Judah, Root of David, and Lamb in Rev 5:5–6, but asserts that "doubtless the Lamb is intended to suggest primarily the passover lamb, for throughout the Apocalypse, and in a passage as close as 5:10, John represents the victory of the Lamb as a new Exodus, the victory which delivers the new Israel." Bauckham, *Climax of Prophecy*, 183–184.

106 Mounce, *Revelation*, 171, 173; Carrez, "Christologie de l'Agneau," 11–12. In Revelation, "blood" is used in three ways: God's judgment upon his enemies (Rev 6:12; 8:7, 8; 11:6; 14:20; 16:3, 4, 6; 19:13), the blood of the saints (Rev 6:10; 16:5–6; 17:6; 18:24; 19:2), and the blood of the Lamb (Rev 1:5–6; 5:9–10; 7:14; 12:11). John makes it explicit when the suffering or martyrdom of the saints is in view by modifying αἷμα with a genitive of source ("of the saints," "of the prophets," "of the bondservants") or couching the phrase in a question from the saints (Rev 6:10). Those instances which speak of the blood of the Lamb refer specifically to Christ's sacrificial death on the cross, through which all believers have received salvation. Beale, *Revelation*, 438. For more discussion of the exodus background of the multitude in Rev 7:9–17, see chapter 7, "They Shall Neither Hunger Nor Thirst (Rev 7:9–17)."

107 Spilsbury, *Throne, the Lamb & the Dragon*, 76; Leopold Sabourin, *The Names and Titles of Jesus* (Macmillan, 1967), 161, 164.

108 "Proportionally Ezekiel ranks second as the most used Old Testament book … although in terms of actual numbers of allusions Isaiah is first, followed by Ezekiel, Daniel, and Psalms," G. K. Beale, "Revelation," in *It Is Written: Scripture Citing Scripture; Essays in Honour of Barnabas Lindars*, ed. D. A. Carson and H. G. M. Williamson (Cambridge University Press, 1988), 318.

109 Jenkins, *OT in Revelation*, 57–60. Jenkins also observes parallels between the fall of Babylon (Rev 17–18) and the fall of Tyre (Ezek 26–28). Scholars vary in their analysis of John's use of Ezekiel's apocalyptic vision. Vanhoye cites eight examples of "utilisations d'ensemble," texts in which the correspondences between Ezekiel and Revelation are more thematic than verbal, and asserts that Revelation goes against the apocalyptic tendency to expand and am-

John has "absorbed something of the character and mind of the prophet [Ezekiel]. This is why he can make so many allusions to the book without ever quoting it.... It is possible that he does not quote it as Scripture because he does not see it as an external source. He has taken on the mind of Ezekiel and writes 'in the spirit' (ἐν πνεύματι)."[110] John's inclination toward Ezekiel may be the result of striking similarities between Ezekiel's general historical circumstances and his own. Ezekiel helped Israel to maintain faith during the exile, and to preserve the community when everything seemed lost;[111] the Apocalypse likewise has a message of hope and eternal salvation for those who remain faithful to Christ amid extreme tribulation.

Yet John does not give the same salvation-historical significance to Ezekiel as he does to the exodus. Perhaps this is due to the contrast between Ezekiel as a vision and the exodus as the primary historical event in the development of the people of God.[112] Indeed, Ezekiel's vision itself seems to draw in some ways on the exodus experience (e.g., the call of Ezekiel, the marking of the faithful, the proclamation of judgment on Egypt, the new covenant with Israel resulting in the rebirth of the nation, the detailed description of the temple). The exodus story was the prototype, the original source from which Israel's expectation of an eschatological deliverance developed; Revelation ultimately draws its message of eschatological hope from this initial account to demonstrate the salvation which has already been inaugurated and which in the last days will be consummated through the Christ event. The OT context of the sealing of the 144,000 must ultimately be understood as God's

---

plify its source material. Rather, John abridges his OT material to draw the reader's attention to the texts' main elements. Albert Vanhoye, "L'utilisation du livre d'Ézéchiel dans l'Apocalypse," *Biblica* 43 (1962): 463–464. For an analysis of Vanhoye's argument, see Jean-Pierre Ruiz, *Ezekiel in the Apocalypse: The Transformation of Prophetic Language in Revelation 16,17–19,10*, European University Studies: Theology 23 (Peter Lang, 1989), 62–78. Goulder attempted a one-to-one correspondence between the two books, asserting that John's inspiration was drawn from the weekly lectionary readings of Ezekiel. He provides a chart which aligns the major sections of Revelation and Ezekiel with the major feasts or celebrations of the Jewish-Christian calendar. M. D. Goulder, "The Apocalypse as an Annual Cycle of Prophecies," *NTS* 27 (1981): 342–367, esp. 353–354.

110 He does go on to acknowledge, however, that the abundant use of various OT traditions in Revelation undoubtedly undermines the argument that John has adopted any one OT 'persona.' Moyise, *OT in Revelation*, 78–80.

111 Jenkins, *OT in Revelation*, 54–57; Ralph W. Klein, *Israel in Exile: A Theological Interpretation*, OBT (Fortress, 1979), 151.

112 John I. Durham, *Understanding the Basic Themes of Exodus*, Quick-Reference Bible Topics (Word, 1990), 5; Jan Fekkes, *Isaiah and Prophetic Traditions in the Book of Revelation: Visionary Antecedents and Their Development*, JSNTSup 93 (JSOT, 1994), 81. Interestingly, the prophet Ezekiel is never mentioned in the NT, though his influence can be seen in the doctrine of resurrection and the Pauline understanding of divine glory. His most profound influence, however, is in the Apocalypse. Block, *Ezekiel*, 45.

protection and deliverance of the Israelites through the Passover and exodus from Egypt. That the Passover undergirds this passage is made clear by the obvious parallels between the Passover (Exod 12) and the marking in Ezek 9, the biblical tendency toward a typological interpretation of history, and John's pervasive use of exodus imagery throughout the Apocalypse to depict the eschatological deliverance of the people of God.

### The Background of Revelation's Lamb

When seeking to interpret the Apocalypse, it is imperative that one understand the central figure of τὸ ἀρνίον, presented by John as "standing, as though it had been slain" (Rev 5:6). The sacrifice of this Lamb has made him worthy to open the scroll (Rev 5:9) and to receive the worship and honor that is normally reserved for the one true God (Rev 5:8, 12–13; 7:9–10; 15:3–4; 22:1, 3). By his blood, the Lamb has ransomed the people of God from every tribe, language, people, and nation (Rev 5:9), set them apart as a kingdom and priests (Rev 5:10), cleansed them of their sins (Rev 7:14), and sealed them from God's righteous judgment (Rev 7:4). The Lamb has the power and authority to unleash the wrath of God upon the earth (Rev 6:1, 16; 8:1; 14:9–10), and as such, becomes the object of imitation by the beast, who attempts to deceive mankind into worshiping him instead of the Lamb (Rev 13:7–8, 11–14). It is through their association with the Lamb that believers are able to persevere through the tribulation (Rev 7:14; 14:4), to conquer the enemy (Rev 12:10–11; 17:14), to stand before his throne (Rev 14:1; 15:2), and to be his Bride (Rev 21:9). Ultimately, it is the Lamb who leads them into the New Jerusalem (Rev 7:17), who provides for every need (Rev 7:16–17; 21:23), whose presence replaces the temple (Rev 21:22), and with whom the saints will reign forever in the New Heaven and the New Earth (Rev 5:10; 20:6; 22:5).

Having demonstrated the considerable paschal overtones within Revelation, it is important to acknowledge that the Passover lamb is not the only background imagery contained in Revelation's Lamb, but is one of three frequently asserted OT or Jewish sources for τὸ ἀρνίον.[113] Apart from the Passover, the most common identification of Revelation's Lamb is Isa 53:7 with its description of the Suffering Servant as a lamb led to the slaughter, a sheep silent

---

113 Johns, *Lamb Christology*, 128. Johns examines a wide range of potential backgrounds for the Lamb in Revelation, including seven possible sources in the OT alone. In addition to the apocalyptic lambs and the Suffering Servant of Isaiah, he explores Daniel's vision of a ram and goat, the Aqedah (Gen 22), the eschatologically victorious lambs of Micah, and "the lamb as a symbol of vulnerability in visions of eschatological peace and elsewhere." However, he finds little support for any OT background to Revelation's Lamb other than a general *Gestalt* of nonresistance and vulnerability.

before its shearers, a view most often held by scholars who maintain that the identification of the Lamb as an expiatory sacrifice precludes it from being a paschal victim.[114] Yet few commentators actually indicate that the Lamb in Revelation should be understood *solely* in light of Isa 53:7.[115]

Other scholars focus on lamb imagery within other apocalyptic literature, overemphasizing the role as the triumphant Davidic Messiah in light of the Lamb's appearance—"with seven horns and with seven eyes" (Rev 5:6)—and two explicitly messianic titles ("Lion of the tribe of Judah" and "Root of David" in Rev 5:5).[116] Yet the apocalyptic lambs are not sacrificial in nature, and thus, as Bauckham asserts, even if Revelation's imagery did evoke other apocalyptic works, the reader "would still be entirely unfamiliar with the notion of a *sacrificial* lamb as a conqueror."[117]

Before making a final determination concerning the origin of Revelation's Lamb imagery, it is critical to recognize the overall NT witness to Christ's death as a sacrificial lamb. As Beasley-Murray states, "if [Revelation] may be viewed as the crown of Biblical eschatology, it requires to be read in conjunction with the books which preceded it."[118] With the exception of Acts 8:32 (a direct quotation of Isa 53:7), each of the NT passages which portray Christ as a lamb (John 1:29, 36; 1 Pet 1:19; 1 Cor 5:7) at least implicitly connects Christ with the paschal sacrifice. First Corinthians 5:7 maintains the

---

114  However, while the early Christians certainly understood Christ's sufferings in light of Isa 53 (cf. Acts 8:32), it is not necessary to go outside the Passover to explain the expiatory and redemptive characteristics of the Apocalypse's depiction of τὸ ἀρνίον.

115  One rare exception is Delitzsch, who claims that "all the references in the New Testament to the Lamb of God (with which the corresponding allusions to the passover are interwoven) spring from this passage." Franz Delitzsch, *Biblical Commentary on the Prophecies of Isaiah*, trans. James Martin, 3rd ed., 2 vols. (Eerdmans, 1877), 2:323. In contrast, Prigent prefers to highlight the differences between the silent victim of Isaiah and the conquering Lamb of Revelation. Prigent, *Commentary on the Apocalypse of St. John*, 249. For more discussion on Isa 53 as the possible source of Revelation's Lamb imagery, see especially Comblin, *Christ dans l'Apocalypse*, 17–47; D'Souza, *Lamb of God*, 27–32.

116  They find the source of John's Lamb imagery within Jewish apocalyptic literature, in which David is represented as a horned lamb (ἀρήν) which becomes a ram (κρίος), a powerful warrior similar to τὸ ἀρνίον in Revelation (e.g., 1 Enoch 89–90; Testament of Joseph 19:8, Testament of Benjamin 3:8). Dodd explicitly affirms that 1 Enoch's portrayal of the conquering lamb is "the prototype of the militant seven-horned 'Lamb' of the Apocalypse of John." Dodd, *Fourth Gospel*, 232; cf. Morris, *Cross in the NT*, 355. For discussion on the apocalyptic background of the Lamb imagery, see Robert H. Mounce, "The Christology of the Apocalypse," *Foundations* 11 (1968): 42–45; Barrett, "Lamb of God," 210–216; D'Souza, *Lamb of God*, 73–77. Yet there is no substantial indication in the OT or Second Temple Judaism that a *messianic* lamb figure was expected, apart from Testament of Joseph 19:3, a single disputed and unconvincing case in a work that maintains evidence of probable Christian interpolation or redaction. Ashby, *Sacrifice*, 87; Barrett, "Lamb of God," 216; etc.

117  Bauckham, *Climax of Prophecy*, 184 (italics original).

118  Beasley-Murray, "How Christian," 284.

most explicit NT reference to Christ in terms of the Passover Lamb by using terminology that specifically denotes the Passover—"for Christ, our Passover lamb, has been sacrificed." Though the vocabulary differs,[119] paschal imagery is prominent throughout the entire context of 1 Pet 1:13–2:10, especially in the adjectives "unblemished and spotless" (1 Pet 1:19, NASB; cf. Exod 12:5), the mention of the blood of a lamb (cf. Exod 12:7), the idea of redemption (cf. Exod 15:13, 16), and the creation of a holy priesthood (1 Pet 2:5; cf. Exod 19:6), most of which also appear in Revelation's exodus typology.[120]

Perhaps the most well-known description of Christ's sacrificial nature in terms of Lamb imagery is found in John's Gospel, "behold, the Lamb of God, who takes away the sin of the world" (John 1:29). Historically, the interpretation of this expression is split between the Latin patristics identifying the Lamb with the paschal victim and the Greek Fathers reading it from the perspective of the Isaianic Servant song.[121] Yet the overall witness of the Gospel of John indicates that the author intentionally presents Christ's death as the sacrifice of the true Passover Lamb (ἀμνός).[122] Ashby claims that the vocabulary of the fourth Gospel is imbedded with sacrificial connotations. The same is true "in the Apocalypse, only with a different word.... The New Testament writers are ... making quite clear that it is the Passover Lamb that they are identifying with Christ."[123] At the same time, there seems to be no theological contrast intended by the different vocabulary. Rather, the Apocalypse is in harmony with the NT testimony to Christ's death as a Passover sacrifice which affects the redemption of men through his blood. Indeed, Osborn

---

119  Aune, *Revelation 1–5*, 361, 371.

120  First Peter 1:18–19 exhibits conceptual parallelism with Rev 5:9; both speak of being ransomed by the blood of the Lamb. Boismard, "Christ the Lamb," 157–159, 163–164. Cf. Marshall, "Concept of Redemption," 161. Dautzenberg disagrees, however, claiming that the simile in 1 Pet 1:19 does not go back to Isa 53 or the Passover lamb but is oriented toward the OT sacrificial system in general. G. Dautzenberg, "ἀμνός, ἀρήν, ἀρνίον," *EDNT* 1:71.

121  D'Souza, *Lamb of God*, 115–116.

122  See chapter 4, "Gospels and Acts." While some scholars (e.g., Johns, *Lamb Christology*, 32) exploit the difference in vocabulary between Revelation and other NT writings, asserting a sharp distinction in meaning between ἀμνός and ἀρνίον in the LXX and NT times, others (e.g., Aune, *Revelation 1–5*, 368) claim that the words were virtually synonymous by the time the NT was written. However, it is important to note that none of the passages (with the exception of the specific quotation in Acts 8:32) refer to Christ as a πρόβατον, the generic word for sheep and the word in closest proximity to the idea of sacrifice in Isa 53:7. There is no conclusive explanation for the Apocalypse's divergence from the typical NT usage of ἀμνός. Hillyer proposes that, in the sense that ἀμνός has unambiguous sacrificial connotations in the LXX, this word is insufficient for the Apocalypse's multifaceted image. Whereas other NT references to the Lamb specifically refer to Christ's sacrifice using ἀμνός, Revelation goes beyond this to portray τὸ ἀρνίον as both sacrifice and warrior, slain and triumphant. Yet, since the Lamb is presented as "standing, as though it had been slain," the sacrificial aspect is prominent still. Hillyer, "The Lamb," 229. Cf. Bauckham, *Climax of Prophecy*, 184; Guthrie, "Lamb in Revelation," 69.

123  Ashby, *Sacrifice*, 88.

boldly asserts that Revelation "does by action what the forerunner of Christ did by speech. Both cry aloud to all the world, 'Behold, the Lamb of God, that taketh away the sin of the world!'"[124]

Ultimately, no single OT or Jewish context is sufficient to account for every facet of Revelation's Lamb imagery. Rather, the images of the Passover lamb (as representative of the entire OT sacrificial system), Isaiah's Suffering Servant, and the warrior lambs of Jewish apocalyptic literature unite to form the Apocalypse's portrayal of Christ as τὸ ἀρνίον.[125] A proper appreciation for Revelation's Lamb imagery must take into account both the sacrificial nature of the Lamb and his messianic role throughout the book as ruler, judge, warrior, and king. Neither the messianic or sacrificial image is adequate on its own, and it is important not to set up a false dichotomy or paradox between the two, for it seems that the author of Revelation has fused these two concepts together in τὸ ἀρνίον. As Bauckham states, Revelation's Lamb is an entirely new symbol, "a symbol of conquest by sacrificial death.... The novelty of John's symbol lies in its representation of the sacrificial death of Christ as the fulfilment of Jewish hopes of the messianic conqueror.... The vision of the Lamb therefore portrays the manner of Christ's victory: through death."[126] Nevertheless, the combination of abundant references to the Lamb's blood and sacrifice with the copious use of exodus typology throughout the Apocalypse reinforces the likelihood that the Passover Lamb was prominent in John's mind as he recorded his vision of τὸ ἀρνίον.

---

124 Thomas Osborn, *The Lion and the Lamb: A Drama of the Apocalypse* (Abingdon, 1922), 193. Cf. D'Souza, *Lamb of God*, 173.

125 See Lioy, *Revelation in Christological Focus*, 119. According to Comblin, "les trois images reunites sous cette figure d'Agneau finessent par composer une sorte de synthèse representative qui fournit un support sensible à une christologie complexe." Comblin, *Christ dans l'Apocalypse*, 34; cf. Hillyer, "The Lamb," 229, 231; Beasley-Murray, "How Christian," 230.

126 Bauckham, *Climax of Prophecy*, 184. Cf. Beasley-Murray, "How Christian," 278; Barrett, "Lamb of God," 210.

## Chapter 7

## Exodus Imagery in Revelation: The Wilderness

Like the Scriptures which precede it, Revelation's use of exodus typology is not limited to the exodus proper but extends to include elements from the broader exodus experience, namely, the wandering of the Israelites in the wilderness. Two of the most significant occurrences are sandwiched between obvious instances of exodus typology—namely, the proleptic view of Yahweh's eschatological provision occurs between the sealing of the 144,000 (Rev 7:1–8) and the commencement of the trumpet judgments (Rev 8), and the vision of the tabernacle filling with the smoke of God's glory (Rev 15:5–8) occurs between the "Song of Moses and the Song of the Lamb" (Rev 15:1–4) and the commencement of the bowl judgments (Rev 16). John also uses wilderness connotations to summarize the salvation-historical conflict between Satan and the people of God in Rev 12. Admittedly, this imagery is less pronounced than the plague traditions and the paschal nature of the Lamb, appearing less in structural allusions and more in thematic or verbal allusions. Yet, with the variety of allusions to events, images, and circumstances related to the Israelites' journey in the wilderness scattered throughout Revelation, including repeated references to the tabernacle/temple and the Sinai theophany, there is no question that wilderness imagery played a substantial role in John's use of exodus typology.

### The Woman and the Dragon: A Survey of Salvation History (Rev 12)

With Rev 12, John begins a new section of the Apocalypse. As Mounce states, "before the seven last plagues of chapter 16, in which the wrath of God is finished (15:1), John turns aside to explain the underlying cause for the hostility about to break upon the church."¹ In metaphorical fashion, Rev 12 surveys the age-old conflict between the people of God and Satan, explains the reason for the persecution of the church, and introduces the major characters in the final battle. This summary of the conflict between Satan and the people of God throughout salvation history is perhaps the most structural of all wilderness allusions in the Apocalypse.

Before delving into the text itself, something must be said about John's use of sources in this passage. The chapter is a virtual amalgamation of ancient images, a "series of interconnecting stories, each of which contributes something significant to the whole."² Many commentators suggest that the undercurrent to all of these stories is an ancient international combat myth³ describing a wicked usurper's attempts to destroy an unborn prince and the protection of that prince from danger until he is old enough to conquer the enemy. This is essentially the story found in Rev 12, though John takes "his account from the OT … reflecting on [the myths] collectively and interpreting them through the lens of the OT and Jewish tradition," and imbedding within it a Christian interpretation.⁴ John's narrative includes allusions to the Scriptural accounts of Eve and the serpent (Gen 3:15), mother Zion struggling to be rescued from Leviathan (Isa 26:16–27:1; Mic 4:10), the birth

---

1 Robert H. Mounce, *The Book of Revelation*, NICNT (Eerdmans, 1977), 234. According to Beale, "chs. 12–22 tell the same story as chs. 1–11 but explain in greater detail what chs. 1–11 only introduce and imply.... In this respect ch. 12 can be seen as introducing the second half of the Apocalypse." G. K. Beale, *The Book of Revelation*, NIGTC (Eerdmans, 1999), 622–623. Osborne labels Rev 12:1–13:8 the "heart of the book, for it establishes the core theme, the war between God/his people and the dragon/his people and between the Lamb and his counterpart, the beast." Grant Osborne, *Revelation*, BECNT (Baker, 2002), 454.

2 Ian Boxall, *The Revelation of Saint John*, BNTC 19 (Hendrickson, 2009), 176. The purpose of this section is not to uncover all of the OT imagery contained in this chapter, for that would far exceed the scope of this project. Rather, this discussion will focus on revealing John's use of exodus typology within Rev 12, bringing in other OT connections only when needed.

3 The label "international myth" recognizes the fact that nearly every ancient religion contains some form of this basic story (e.g. those from Asia Minor, Persia, Babylon, Egypt, Ugarit, and Greece). Robert W. Mol, "Sources and Their Use in Revelation 12:1–17" (MA thesis, Trinity Evangelical Divinity School, 1981), 131; Richard Bauckham, *The Theology of the Book of Revelation*, New Testament Theology (Cambridge University Press, 1993), 89; etc.

4 Beale, *Revelation*, 624–625. According to Boxall, "Israel had already reworked such traditions to express its conviction that YHWH had defeated the forces of chaos (e.g., Gen. 1:1—2:3; Ps. 74:13–14; Isa 27:1; 51:9–10), and John is almost certainly drawing on this biblical tradition." Boxall, *Revelation*, 176. He goes on to say that "what would be most shocking to the first hearers of Revelation, however, is the way in which John's vision retells and radically subverts such myths." Ibid., 177. Mounce is even less inclined to believe John intentionally drew upon pagan mythology—"Would a writer who elsewhere in the book displays such a definite antagonism toward paganism draw extensively at this point upon its mythology? As always, John is a creative apocalyptist who, although gathering his imagery from many sources, nevertheless constructs a scenario distinctly his own." Mounce, *Revelation*, 235.

of Israel's Messiah to Mary, and Satan's underlying opposition to Yahweh, his people, and his son. In addition, he recalls the exodus tradition of Pharaoh's pursuit of the Israelites and their protection by Yahweh in the wilderness. Through this kaleidoscopic array of OT stories, John places the coming conflict squarely within the context of the timeless war of evil against God and those faithful to him.[5]

Revelation 12 naturally divides into three segments. In Rev 12:1–6, John sets the stage by introducing the main characters in this battle—the woman and the dragon—through two signs in heaven; their story resumes in Rev 12:13–17. This narrative frames the middle section, Rev 12:7–12, which delineates the heavenly skirmish between Satan and the archangel Michael and "provides the central interpretation and theological underpinning"[6] for the conflict between the woman and the dragon.

The chapter begins with a sign in heaven—a woman arrayed with the sun, moon, and twelve stars, caught in the throes of giving birth (Rev 12:1–2). The twelve stars perhaps represent the whole of Israel, recalling Joseph's dream in which Jacob, his wife, and eleven tribes appear as the sun, moon, and eleven stars bowing down to him, the twelfth tribe (Gen 37:9).[7] Elsewhere, Solomon's queen (identified with Jerusalem) is also described as "beautiful as the moon, bright as the sun" (Song 6:10), imagery that was later applied to Israel (e.g., Isa 60:19–20; Midr. Exod 15:6; Midr. Num. 2:4; 9; 14; Midr. Ps. 22:11–22; Pirqe R. El. 42) to emphasize her faithfulness to God in both the wilderness and the exile.[8] The woman is the personified people of God, a picture of the faithful community both before and after Christ (rather than a picture of Mary or ethnic Israel), who "cannot be corrupted during her wilderness wandering in the last days, which is portrayed in vv 6, 13–17."[9] The woman is in direct contrast

---

5 Bauckham, *Theology of Revelation*, 89; Boxall, *Revelation*, 176. Beale argues that John's purpose in Rev 12 is to urge readers to persevere through their persecution, protected from Satan through Christ's ultimate victory in his death and resurrection. Beale, *Revelation*, 624.
6 Beale, *Revelation*, 624; cf. Boxall, *Revelation*, 174.
7 Beale, *Revelation*, 625.
8 Ibid., 625–626.
9 Ibid., 625. Patterson argues that since the Messiah must be born to the offspring of Israel, "the only effective and appropriate identification of the radiant woman, then, is to see her as the ethnic offspring of Abraham, the Jewish people." Paige Patterson, *Revelation*, NAC 39 (Broadman & Holman, 2012), 262. Yet, contrary to the traditional dispensationalist viewpoint, John does not distinguish between Israel and the church in his depiction of the community of the faithful, so both are included within this image. For an explanation of the interpretations of Israel/the church held by the various millennial views, see Darrell L. Bock, "Summary Essay," in *Three Views on the Millennium and Beyond*, ed. Darrell L. Bock, Counterpoints (Zondervan, 1999), 290–293, 296–297. While it has been strongly argued (by the Catholic church in particular) that the woman in Rev 12 represents Mary, mother of Jesus, it is unlikely that a particular individual woman was John's primary focus. Like the other women in this section of Revela-

with the whore of Babylon, which in Revelation 17 represents the unbelieving community; therefore the righteous woman here must symbolize the believing community, made up of both Jews and Gentiles. The idea that she is the persecuted people of God fits the context, since the emphasis is on her labor pains (βασανιζομένη), used elsewhere in Scripture to indicate the distress of God's people through oppression.[10] This picture of God's persecuted people hearkens back to the suffering of the Israelites during their bondage in Egypt.

In Rev 12:3–4, John sees a "a great red dragon, with seven heads and ten horns, and on his heads seven diadems.... And the dragon stood before the woman who was about to give birth, so that when she bore her child he might devour it." While this imagery clearly resembles the ancient combat myths, John's source is not necessarily found outside of the Scriptures. The dragon's description draws upon a mosaic of OT contexts in which the powers of evil oppressing God's people are symbolized by a dragon or sea monster. This is especially true of Pharaoh and Egypt, represented throughout Scripture as an evil sea monster (identified as Leviathan or Rahab) who is defeated through God's mighty acts in the exodus (e.g., Pss 74:13–14; 89:10; Isa 51:9–10; Ezek 29:3; 32:2–3). The fact that the dragon in Rev 12:3 is "great" (δράκων μέγας) reinforces the link with Egypt, for only in Ezek 29:3, in a passage clearly referring to Pharaoh, is this adjective used to describe the OT dragon ("the great dragon," τὸν δράκοντα τὸν μέγαν).[11]

The evil nature of the dragon is highlighted by its stance, perched to devour the child at the moment of his birth (Rev 12:4). This seems to echo the slaughter of innocent children in Bethlehem by Herod at the time of Christ's birth (Matt 2:16), an atrocity that has multiple parallels in Pharaoh's attempts

---

tion (the bride of Christ, Babylon), she has a corporate identity. Boxall, *Revelation*, 178–179; Beale, *Revelation*, 628, 630.

10 Isaiah describes Israel in bondage as a "a pregnant woman who writhes and cries out in her pangs when she is near to giving birth" (Isa 26:17; cf. 66:7; Mic 4:10). Nowhere within biblical and extrabiblical literature is βασανίζειν used in a literal sense to refer to a woman's birth pains. Osborne, *Revelation*, 457–458; Beale *Revelation*, 629. Rather, βάσανος and its derivatives are used to denote both the afflictions which the ungodly force upon the righteous, and the just suffering which the ungodly will experience in eternity as a punishment for his actions. Occasionally (e.g., Wis 3:1; Ezra 12:18; Luke 16:23, 28) there is embedded within this language a sense of eschatological torment or torture, particularly in the form βασανίζειν (e.g. Wis 11:9; Matt 8:6; 2 Pet 2:8). Johannes Schneider, "βάσανος, βασανίζω, βασανισμός, βασανιστής," *TDNT* 1:562.

11 Stephen S. Smalley, *The Revelation to John: A Commentary on the Greek Text of the Apocalypse* (InterVarsity, 2005), 317. Like Pharaoh, Nebuchadnezzar is called a "sea monster" (Jer 51:34 HCSB; ESV = "monster"; NIV = "serpent"; KJV = "dragon")—both rulers tended to "devour" nations and were clearly enemies of God's people. Osborne, *Revelation*, 459. Cf. Psalms of Solomon 2:29–30, where the sea monster is identified as the Roman commander Pompey lying "on the mountains of Egypt." G. K. Beale and Sean M. McDonough, "Revelation," in *Commentary on the New Testament Use of the Old Testament*, ed. G. K. Beale and D. A. Carson (Baker, 2007), 1123.

to destroy all the male Hebrew children in the days of Moses (Exod 1:15–2:10).[12] The male child born to the woman in Rev 12:5 is Jesus the Messiah, born to the community of God's faithful believers (cf. Isa 66:7–8) to rule all the nations (cf. Ps 2:9), who was persecuted by Satan not only at the moment of his birth but also in the schemes by the Jewish leaders to arrest and kill him at the end of his life.[13] Like the infant Jesus whose family fled from Bethlehem to avoid Herod's evil designs (Matt 2:16), this male child is "caught up to God and his throne" (Rev 12:5) before the dragon was able to accomplish his murderous plot.[14] It is possible to view this as an allusion to Christ's ascension (cf. Acts 1:2, 11, 22; 1 Tim 3:16), such that "the life and earthly ministry of Jesus appear in a very truncated form, with a jump in timescale from the birth to the exaltation of the Messiah, and with everything in between (including the passion) omitted."[15] The passion, however, is likely implied, for it was through the death, burial, and resurrection of Christ that Satan's downfall was secured. He is still able to wreak havoc for a time, as the dragon does in Rev 12:13–17, but God's victory is certain, and Satan's ultimate demise is guaranteed.

While the child is snatched up to the throne of God, "the woman fled into the wilderness, where she has a place prepared by God, in which she is to be nourished for 1,260 days" (Rev 12:6).[16] The exodus parallels in this verse alone are striking—God's faithful people, the Israelites, fled the evil dragon

---

12 According to Tyconius, the dragon is "the devil. It was he who inflamed Herod with the fire of envy so that he would feign to adore the Christ even while seeking with all his power to kill Christ whom he knew was to be born king of the Jews." Tyconius, *Commentarius in Apocalypsin*, ed. A. W. Adams (Brepols, 1985), 12.3, translated in William C. Weinrich, ed., *Revelation*, ACCS New Testament 12 (InterVarsity, 2005), 177. Cf. Oecumenius, *Oecumenii Commentarius in Apocalypsin*, ed. Marc de Groote (Peters, 1999), 12.3–6, in Weinrich, *Revelation*, 180.

13 Osborne, *Revelation*, 462; Beale, *Revelation*, 628; etc. Cf. Tyconius, *Apocalypsin* 12.5, in Weinrich, *Revelation*, 181–182.

14 "The poisonous dragon lay in wait and incited Herod to kill the children in Bethlehem, thinking that certainly among them he would locate the Lord. But by the providence of the Father the child escaped the plot. For Joseph heard a warning from heaven and took the child and its mother and fled into Egypt, since Herod was seeking the life of the child." Oecumenius, *Apocalypsin* 12.3–6, in Weinrich, *Revelation*, 182.

15 Smalley, *Revelation*, 320; cf. Mounce, *Revelation*, 238–239; Primasius, *Commentarius in Apocalypsin*, ed. A. W. Adams (Brepols, 1985), 12.3, translated in Weinrich, *Revelation*, 182.

16 At first glance, the 1260 days (which equals 3.5 years or 42 months) seems to have nothing to do with the exodus. It is a symbolic figure for the eschatological period of tribulation prophesied in Dan 7:25. In the Apocalypse, the three-and-a-half years illustrates that while the present age is a time of tribulation, God is faithful to protect and sustain those who put their trust in him, just as the Israelites learned in the wilderness. The number forty-two may have specific ties to the exodus motif, for the wilderness wanderings included forty-two encampments. Additionally, the time in the wilderness could technically be counted as forty-two years, since it is likely that two years passed before Israel incurred the forty-year penalty (Num 14:20–35). Given the exodus connotations imbedded throughout this passage, it seems likely that Yahweh's provision for his people in the wilderness during the exodus is typologically articulated in each of Revelation's four references to three-and-a-half years (Rev 11:2; 12:6, 14;

Pharaoh into the wilderness (ἔρημον),[17] the place appointed by God (see Exod 3:18; 13:17–18); while there, Yahweh provided for their every need, turning bitter water to sweet, bringing forth water from the rock, providing manna and even quail when bread alone did not satisfy, and of course, protecting them from their enemies. Similarly, the wilderness in Rev 12 is a place of refuge, of dependence upon God. John is in harmony here with the OT prophets who portrayed Israel's eschatological return from captivity in terms of a new exodus (e.g., Isa 32:15; 35:1; 40:3; 41:18; 43:19–20; 51:3; Jer 31:2; Ezek 34:25; Hos 2:14–15 [16–17 LXX]), a time when Yahweh would again protect and nourish them in the wilderness.[18]

Just as the action seems to be picking up speed, John interrupts the narrative and shifts the scene from earth to heaven with an apocalyptic rehearsal of the heavenly battle between Satan and the archangel Michael (Rev 12:7–12). This battle represents the counterpart to the earthly events recorded in Rev 12:1–6 (see Dan 10:13, 21; 12:1, etc., where good and bad angels represent Israel and evil nations respectively)—the conflict between God's faithful believers and the dragon is mirrored here in the heavenly battle.[19] Where first the reader is given a glimpse of the victory and ascension of Christ (Rev 12:5), here the reader witnesses the decisive defeat of the dragon (Rev 12:8–9). The outcome of the battle has already been decided, though it is not yet finalized on earth. John also removes any doubt as to the true identity of the dragon—he is "the devil and Satan, the deceiver of the whole world" (Rev 12:9; cf. 20:2). This dragon, described in Rev 12:3–4 with symbols linked to Pharaoh and other OT forces in opposition to God's people, is revealed to be Satan, the ultimate adversary of God and behind-the-scenes instigator of all the evil rulers and kingdoms who throughout history have sought to oppress the people of God.[20] However, as Michael and his angels emerge from the battle victorious,

---

13:5). Paul Spilsbury, *The Throne, the Lamb & the Dragon: A Reader's Guide to the Book of Revelation* (InterVarsity Press, 2002), 83–84; Beale, *Revelation*, 565, 647.

17 The LXX and NT repeatedly use the word ἔρημος when referring to the Israelites' wilderness sojourn (for just a few examples, see Exod 15:22; 16:2; 19:2; Num 9:5; 14:2; Deut 1:40; 2:7; Josh 5:6; Pss 106:9 [105:9 LXX]; 136:16 [135:16 LXX]; Amos 2:10; Isa 63:13; Jer 2:6; Ezek 20:13; John 3:14; 6:31, 49; Acts 7:30, 36; 1 Cor 10:5; Heb 3:17). This is by no means the only context for the word "wilderness" in Scripture, but it is certainly prominent, and John's explicit use of the word here, when surrounded by other exodus/wilderness allusions, reinforces the imagery.

18 Beale, *Revelation*, 643, 647; Beale and McDonough, "Revelation," 1124; Mounce, *Revelation*, 239.

19 Beale, *Revelation*, 650. According to Beale, Jewish writings indicate that during the exodus from Egypt, Israel's angels executed judgment upon Egypt's guardian angels at the Red Sea (e.g., Midr. Exod 9:9; 23:15; Midr. Isa 24:21). Therefore, "it is appropriate that such angelic combat would occur again to launch the new Israel's exodus through the wilderness of the world." Beale, *Revelation*, 650–651.

20 Mounce, *Revelation*, 242.

the dragon "was thrown down to the earth, and his angels were thrown down with him" (Rev 12:9).

John's apocalyptic vision of the dragon's climactic downfall is interpreted in a brief hymn of praise (Rev 12:10–12):

> And I heard a loud voice in heaven, saying, "Now the salvation and the power and the kingdom of our God and the authority of his Christ have come, for the accuser of our brothers has been thrown down, who accuses them day and night before our God. And they have conquered him by the blood of the Lamb and by the word of their testimony, for they loved not their lives even unto death. Therefore, rejoice, O heavens and you who dwell in them! But woe to you, O earth and sea, for the devil has come down to you in great wrath, because he knows that his time is short!"

In a pattern typical of Revelation, this hymn functions "like a Greek chorus in a play, not only celebrating but also interpreting the significance of the narratives."[21] If the connection between the child being caught up to the throne and the passion and ascension of Christ was previously unclear, here John makes it explicit. Christ has come, manifesting the power, authority, and salvation of God, and has conquered the dragon with his blood (Rev 12:10). This is not a reference to the second coming of Christ but to the historical incarnation and passion of the living Son of God. As the hymn continues, the conclusion to the story which began in Rev 12:1–6 is revealed. While the dragon will persecute God's people relentlessly on earth, his time is limited because of the cross of Christ, and the faithful community will emerge victorious because of their identification with the blood of the Lamb (Rev 12:11–12).

After this hymnic interlude the narrative action resumes, with the soon-to-be-conquered dragon pursuing the woman into the wilderness—"the woman was given the two wings of the great eagle so that she might fly from the serpent into the wilderness, to the place where she is to be nourished for a time, and times, and half a time" (Rev 12:14). Through John's choice of vocabulary, he calls to mind the metaphorical depiction of God's deliverance of his people in the exodus as an eagle protecting his children; God himself says, "I bore you on eagles' wings and brought you to myself" (Exod 19:4).[22]

---

21 Osborne, *Revelation*, 473.
22 See also Deut 32:11 which describes Yahweh as an eagle carrying its young on his wings. Beale, *Revelation*, 490–491; Ian Paul, "The Use of the Old Testament in Revelation 12," in *The Old Testament in the New Testament; Essays in Honour of J. L. North*, ed. Steve Moyise, JSNTSup 189 (Sheffield, 2000), 268. Compare the use of πτέρυξ and ἀετός in Exod 19:4 LXX (πτερύγων ἀετῶν) and Rev 12:14 (πτέρυγες τοῦ ἀετοῦ τοῦ μεγάλου). Both verses emphasize removal from a place of

The wilderness imagery from Rev 12:6 is reinforced through the remainder of the passage. Not only does God provide nourishment for the woman as he did for the Israelites in the wilderness, but the ground itself opens to protect her from her enemies (Rev 12:16). While it is possible that this alludes to the earth swallowing the Israelites who rebelled against Moses in the desert (Num 16:31–33), the context suggests it is more likely an allusion to the Red Sea crossing, of which the Song of Moses proclaims, "You stretched out your right hand; the earth swallowed them" (Exod 15:12).[23]

Although the cosmic interlude (Rev 12:7–12) announces the ultimate defeat of the dragon, he has not yet been fully bound on earth, though "he knows that his time is short" (Rev 12:12). Thus Rev 12 concludes with the dragon going off in fury "to make war on the rest of [the woman's] offspring" (Rev 12:17). Through the telescoping of time, John has given his readers a look into the distant future and portrayed the culmination of history, Yahweh's defeat of the great dragon, through the lens of exodus typology. In the end, Satan will meet the same demise as Pharaoh's forces, who were utterly destroyed as they attempted to pursue and oppress the Israelites (Exod 14:23–28). As Isa 27:1 states of the end times, "In that day the Lord with his hard and great and strong sword will punish Leviathan the fleeing serpent, Leviathan the twisting serpent, and he will slay the dragon that is in the sea." At the same time, Yahweh's care for his people continues; as with the Israelites, he will protect and provide for the community of the faithful—"those who keep the commandments of God and hold to the testimony of Jesus" (Rev 12:17)—in the wilderness, even as they face persecution and hardship.

### They Shall Neither Hunger nor Thirst (Rev 7:9–17)

The promise that Yahweh will nourish faithful believers during their time in the wilderness is not limited to Rev 12. To the church at Pergamum, God promised, "To the one who conquers I will give some of the hidden manna

---

danger/oppression via wings of eagles, and God's protection in the new place. The expression "wings of an eagle" may also bring to mind the more popular Isa 40:31, "but they who wait for the Lord shall renew their strength; they shall mount up with wings like eagles; they shall run and not be weary; they shall walk and not faint," a prediction of future Israel's return from exile (cf. 1 Enoch 96:2; Assumption of Moses 10:8). Beale, *Revelation*, 670.

23 According to Beale, "the *Tg. Ps.-J.* to Exod. 15:12 expands on the MT and repeats that 'the earth opened its mouth and consumed them.'" Beale and McDonough, "Revelation," 1126. Whereas in Exodus, Yahweh controlled the waters, parting the sea until the Israelites crossed and then causing the water to rush back over the Egyptians, here the serpent spews forth a flood to sweep the woman away but the earth comes to her aid, swallowing the menacing river. Could this perhaps be an instance of imitation? (For more on this motif, see chapter 8, "Motif of Imitation and Fraud.")

(μάννα)" (Rev 2:17), while in Rev 21:6 he vows, "to the thirsty (τῷ διψῶντι) I will give from the spring of the water (ὕδωρ) of life without payment" (cf. Rev 22:17).[24] More significantly, within the twofold vision of the people of God in Rev 7, John recounts a proleptic glimpse of a vast multitude worshiping in the heavenly throne room and receiving God's unending provision after their final deliverance (Rev 7:9–17), just as the Israelites experienced Yahweh's presence and divine care in the wilderness. As we have already seen in this passage inundated with exodus typology, this same group is alternately described in Rev 7:1–8 as the 144,000, set apart as God's possession and sealed as a signal of God's ownership and a means of protection from God's wrath.

The identity of this multitude is quickly confirmed. While they wear robes of white[25] and wave palm branches,[26] the defining characteristic of the multitude in Rev 7:9–17 is its identification with the blood of the Lamb. As one of the elders announces to John, these are "the ones coming out of the great tribulation. They have washed their robes and made them white in the blood of the Lamb" (Rev 7:14).[27] Just as the Hebrew people were redeemed from slavery in Egypt (Exod 20:2; Deut 5:6) through the sign of the paschal lamb's blood on the doorposts, so Christ's disciples, sealed with the blood of the Lamb (Rev 14:1), are redeemed from the earth (Rev 14:3) and bondage to sin or rebellion against God, and won for God (cf. 1 Pet 1:19; John 1:29).[28]

---

24  This is a possible thematic allusion to God's provision of water (ὕδωρ) from the rock when the Israelites complained of their thirst (ἐδίψησεν) in the wilderness (Exod 17:1–7).

25  The white robes indicate purity, victory of faith, and worthiness to receive eternal life. At various points in Revelation, the people of God are clothed in white (Rev 6:11; 7:9, 13, 14; 19:14) or promised such if they persevere in their faith (Rev 3:4, 5, 18). White also possibly alludes to the righteousness of Christ—it is the color of the exalted Son of Man's hair (Rev 1:14), the horse upon which Christ rides into battle with the beast (Rev 19:11), and the great throne of God (Rev 20:11). Smalley, *Revelation*, 191; Dan Lioy, *The Book of Revelation in Christological Focus*, SBL 58 (Peter Lang, 2003), 137–139.

26  Palm branches were not an image of persecution and martyrdom but of victory, conquest, and festive joy (e.g., 1 Macc 13:51; 2 Macc 10:7; 14:4). They were used by the Israelites in the Feast of Tabernacles, as well as by Jesus' followers welcoming him to Jerusalem during his triumphal entry (John 12:13). Smalley, *Revelation*, 191; Pierre Prigent, *Commentary on the Apocalypse of St. John*, trans. Wendy Pradels, rev. ed. (Mohr Siebeck, 2001), 289–290; Lioy, *Revelation in Christological Focus*, 139; etc.

27  It is possible that this reference to "washing (ἔπλυναν)" their robes in the blood (Rev 7:14) immediately prior to the statement that "they are before the throne of God" (Rev 7:15) is a thematic allusion to the Israelites preparing to meet with God at Mount Sinai. Scripture recalls that Moses consecrated the people; and they washed (ἔπλυναν) their garments. And he said to the people, "Be ready for the third day; do not go near a woman" (Exod 19:10, 14–15). Compare Rev 22:14, "blessed are those who wash their robes, so that they may have the right to the tree of life and that they may enter the city" where God's presence resides. In addition, Rev 19:7–8 states that the Bride has made herself ready for the return of Christ and is clothed in "fine linen, bright and pure."

28  Spilsbury, *Throne, the Lamb & the Dragon*, 76, Leopold Sabourin, *The Names and Titles*

In a poetic amalgamation of OT images, the elder continues his portrait of the multitude, focusing on the blessings they receive through identification with the Lamb:

> Therefore they are before the throne of God, and serve him day and night in his temple; and he who sits on the throne will shelter them with his presence. They shall hunger no more, neither thirst anymore; the sun shall not strike them, nor any scorching heat. For the Lamb in the midst of the throne will be their shepherd, and he will guide them to springs of living water, and God will wipe away every tear from their eyes (Rev 7:15–17).

The language of promise that God will "shelter them with his presence" in Rev 7:15 is significant. Literally, σκηνώσει ἐπ' αὐτούς translates as "will spread his tabernacle over them" (NASB; or more simply, "will tabernacle over them") and immediately evokes memories of the tabernacle, the means by which God dwelt among the Israelites as they sojourned in the wilderness (Exod 25:8). It was in this tent that the Lord spoke with Moses face to face, revealing his will for his people (Exod 25:21–22; 33:9–11). Interestingly, a very similar expression occurs in the prologue of the Fourth Gospel—"The Word became flesh and dwelt among us (ἐσκήνωσεν ἐν ἡμῖν)" (John 1:14; cf. Rev 7:15, σκηνώσει ἐπ' αὐτούς).[29] The tabernacle represents the immediate presence of God (cf. Isa 4:5–6). In this proleptic vision, John has seen the fulfillment of the goal of the exodus, the promise that God will dwell in the midst of his people (Exod 25:8; 29:45–46; Ezek 37:27; Zech 2:10; cf. Rev 21:3, the dwelling place [ἡ σκηνὴ] of God is with man. He will dwell [σκηνώσει] with them).[30]

For the multitude in heaven, the blessings continue. In Rev 7:16–17, John includes a strong verbal allusion to Isa 49:10, a passage in which the prophet describes the future day of Israel's restoration—"they shall not hunger or thirst, neither scorching wind nor sun shall strike them, for he who has pity on them will lead them, and by springs of water will guide them."[31] The similarities abound, particularly when one recognizes that Revelation draws upon the OT shepherding motif (e.g., Isa 49:9; Ps 23), referring to the Lamb as their shepherd rather than "he who has pity on them" as their guide (Isa

---

*of Jesus* (Macmillan, 1967), 161, 164; Jan Fekkes, *Isaiah and Prophetic Traditions in the Book of Revelation: Visionary Antecedents and Their Development*, JSNTSup 93 (JSOT, 1994), 167.

   29  Young's Literal Translation reads "the Word became flesh, and did tabernacle among us."

   30  Mounce, *Revelation*, 175; Smalley, *Revelation*, 192; Beale, *Revelation*, 428; J. Massyngberde Ford, *Revelation*, AB 38 (Doubleday, 1975), 119.

   31  According to Fekkes, the reference to Isa 49:10 in Rev 7:16–17 is one of forty-one certain/virtually certain allusions to the book of Isaiah in the Apocalypse. Fekkes, *Prophetic Traditions*, 280–281.

49:10).[32] John has picked up on Isaiah's innovative transformation of the benefits which the Israelites received in the wilderness into eschatological blessings to be enjoyed by the true Israel in the coming new exodus. The Israelites in the wilderness experienced God's provision of manna, quail, and water, God's protection from their enemies, and God's presence in the pillar of cloud and fire and later in the tabernacle; in the same way, in the final, eschatological restoration the people of God will receive divine nourishment, protection, and most importantly, God's divine presence guiding them on their journey.

The function of John's use of exodus typology within Rev 7 as a whole is buttressed by Ulfgard's proposal regarding Rev 7:9–17. In Exodus, God provides a reason for Israel's liberation—"Let my people go, that they may hold a feast to me in the wilderness" (Exod 5:1; cf. 4:23; 7:16). It is possible that the scene of worship in the latter half of Rev 7 corresponds to this feast that was to take place after the Israelites left Egypt.[33] This celebration, known as the Feast of Tabernacles, celebrated God's victory over his enemies and the presence, provision, and protection of Yahweh which the Israelites experienced during the wilderness wanderings. The Feast of Tabernacles took place at the time of reaping, when God's abundant goodness received tangible expression in the bountiful harvest (Lev 23:33–43; Deut 16:13–15). As part of the festival observance, the Israelites lived in booths for seven days (Lev 23:42) and carried palm branches in and around the Temple (Lev 23:40, 43; Neh 8:15; 2 Macc 10:7).[34]

---

32  Only the mention of God wiping away their tears in Rev 7:17 is completely missing from Isa 49:10. This, however, alludes to yet another passage from Isaiah—"He will swallow up death forever; and the Lord God will wipe away tears from all faces, and the reproach of his people he will take away from all the earth, for the Lord has spoken" (Isa 25:8).

33  Håkan Ulfgard, *Feast and Future: Revelation 7:9–17 and the Feast of Tabernacles*, ConBNT 22 (Almqvist & Wiksell, 1989), 40. In Rev 18:4, John hears a voice from heaven saying "Come out (ἐξέλθατε) of her, my people, lest you take part in her sins, lest you share in her plagues (πληγή)." This call for God's people to come out may allude to the prophets' appeals to the Israelites to depart the cultures in which they were exiled (e.g., Isa 52:11; Jer 51:6–9, 45). However, when combined with the use of the word "plagues," Rev 18:4 also calls to mind the call for the Israelites to leave Egypt, where the people of God are likewise called to separate themselves from an idolatrous oppressor. While the specific reasons for departure are not the same—in Exodus, the purpose is to worship God in the wilderness; in Revelation, the purpose is so that believers will not be punished for the sins of unbelievers—both reflect the worship of the one true God. The connection is reinforced in the following verse, in which John is assured that Babylon's "sins are heaped high as heaven, and God has remembered (ἐμνημόνευσεν) her iniquities" (Rev 18:5), a creative contrast to the reminder that Yahweh "remembered (ἐμνήσθη) his covenant with Abraham, with Isaac, and with Jacob" in Exod 2:24. In both cases, God's remembering results in the salvation/protection of those who believe in God and the judgment of those who seek to oppress them.

34  Ibid., 146.

There is evidence as early as Zech 14:16 that the Feast of Tabernacles had eschatological significance, not only looking back to God's protection in the wilderness but also forward with the expectation of a future reward for the righteous on the coming day of the Lord—"then everyone who survives of all the nations that have come against Jerusalem shall go up year after year to worship the King, the Lord of hosts, and to keep the Feast of Booths."[35] Draper asserts that Rev 7 is deeply indebted to the eschatological nature of Zech 14 and should be understood as the "envisaged fulfilment of the prophecy in a heavenly Feast of Tabernacles."[36] For Ulfgard, however, "it is not the Feast of Tabernacles in itself which is in focus in 7:9–17, but what it represents," namely the joyful celebration of God's acts of salvation in the exodus.[37] Those pictured in Rev 7:1–8 as protected and brought through the tribulation by the seal of God are now seen praising God in the heavenly throne room in the very presence of God and the Lamb.

In the exodus, the Hebrews were identified as God's chosen people and protected from his righteous wrath through the blood of the paschal lamb (Exod 12). They were delivered from slavery and oppression by the power of Yahweh (Exod 13–14) and rejoiced over God's mighty acts of salvation in a song of praise (Exod 15). In the wilderness the Israelites received God's supernatural provision of water (Exod 15:22–27; 17:1–7), manna, and quail (Exod 16); the presence of Yahweh went before them to lead them (Exod 14:19–20; 23:20–23; 33:14–16) and dwelt among them in the tabernacle (Exod 40:34–38). Likewise, in Rev 7:1–8 John presents the servants of God on earth, sealed by the living God for protection from the coming judgments. In a scene reminiscent of the ancient Feast of Tabernacles, Rev 9–17 form a proleptic look at the same group having come out of the tribulation, extolling God for his acts of deliverance in bringing them through a new, greater exodus (Rev 7:12). John draws upon Isaiah to present the eschatological gifts enjoyed by those who persevere in terms which recall Yahweh's divine protection, provision, and presence in the wilderness (Rev 7:14–17).[38]

---

35 Ulfgard, *Feast and Future*, 146; Francis Foulkes, "The Acts of God: A Study of the Basis of Typology in the Old Testament," in *The Right Doctrine from the Wrong Texts? Essays on the Use of the Old Testament in the New*, ed. G. K. Beale (Baker, 1994), 359.

36 J. A. Draper, "The Heavenly Feast of Tabernacles: Revelation 7.1–17," *JSNT* 19 (1983): 133–147.

37 Ulfgard, *Feast and Future*, 150; David E. Aune, *Revelation 6–16*, WBC 52b (Thomas Nelson, 1998), 449.

38 See Fekkes, *Prophetic Traditions*, 167, 173–174; Ford, *Revelation*, 119. Similarly, the 144,000 sealed who sing a "new song before the throne" in Rev 14:1–5 should be understood as one and the same with "those who were victorious over the beast and his image and the number of his name" (Rev 15:2, NASB) who actually sing the song of Moses and of the Lamb. Beale, *Revelation*, 791; Smalley, *Revelation*, 386.

## "The Temple of the Tabernacle of Meeting"

As we have seen, Revelation promises the eschatological fulfillment of the goal of the exodus, namely God dwelling among his people, as "he who sits on the throne will spread his tabernacle over them" (Rev 7:15, NASB). The Apocalypse is saturated with temple and tabernacle imagery, which ultimately derives from the establishment of the tabernacle in Exod 25–31, 35–40. The Hebrew word for "tabernacle" comes from the Hebrew root שׁכן ("to settle, to dwell"), referring to Yahweh's active and intimate presence among his people.[39] When Moses was at last granted permission to build the tabernacle, the divine presence was no longer hidden from the Israelites, confined to a tent outside the camp in which Moses alone could commune with Yahweh. Rather, the tabernacle was built in the midst of the Israelite camp, where all of God's people could draw close to worship him.[40] Yet the tabernacle was never intended to be an established sanctuary or fixed structure such as the temples of ancient deities; it was designed for transport by the Israelites throughout their wilderness march.[41] The movable nature of the tabernacle emphasized that Yahweh was not subject to any limitation of space, and his presence could not be permanently fixed in any one place. Yahweh was present with a chosen people rather than in any particular location.[42]

Under the vision of King David and during the reign of Solomon, the portable tabernacle of the wilderness was replaced with a stationary temple in Jerusalem, a more permanent but "recognizable variant on the tabernacle."[43] The two structures shared a similar floor plan of an outer court, the holy place, and the innermost Holy of Holies, as well as the same furnishings (Exod 25–30; 1 Kgs 6–8; 1 Chr 28:18). The cloud of God's glory present in both structures provides clear evidence of the continuity between the temple and the tabernacle.[44] When the building of the tabernacle and its furnishings was complete, Yahweh majestically entered the symbol of his presence (Exod 40:34–38). At the completion of the Jerusalem temple a similar

---

39  Michael E. Lodahl, *Shekhinah/Spirit: Divine Presence in Jewish and Christian Religion* (Paulist, 1992), 52.

40  R. W. L. Moberly, *At the Mountain of God: Story and Theology in Exodus 32–34* (JSOT, 1983), 106.

41  William J. Dumbrell, *The End of the Beginning: Revelation 21–22 and the Old Testament* (Lancer, 1985), 44.

42  James Plastaras, *The God of Exodus: The Theology of the Exodus Narratives* (Bruce Publishing, 1966), 260, 268, 274.

43  Andrea Spatafora, *From the "Temple of God" to God as the Temple: A Biblical Theological Study of the Temple in the Book of Revelation*, TGST 27 (Editrice Pontificia Università Gregoriana, 1997), 16–18, 28; Dumbrell, *End of the Beginning*, 38, 45.

44  Dumbrell, *End of the Beginning*, 52.

event occurred, "so that the priests could not stand to minister because of the cloud, for the glory of the Lord filled the house of the Lord" (1 Kgs 8:11). Thus the promise of God announced in Exod 25:8, "that I may dwell in their midst," was seen in both the tabernacle and the temple.

Revelation's diverse use of temple and tabernacle imagery sets the backdrop for the unfolding events of the prophecy. One of the most explicit allusions to the tabernacle occurs in chapter 15, immediately following the Song of Moses and the Song of the Lamb. As the song concludes, John sees the heavenly temple open (Rev 15:5), from which proceed the seven angels holding the seven plagues, clothed in pure linen with golden sashes (Rev 15:6). When they have received the bowls of God's wrath from the four living creatures, the tent fills with the smoke of God's glory and power, and entry into the sanctuary is prohibited until the bowl judgments are completed (Rev 15:8). Sandwiched between two prominent occurrences of exodus typology (the conquerors standing on the sea singing the "Song of Moses ... and of the Lamb" in Rev 15:1–4 and the bowl judgments in Rev 16:1–21), it should come as no surprise that this brief temple scene is likewise imbedded with images from the exodus experience.

The exodus/tabernacle connotations in this passage are immediate and abundant, starting with the opening of the "the temple of the tabernacle of testimony in heaven" (Rev 15:5, NASB).[45] This vision seems to parallel the events in Rev 11:19, in which the temple in heaven opens to reveal the ark of the covenant.[46] While the ark of the covenant receives much attention in the Pentateuch and the writings of the former prophets, it is almost completely absent from the rest of Scripture, appearing only twice in the NT. Thus it is especially significant that one of its two NT appearances occurs in Rev 11:19.[47] The ark of the covenant was the most sacred and essential furnishing of the tabernacle and temple. It was the first object mentioned in God's blueprint (Exod 25:10–22), for it was to be the focal point of God's presence among his

---

45 The fact that John refers specifically to the tabernacle is significant in itself. Other than an occurrence within the recollection of Israel's history in Acts 7 and the discussion of Christ as the typological fulfillment of the tabernacle in Heb 9, the tabernacle is rarely mentioned in the NT. It seems clear that John was intentionally drawing the reader's attention back to the wilderness and the tabernacle's role in the Israelites' sojourn. M. J. Harris, "Tent, Tabernacle (σκηνή)," *NIDNTT* 3:811–816.

46 Osborne, *Revelation*, 569. It is also possible that this imagery may hearken back to the moment of Jesus' death, in which the veil of the temple was torn in two as a symbol of judgment (cf. Matt 27:51 par.). In both Rev 11 and Matt 27, the opening of the temple is accompanied by an earthquake.

47 Robert A. Briggs, *Jewish Temple Imagery in the Book of Revelation*, Studies in Biblical Literature 10 (Peter Lang, 1999), 92–93. The only other NT reference to the ark of the covenant occurs in Heb 9:4.

people, the depiction of his power and authority in the Israelite camp. The ark served to remind the people that they had no king but Yahweh. It was carried before the Israelites into battle, reassuring them that Yahweh himself went before them. For John, as well as his Jewish readers, the reference to the ark of the covenant would immediately call to mind God's awesome power against Israel's enemies, his holy presence dwelling among his chosen people, and the regular atonement of the nation's sins on the annual Day of Atonement (Lev 16).[48]

The use of exodus typology in Rev 15:5 becomes clearer through the accompanying description of the temple as "the tabernacle of testimony," an obvious verbal allusion to the tabernacle. In the wilderness, the tabernacle was customarily referred to as the "tent of witness" or "tabernacle of testimony" (Exod 27:21; cf. Exod 30:36; 33:7; 40:26, 34–35),[49] due to the fact that it contained the ark of the covenant and the "two tablets of the testimony" which Moses received at Sinai (Exod 32:15; Deut 10:5).[50] As in the exodus, "God is about to reveal his just will from his heavenly dwelling place by sending forth judgments on the earth against those who reject his testimony."[51]

The seven angels whom John observed having the seven plagues in Rev 15:1 now proceed from the sanctuary, adorned in "pure, bright linen, with golden sashes around their chests" (Rev 15:6), attire which connects them to the vision of "one like a son of man" in Rev 1:12–16. There are indications that the multi-faceted description of this celestial figure is intended to set forth the high-priestly function of Christ. The garments in Rev 1:13—a long robe (ποδήρη) and a golden sash—are particularly reminiscent of the priestly vestments designed for Aaron and his sons for their ministry in the tabernacle (a coat of fine linen and sash embroidered with needlework; Exod 28:39–43). In the LXX, the term ποδήρης ("long robe") always refers to the garment of the High Priest.[52] Like the "one like a son of man," the angels in Rev 15:5 are rep-

---

48 Plastaras, *God of Exodus*, 266–268. Yahweh's presence was primarily linked to the cover of the ark, also called the mercy seat (כַּפֹּרֶת, Exod 25:17), which seemed to function as a throne. It was above this cover that "the heavenly met the earthly in the mediation of the revelation and in the forgiving divine grace." Edward R. Dalglish, *The Great Deliverance: A Concise Exposition of the Book of Exodus* (Broadman, 1977), 117; Spatafora, *God as the Temple*, 27.

49 According to Beale, of the approximately 140 occurrences of this phrase in the Greek OT, 130 are found in Exodus through Deuteronomy, 34 of which occur in Exod 27:21–40:35. Beale, *Revelation*, 801.

50 Mounce, *Revelation*, 289; Oecumenius, *Apocalypsin* 15.5–16.1, in Weinrich, *Revelation*, 241; etc.

51 Beale, *Revelation*, 802; Smalley, *Revelation*, 390. According to Mounce, this emphasizes that "the final plagues come from the presence of God and are the expression of his unalterable opposition to sin." Mounce, *Revelation*, 289.

52 While the attire is not identical, the similarities are clear, and both function to set the

resentatives of God, exuding holiness and glory and tasked with pouring out his judgment on the earth.[53]

According to John's vision, when the angels receive the seven golden bowls full of God's wrath, the sanctuary filled with the smoke of God's glory and power, and no one was allowed to enter into the tabernacle until the seven plagues were poured out (Rev 15:7–8). This scene is distinctly similar to those occasions throughout the OT in which God's presence in the form of a cloud or smoke restricts entry into the tabernacle or temple (Exod 40:34–35; 1 Kgs 8:10–11; 2 Chr 5:13; Isa 6:1,4). This strengthens the priestly interpretation of the seven angels, for in the OT, it is the priests who were unable to stand in the presence of God's glory.[54] According to Beale, while all of these OT scenes are drawn to mind by the imagery here, the immediate context may specifically refer to Ezek 10:2–4, in which a scene of judgment is introduced by the appearance of an angelic being clothed in linen and the cloud of God's glory filling the temple.[55]

The correlation between the temple filling with God's glory and the ensuing judgment poured out upon the earth certainly seems to highlight the connection with Ezekiel in this final image of Rev 15. Yet given the exodus typology imbedded throughout the broader context, it is equally likely that John is using a "collective echo" of similar OT scenes, the first of which takes place during the broader exodus event. This particular vision—seven angels attired in the priestly garments lined out in Exod 28, holding judgments described as "plagues," prohibited from entering the "temple, namely the tabernacle of witness" due to the presence of the cloud of God's glory—occurs immediately after the conquerors are seen standing by (or on) the sea singing the "song of Moses and the song of the Lamb," a song with clear thematic correlations to the hymn sung by the Israelites after crossing the Red Sea. Immediately after this vision, the exodus typology escalates as the seven bowl judgments are described through the paradigm of the plagues sent upon Egypt. The cumulative effect is one in which the reader cannot help but recognize the influence of the exodus events.

---

figure apart from the people and to symbolize his purity and position. The high priestly office of "the one like a son of man" is further reinforced by the presence of the seven lampstands (Rev 1:12), as it was the High Priest's duty to set up and tend the lamps which were part of the temple and tabernacle furniture (Num 8:1–3). While this vision is a composite of numerous OT allusions (including Ezekiel, Judges, and especially Dan 7, 10), one cannot discount the presence of temple and priestly imagery in John's depiction of the risen Christ. Prigent, *Apocalypse of St. John*, 134–136; Boxall, *Revelation of Saint John*, 221; etc.

53 Beale, *Revelation*, 804; Osborne, *Revelation*, 570.
54 Beale, *Revelation*, 807.
55 Beale and McDonough, "Revelation," 1134; Osborne, *Revelation*, 571.

## The Sinai Theophany

Revelation's wilderness imagery is not limited to the obvious structural allusion to the Israelites' journey in the wilderness (Rev 12), the significant verbal allusion to God's provision and protection in the wilderness as eschatological blessings in a scene reminiscent of the Feast of Tabernacles (Rev 7:9–17), and the reference to the ark of the covenant (Rev 11:19) and tabernacle/temple imagery (e.g., Rev 15:5–8). Apart from these passages, the Apocalypse contains several possible allusions to the Sinai theophany and the events that took place at the mountain, which are perhaps less significant but still contribute to the overall impact of exodus typology upon the book.

At the beginning of the covenant ceremony at Mount Sinai, a critical juncture in the formation of Israel, Yahweh vowed, "if you will indeed obey my voice and keep my covenant, you shall be my treasured possession among all peoples, for all the earth is mine; and you shall be to me a kingdom of priests and a holy nation" (Exod 19:5–6). These words were God's pledge to a people who would trust him and obey his commandments. The Israelites were to become "a community of persons invested with the powers of sovereignty,"[56] a body of priests in daily communion with the one true God. Three times within the Apocalypse, John recalls this promise and applies it to believers in Christ by alluding to the phrase "a kingdom of priests" (βασίλειον ἱεράτευμα, Exod 19:6 LXX). In Rev 5:9–10, a passage already established as being fraught with exodus typology and significant in determining the paschal nature of Revelation's Lamb, the inhabitants of the throne room worship the one who has "made them a kingdom and priests to our God" (βασιλείαν καὶ ἱερεῖς). Likewise, in the prologue, John refers to his readers as "a kingdom, priests to his God and Father" (βασιλείαν, ἱερεῖς), a status granted by the one who has "freed us from our sins by his blood" (Rev 1:5–6). In both texts, "the redemption from among humankind of a people to become a kingdom and priests to God is effected by the sacrifice of the Lamb and is presented in a pattern moulded by the Exodus tradition of redemption."[57]

The final example of the royal, priestly promise occurs in Rev 20:6—"they will be priests (ἱερεῖς) of God and of Christ, and they will reign (βασιλεύσουσιν)

---

56 James Murphy, *A Critical and Exegetical Commentary on the Book of Exodus* (1868; reprint, James Publications, 1979), 207 (page citations are to the reprint edition); Steven J. Friesen, *Imperial Cults and the Apocalypse of John: Reading Revelation in the Ruins* (Oxford University Press, 2001), 181.

57 Jay Casey, "The Exodus Theme in the Book of Revelation against the Background of the New Testament," in *Exodus: A Lasting Paradigm*, ed. Antonius G. Weiler, Marcus Lefébure,- & Bastiaan Martinus Franciscus van Iersel (T&T Clark, 1987), 35–36.

with him for a thousand years." While the immediate context of this passage does not necessarily invoke images of the exodus, the cumulative effect of the three allusions to Exod 19:6 provides persuasive evidence toward that end. This repeated description of the church calls to mind the ritual purity of the priests, denoting believers as a holy people set apart from the world for worship and service to God, a concept that is supported in the final few chapters of the Apocalypse. The picture of "his name ... on their foreheads" (Rev 22:4) brings to mind the words "Holy to the Lord" which the High Priest bore on his forehead as he served in the tabernacle (Exod 28:36–38).[58] It is possible that the overwhelming similarities between the twelve precious stones on the city walls (Rev 21:18–21) and those on the priestly breastplate (Exod 28:17–20) imply that followers of the Lamb are to act as priests to the rest of humankind.[59] John does not neglect the regal aspect of this promise, however; in this final allusion to Exod 19:6 he shifts the emphasis to kingship by separating the two elements, proclaiming that believers will participate in the dominion of the victorious Son of Man.[60] The culmination of John's vision is a kingdom in which "every knee will bow ... and that every tongue will confess that Jesus Christ is Lord" (Phil 2:10–11, NASB), and those who trust in Christ will reign with him forever (Rev 22:5).

Along with allusions to Exod 19:6, John's primary means of recalling the events at Mount Sinai appears in the use of theophanic elements. Following Moses' instructions, the Israelites prepared to meet with Yahweh at Sinai through consecration and cleansing (Exod 19:14–15). On the third morning, "there were thunders and lightnings and a thick cloud on the mountain and a very loud trumpet blast.... Mount Sinai was wrapped in smoke because the Lord had descended on it in fire ... and the whole mountain trembled greatly" (Exod 19:16, 18).[61] Throughout Scripture, theophanic elements signify the visible or audible presence and glory of the holy God among his people. This

---

58 David Mathewson, *A New Heaven and a New Earth: The Meaning and Function of the Old Testament in Revelation 21:1–22:5*, JSNTSup 238 (JSOT, 2003), 208–209; Margaret Barker, *The Great High Priest: The Temple Roots of Christian Liturgy* (T&T Clark, 2003), 79, 139.

59 Michael Gilbertson, *God and History in the Book of Revelation: New Testament Studies in Dialogue with Pannenberg and Moltmann* (Cambridge University Press, 2003), 192. Isaiah 54:11–12 also alludes to the twelve stones in the breastplate in its reference to the foundations of the new Jerusalem. "In addition, the appearance of the stones from the breastplate in the future restored Jerusalem (Rev. 21:18–20) may reflect the tradition of the stones from the highpriest's breastplate being kept safe until the future when their function would be restored (*2 Apoc. Bar* 6:7–9; *LAB 26:12*; *b. Sota* 49b)." David Mathewson, "Assessing Old Testament Allusions in the Book of Revelation," *EvQ* 75 (2003): 323–324.

60 Friesen, *Imperial Cults*, 181–182; Dumbrell, *End of the Beginning*, 159.

61 While the MT states "and the whole mountain trembled greatly," the Greek in contrast reads "and all the people were greatly amazed" (Exod 19:18).

can be seen in several ways in the exodus experience alone—e.g., the burning bush which Moses encountered on Mount Horeb (Exod 3), the pillar of cloud and fire guiding the Israelites out of Egypt into the wilderness (Exod 13:21–22), and the cloud of glory filling the tabernacle (Exod 40:34–35). This same symbolism can be found in the NT in the cloud overshadowing the disciples on the Mount of Transfiguration (Mark 9:7–8; Matt 17:5–6; Luke 9:34–36), the earthquake at the moment of Jesus' death (Matt 27:45–54),[62] and the tongues of fire filling the believers with the Spirit at Pentecost (Acts 2:1–4).

Likewise, within the Apocalypse certain theophanic elements accompany the appearance of divine figures. In Rev 1, the Son of Man is introduced by a "loud voice like a trumpet" (Rev 1:10), while in the throne room vision, "flashes of lightning, and rumblings and peals of thunder" proceed from the throne of God (Rev 4:5). Just before Christ returns on the white horse for the final battle against the dragon's minions (Rev 19:11), John hears "what seemed to be the voice of a great multitude ... like the sound of mighty peals of thunder" crying out in praise of God's might and glory (Rev 19:6), while the mighty angel in Rev 10 comes "down from heaven, wrapped in a cloud, with a rainbow over his head, and his face was like the sun, and his legs like pillars of fire" (Rev 10:1). This combination of the cloud (νεφέλην) and "pillars of fire" (στῦλοι πυρός) calls to mind God's presence guiding the Israelites out of Egypt and protecting them in the wilderness with "the pillar of cloud by day and the pillar of fire by night" (ὁ στῦλος τῆς νεφέλης ἡμέρας καὶ ὁ στῦλος τοῦ πυρὸς νυκτός, Exod 13:22 LXX). God's faithfulness resounds with the addition of the rainbow (Gen 9:16); God has been faithful to deliver the Israelites from their suffering; the angel in Revelation anticipates that he will continue to honor his covenant with those who follow him.[63]

Even more significant is the strong verbal allusion to the Sinai events through the collective and escalating use of theophanic elements following the seventh seal, trumpet, and bowl judgments. As the seventh seal concludes, one of the angels who stands before God fills a censer with fire from the altar and throws it on the earth, bringing about "peals of thunder, rumblings, flashes of lightning, and an earthquake" (Rev 8:5). This storm theophany recurs at the close of the trumpet judgments with the addition of "heavy hail" and the

---

62 At the moment Jesus gave up his spirit, an earthquake caused the rocks to split, the temple veil to rip in two, and the tombs to open. Upon witnessing these events, the centurion and those keeping watch over Jesus were filled with awe and acknowledged, "Truly this was the Son of God!"

63 Beale, *Revelation*, 525. The angel promises "that in the days of the trumpet call to be sounded by the seventh angel, the mystery of God would be fulfilled, just as he announced to his servants the prophets" (Rev 10:7).

rare glimpse of the ark of the covenant (Rev 11:19). Once more the scene is repeated at the culmination of the seventh bowl, when a loud voice from the temple proclaims, "It is done!" Here, the earthquake is described as "a great earthquake such as there had never been since man was on the earth," and the hailstones weigh in at "one hundred pounds each" (Rev 16:17–21). There is no question that Yahweh is in charge—it is his presence, majesty, and glory that is at work in bringing about judgment upon the earth. In each case, "the emphasis of the storm imagery is on the eschaton as God is in process of bringing the history of this world to a close."[64]

One final instance of Revelation's use of wilderness imagery is the list of vices found in Rev 21:8, which includes several parallels with the Ten Commandments (Exod 20:1–17). Both lists include murder (Rev 21:8; Exod 20:15 LXX), sexual immorality (Rev 21:8; Exod 20:13 LXX), idolatry (Rev 21:8; Exod 20:4–6 LXX), and lying (Rev 21:8; Exod 20:16 LXX). At the very least, Rev 21:8 reflects an early Christian use of the Ten Commandments as stipulations of appropriate behavior for believers.[65] Yet the relationship between these two lists extends beyond a mere verbal connection. It is not insignificant that both inventories occur immediately prior to a detailed vision of the "dwelling place of God," both of which were received upon a mountain. Directly after the list of vices in Revelation, John is carried away "to a great, high mountain" (Rev 21:10) where he is shown the majesty of the heavenly city, complete with measurements and materials (Rev 21:10–21), in a scene reminiscent of Yahweh prescribing to Moses the blueprint for the tabernacle on Mount Sinai following the giving of the Ten Commandments (Exod 25–27). The "ten words" were an integral part of the Sinai experience, principles guiding not only Israel's fellowship with their God, but also their relationships with one another and the world as a whole.[66] Revelation 21:8 likewise establishes guidelines for the followers of God by presenting an account of those men who will have no place in the New Jerusalem and who will spend an eternity devoid of any fellowship with the Almighty God.

---

64 Osborne, *Revelation*, 347. Certainly, other OT theophanies have resemblances to the events at Sinai and those recorded throughout Revelation. For example, Ps 18 describes David's rescue from Saul in very similar theophanic imagery (Ps 18:7–19). This does not discount the Sinai connections, however, when one considers the cumulative picture of exodus/wilderness imagery within the Apocalypse.

65 Mathewson, *New Heaven and a New Earth*, 91; David E. Aune, *Revelation 17–22*, WBC 52c (Thomas Nelson, 1998), 1131. The Ten Commandments appear to also be in mind in Rev 22:15, which likewise lists those outside the city gates as "dogs and sorcerers and the sexually immoral and murderers and idolaters, and everyone who loves and practices falsehood."

66 John I. Durham, *Understanding the Basic Themes of Exodus*, Quick-Reference Bible Topics (Word, 1990), 60; Dumbrell, *End of the Beginning*, 42.

## "The Face of God"

Throughout the book of Exodus, readers are confronted with the fact that Yahweh is actively present in and among his chosen people. The exodus was the crucial experience in the history of Israel, for it was in these events that Israel came to know Yahweh as the God who is truly present.[67] At the risk of sounding sermonic, it can be maintained that God's presence was displayed in Exodus through his power in protecting and delivering the Israelites, his provision throughout the wilderness wanderings, and the privileged relationship established at Mount Sinai. The goal of the entire exodus episode is found in the statement, "I will dwell among the people of Israel and will be their God. And they shall know that I am the Lord their God, who brought them out of the land of Egypt that I might dwell among them. I am the Lord their God" (Exod 29:45–46).[68]

Perhaps one phrase sums up the presence of Yahweh in both Exodus and Revelation—"the face of God." Aware of the awesome power of God, Moses vacillates between a fear of looking at God and a desire to see his glory. His initial reaction upon realizing that he was in the presence of Yahweh in the burning bush episode was to hide his face, afraid to see God (Exod 3:6). Fear was the typical response to the overwhelming intensity of an encounter with the divine presence—"the unique, transcendent, supernatural holiness of the Divine Presence is an experience felt to be almost beyond the human capacity to endure."[69] The Israelites had a similar reaction when God merely spoke to them at Mount Sinai (Exod 20:18–21). Yet later, emboldened by his dialogue with the living God, Moses made a dramatic request to see God's glory (Exod 33:18). In what may be the most intimate, exceptional experience of God by an individual in Scripture, Yahweh agreed to pass before Moses in all his glory; at the same time he prepared for Moses' protection, saying, "You cannot see my face, for man shall not see me and live" (Exod 33:20). Thus Yahweh hid Moses in the cleft of the rock, covering him with his hand so that Moses could see only his back. Moses responded in the only manner appropriate after an encounter with God's presence—he fell prostrate on the ground in worship (Exod 34:8).[70]

---

67 Augustine Stock, *The Way in the Wilderness: Exodus, Wilderness, and Moses Themes in Old Testament and New* (Liturgical Press, 1969), 18; Durham, *Basic Themes of Exodus*, 5.

68 Antonius Gerardus Weiler and Marcus Lefébure, eds., *Exodus—A Lasting Paradigm* (T&T Clark, 1987), 20.

69 Nahum M. Sarna, *Exploring Exodus: The Origins of Biblical Israel* (1986; repr., Pantheon Books, 1996), 45; Samuel Terrien, *The Elusive Presence: The Heart of Biblical Theology* (Harper & Row, 1978), 112.

70 Durham, *Basic Themes of Exodus*, 75–76; Lester Meyer, *The Message of Exodus: A Theo-*

In Revelation, the divine presence and power also results in both fear and the desire for a closer relationship. Upon first sight of the "one like a son of man" (Rev 1:13), John, too, "fell at his feet as though dead" (Rev 1:17). Being well versed in the OT Scriptures, John was aware that man could not look on the face of God and still live. In Isaiah's vision of the Lord, he, too, cried out, "Woe is me ... for my eyes have seen the King, the Lord of hosts" (Isa 6:5). It is possible that John's experience is patterned after Daniel 10, for his reaction to the vision is similar to Daniel's response to the angelic figure (Dan 10:7–9).[71] In both instances the seer is told, "fear not" (μὴ φοβοῦ, Dan 10:12 LXX; Rev 1:17). Yet Daniel is not permitted to look upon the face of Yahweh. The eschatological promise is not yet fulfilled.

Within the Apocalypse, however, the prohibition against seeing the face of God is finally lifted. The divine figure in John's vision is none other than the risen Christ. He is identified as such by the repeated use of the phrase, "I am," (possibly derived from the OT personal name of God; compare the "I am" sayings by Jesus in the Gospel of John) as well as reference to other divine attributes in the statement, "I am the first and the last, and the living one. I died, and behold I am alive forevermore, and I have the keys of Death and Hades" (Rev 1:17–18).[72] John is permitted to witness more of God's glory than any man before him, including a vision of the eschatological presence of God. More significantly, we are told that in the end, those who dwell in the New Jerusalem "will see His face" (Rev 22:4), thereby reversing that which was denied to Moses at Mount Sinai (Exod 33:20, 23). Seeing God's face constituted the highest expression of Yahweh's presence among his people, the eschatological goal of the worshiping people throughout Scripture, which is ultimately reached in Revelation with the saints serving God face to face.[73]

---

*logical Commentary* (Augsburg, 1983), 161–162. "Prostration to the earth was a frequent reaction of those who received visions and the accompanying supernatural manifestations (cf. Ezek. 1:28; 3:23; 9:8; 11:13; 43:3; 44:4; Dan. 2:46; 8:17; 10:9; Matt. 17:6; Luke 5:8; Acts 26:14)." Robert L. Thomas, *Revelation 1–7: An Exegetical Commentary*, ed. Kenneth Barker (Moody, 1992), 109.

71 Thomas, *Revelation 1–7*, 109. Certainly the description of the heavenly being in Rev 1 is woven together of images from Dan 7 and 10. Scholars are divided on the identity of the heavenly figure in Dan 10, as the description is appropriate to depict an angel or the preincarnate Christ. According to Lucas, however, "it is generally assumed that the being in question is Gabriel, as in Dan. 8–9, but this is not made explicit." Ernest Lucas, *Daniel*, ApOTC (InterVarsity, 2002), 275; Alexander A. Di Lella, *The Book of Daniel*, AB 23 (DoubleDay, 1978), 279–280; etc.

72 Thomas, *Revelation 1–7*, 110–11; Christopher R. Seitz, *Figured Out: Typology and Providence in Christian Scripture* (Westminster John Knox, 2001), 137–138.

73 Mathewson, *New Heaven and a New Earth*, 206–207. Note another interesting parallel—when Moses descended the mountain after this divine encounter, "his face shone (δεδόξασται, from δοξάζω) because he had been talking with God" (Exod 34:29). This visible manifestation of God's presence is sometimes called the shekhinah glory. Likewise, John sees

## The Wilderness—A Summary

The sojourn in the wilderness following the exodus from Egypt was a time in which the Israelites encountered Yahweh in unique and powerful ways. His power protected them from their enemies, both at the Red Sea and beyond. His provision of food and water sustained them in their time of need. Most importantly, the Israelites repeatedly experienced the visible manifestation of his presence in the pillar of cloud and fire, the Sinai theophany, and the tabernacle. In response, the Israelites made a covenant to follow God's commandments and Yahweh pledged to make them a kingdom of priests, his treasured possession. In Revelation, John imbeds his vision of eschatological deliverance with each of these wilderness connotations, making it clear that the power, provision, and presence of God is constant—the same yesterday, today, and tomorrow.

It has been asserted that the goal of the entire exodus experience was the presence of God dwelling among his people, and that goal extends throughout Scripture. While the tabernacle was the scene of Israelite worship in the wilderness, and the Jerusalem temple seemed to identify the dwelling place of God's presence under the old covenant, the Gospel of John emphasizes Jesus Christ as the new temple. In the new covenant, the majesty associated with the OT temple and tabernacle is now manifested in Jesus, in whom the glory of God had "tabernacled" (John 1:14). Through the resurrection of Christ and the power of the Holy Spirit, God is present in and among believers, in whom full access to God is eschatologically realized. Thus in Revelation, the new temple is conspicuously absent in the New Jerusalem; John plainly states that there is no temple in the New Jerusalem, "for the Lord God Almighty and the Lamb are its temple" (Rev 21:22, NIV). The entire heavenly city is the dwelling place of God, the Holy of Holies, the center of universal worship and the symbol of unity under divine kingship. The people of God finally experience his presence dwelling among them as he promised during the exodus, and as they only glimpsed in the wilderness.

---

the New Jerusalem, the place in which God's presence will dwell among man (Rev 21:3), "coming down out of heaven from God, having the glory (δόξαν) of God" (Rev 21:10–11).

CHAPTER 8

# HERMENEUTICAL SIGNIFICANCE AND ANALYSIS OF REVELATION'S EXODUS TYPOLOGY

WE HAVE NOW REACHED the point where it is possible (and indeed, necessary) to engage in hermeneutical analysis of all that has been discussed thus far. It is not enough simply to make observations about how images, ideas, events, and traditions from the exodus experience appear throughout the Apocalypse, without also asking the "so what?" questions. If the study does not enlighten our understanding of John's purpose in employing exodus typology, clarify his rhetorical goals in writing the Apocalypse, illuminate the complex symbolism for which Revelation is known, or reveal how exodus typology ties together the Scriptural portrait of salvation history, it has been in vain.

As shown in the previous three chapters, John's typological employment of exodus imagery is pervasive, incorporating verbal, thematic, and structural parallels from every stage of the exodus experience, most especially the ten plagues, the Passover, and the wilderness sojourn. This exodus influence can be noted throughout the entire text of Revelation at strategic structural junctures, including the letters to the churches (Rev 2–3), the throne room vision (Rev 4–5), the trumpet and bowl judgments on God's enemies (Rev 8–9, 16), the sealing of believers (Rev 7), the destruction of Babylon and the Marriage Supper of the Lamb (Rev 17–19), and the inauguration of the New Heaven and New Earth (Rev 21–22). Indeed, John unified his revelation by employing exodus typology in each of the four visions (Rev 1:9–3:22; 4:1–16:21; 17:1–21:8; 21:9–22:5) which make up the Apocalypse.[1] The frequency, contextual significance, and theological relevance of exodus typology within Revelation combine to

---

1 The Apocalypse actually consists of four distinct visions, plus a prologue (Rev 1:1–8) and epilogue (Rev 22:6–21). The visions can be identified by an introductory formula including identification of the recipient, a change of location, a loud voice (missing from visions 3 and 4), and a reference to the Spirit such as "I was in the Spirit" (ἐγενόμην ἐν πνεύματι) or "he carried me

enhance the reader's appreciation and understanding of John's visions. It is clear that John's use of exodus imagery is neither haphazard nor accidental, but instead is structured, purposeful, and significant to his rhetorical program. Indeed, one could identify exodus typology as one of the primary hermeneutical axioms upon which the book of Revelation stands.

### Theme and Purpose: Allegiance in a Compromising and Persecuted World

Much has been said about the purpose and theme(s) of the Apocalypse. The traditional, long-accepted view is that John wrote Revelation to encourage believers to remain steadfast during a time of pervasive and horrific persecution of Christians under the emperor Domitian.[2] It is true that first-century Rome was intensely idolatrous, with an abundance of mystery religions, pagan cults, and Olympian deities, as well as a developing imperial cult which may have reached its pinnacle during Domitian's reign.[3] John himself was in a sense a victim of persecution; he identifies himself as a "brother and partner in the tribulation and the kingdom and the patient endurance that are in Jesus" and claims that his exile was "on account of the word of God and the testimony of Jesus" (Rev 1:9). Yet the existence of widespread, official Roman

---

away in the Spirit" (ἀπήνεγκέν με ... ἐν πνεύματι). Compare Rev 1:9–10; 4:1–2; 17:1–3, and 21:9–10. G. K. Beale, *The Book of Revelation*, NIGTC (Eerdmans, 1999), 111.

2 Revelation "is a book written for the consolation and encouragement of Christians suffering persecution, in order to assure them that their oppressors will be judged and they will be vindicated in the end." Richard Bauckham, *The Theology of the Book of Revelation*, New Testament Theology (Cambridge University Press, 1993), 15. Most scholars claim that Revelation was written in the last third of the first century AD, between the beginning of the reign of Nero (AD 54–68) and the end of Domitian's reign (AD 81–96). Grant R. Osborne, *Revelation*, BECNT (Baker, 2002), 6–9; cf. Ian Boxall, *The Revelation of Saint John*, BNTC 19 (Hendrickson, 2009), 13.

3 Marvin C. Pate, ed. *Four Views on the Book of Revelation* (Zondervan, 1998), 139; William Bert Tolar, "Re-Evaluation of the Evidences that the Domitianic Persecutions Served as the Background for the Book of Revelation" (ThD thesis, Southwestern Baptist Theological Seminary, 1966), 118–124. As a rule, Roman emperors were not deified until their death. While temples were commonly built to worship deceased emperors during the first century, it was rare for living emperors to be worshiped as divine. However, many scholars recognize within Domitian an arrogant claim of divinity, as indicated by the construction of the temple of Sebastoi in Ephesus and its dedication to the worship of Domitian during his lifetime, the two months of the year which he named after himself, various coins bearing the image of his deified son and the title "*Deus et Dominus*," and the use of this same title in writing and personal address. The title *Dominus* was not in itself offensive or unusual, as it conveyed nothing of autocratic mastery; "it was the lengths to which Domitian went in insisting on respect and reverence that finally offended Roman dignity." Pat Southern, *Domitian: Tragic Tyrant* (Indiana University Press, 1997), 45; J. Daryl Charles, "Imperial Pretensions and the Throne-Vision of the Lamb: Observations on the Function of Revelation 5," *CTR* 7 (1993): 93; Steven J. Friesen, *Imperial Cults and the Apocalypse of John: Reading Revelation in the Ruins* (Oxford University Press, 2001), 147–148; etc.

persecution during the time of Domitian is a matter of significant debate for which there is no conclusive evidence. At the same time, as Lewis insightfully states, "the fact that the persecutions of Domitian's reign are not officially reported should not surprise us at all. Oppressive governments certainly do not label their actions in a negative fashion or draw attention to them."[4]

Whether or not the persecution of Christians was an official Roman practice at the time Revelation was written, there was clearly social and economic pressure on first-century Christians to participate to some degree in the trade guilds, cultic practices, and imperial worship that was a part of daily Roman life (Rev 13:15; 20:4).[5] Rome allowed Judaism the distinct privilege of being a permitted religion, exempting them from the imperial cult and allowing them the right to observe their legal tradition and gather for worship at the synagogue. As the Christian church grew predominantly more Gentile, it became increasingly separated from Judaism and less tolerated in the eyes of Roman law. This resulted in a certain amount of assimilation to the culture and the temptation to compromise the truth of the Gospel, as believers either returned to the synagogues to gain the freedom which Judaism offered or engaged in pagan customs without recognizing the spiritual danger they faced. Thus, many scholars have determined that the Apocalypse was actually intended to jolt accommodating Christians "back into the reality of their faith and the seriousness of their sin by telling them that they could not be loyal to two masters but only one. The false teachers who were teaching that Christians could identify with pagan cults and still be considered faithful had to be refuted."[6]

It is not necessary to choose between persecution and spiritual assimilation as the historical background of Revelation. Indeed, as DeSilva suggests, both situations are true; "each different audience ... will continue to deepen its reading of its own situation and options" in light of Revelation's demand for faithfulness to the cause of Christ.[7] As the early Christians faced the

---

4 Scott M. Lewis, *What Are They Saying about New Testament Apocalyptic?* (Paulist: 2004), 59. According to Beale, "a viable middle position can be taken with respect to the debate concerning the situation of persecution. All agree that oppression of Christians had been sporadic before John wrote. But John may foresee not only that persecution will intensify in the future but also that it is already in the process of slowly intensifying to some degree." Beale, *Revelation*, 29.

5 Osborne, *Revelation*, 11.

6 Beale, *Revelation*, 30; Lewis, *New Testament Apocalyptic*, 57–59; John Benjamin Lawrence, *New Heaven and a New Earth: A Contemporary Interpretation of the Book of Revelation* (American, 1960), 38–39.

7 David A. DeSilva, "Final Topics: The Rhetorical Functions of Intertexture in Revelation 14:14–16:21," in *The Intertexture of Apocalyptic Discourse in the New Testament*, ed. Duane F. Watson, SBL Symposium Series 14 (SBL, 2002), 219–220. For Beale, "John's purpose in writing is,

dilemma of compromising their beliefs and forsaking Christ or persevering in their faith despite the tyranny of oppression, the Apocalypse serves both as a comforting balm for those experiencing persecution and as a rallying cry to Christians to be so faithful that they find themselves the subjects of such persecution.[8] This twofold purpose is demonstrated in the seven letters to the churches (Rev 2–3), which contain both praise and encouragement for churches that withstood the demand to worship Caesar (Smyrna and Philadelphia) and warnings to those that failed to remain entirely faithful to God (Ephesus, Pergamum, Thyatira, Sardis, and Laodicea).

MOTIF OF IMITATION AND FRAUD

It is possible that the worship of the antichrist portrayed in Revelation is reminiscent of the emperor worship of the first century. Yet striking similarities also exist between the historical setting of Revelation and the Israelites' circumstances in Egypt. John understood the present and future persecution as an element of continuity with the history of the people of God, in which powers of oppression and injustice that appeared to be in command were overthrown by the saving work of God. Clearly, John was canonically oriented, setting his Apocalypse within the context of God's mighty acts of history, drawing upon the entire canon up to that point, and utilizing OT imagery to portray both the present and eschatological action of God. It is not surprising, then, that the OT texts John alludes to most frequently are associated with God's sovereign deliverance of his people, whether actual or anticipated. Thus, while the worship of the antichrist within Revelation does bring to mind the imperial cult, it is also related to the worship of Pharaoh in the days of the exodus.[9] The Egyptian civilization during the exodus and the society portrayed in the Apocalypse are connected by the worship of idols and the claims of deity by false gods.[10] This link is reinforced by the prevalence of imitation and fraud

---

therefore, to encourage those not compromising with idolatry to continue in that stance and to jolt those who are compromising out of their spiritual anesthesia so that they will perceive the spiritual danger they are in and repent and become witnesses to the risen Christ as Lord. For those who never respond, only judgment will ensue…. Therefore, the focus of the book is exhortation to the church community to witness to Christ in the midst of a compromising, idolatrous church and world." Beale, *Revelation*, 33.

    8 Boxall, *Revelation*, 13. Osborne describes the future portrayed in the Apocalypse as "a counterreality to the prevailing reality of the Roman world, a transcendent realm in which the people of God are part of a counterculture and are willing to suffer for it." Osborne, *Revelation*, 11.

    9 M. Eugene Boring, "The Theology of Revelation: 'The Lord Our God the Almighty Reigns,'" *Interpretation* 40 (1986): 263.

    10 The Egyptians did not accept Yahweh as the one true God, for theirs was a world of

throughout Revelation, a motif which carries over from the exodus and highlights God's complete authority over nature and every being in heaven and on earth. This theme of deception appears at critical moments throughout Revelation, often in conjunction with John's use of exodus typology.

The first title given to Jesus in the Apocalypse is "the faithful witness" (Rev 1:5). Yet the beast is consistently depicted throughout Revelation as a fraud who imitates the actions and persona of the almighty God, assumes divine characteristics, disguises himself as the true bearer of power and authority, and confuses people into worshiping a false god. Indeed, Revelation outright identifies the dragon as the "deceiver of the whole world" (Rev 12:9). John consistently contrasts the influence of the dragon and the beast, based on deception and force, with the authority of God and the Lamb, founded on God's nature as creator and on Jesus' redeeming sacrifice.[11]

Imitation is clearly found within the sixth bowl judgment, one of Revelation's most creative examples of exodus imagery, in which demonic spirits that look like frogs spew forth from the mouths of the dragon, the beast, and the false prophet (Rev 16:13).[12] The signs performed by the frogs are an arrogant display of fraudulent power and imitation and a clever use of exodus typology, recalling the fact that the plague of frogs was one of two that Pharaoh's magicians were able to reproduce through their "secret arts" (Exod 8:7).[13] Yet fraudulent signs are not limited to the demonic frog-like spirits. The primary action of the beast is to deceive those who dwell on earth and cause men to worship him (Rev 19:20),[14] a feat that is accomplished through the great signs

---

idolatry and a culture of innumerable deities. Pharaoh was widely believed to be the "guarantor of the fertility of the land, defeator of the forces of chaos, divine celebrant of the cult, upholder of the order of the universe," attracting and eventually demanding the worship of his people. Donald B. Redford, *The Ancient Gods Speak: A Guide to Egyptian Religion* (Oxford University Press, 2002), 366; Robert Kirk Kilpatrick, "Against the Gods of Egypt: An Examination of the Narrative of the Ten Plagues in the Light of Exodus 12:12" (ThD diss., Mid-America Baptist Theological Seminary, 1995), 3. Tolar describes the Roman religion as influenced by "the Egyptian, Greek, and Oriental practice of deifying kings." Tolar, "Domitianic Persecution," 99.

11 Friesen, *Imperial Cults*, 203–204.

12 The fact that the evil spirits go about "performing signs" (Rev 16:14) reinforces the exodus background, for in ancient Judaism and early Christianity, the concept of "signs" carried an underlying connotation of Yahweh's miraculous deeds during the exodus, executed to demonstrate his sovereign authority. Robert Houston Smith, "Exodus Typology in the Fourth Gospel," *JBL* 81 (1962): 334.

13 It is significant, however, that neither Pharaoh's magicians nor the frog-like spirits in Revelation attempted to stop or reverse the judgments. Their only success was in duplicating the plagues, which in Exodus only worsened their state of affairs and served to undermine the Egyptians' faith in what they accepted as divine. Lester Meyer, *The Message of Exodus: A Theological Commentary* (Augsburg, 1983), 73; Nahum M. Sarna, *Exploring Exodus: The Origins of Biblical Israel* (Schocken Books, 1986; repr., Pantheon Books, 1996), 80.

14 That his fraud is successful in garnering worship is evidenced by their exaltation, "Who is like the beast, and who is able to wage war with him?" (Rev 13:4, NASB), an overt satire of the

he works (Rev 13:12–14). The one sign Revelation mentions outright, namely "making fire come down from heaven to earth in front of people" (Rev 13:13), is itself a pale imitation of several of Yahweh's trumpet and bowl judgments.[15]

The theme of mimicry highlights the distinction between the beast and the one true God. In reading Revelation, one becomes aware of an "unholy trio", made up of "the dragon [Satan] and … the beast and … the false prophet" (Rev 16:13). One need not look far to see this as an imitation of the Holy Trinity. Just as the One on the Throne and the Lamb are worshiped together in Rev 15:3–4 (cf. Rev 4–5), so are the dragon and the beast in Rev 13:4. Like the Lamb who was slain yet lives (Rev 5:6), the beast appears to survive in spite of a mortal wound (Rev 13:12, 14), and this imitation of Christ's resurrection becomes the basis for mankind's worship of the beast (Rev 13:3).[16] The beast rising from the sea in Rev 13:11 even takes on the appearance of a lamb, the only occurrence of ἀρνίον in the Apocalypse which does not refer to Christ.[17] John makes sure to distinguish between the true God and the imposter, revealing the association between Babylon and the beast who "was and is not and is to come (ἦν καὶ οὐκ ἔστιν καὶ παρέσται)" (Rev 17:8). This description parodies the title attributed to both God and Jesus, "who is and who was and who is to come" (ὁ ὢν καὶ ὁ ἦν καὶ ὁ ἐρχόμενος, Rev 1:8; cf. 1:4; 4:8; 11:17; 16:5), which itself may be an allusion to the divine name, "I am who I am" (ἐγώ εἰμι ὁ ὤν), revealed to Moses in Exod 3:14.

The image of the beast created for worship (Rev 13:14–15) is yet another example of imitation and fraud when examined against the backdrop of the golden calf episode (Exod 32). The golden calf functioned as a contrast to the tabernacle in the wilderness, a poor substitute for a divine gift—"Instead of the unique, revolutionary idea of the Divine Word enshrined in the Holy of Holies … there was a profane, plastic image which could easily be recognized as falling within the orbit of paganism."[18] This description could just as easily be attributed to the image of the beast in Revelation. God desires all men to

---

song of the Lamb, in which the saints sing, "Who will not fear, O Lord, and glorify your name? For you alone are holy. All nations will come and worship you, for your righteous acts have been revealed" (Rev 15:3–4). David A. DeSilva, *Seeing Things John's Way: The Rhetoric of the Book of Revelation* (Westminster John Knox, 2009), 201.

15 Trumpet 1, "hail and fire, mixed with blood … thrown upon the earth;" trumpet 2, "something like a great mountain, burning with fire, was thrown into the sea;" bowl 4, "the sun and it was allowed to scorch people with fire."

16 He is "wounded by the sword and yet lived" (Rev 13:14). Mathias Rissi, *Time and History: A Study on the Revelation* (John Knox, 1966), 64–65.

17 Maurice Carrez, "Le Déploiement de la Christologie de l'Agneau dans l'Apocalypse," *RHPR* 79 (1999): 10.

18 Sarna, *Exploring Exodus*, 200–203, 217–219; cf. Richard J. Clifford, "The Tent of El and the Israelite Tent of Meeting," *CBQ* 33 (1971): 226.

worship him freely and abide with him in the land he provides, yet those who dwell on the earth yield to their present desires and worship the graven image rather than waiting for God's awesome provision in the near future.[19]

There is no neutrality in Revelation—one is a follower either of God or of Satan; there is now no middle ground. This is demonstrated by the mark of the beast on unbelievers (Rev 13:17), which functions as an antithetical foil for the sealing of the 144,000.[20] The seal (σφραγίς) is the name of God and of Christ (Rev 14:1), thus linking these servants of God with the victors in Rev 3:12,[21] while the mark (χάραγμα) of the beast is the name of the beast (Rev 13:17).[22] Those who take the mark of the beast are permitted to participate in commerce (Rev 13:16–17), but they are also subject to God's wrath and judgment (Rev 14:9; 16:2) and eternal torment (Rev 14:10–11); those who are sealed as God's servants may undergo temporary persecution at the hands of the beast and his followers (Rev 13:14–17), but ultimately experience the presence of God, dwelling and reigning with him through the millennium and forever (Rev 20:4; 22:5). Thus John purposefully contrasts the sealing of the 144,000 with the mark of the beast in order to impress upon mankind the urgency to choose for all eternity the object of their devotion and allegiance.

THE PLAGUES AND ALLEGIANCE

John's double challenge to his readers—to denounce pagan culture and to remain faithful to Christ in spite of persecution—underscores what may be

---

19 Interestingly, in Exodus those who worshiped the golden calf are killed at the hand of those who are "on the Lord's side" (Exod 32:26–28), whereas in Revelation it is those who refuse to worship the image of the beast who face death (Rev 13:14–15).

20 Osborne, *Revelation*, 310.

21 "The one who conquers, I will make him a pillar in the temple of my God. Never shall he go out of it, and I will write on him the name of my God, and the name of the city of my God, the new Jerusalem, which comes down from my God out of heaven, and my own new name" (Rev 3:12). Beale notes that the covenant background for the joining of God's "seal" and his "name" is Exod 28:11–21, in which the "names of the twelve tribes are written on the stones to name the members of the Israelite covenant community. These twelve stones are called 'seals' (σφραγίς) worn on the high priest's shoulders ... [and] correspond to the 'seal' (σφραγίς) placed on Aaron's *forehead*, which also represented Israel." Beale, *Revelation*, 411–412. Cf. Stephen S. Smalley, *The Revelation to John: A Commentary on the Greek Text of the Apocalypse* (InterVarsity, 2005), 184; Dennis E. Johnson, *Triumph of the Lamb: A Commentary on Revelation* (P & R, 2001), 129; etc.

22 Scholars often note the significantly different vocabulary in these two accounts—the word σφραγίς implies security through the protective authority of God, while the beast's χάραγμα, with its underlying idea of inscription or branding, makes no such guarantee. Ralph P. Martin, "Mark, Brand," *NIDNTT* 2:572–573; Edwin A. Judge, "The Mark of the Beast, Revelation 13:16," *TynBul* 42.1 (1991): 158–160; Johnson, *Triumph of the Lamb*, 130. See chapter 6, "Sealing of the 144,000 (Rev 7:1–8)," for more.

the principal theme within the Apocalypse, namely a call for allegiance to the one true God. It is true that Revelation highlights a number of themes, including the sovereignty of God, the futility of Satan, Christology, the Holy Spirit, cosmic war, theodicy, mission, the perseverance of the saints, and worship.[23] Yet in some way or another, all of these themes can be absorbed under the overarching theme of "allegiance." John contrasts the supremacy of Christ and sovereignty of God with the futility of Satan, largely through the element of imitation and fraud. Satan's unwillingness to admit defeat results in cosmic war, in which those who worship the beast are faced with God's wrath and judgment while those who are sealed as God's servants (indwelt with the Spirit) and persevere in their faith receive salvation and God's eternal presence. Ultimately, it all comes down to allegiance—do you worship the Lamb or the beast?

The use of exodus typology throughout the Apocalypse buttresses John's call to unwavering allegiance in two ways. First, it validates John's vision of the end times by linking it within a familiar and awe-inspiring historical event and reminds his readers of the consequences of idolatry and feeble commitment. Second, it provides a historical and theological framework for understanding God's faithfulness and the privilege of his eternal presence in the lives of those believers who remain true to the one true God.

Throughout the Bible, especially throughout the NT, there is a recurring message of the hope which believers maintain—an expectation for the future, a trust or confidence in God, and an element of "patience, a reinforcement of the power to endure the difficulties and hardships of the present in the prospect of better things to come."[24] This overall picture of hope is presented in the Apocalypse as well, most explicitly through the lens of exodus typology. John calls to the mind of his readers the epic story of the Israelites' deliverance from enslavement in Egypt through God's mighty acts of judgment upon their enemies, as well as their reliance on Yahweh and his protection of them through both the plagues and the wilderness experience, in order to cement within the hearts of believers the fact that God will forever be the same. He is consistent in his protection of his people, as well as in his attitude toward good and evil. The same God who sent ten progressively disastrous plagues upon the land of Egypt in order to deliver his children from oppression will ultimately affect the final victory over

---

23 Osborne asserts that "the primary theme of the book is the sovereignty of God, which is a major theme in virtually all Jewish and Christian apocalypses." Yet he goes on to outline in some detail how Revelation's theology also emphasizes each of the other themes mentioned here. Osborne, *Revelation*, 31–49.

24 Allan Barr, "'Hope' ('ΕΛΠΙΣ, 'ΕΛΠΙΖΩ) in the New Testament," *SJT* 3.1 (1950): 69.

evil.[25] While the scale of deliverance and judgment is surely grander in Revelation than in Exodus (an example of the escalation that often characterizes typology), the motivation behind the divine action remains constant.[26] This is perhaps best expressed in the description of God as the One "who is and who was and who is to come" (Rev 1:4, cf. 1:8; 4:8; 11:17; 16:5).[27]

There is little question that the exodus plagues serve as the paradigm for Revelation's trumpet and bowl judgments, as suggested by the repeated use of the word "plague" to describe the judgments, both individually and as a collective whole, particularly in scenes which are imbedded with other occurrences of exodus typology (e.g., Rev 15). More telling, however, is the fact that the majority of the trumpet and bowl judgments contain striking similarities to the ten plagues in Egypt. Even those judgments which contain no overt comparison to the plagues have exodus implications. But Revelation's use of the plague paradigm is not limited to God's judgment of his enemies. John recognized the fact that in many of the exodus plagues, Yahweh set the Hebrew people apart from the Egyptians and protected them from the plagues (e.g., "I will set apart the land of Goshen, where my people dwell, so that no swarms of flies shall be there.... Thus I will put a division between my people and your people," Exod 8:22–23). The distinction is even more apparent at the Red Sea, where God made a pathway for his people to cross on dry land but allowed the waters to swallow Pharaoh and his army. Yahweh's protection of those who are faithful to him and follow his commands likewise appears in tandem with the judgments in the Apocalypse, in the sealing of the 144,000 from the wrath of God, as well as in explicit statements that the judgments were to harm "only those people who do not have the seal of God on their foreheads" (Rev 9:4; cf. 16:2, 6, 10). Thus, the rhetorical force of the plague imagery in Revelation functions to sharpen John's point that readers must make a choice between the Lamb and the beast. The resulting narrative appeals for the readers to join the people of God through repentance of their sins (e.g., Rev 9:20–21; 16:9, 11) and allegiance to the Lamb, and unequivocally portrays

---

25  Kenneth Albert Strand, *Interpreting the Book of Revelation: Hermeneutical Guidelines, With Brief Introduction to Literary Analysis* (Ann Arbor, 1976), 21.

26  David Mathewson, *A New Heaven and a New Earth: The Meaning and Function of the Old Testament in Revelation 21:1–22:5*, JSNTSup 238 (JSOT, 2003), 218; DeSilva, "Final Topics," 233.

27  It is possible that this expansion of the divine name ("I Am") to "the one who is, who was, and is coming" (Rev 1:8, HCSB) is yet another occurrence of escalation and amplification, in which the significance of the name is increased to include past, present, and future. Yet John's use of this construction may have been intended "to show the solidarity of his work with that of God's revelation in the OT", for the divine name "was also expanded in a threefold manner by later Jewish tradition, most notably *Tg. Ps.-J.* Deut. 32:39, 'I am he who is and who was, and I am he who will be.'" G. K. Beale and Sean M. McDonough, "Revelation," in *Commentary on the New Testament Use of the Old Testament*, ed. G. K. Beale and D. A. Carson (Baker, 2007), 1089.

the outcome for those who do not—"if anyone's name was not found written in the book of life, he was thrown into the lake of fire" (Rev 20:15).[28]

## The Passover and Allegiance

Paschal imagery figures prominently throughout Revelation, most particularly in the figure of the Lamb. In passages such as the throne room vision, Revelation links the nature and role of τὸ ἀρνίον with the original Passover lamb and presents Christ's sacrificial death as a means of redemption and transformation for those who identify themselves with him through faith. The blood of the Lamb brings freedom from sins (Rev 1:5) and redemption from the world (Rev 5:9), in both cases enabling the establishment of a kingdom of priests (Rev 1:6; 5:10). The blood is a sign of protection for the servants of God (Rev 7), preserving them from the wrath of God sent down in his judgments (cf. Rev. 9:4). It is the believers' source of victory over the beast (Rev 12:11), and the basis for entrance into the heavenly throne room in Rev 7:14. Identification with the blood results in one's name being recorded in the Lamb's book of life (Rev 13:8), sets believers apart as the bride of the Lamb (Rev 19:7, 9), and enables them to reign eternally in the New Jerusalem in the presence of God and the Lamb (Rev 21:22–26; 22:1–5).

The presence of the paschal imagery in the Apocalypse serves to cement the foundational belief that God will forever be the same. He is consistent in his protection of his people, as well as his desire to create for himself a chosen people with whom he will dwell and share a distinctive communion (Exod 29:45–46; Rev 21:3). The sealing of the 144,000 in Rev 7 functions in much the same way as the sign of the blood in the original Passover; they are marks of distinction, designating the bearers as followers of the one true God and setting them apart from the idolaters of their time. Though believers may undergo periods of misery, tribulation and strife, God will reward those who faithfully endure by bringing them into unique and everlasting fellowship with him.[29]

Through his use of exodus typology in Revelation, John reminds the reader that God has redeemed all who trust in him from bondage to sin and death

---

28  Compare Exod 32:33 in the aftermath of the golden calf episode—"But the Lord said to Moses, 'Whoever has sinned against me, I will blot out of my book.'"

29  According to Mounce, "the faithful are to live with the assurance that God is in command of his universe. At the moment it may appear that the forces of evil have gained the edge, but the one who defeated those very forces by means of his sacrificial death on the cross will return at the end of time to claim his own people and destroy forever all that stands in opposition." Robert H. Mounce, *The Book of Revelation*, NICNT (Eerdmans, 1977), 153. Cf. Osborne, *Revelation*, 339; Beale, *Revelation*, 556, 818.

through the sacrificial blood of the true Paschal Lamb, Jesus Christ. As in the exodus itself, God will continue to provide for his children and protect them from the ploys of the evil one. The same God who delivered his children from Egypt and who guards over his people in the present world will eventually complete the final victory over evil, a triumph that was inaugurated and verified through the sacrificial death of Christ on the cross.

Yet alignment with the blood of the Lamb is not an automatic assumption. In both Exodus and Revelation, it requires a choice. Before the tenth and final plague of death, Yahweh commanded the Hebrew people to

> take some of the blood and put it on the two doorposts and the lintel of the houses in which they eat it. They shall eat the flesh that night, roasted on the fire; with unleavened bread and bitter herbs they shall eat it.... Let none of it remain until the morning; anything that remains until the morning you shall burn. In this manner you shall eat it: with your belt fastened, your sandals on your feet, and your staff in your hand. And you shall eat it in haste. It is the Lord's Passover (Exod 12:7–11).

The Israelites had to choose to comply with Yahweh's instructions; if they did not, they, like the Egyptians, would be subject to God's judgment. They were set apart only by their obedience in marking their homes with the blood of the lamb. As Yahweh promised, "The blood shall be a sign for you ... when I see the blood, I will pass over you, and no plague will befall you to destroy you, when I strike the land of Egypt" (Exod 12:13).

In the same way, Revelation presents readers with a choice to give their allegiance to Christ by professing true, living, and enduring faith in Jesus and remaining faithful through the threat of persecution and the wiles of the world. The most explicit manifestation of this choice is found in the mark of the beast, the antithesis of the sealing of the 144,000. As in the exodus, those who elect to place their faith in God and refuse the mark of the beast will experience salvation and protection through the blood of the true Passover Lamb.

## THE WILDERNESS AND ALLEGIANCE

As the Israelites traversed through the desert, they endured a number of trials and difficulties, such as enemy encounters and a lack of food and water. Yet God reminded them daily of his protection and guidance toward the Promised Land. More than any other people, the exodus generation experienced the divine presence as a known, manifest reality. Not only did they witness the pillar of cloud and fire, they heard God's voice at Mount Sinai, received a covenant obliging them to obey his commands, and were granted the opportunity to build and serve him in the tabernacle, the symbol of God's dwelling among his people.

The presence of God in and among the Israelites was a unique privilege, for no other nation had the living God abiding within their midst. There is a most poignant correlation between the divine presence and national identity, for without Yahweh's presence the Israelites would no longer be set apart from other nations (Exod 33:16). It is God's presence that created the Israelites, and without him the chosen people of God would cease to exist.[30] John thus draws upon this second half of the exodus epic to emphasize the unique eschatological communion between God and believers in Christ. The Israelites' celebration of the presence of God amongst them was limited to corporate worship, as only the High Priest was granted access to the inner sanctum of the tabernacle. The essential goal of the Apocalypse, however, is a city in which all believers enjoy access and the opportunity to experience the presence of God and the Lamb personally, living and ruling alongside him in the heavenly city.

Like the plagues and Passover, the wilderness imagery in Revelation serves to reinforce the necessity of choosing where one's allegiance lies. While worshiping the beast and taking his mark provides the ability to buy and sell (Rev 13:17), this is but a temporary attainment, for Babylon will fall and with it the economic success of all who participated in its trade. Yet, just as Yahweh provided water, manna, protection, and even the tabernacle in the wilderness, in Revelation God protects and nourishes his people in the wilderness (Rev 12:6, 14), and ultimately transforms the physical gifts into eschatological blessings in the New Jerusalem. More significantly, however, allegiance determines one's access to the presence of God. Revelation makes it clear that those who take the mark of the beast, who persecute God's people and break his commandments, will not gain entry into the New Jerusalem, a city in which evil is banished (Rev 19:2; 21:8, 27; 22:15). Yet those who place their faith in God, refuse the mark of the beast, and wash their robes in the blood of the Lamb, will see the fulfillment of the goal of the exodus (Exod 29:45–46) and all of Scripture—they will reign with God forever as his presence dwells

---

30 Thomas W. Mann, *Divine Presence and Guidance in Israelite Traditions: The Typology of Exaltation* (Johns Hopkins University Press, 1977), 157–158; Samuel Terrien, *The Elusive Presence: The Heart of Biblical Theology* (Harper & Row, 1978), 124. Exodus 33:16 reads, "is it not in your going with us, so that we are distinct, I and your people, from every other people on the face of the earth?"

among them in the New Heaven and New Earth, and will receive the ultimate privilege of seeing his face (Rev 20:4–6; 21:3–7; 22:3–5, 14).

"CHOOSE THIS DAY WHOM YOU WILL SERVE"

Thus, through his use of exodus typology, John strengthens the rhetorical argument of his Apocalypse, emphasizes the theme of allegiance, and heightens his ability to accomplish his purpose of engendering faithfulness to God in spite of persecution and an idolatrous society. By alternating between scenes of judgment and salvation, many of which are imbedded with exodus imagery, John presents his readers with a challenge: choose today whom you will serve—worship the beast and face eternal judgment as an enemy of God; worship and remain faithful to the Almighty God, and rule with him for all eternity. As Smalley states,

> The seer's chief concern is to present a drama about God's salvation through his judgement to a community which was *itself* infected with falsehood.... The prophet-seer therefore warns his readers about the dangers of idolatry in any form: social, political, ecclesiastical or economic.... By contrast, and by means of a testimony which is relevant to any Christian group in any age, John urges his congregations to worship God, rather than the beast, and to reject the wiles of Satan by following the exalted Lamb.[31]

Throughout Revelation, beginning in each of the seven letters, John repeatedly urges genuine believers to take a stand against idolatry and pledge their loyalty to God (e.g., Rev 2:3–5, 9–10, 13–17, 19–26; 3:3–5, 8–12, 19–21; 7:14–15; 12:11; 14:12; 19:1–5), who demonstrated his worthiness in the exodus by judging his enemies, delivering the Israelites, and protecting and sustaining them in the wilderness, and to Christ, whose sacrificial death and resurrection is highlighted in the figure of the Lamb. At the same time, as the Apocalypse progresses, there emerges a beast who is in direct opposition to the Lamb (Rev 14:9–10; 17:10–14), believing himself to be divine and demanding that all mankind worship him as such (Rev 13:4–8), yet defeated in the end by the God who has proven himself throughout history to be the divine protector and judge. There should be no further catalyst needed to incite believers to remain faithful to this sovereign Lord, and to encourage others to turn to him in repentance.

---

31  Smalley, *Revelation*, 6. Emphasis in the original.

The counterpoint between "Jesus Christ the faithful witness" (Rev 1:5) and "Satan, the deceiver of the whole world" (Rev 12:9) confronts the reader with a choice to worship either the Lamb or the beast. This choice is not to be taken lightly, for it affects one's entire existence, both on earth and beyond. As Spilsbury stresses, Revelation

> is not a book for the faint-hearted. Its message is deeply disturbing. It unsettles us. It urges us to reevaluate the most fundamental of our convictions, our loyalties and commitments. What are our true values? What is really the most important thing in our lives? What would we be willing to die for?... At its most basic level Revelation calls us to worship God.[32]

Like Joshua, who rehearsed the history of Israel as a stimulus for covenant renewal at Shechem, John reminds his readers of all that God has done in the exodus and wilderness wanderings to preserve his people and exhorts his readers to "choose this day whom you will serve ... but as for me and my house, we will serve the Lord" (Josh 24:15).

## Is Revelation's Exodus Typology Isaianic?

One question which arises out of the conclusion that John appealed to exodus typology to further his agenda of presenting a call for allegiance to Christ is how this presentation fits within the canonical witness to the expectation of a new exodus. This is particularly true regarding Isaiah's portrayal of the return from exile in terms of a new exodus, given Watts's assertion that in Isa 40–55 the new exodus "replac[es] the first Exodus as *the* saving event."[33] As discussed previously, however, uncertainty remains as to whether Isaiah's use of exodus imagery depicts an imminent deliverance in the literal return from Babylonian exile, or the eschatological, final salvation and restoration of the people of God.[34] While certain similarities between the historical exodus and the return from Babylonian exile suggest that this was Isaiah's immediate focus, the course of history has highlighted the eschatological overtones of Isaiah's prophecy, making it clear that this new exodus event has yet to take place.

Recent scholarly interest in this Isaianic new exodus has produced a number of studies detailing the influence of Isaiah's expectations upon the

---

32 Paul Spilsbury, *The Throne, the Lamb & the Dragon: A Reader's Guide to the Book of Revelation* (InterVarsity, 2002), 15.

33 Rikki E. Watts, *Isaiah's New Exodus and Mark*, WUNT 2nd series 88 (Mohr Siebeck, 1997), 79–80.

34 See chapter 4, "The Isaianic New Exodus."

NT, perhaps the most significant being Pao's *Acts and the Isaianic New Exodus* and Watts's *Isaiah's New Exodus in Mark*.³⁵ Both Pao and Watts emphasize the prologue to "Deutero-Isaiah" (Isa 40:1–11) as a programmatic or summary statement for the entire Isaianic new exodus,³⁶ particularly stressing Isaiah's use of "way" (ὁδός) terminology in this context. They understand the phrase "the way of the Lord" (Isa 40:3) as drawing upon the exodus tradition of the pillar of cloud and fire leading the Israelites "along the way" (Exod 13:21; cf. Exod 23:20) and thus pointing to the coming salvation of God. As Yahweh's presence shepherded the Israelites out of Egypt and through the wilderness, he will do so again in the new exodus. Thus, "'the Way' symbolizes the presence of God in the ancient Exodus story as well as the anticipated eschatological event."³⁷

---

35  Pao's overriding thesis is that, "as the Exodus traditions are utilized in the construction of the Isaianic vision in the context of the rebuilding of the exilic community, so the Exodus traditions as transformed in the Isaianic corpus are evoked by Luke in the articulation of an identity claim in the development of the early Christian community." David W. Pao, *Acts and the Isaianic New Exodus*, WUNT 2nd series 130 (Mohr Siebeck, 2000), 249. In his monograph, Watts argues that Mark's opening citation of Isa 40:3 indicates "a positive schema whereby Jesus' identity and ministry is presented in terms of Isaiah's New Exodus." Watts, *Isaiah's New Exodus and Mark*, 4.

36  Pao finds significance in Luke's repeated allusions to Isa 40:1–11 (Luke 1:17, 76; 2:30; Acts 13:23–36; 28:28) and asserts that the quotation of Isa 40:3–5 in Luke 3:4–6 "functions as a hermeneutical lens without which the entire Lukan program cannot be properly understood." Pao, *Acts and the Isaianic New Exodus*, 37. According to Pao, Luke's use of Isa 40:3–5 evokes the wider context of the Isaianic new exodus (Isa 40–55), characterized by four primary themes—the restoration of Israel, the universal offer of salvation, the Word of God, and the polemic against idols. Pao suggests that these prominent themes were initially appropriated by Isaiah from the original exodus paradigm. Likewise, Watts claims that Isa 40:1–11 (and in particularly 40:3) "came to be understood as encapsulating the critical event upon which the whole of the NE depends: the call made by an unidentified 'messenger' to prepare the way in the desert for the coming of Yahweh whose advent as warrior and shepherd presages the redemption of his people." Watts, *Isaiah's New Exodus and Mark*, 82. Rather than focusing on the themes found in Isa 40:1–11 (as Pao), Watts (50) identifies between the first exodus and the Isaianic new exodus a common schema of deliverance, journey, and arrival at Yahweh's dwelling place.

37  Pao, *Acts and the Isaianic New Exodus*, 41, 52; Watts, *Isaiah's New Exodus and Mark*, 80–81. Isaiah 40:3 reads "A voice cries: 'In the wilderness prepare the way (τὴν ὁδὸν) of the Lord; make straight in the desert a highway for our God.'" According to Pao, the use of ὁδός language in Isaiah's prologue as well as its appearance in the context of the exodus paradigm throughout Isaiah contributes to the development of a unique use of the term "to point to the coming of Yahweh for his people as well as the return of the people from captivity." Pao, *Acts and the Isaianic New Exodus*, 53. With regard to Acts, Pao states that "the use of ὁδός terminology in an ecclesiological sense is also dependent upon the context of Isa 40:3–5; and it is used to evoke the Isaianic tradition to establish the identity of the early Christian movement." Ibid., 45. Similarly, Watts understands Isaiah's "way" language in both spatial and sapiential terms; thus "the 'way' of the NE is not only the 'way' of the returning exiles to Jerusalem but is also a matter of rejecting the idolatrous wisdom of the past and embracing Yahweh's teaching … the attaining of that wisdom which signals fidelity to Yahweh and therefore the return to his presence." Watts, *Isaiah's New Exodus and Mark*, 242–243. Like Luke, Mark quotes Isa 40:3 in his opening statement,

Given the significant influence of the historical exodus upon the OT prophets and the eschatological nature of the Isaianic new exodus, as well as the apparent impact of Isaiah's new exodus expectation upon NT writers such as Mark and Luke, one must inquire whether Revelation's use of exodus typology could, and indeed should, be considered within this framework of the "Isaianic new exodus." Does Revelation draw upon and accentuate the particular aspects of the original exodus that are generally highlighted in Isaiah, or is Revelation's use of exodus imagery characterized by different features of the exodus, thereby creating its own unique emphases? Was John, as he recorded his visions of the end-time events, dependent upon Isaiah's portrayal of the return from exile in terms of an exodus-type deliverance that exceeds even the original event, or was the prototype, the original exodus from Egypt, in the forefront of his mind?

Since both Pao and Watts highlight the importance of Isa 40:1–11 as a summary statement for the whole of the Isaianic new exodus, and focus on ὁδός language from Isa 40:3–5 as one of the primary ways this Isaianic new exodus appears in Mark and Acts, the first step in determining whether Revelation's exodus typology is Isaianic is to look for ὁδός language and allusions to Isa 40:1–11 (especially 40:3–5) within the Apocalypse. According to Pao, ὁδός language occurs fifty-one times throughout Isaiah (twenty-one times in chapters 40–55 alone). While "way" is also used with other meanings in Isa 40–55 (e.g., Isa 40:14, 27; 42:24; 53:6), Pao and Watts understand its primary function as pointing to both the coming of Yahweh/return of his presence and the people's return from exile.[38] Yet within the Apocalypse, ὁδός language occurs only twice. In Rev 15:3, the word is used within the Song of Moses and the Song of the Lamb to refer to Yahweh's righteous character and actions on behalf of his people—"Great and amazing are your deeds, O Lord God the Almighty! Just and true are your ways [ὁδοί], O King of the nations!" In Rev 16:12, in the sixth bowl judgment, the Euphrates River dries up "to prepare the

---

which Watts takes as "indicat[ing] that the overall conceptual framework for his Gospel is the Isaianic NE, the prophetic transformation of Israel's memory of her founding moment into a model for her future hope" (90). Mark also strategically clusters "way" terminology throughout 8:27–11:1 in what has been called his "Way/journey" section (Mark 8:27; 9:33, 34; 10:17, 32, 46, 52), describing Jesus and his disciples' journey to Jerusalem. Mark's purpose in using "way" language appears to be multifaceted. According to Watts, based on Mark's use of Isa 40:3 in his opening statement, the "'Way' seems clearly to be the 'way' of Yahweh's INE coming." However, the sapiential connotations elsewhere in Mark indicate that he is using "the way" to show that participation in the new exodus requires "acceptance of Yahweh's wisdom, namely, that the Messiah, S/son of God, must go the 'way' of the cross." Ibid., 256–257.

38  Pao, *Acts and the Isaianic New Exodus*, 53. Watts asserts that the prominence of the summons to prepare a way for Yahweh (Isa 40:3) "indicates that the emphasis of the NE lies on the return of Yahweh's actual presence." Watts, *Isaiah's New Exodus and Mark*, 80.

way [ἡ ὁδός] for the kings from the east." Incidentally, in this case "the way" appears to have an opposite effect from Pao and Watts's understanding from Isaiah; rather than ushering in the presence of Yahweh, here it enables the assembly of his enemies.

Unlike Luke and Acts, both of which quote Isa 40:3 in passages that identify John the Baptist as preparing the way for Jesus' earthly ministry (Mark 1:3; Luke 3:4–6), neither of the uses of ὁδός within Revelation occur within quotations or even allusions to this verse.[39] Indeed, while Watts and Pao claim Isa 40:1–11 to be programmatic for the entire Isaianic new exodus, Revelation contains only two possible allusions to this passage (Rev 12:6; 22:7, 12).[40] Beale suggests that the description of the woman fleeing to a place prepared for her in the wilderness (Rev 12:6) alludes to the expectation of an "end-time exodus or restoration when Israel would return in faith to the Lord and again be protected and nourished by him in the wilderness (Isa. 32:15; 35:1; 40:3 ...)."[41] While this verse does contain verbal similarities to Isa 40:3 in its use of the word "wilderness" (ἔρημος) and a form of the verb "to prepare" (ἑτοιμάζω), the fact that the whole of Rev 12 is imbedded with exodus typology tends to minimize the impact of a potential allusion to Isaiah here. John is in harmony with, but not necessarily dependent upon, the prophetic anticipation of a new exodus event.

The final chapter of the Apocalypse does contain a probable allusion to this Deutero-Isaianic prologue, particularly Isa 40:10, which reads "Behold, the Lord God comes with might, and his arm rules for him; behold, his reward is with him, and his recompense before him." Revelation 22:12 proclaims, "Behold, I am coming soon, bringing my recompense with me, to repay each one for what he has done." The allusion in Rev 22:12 is quite strong verbally; John repeats Isaiah's use of ἰδού plus a present indicative form of the deponent verb ἔρχομαι, transferred into first person singular to fit the dialogue, and

---

39 Interestingly, however, both uses of "way" in Revelation occur in passages characterized by exodus typology (Rev 15, the Song of Moses and the Song of the Lamb; Rev 16, the bowl judgments).

40 In addition to the allusions discussed above, the list of NT references to the OT in the 4th edition of Aland et al., *Greek New Testament* (Barbara Aland et al., eds., *The Greek New Testament*, 4th rev. ed. [Deutsche Bibelgesellschaft, 1994], 793) suggests an allusion in Rev 1:5b to Isa 40:2b. Certainly, there is thematic continuity between these two verses, as both speak of the forgiveness of sins (Rev 1:5b = "To him who loves us and has freed us from our sins by his blood" [Τῷ ἀγαπῶντι ἡμᾶς καὶ λύσαντι ἡμᾶς ἐκ τῶν ἁμαρτιῶν ἡμῶν ἐν τῷ αἵματι αὐτοῦ]; Isa 40:2b = "... that her iniquity is pardoned, that she has received from the Lord's hand double for all her sins" [λέλυται αὐτῆς ἡ ἁμαρτία ὅτι ἐδέξατο ἐκ χειρὸς Κυρίου διπλᾶ τὰ ἁμαρτήματα αὐτῆς]. However, there is not enough similarity in phrasing to make an allusion certain.

41 Beale and McDonough, "Revelation," 1124. Interestingly, Fekkes does not even consider the possibility of an allusion to Isa 40:3 in Rev 12:6. Jan Fekkes, *Isaiah and Prophetic Traditions in the Book of Revelation: Visionary Antecedents and Their Development*, JSNTSup 93 (JSOT, 1994).

follows this with the first person singular equivalent of Isaiah's "his reward is with him" (ὁ μισθὸς αὐτοῦ μετ' αὐτοῦ).[42] Yet John's apparent allusion to Isa 40:10, with the understanding that God will reward the faithful with salvation and punish the unfaithful with judgment,[43] does not necessitate the conclusion that his exodus typology is formulated upon the Isaianic new exodus.

There is no question that Revelation draws upon the text of Isaiah frequently. According to Fekkes, Isaiah is one of five "OT traditions which are widely recognized as dominant in the prophet's visionary consciousness and expression."[44] Yet how prominent is Isa 40–55, which both Pao and Watts recognize as the core of the Isaianic new exodus? In his highly detailed analysis concerning the occurrence and probability of Isaianic allusions in the Apocalypse, Fekkes suggests that Revelation's forty-one virtually certain Isaianic allusions derive from approximately twenty-three general sections of Isaiah, with four passages considered "especially prominent"—Isa 6:1–4 (Isaiah's commission); Isa 34:4–14 (judgment against the nations); Isa 60:1–19 (the glory of Zion; and Isa 65:15–20a (the glorious new creation). Yet not one of these four highly significant passages is from Isa 40–55. Indeed, Fekkes determined that of those forty-one "certain or virtually certain" allusions to Isaiah, only ten were from chapters 40–55 (24.4%), while only three of the nine "probable or possible" Isaianic allusions were from these chapters (33.3%). Thus, Revelation alludes to Isa 40–55 in roughly a quarter of its fifty possible or virtually certain Isaianic allusions.[45]

Fekkes engages in the thematic categorization of Isaianic allusions in Revelation, arguing that "not only does it appear that these Isaiah texts are consciously *selected* according to subject, but they are also *applied* according to subject."[46] He concludes that allusions from Isa 40–55 are almost exclusively classified as statements of eschatological salvation. Rarely does John use passages from Deutero-Isaiah containing eschatological judgment or Christological titles and descriptions, and visionary experience and language from Isa 40–55 is entirely absent from the Apocalypse. Interestingly it is precisely in the context of Christological titles and eschatological judgment that we find some of Revelation's most explicit uses of exodus imagery (the plagues

---

42 Fekkes, *Prophetic Traditions*, 276–278.
43 Beale and McDonough, "Revelation," 1156–1157.
44 Fekkes, *Prophetic Traditions*, 13. The following statistics are based on Fekkes's summary and conclusion (chapter eight), especially the charts on pp. 280–281.
45 In contrast, Fekkes categorized twenty-three "doubtful or unlikely" allusions to Isaiah in Revelation, nearly half of which relate to Isa 40–55 (47.8%). Interestingly, 36.6% of the virtually certain allusions and 22.2% of the possible allusions refer to Isa 60–66. Thus 34% of the 50 Isaianic allusions in Revelation are drawn from the final seven chapters, whereas only 26% come from the sixteen chapters of "Deutero-Isaiah."
46 Ibid., 282, italics original.

and the paschal lamb). Yet allusions to Isaiah are conspicuously absent from the trumpet sequence (Rev 8–9), and only two possible allusions can be found within the bowl sequence (Rev 16), neither of which are Deutero-Isaianic (Isa 11:15–16 in Rev 16:12; Isa 14:13 in Rev 16:16).

Mathewson has stated that in Revelation, "the Isaian and prophetic story of God's salvation of Israel becomes the story of God's salvation of the Christian community, providing a framework for understanding their own situation, and providing a lens of perception for how God will act on their behalf in the future."[47] Similarly, Watts argues that Israel's recollection of her founding moment (the exodus) was profoundly influenced by the prophetic transformation of that tradition in their vision of a greater, final new exodus.[48] Thus he suggests it is the shared schema of deliverance, journey, and arrival between the original exodus and the Isaianic portrayal of a new exodus, rather than various "icons" associated with the exodus itself (e.g., paschal lamb, 'forty years', manna, fiery cloud), that signals new exodus connotations within later texts—"it is this simple pattern, rather than the more convoluted accounts that we find in the Exodus narratives themselves ... to which we should be looking."[49]

Yet the question remains, is this true for John's record of his eschatological visions within the Apocalypse? There is little question that many prominent themes from the Isaianic new exodus (e.g., divine provision, rejection of idolatry, restoration of the people of God, rebuilding of the city of Jerusalem, return of the glory/presence of Yahweh) are likewise emphasized in Revelation. Yet in many cases, the author of Revelation uses these same themes for different purposes. For example, the idea of rejection of idolatry in Revelation is not immediately a call for repentance from those who engaged in idolatry (as Watts claims is true in Isaiah[50]), but is primarily a call to those who worship Yahweh to maintain this allegiance in the midst of their idolatrous surroundings and a reminder that he will eventually bring them out of that situation.

Revelation also draws upon significant elements (or "icons," as Watts calls them) of the exodus tradition which are lacking or not developed in Isaiah's new exodus expectation. Perhaps the most noteworthy example is Revelation's modification of the exodus plague accounts in the trumpet and bowl judgments (Rev 8:6–9:21; 16:1–21), transforming the plagues upon Egypt into eschatological catastrophes. By employing the exodus plagues as a literary and theological model for the trumpet and bowl sequences, John lends

---

47  Mathewson, *New Heaven and a New Earth*, 71.
48  Watts, *Isaiah's New Exodus and Mark*, 49.
49  Ibid., 50.
50  Ibid., 247.

validity to his vision of the future judgment through historical rehearsal, calling upon a familiar historical event to remind his readers of God's past acts of judgment and redemption.[51] In contrast, the judgments in Isaiah generally conform to the typical pattern of apocalyptic judgments as seen in the synoptic mini-apocalypses and even Revelation's seal judgments; a dependence upon the plague tradition is notably absent in Isaiah.[52] Revelation also uses exodus imagery to portray its most central figure, the Lamb. Just as the sign of the paschal blood on the doorposts provided the means of redemption and deliverance from bondage in Egypt, so believers in Christ, marked by the blood of the Lamb, are redeemed from the world of rebellion against God, and set apart for his purposes.[53] While the Passover lamb seemed to play no role in Jewish eschatological expectation, occurring nowhere in Isaiah's portrayal of the new exodus, Revelation's use of paschal imagery is in harmony with other NT writers (e.g., John 1:29, 36; Acts 8:32; 1 Pet 1:19) who linked the Suffering Servant of Isaiah (Isa 53:7) with the Passover lamb in their depictions of Christ's sacrificial death and salvific purposes.[54]

These two key aspects of the original exodus (the plagues and the Passover lamb) are virtually ignored in Isaiah's new exodus portrayal, yet are strategically developed and highlighted with Revelation's use of exodus imagery. Other less obvious examples of exodus "icons" which are present within Revelation yet missing from the Isaianic new exodus include God's marking his people for protection and deliverance (cf. the blood of the paschal lamb with the sealing of the 144,000) and the identification of God's people as a "kingdom of priests" (cf. Exod 19:6 with Rev 1:5–6; 5:10; 20:6). While perhaps in isolation these Revelation images would not evoke exodus connotations, their cumulative effect alongside the unmistakable exodus images of the plagues and the lamb provides persuasive evidence toward that end.

---

51 Revelation's countless symbols are couched in terms of the OT Scriptures, thus enabling the readers to understand what is to come "by describing it in terms of what they know." John Goldingay, *Israel's Faith*, vol. 2 of *Old Testament Theology* (InterVarsity, 2006), 2:426; Mark Adam Elliott, *The Survivors of Israel: A Reconsideration of the Theology of Pre-Christian Judaism* (Eerdmans, 2000), 356; Elisabeth Schüssler Fiorenza, "The Phenomenon of Early Christian Apocalyptic: Some Reflections on Method," in *Apocalypticism in the Mediterranean World and the Near East: Proceedings of the International Colloquium on Apocalypticism, Uppsala, August 12–17, 1979*, ed. David Hellholm, 2nd ed. (Mohr, 1989), 300.

52 See Isa 10:16–19; 13:8–22; 19:2; 28:2; 29:6; 30:27–30; 32:19; 33:3–4; 34:2–10; 50:2–3; 51:19–20; 66:15–16. While Isa 19:5–8 may contain a vague allusion to the first plague, one ambiguous, possible allusion to a single plague does not begin to approach the cumulative effect of continuous allusions to at least six of the ten exodus plagues in Revelation.

53 See Leon Leon Morris, *The Apostolic Preaching of the Cross*, 3rd rev. ed. (Eerdmans, 1994), 113–143 for an intriguing discussion of the biblical meaning of "blood" and the "Lamb of God."

54 Bauckham, *Theology of Revelation*, 71; Godfrey Ashby, *Sacrifice: Its Nature and Purpose* (SCM, 1988), 82–83; Pate, *Four Views*, 143.

In conclusion, the OT anticipation of a future eschatological exodus is perhaps most prominent in the Isaianic new exodus, where it emphasizes the prophet's themes of exile, homecoming, and restoration. Many NT authors demonstrate an awareness of this expectation, frequently employing exodus or Isaianic new exodus imagery in their own writings. Certainly, John's readers were aware of God's reputation of judgment and redemption, as presented in the exodus account as well as throughout Scripture. Indeed, the presence of exodus imagery throughout Scripture makes it evident that it was nothing less than the historical nature of the exodus from Egypt which provided the Jewish pattern and hope for a more dramatic future deliverance. John's application of the expected eschatological exodus to believers in Revelation is consistent with the exodus imagery found elsewhere in the NT, in which the Christian church represents the true Israel of God through the passion, death, and resurrection of Jesus Christ.[55] Yet Revelation's adaptation of the exodus traditions is distinct in a variety of ways from these other NT books and from the Isaianic new exodus as a whole. There is no denying that the Apocalypse was influenced to a large degree by Isaiah. Yet evidence seems to suggest that, in its portrayal of the anticipated eschatological exodus, Revelation draws primarily upon aspects of the exodus tradition which Isaiah neglects (e.g., the plagues and the Passover lamb), and hence John bases his exodus typology upon the paradigm of the original, historical exodus rather than the Isaianic model.[56]

## The Past Is Yet to Come: The Apocalypse as the Culmination of Salvation History

We have explored the development of exodus typology throughout the OT and NT, most particularly in the prophetic writings, and analyzed the hermeneutical function of the person of the Lamb and other paschal imagery,

---

55  C. H. Dodd, *According to the Scriptures: The Sub-Structure of New Testament Theology* (Nisbet, 1952), 111–113.

56  Kee states that, though the biblical writers "drew upon the same basic biblical material—the stories of the patriarchs and the exodus, of the conquest of Canaan and the establishment of the monarchy—they each interpret the stories in ways that serve their own distinctive ends in their own specific time and cultural circumstances. In each case there are overarching assumptions about God and the creation, about human knowledge, about divine purpose for the creation, and for God's people. In each case cultural and social conditions of the writer's time influence directly and pervasively the ways in which the biblical material is understood and its meaning inferred." Howard Clark Kee, "Appropriating the History of God's People: A Survey of Interpretations of the History of Israel in the Pseudepigrapha, Apocrypha and the New Testament," in *The Pseudepigrapha and Early Biblical Interpretation*, ed. James H. Charlesworth and Craig A. Evans, JSPSup 14, SSEJC 2 (Sheffield, 1993), 63.

the plague-like trumpet and bowl judgments, and the myriad of allusions to Yahweh's provision and presence in the wilderness wanderings in Revelation's use of exodus typology. In so doing, we have demonstrated that John's Apocalypse was indeed in harmony with the Jewish expectation of an eschatological exodus and the Christian understanding of the Christ event as the inauguration of that long-awaited new deliverance. In addition, our examination of certain key emphases of the Isaianic new exodus and the absence of these features in Revelation, particularly within the sections most imbedded with exodus typology, as well as the presence within Revelation of certain trademark exodus elements that do not emerge in the Isaianic new exodus, reveals that John exceeds other presentations of a new exodus, fleshing out aspects of the Isaianic/prophetic hope of restoration in his portrayal of the eschaton. But to what end?

It can be suggested that John employed exodus typology throughout his Apocalypse as a means of representing the eschaton as the culmination of salvation history[57] and a re-creation or reinstatement of God's initial purposes and ideals for mankind and the world. Through his portrayal of the end-times exodus, John demonstrates that God has finally brought to completion his salvific purposes. From the time of the Fall (Gen 3), God has been working to create for himself a chosen people and to provide for them an Edenic existence—and in all of this, to bring man back into proper fellowship with himself, a relationship marked by the presence of God dwelling in their midst (Gen 3:8). Through the Abrahamic covenant, God promised to Abram innumerable descendants and a land in which they will be both blessed and a blessing (Gen 12:1–3; cf. 13:16; 15:5). Later, at Sinai, Yahweh covenanted with Moses and all of the Israelites that they would be his "treasured possession among all peoples … a kingdom of priests and a holy nation" (Exod 19:5–6) and that he would drive out their enemies until they could possess the land (Exod 23:30–31). While they were still in the wilderness, he provided a symbol of his divine presence in the tabernacle, so that they "shall know that I am the Lord their God, who brought them out of the land of Egypt that I might dwell among them" (Exod 29:46).

---

57 This use of the term "salvation history" is by no means related to the modern characterization of the Scriptures not as historical in themselves but rather a metanarrative illustrating "the individual's personal journey to faith (e.g., Bultmann), or … the history of the proclamation of salvation (e.g., von Rad)." Instead, the present understanding of salvation history acknowledges "(1) that God has acted in human history; and (2) that the books of the Bible, while not uniformly historical in form, all relate to an unfolding narrative of these events. It follows not only that salvation is historic, but also that history is salvific, itself revelation." Brian S. Rosner, "Salvation, History of," in *Dictionary for Theological Interpretation of the Bible*, ed. Kevin J. Vanhoozer (Baker, 2005), 714.

Though Israel did indeed enter the land of Canaan under Joshua's leadership, the people were unfaithful and did not keep the covenant with Yahweh. As a result, they were ultimately sent into exile under Assyria and Babylon, and more significantly, the Lord "cast them out from his presence" (Jer 52:3). But the story did not end there, for Yahweh himself was not unfaithful. He vowed that at the end of seventy years he would fulfill his promise and bring them out of exile (Jer 29:10, 14) in a deliverance so great that the people will no longer say, "'As the Lord lives who brought up the people of Israel out of the land of Egypt,' but 'As the Lord lives who brought up and led the offspring of the house of Israel out of the north country and out of all the countries where he had driven them.' Then they shall dwell in their own land" (Jer 23:7–8). Yahweh also pledged to forge a new covenant with Israel, in which his law will be written on their hearts, their sins will be forgiven, and they will be his people and he will be their God (Jer 31:31–35).[58] Thus Sinai became the model for the new covenant, just as the paradigm for coming deliverance was found in the exodus from Egypt.[59]

While God did indeed bring his people out of Babylon, the words of Scripture and the witness of history make it clear that this post-exilic return to Jerusalem was not the grand deliverance which the prophets foretold. Rather, they were looking toward an eschatological, final redemption which would supersede all of God's salvific acts in the past. Both that long-awaited event and the new covenant are consummated in the Christ event (Luke 22:20; Heb 8:6–13; 9:15). With Christ's birth, God took on flesh and tabernacled among men (John 1:14); with his death, access to the divine presence is eternally assured.[60] Believers in Christ become the true Israel of God, a chosen people from every nation, and heirs of the promises that the Israelites rejected in their disobedience (1 Pet 2:9–10; Gal 4:21–31; 6:16; Rom 9:6–8, 24–26).[61]

Yet there is a sense of "already but not yet" to this deliverance. While the new covenant has been inaugurated in the Christ event, and salvation is secured for the true people of God, believers are still sojourners in a land marked by the Fall and subject to the wiles of evil forces on earth. Yet Scripture assures that there is more to come. In the fullness of time Christ will

---

58 According to Dumbrell, the hallmark of the new covenant is God's presence among men. William J. Dumbrell, *The End of the Beginning: Revelation 21–22 and the Old Testament* (Lancer, 1985), 79.

59 Ibid., 88.

60 Ibid., 115.

61 Scripture makes it clear that through the life, death, and resurrection of Jesus Christ, "the special, elect people of God is the universal church. Thus, in Christian theology 'Israel' refers to the ethnic nation that becomes the spiritual body of Christ." Scot McKnight, "Israel," in Vanhoozer, *Dictionary for Theological Interpretation of the Bible*, 346.

return to judge the living and the dead, to deliver his people out of the persecution and temptation of this world, and to bring to completion all that God has purposed and promised. It is this final culmination of salvation history, this grand new deliverance by the Christ who accomplished salvation in his death and resurrection, that the Apocalypse portrays through the lens of exodus typology. As Ladd says, "Revelation outlines the consummation of the redemptive work of Christ for the world and human history, which is made possible because of what he has done in history (Rev. 5)."[62]

Through his use of exodus typology in Revelation, John forges a link between the renowned history of God's mighty deeds and his eschatological acts of salvation on behalf of believers. Through the paradigm of the exodus, he demonstrates that God is the same yesterday, today, and tomorrow, and that there will be profound continuity between God's actions in the future and those of the past. In the culmination of salvation history, God will pour out his wrath in plague-like judgments upon his enemies while at the same time protecting his children through the blood of the ultimate sacrificial Lamb. He will provide for and preserve his people through the trials of the eschatological wilderness, knowing that those who remain faithful to him will soon enter the New Jerusalem, reign with him forever, and receive the ultimate privilege of seeing his face.

Here the promises to Abraham, Moses, Israel, and all of God's children are realized. God's people, an innumerable multitude from every tribe, language, people, and nation, stand in the presence of God and the Lamb, praising his mighty acts of salvation (Rev 7:9–10; 22:3–4). In the New Jerusalem, God's people finally fulfill the covenantal status of a "kingdom of priests" (Exod 19:6; Rev 1:6; 5:10; 20:6). In the New Heaven and the New Earth, God at last restores to his people a land of Edenic glory, a paradise where Satan and evil have no place (Rev 20:10; 21:27), where the Fall's curses are reversed (Rev 21:4; 22:3, 5), where access to the tree of life is reinstated (Rev 22:14), and where man once again walks with God face to face (Rev 21:3; 22:4). In the eschatological new creation revealed by John in Revelation, the ultimate goal of the exodus is accomplished—God indeed dwells among his people, and they irrefutably acknowledge him as their God (Exod 29:45).

---

62 George Eldon Ladd, *A Theology of the New Testament*, rev. ed. (Eerdmans, 1993), 23. Dumbrell rightly asserts that the finality of the new covenant experience is found in Christ's triumphant return. Dumbrell, *End of the Beginning*, 116.

# Chapter 9

# Conclusion and Further Reflections

## Summary of the Current Project

The current study represents an attempt at a biblical theological analysis of the significance of exodus typology upon the conclusion of Scripture, namely, Revelation. After a brief introduction to the project in chapter 1, chapter 2 focuses on background matters related to intertextuality and outlining the presuppositions behind the use of typology which is the basis for this study. Building upon this foundation, chapter 3 examines the Scriptural witness to determine that exodus typology incorporates the events surrounding the departure from Egypt, including the wilderness wanderings, while excluding the conquest of Canaan. Chapter 4 surveys the development of a new exodus expectation within canonical and extracanonical writings, with special attention upon the prophetic era and the NT.

Chapters 5 through 7 represent the heart of this study. It is here that the attention turns to the Apocalypse itself. Drawing upon the historical record of the original exodus, we determined that John typologically incorporates images from each major stage of the exodus (the plagues, the Passover, and the wilderness sojourn) in his presentation of his end-time visions. The Egyptian plagues function as the general paradigm for the trumpet and bowl judgments, as seen in the repeated use of the word πληγή ("plague") as well as the cumulative allusions to the plagues in the descriptions of the judgments (Rev 8–9, 16). Allusions to the Passover predominate in the Christological figure of the Lamb, whose blood accomplishes the redemption of mankind (Rev 5:6–10) and seals believers from the disastrous consequences of God's wrath upon the unrighteous (Rev 7). Lastly, wilderness connotations are prominent in the repetition of temple/tabernacle and Sinai imagery (e.g., Rev 8–9, 15, 16), the summary of the salvation-historical conflict between Satan and the people of God (Rev 12), and the eschatological blessings (Rev 7). Read in this way, Revelation's structured and purposeful use of exodus typology enhances the reader's appreciation and understanding of John's visions.

Finally, chapter 8 contains a hermeneutical analysis of the exodus typology within the Apocalypse. It is argued that the primary theme of Revelation is an exhortation to allegiance to the Lamb in the face of persecution and a compromising culture. Through exodus typology, John demonstrates Yahweh's faithfulness to redeem and protect his people from the righteous wrath he rains down upon his enemies. Ultimately there will be no neutrality—one either worships the beast or the Lamb—and John urges his readers to "choose this day whom you will serve." Revelation's use of exodus typology represents the eschaton as the culmination of salvation history, a reinstatement of God's initial purposes and ideals for his creation. Through the end times deliverance, Yahweh's relationship with his people is once again marked by his presence dwelling in their midst, as they are restored to a land of Edenic glory to reign with God forever. At last, all that was inaugurated through Christ's redemptive death on the cross is completed, the covenants throughout Scripture are fulfilled, and the goal of the exodus is accomplished.

## Areas of Further Study

This study has sought to make a significant contribution both to the present understanding and future study of the Apocalypse. While the conclusions of this project may not be universally accepted, they may certainly have some influence upon other aspects of Revelation scholarship, in particular the historical and theological debates regarding the background and eschatological stance of the Apocalypse. Recognizing Revelation's use of exodus typology may highlight the viability of one position over another and enable more informed hypotheses based on the evidence of the text itself. Two areas in particular might be impacted by understanding the presence and purpose of exodus typology in the Apocalypse.

First, if it is determined that Revelation and the Gospel of John utilize exodus imagery in similar fashion, might this lend some credence to the possibility that the two share a common author? The authorship of Revelation is a matter of substantial disagreement among modern scholars, who assert various proofs against the apostle John, despite the fact that John was almost universally accepted as the author by the early church.[1] The most frequent

---

1 William C. Weinrich, ed., *Revelation*, ACCS New Testament 12 (InterVarsity, 2005), xvii, xix.

argument against authorship by the apostle John concerns supposed differences from the fourth Gospel, particularly inconsistencies in theology and vocabulary. For example, Osborne points out the false contrast between "the God of John [as] a God of love who seeks the conversion of the 'world' … while the God of Revelation is a God of wrath and judgment."[2] In addition, there are those who claim that the use of different words for "Lamb" (ἀμνός in John, ἀρνίον in Revelation) is evidence against a common author, whether or not the words were virtually synonymous at the time the NT was written.[3] While variations such as these could be explained (even expected?) by their distinctly different genres, purposes, and occasions,[4] Smalley actually asserts that John and Revelation are so similar in their use of the Lamb of God, as well as the Word and the Son of Man, that a common author is likely.[5] For example, in both John and Revelation, the Lamb is said to have the power to forgive sins (John 1:29, "Behold, the Lamb of God, who takes away the sin of the world"; Rev 1:5, "To him who loves us and has freed us from our sins by his blood"; cf. the parallel passage, Rev 5:9–10, in which the Lamb is explicitly mentioned). Indeed, both John and Revelation portray Christ as the perfect paschal victim whose willing sacrifice accomplishes the redemption of mankind. While these consistencies certainly cannot answer all the objections against Johannine authorship of the Apocalypse, acknowledging that John and Revelation are comparable in the use of "the Lamb" as a Christological title and the function of Passover imagery within their narration perhaps removes a key objection to common authorship. Further study is necessary to make any conclusive determinations regarding the impact of Revelation's exodus typology upon assertions of authorship.

Second, acknowledging the programmatic use of exodus typology within major structural sections of the Apocalypse may force scholars to reconsider their stance regarding the tribulational debate. The fact that the Egyptian

---

2 Grant R. Osborne, *Revelation*, BECNT (Baker, 2002), 4. Osborne argues against such a strong dichotomy, recognizing that judgment and repentance are present in both John's Gospel and Revelation.

3 E.g., Loren L. Johns, *The Lamb Christology of the Apocalypse of John: An Investigation into Its Origins and Rhetorical Force*, WUNT 2nd series 167 (Mohr Siebeck, 2003), 32.

4 G. K. Beale, *The Book of Revelation*, NIGTC (Eerdmans, 1999), 35. According to Fee, "even though [Revelation] has several linguistic and grammatical differences from the Gospel and Epistles that bear John's name, these differences are no more severe than those between Galatians and Romans, both of which almost all living scholars assume to be Pauline. And with regard to the Revelation, one could argue further that the small differences between it and the Gospel of John can easily be attributed to John's exile on Patmos, where he probably had to write on his own without an amanuensis." Gordon D. Fee, *Revelation*, New Covenant Commentary Series (Wipf and Stock, 2010), xix.

5 Stephen S. Smalley, "John's Revelation and John's Community," *BJRL* 69 (1988): 556–558.

plagues function as the paradigm for Revelation's trumpet and bowl judgments is key to this question. Certain premillennialists hold to a pretribulational rapture, in which the rapture is "temporally distinct from, or is a temporal phase of, the Second Coming," occurring prior to the period of apocalyptic judgment known as the tribulation.[6] In this model, believers who are still alive at the time of the rapture will be "caught up" into Christ's presence before the tribulation, and thus will not be required to experience the events of God's judgment upon mankind and the beast's rule of terror on the earth. However, recognizing the influence of exodus typology upon the Apocalypse, particularly within the judgment sequences, should cause scholars to take note of the events leading up to the Israelites' departure from Egypt. Throughout the ten plagues, Yahweh rained judgment upon the Egyptians, causing them to endure economic, physical, spiritual, social, and familial turmoil. At the same time, Scripture highlights the fact that God shielded the Hebrew people from the plagues, and even provided a way to ensure their protection in the Passover. It was only after the final plague that Yahweh delivered the Israelites from Egypt. When one reads the Apocalypse through the lens of exodus typology, it becomes necessary to at least acknowledge that God may once again choose to protect his people during his judgment upon his enemies rather than taking them out of the situation beforehand.

One cannot expect to answer every question about Revelation through examining its use of exodus typology, nor can the entire purpose and message of the book be summed up through this framework. Yet there is no question that exodus imagery appears pervasively throughout the book and that its presence provides a unifying link for an otherwise mystifying text, and is certainly a prominent and effective tool in communicating John's message. While we certainly cannot claim to solve the debates related to Revelation's authorship and the tribulation, we would be remiss not to recognize this study's potential contributions to these weighty debates. Regardless of whether the Apocalypse was written by the apostle John or another individual, or whether one holds to a pre-, mid-, or post-tribulational rapture, the fact remains that exodus typology features prominently throughout Revelation as John builds upon the prophetic hope to represent the eschaton as a new exodus even greater than anything that has come before, and as such, as the culmination of salvation history.

---

6 Craig A. Blaising, "Premillennialism," in *Three Views on the Millennium and Beyond*, ed. Darrell L. Bock (Zondervan, 1999), 158. An alternative position is "midtribulationism," which holds that the rapture occurs in the midst of the tribulational period.

# Bibliography

Aland, Barbara, Kurt Aland, J. Karavidopoulos, Carlo M. Martini, and Bruce M Metzger, eds. *The Greek New Testament*. 4th rev. ed. Deutsche Bibelgesellschaft, 1994.

Allen, Leslie C. *Ezekiel 1–19*. WBC 28. Word, 1994.

Anderson, Bernhard A. "Exodus and Covenant in Second Isaiah and Prophetic Tradition." Pages 339–360 in *Magnalia Dei: The Mighty Acts of God: Essays on the Bible and Archaeology in Memory of G. Ernest Wright*. Edited by Frank Moore Cross, Werner E. Lemke, and Patrick D. Miller, Jr. Doubleday, 1976.

Anderson, Bernhard A. "Exodus Typology in Second Isaiah." Pages 177–195 in *Israel's Prophetic Heritage: Essays in Honor of James Muilenburg*. Edited by Bernard A. Anderson and Walter Harrelson. Harper, 1962.

Anderson, Gary A. "Sacrifice & Sacrificial Offerings (OT)." Pages 870–886 in *Anchor Bible Dictionary*. Vol. 5. Edited by David Noel Freedman. Doubleday, 1992.

Andrew of Caesarea. *Commentary on the Apocalypse*. Vol 1. of *Studien zur Geschichte des griechischen Apokalypse-Testes*. Edited by Josef Schmid. K. Zink, 1955–56.

Annen, Franz. "θαυμαστός." Pages 135–136 in *EDNT*. Vol. 2. Edited by Horst Balz and Gerhard Schneider. Eerdmans, 1990.

Aristotle. *The "Art" of Rhetoric*. Translated by J. H. Freese. LCL 193. Harvard University Press, 1926.

Ashby, Godfrey. *Sacrifice: Its Nature and Purpose*. SCM, 1988.

Aune, David E. *Revelation 1–5*. WBC 52a. Word, 1997.

Aune, David E. *Revelation 6–16*. WBC 52b. Thomas Nelson, 1998.

Aune, David E. *Revelation 17–22*. WBC 52c. Thomas Nelson, 1998.

Bacon, Benjamin W. *Studies in Matthew*. Constable & Company, 1930.

Baker, David L. "Typology and the Christian Use of the Old Testament." Pages 313–330 in *The Right Doctrine from the Wrong Texts? Essays on the Use of the Old Testament in the New*. Edited by G. K. Beale. Baker, 1994.

Baldwin, Joyce G. "*SEMAH* as a Technical Term in the Prophets." *VT* 14 (1964): 93–97.

Balentine, George L. "Death of Jesus as a New Exodus." *RevExp* 59 (1962): 27–41.

Barker, Margaret. *The Great High Priest: The Temple Roots of Christian Liturgy*. T&T Clark, 2003.

Barr, Allan. "'Hope' (ἘΛΠΙΣ, ἘΛΠΙΖΩ) in the New Testament." *SJT* 3.1 (1950): 68–77.

Barrett, C. K. "The Lamb of God." *NTS* 1 (1954–1955): 210–218.

Barstad, Hans M. *A Way in the Wilderness: The "Second Exodus" in the Message of Second Isaiah*. Journal of Semitic Studies Monograph 12. University of Manchester Press, 1989.

Bauckham, Richard. *The Climax of Prophecy: Studies on the Book of Revelation*. T&T Clark, 1993.

Bauckham, Richard. *James: Wisdom of James, Disciple of Jesus the Sage*. New Testament Readings. Routledge, 1999.

Bauckham, Richard. "The List of the Tribes in Revelation 7 Again." *JSNT* 42 (1991): 99–115.

Bauckham, Richard. "The Rise of Apocalyptic." *Them* 3.2 (1978): 10–23.

Bauckham, Richard. *The Theology of the Book of Revelation*. New Testament Theology. Cambridge University Press, 1993.

Beale, G. K. *The Book of Revelation*. NIGTC. Eerdmans, 1999.

Beale, G. K. "The Eschatological Conception of New Testament Theology." Pages 11–52 in *"The Reader Must Understand": Eschatology in Bible and Theology*. Edited by K. E. Brower and M. W. Elliott. Apollos, 1997.

Beale, G. K. *John's Use of the Old Testament in Revelation*. JSNTSup 166. Sheffield, 1998.

Beale, G. K. "Positive Answer to the Question: Did Jesus and His Followers Preach the Right Doctrine from the Wrong Texts? An Examination of the Presuppositions of Jesus' and the Apostles' Exegetical Method." Pages 387–404 in *The Right Doctrine from the Wrong Texts? Essays on the Use of the Old Testament in the New*. Edited by G. K. Beale. Baker, 1994.

Beale, G. K. "Revelation." Pages 318–336 in *It Is Written: Scripture Citing Scripture; Essays in Honour of Barnabas Lindars*. Edited by D. A. Carson and H. G. M. Williamson. Cambridge University Press, 1988.

Beale, G. K. "Solecisms in the Apocalypse as Signals for the Presence of Old Testament Allusions: A Selective Analysis of Revelation 1–22." Pages 421–445 in *Early Christian Interpretation of the Scriptures of Israel: Investigations and Proposals*. Edited by Craig A. Evans. JSNTSup 148, SSEJC 5. Sheffield, 1997.

Beale, G. K. *The Use of Daniel in Jewish Apocalyptic Literature and in the Revelation of St. John*. University Press of America, 1984.

Beale, G. K. *We Become What We Worship: A Biblical Theology of Idolatry*. InterVarsity, 2008.

Beale, G. K., and Sean M. McDonough. "Revelation." Pages 1081–1161 in *Commentary on the New Testament Use of the Old Testament*. Edited by G. K. Beale and D. A. Carson. Baker Academic, 2007.

Beall, Todd S. "Essenes." Pages 342–348 in *Dictionary of New Testament Background*. Edited by Craig A. Evans and Stanley E. Porter. InterVarsity, 2000.

Beasley-Murray, G. R. "How Christian Is the Book of Revelation?" Pages 275–285 in *Reconciliation and Hope: New Testament Essays on Atonement and Eschatology, Presented to L. L. Morris on his 60th Birthday*. Edited by Robert Banks. Paternoster, 1974.

Bergmeier, Roland. "Die Buchrolle und das Lamm (Apk 5 und 10)." *Zeitschrift für die neutestamentliche Wissenschaft und die Kunde der Älteren Kirche* 76 (1985): 225–242.

Betz, Otto. "The Eschatological Interpretation of the Sinai-Tradition in Qumran and in the New Testament." *Revue de Qumran* 6 (1967): 89–107.

Blaising, Craig A. "Premillennialism." Pages 155–227 in *Three Views on the Millennium and Beyond*. Edited by Darrell L. Bock. Zondervan, 1999.

Block, Daniel I. *The Book of Ezekiel, Chapters 1–24*. NICOT. Eerdmans, 1997.

Blount, Brian K. *Revelation: A Commentary*. New Testament Library. Westminster John Knox, 2009.

Bock, Darrell L. "Summary Essay." Pages 277–309 in *Three Views on the Millennium and Beyond*. Edited by Darrell L. Bock. Counterpoints. Zondervan, 1999.

Boismard, M.-E. "Christ the Lamb, Redeemer of Men." Pages 156–167 in *Theology of the Atonement: Readings in Soteriology*. Edited by John R. Sheets. Prentice-Hall, 1967.

Bokser, Baruch M. "Unleavened Bread and Passover, Feasts of." Pages 755–765 in *Anchor Bible Dictionary*. Vol. 6. Edited by David Noel Freedman. Doubleday, 1992.

Boring, M. Eugene. "The Theology of Revelation: 'The Lord Our God the Almighty Reigns'." *Interpretation* 40 (1986): 257–269.

Boxall, Ian. *The Revelation of Saint John*. BNTC 19. Hendrickson, 2009.

Briggs, Robert A. *Jewish Temple Imagery in the Book of Revelation*. SBL 10. Peter Lang, 1999.

Bruce, F. F. *The New Testament Development of Old Testament Themes*. Eerdmans, 1968.

Brueggemann, Walter. *The Land*. Fortress, 1977.

Bullock, C. Hassell. *An Introduction to the Old Testament Prophetic Books*. Moody, 1986.

Büchsel, Friedrich. "ἀγοράζω, ἐξαγοράζω." Pages 124–128 in *TDNT*. Vol. 1. Edited by Gerhard Kittel. Translated by Geoffrey W. Bromiley. Eerdmans, 1967.

Büchsel, Friedrich. "λύω." Pages 328–359 in *TDNT*. Vol. 4. Edited by Gerhard Kittel. Translated by Geoffrey W. Bromiley. Eerdmans, 1967.

Caird, G. B. *A Commentary on the Revelation of St. John the Divine*. HNTC. Harper & Row, 1966.

Caird, G. B. *The Revelation of St. John the Divine*. 2nd ed. BNTC. Black, 1984.

Campbell, Antony F. *Joshua to Chronicles: An Introduction*. Westminster John Knox, 2004.

Carrez, Maurice. "Le Déploiement de la Christologie de l'Agneau dans l'Apocalypse." *RHPR* 79 (1999): 5–17.

Carson, D. A., and Douglas J. Moo. *An Introduction to the New Testament*. 2nd ed. Zondervan, 2005.

Casey, Jay. "The Exodus Theme in the Book of Revelation against the Background of the New Testament." Pages 34–43 in *Exodus: A Lasting Paradigm*. Edited by Antonius G. Weiler, Marcus Lefébure, & Bastiaan Martinus Franciscus van Iersel. T&T Clark, 1987.

Casey, Jay. "Exodus Typology in the Book of Revelation." PhD diss., The Southern Baptist Theological Seminary, 1981.

Casey, Maurice. "Christology and the Legitimating Use of the Old Testament in the New Testament." Pages 42–64 in *The Old Testament in the New Testament: Essays in Honour of J.L. North*. Edited by Steve Moyise. JSNTSup 189. Sheffield, 2000.

Charles, J. Daryl. "An Apocalyptic Tribute to the Lamb (Rev 5:1–14)." *JETS* 34 (1991): 461–473.

Charles, J. Daryl. "Imperial Pretensions and the Throne-Vision of the Lamb: Observations on the Function of Revelation 5." *CTR* 7 (1993): 85–97.

Charles, R. H. *A Critical and Exegetical Commentary on The Revelation of St. John: With Introduction, Notes, and Indices, also The Greek Text and English Translation*. 2 vols. ICC. T&T Clark, 1920.

Charlesworth, James H., ed. *Damascus Document, War Scroll, and Related Documents*. Vol. 2 of *The Dead Sea Scrolls: Hebrew, Aramaic, and Greek Texts with English Translations*. J. C. B. Mohr, 1995.

Charlesworth, James H., and James R. Mueller. *The New Testament Apocrypha and Pseudepigrapha: A Guide to Publications, with Excursuses on Apocalypses.* ATLA Bibliography Series 17. American Theological Library Association, 1987.

Cheon, Samuel. *The Exodus Story in the Wisdom of Solomon: A Study in Biblical Interpretation.* Sheffield, 1997.

Childs, Brevard S. *The Book of Exodus: A Critical, Theological Commentary.* OTL. Westminster, 1974.

Chisholm, Robert B., Jr. "Divine Hardening in the Old Testament." *BSac* 153 (1996): 410–434.

Clifford, Richard J. "The Exodus in the Christian Bible: The Case for 'Figural' Reading." *Theological Studies* 63 (2002): 345–361.

Clifford, Richard J. "The Tent of El and the Israelite Tent of Meeting." *CBQ* 33 (1971): 221–227.

Collins, John Joseph, ed. *Apocalypse: The Morphology of a Genre.* Semeia 14. Scholars, 1979.

Collins, John Joseph. *The Apocalyptic Imagination: An Introduction to Jewish Apocalyptic Literature.* 2nd ed. The Biblical Resource Series. Eerdmans, 1988.

Comblin, J. *Le Christ dans l'Apocalypse.* Théologie Biblique. Desclée, 1965.

Cooper, Lamar Eugene. *Ezekiel.* NAC 17. Broadman & Holman, 1994.

Dalglish, Edward R. *The Great Deliverance: A Concise Exposition of the Book of Exodus.* Broadman, 1977.

Dalman, Roger. *A People Come Out of Egypt: Studies in the Books of Exodus, Deuteronomy and Judges.* Send the Light Press, 2002.

Daly, Robert J. *The Origins of the Christian Doctrine of Sacrifice.* Fortress, 1978.

Daniélou, Jean. *From Shadows to Reality: Studies in the Biblical Typology of the Fathers.* Translated by Wulstan Hibberd. Burns & Oates, 1960.

Danker, Frederic William, ed. *A Greek-English Lexicon of the New Testament and Other Early Christian Literature*, 3rd ed. University of Chicago Press, 2000.

Daube, David. *The Exodus Pattern in the Bible.* Faber and Faber, 1963.

Dautzenberg, G. "ἀμνός, ἀρην, ἀρνίον." Pages 70–72 in *EDNT*. Vol. 1. Edited by Horst Balz and Gerhard Schneider. Eerdmans, 1990.

Davidson, Richard M. *Typology in Scripture: A Study of Hermeneutical τύπος Structures.* Andrews University Seminary Doctoral Dissertation Series 2. Andrews University Press, 1981.

Delitzsch, Franz. *Biblical Commentary on the Prophecies of Isaiah.* 3rd ed. Translated by James Martin. 2 vols. Eerdmans, 1877.

Dempster, Stephen G. *Dominion and Dynasty: A Theology of the Hebrew Bible.* New Studies in Biblical Theology. InterVarsity, 2003.

Dempster, Stephen G. "Exodus and Biblical Theology: On Moving into the Neighborhood with a New Name." *Southern Baptist Journal of Theology* 12.3 (2008): 4–23.

DeSilva, David A. "Final Topics: The Rhetorical Functions of Intertexture in Revelation 14:14–16:21." Pages 215–241 in *The Intertexture of Apocalyptic Discourse in the New Testament.* Edited by Duane F. Watson. SBL Symposium Series 14. SBL, 2002.

DeSilva, David A. *Introducing the Apocrypha: Message, Context, and Significance.* Baker, 2002.

DeSilva, David A. *Seeing Things John's Way: The Rhetoric of the Book of Revelation.* Westminster John Knox, 2009.

Di Lella, Alexander A. *The Book of Daniel.* AB 23. DoubleDay, 1978.

Draper, J. A. "The Heavenly Feast of Tabernacles: Revelation 7.1–17." *JSNT* 19 (1983): 133–147.

Dodd, C. H. *According to the Scriptures: The Sub-Structure of New Testament Theology.* Nisbet, 1952.

Dodd, C. H. *Interpretation of the Fourth Gospel.* Cambridge University Press, 1960.

D'Souza, John. *The Lamb of God in the Johannine Writings.* St. Paul, 1968.

Dumbrell, William J. *Covenant and Creation: A Theology of Old Testament Covenants.* Biblical and Theological Classics Library 12. Paternoster, 1984.

Dumbrell, William J. *The End of the Beginning: Revelation 21–22 and the Old Testament.* Lancer, 1985.

Durham, John I. *Exodus.* WBC 3. Word, 1987.

Durham, John I. *Understanding the Basic Themes of Exodus.* Quick-Reference Bible Topics. Word, 1990.

Elliott, Mark Adam. *The Survivors of Israel: A Reconsideration of the Theology of Pre-Christian Judaism.* Eerdmans, 2000.

Enns, Peter. "Wisdom of Solomon and Biblical Interpretation in the Second Temple Period." Pages 212–225 in *The Way of Wisdom: Essays in Honor of Bruce K. Waltke.* Edited by J. I. Packer & Sven K. Soderlund. Zondervan, 2000.

Ericson, Norman R. "The NT Use of the OT: A Kerygmatic Approach." *JETS* 30 (1987): 337–342.

Eslinger, Lyle M. "Freedom or Knowledge: Perspective and Purpose in the Exodus Narrative (Exodus 1–15)." *JSOT* 52 (1991): 43–60.

Evans, Craig A. "The Old Testament in the New." Pages 130–145 in *The Face of New Testament Studies: A Survey of Recent Research.* Edited by Scot McKnight and Grant R. Osborne. Baker, 2004.

Evans, Craig A. "Typology." Pages 862–866 in *Dictionary of Jesus and the Gospels.* Edited by Joel B. Green and Scot McKnight. InterVarsity, 1992.

Fairbairn, Patrick. *The Typology of Scripture: Two Volumes in One, Complete and Unabridged.* Zondervan, 1967.

Fee, Gordon D. *Revelation.* New Covenant Commentary Series. Wipf and Stock, 2010.

Fekkes, Jan. *Isaiah and Prophetic Traditions in the Book of Revelation: Visionary Antecedents and Their Development.* JSNTSup 93. JSOT, 1994.

Feuillet, A. "Les 144,000 Israelites marques d'un sceau." *NovT* 9 (1967): 191–224.

Fisher, Fred L. "The New and Greater Exodus: The Exodus Pattern in the New Testament." *SwJT* 20 (1997): 69–79.

Fitzer, Gottfried. "σφραγίς." Pages 939–953 in *TDNT.* Vol. 8. Edited by Gerhard Kittel. Translated by Geoffrey W. Bromiley. Eerdmans, 1967.

Ford, J. Massyngberde. *Revelation.* AB 38. Doubleday, 1975.

Foulkes, Francis. "The Acts of God: A Study of the Basis of Typology in the Old Testament." Pages 342–371 in *The Right Doctrine from the Wrong Texts? Essays on the Use of the Old Testament in the New.* Edited by G. K. Beale. Baker, 1994.

France, R. T. *Jesus and the Old Testament: His Application of Old Testament Passages to Himself and His Mission.* Tyndale, 1971.

Fretheim, Terence E. "'Because the Whole Earth is Mine': Theme and Narrative in Exodus." *Interpretation* 50 (1996): 229–239.

Friedman, Richard Elliott. *The Hidden Face of God.* HarperCollins, 1996.

Friesen, Steven J. *Imperial Cults and the Apocalypse of John: Reading Revelation in the Ruins.* Oxford University Press, 2001.

Geyser, Albert. "The Twelve Tribes in Revelation: Judean and Judeo–Christian Apocalypticism." *NTS* 28 (1982): 388–399.

Gilbertson, Michael. *God and History in the Book of Revelation: New Testament Studies in Dialogue with Pannenberg and Moltmann.* Cambridge University Press, 2003.

Goldingay, John. *Israel's Faith.* Vol. 2 of *Old Testament Theology.* InterVarsity, 2006.

Goppelt, Leonhard. *Typos: The Typological Interpretation of the Old Testament in the New.* Translated by Donald H. Madvig. Eerdmans, 1982.

Goulder, M. D. "The Apocalypse as an Annual Cycle of Prophecies." *NTS* 27 (1981): 342–367.

Gray, George Buchanan. *Sacrifice in the Old Testament: Its Theory & Practice.* Clarendon, 1925.

Grimsrud, Ted. *Triumph of the Lamb: A Self–Study Guide to the Book of Revelation.* Herald, 1987.

Grundmann, Walter. "Στήκω, ἵστημι," Pages 636–653 in *TDNT*. Vol 5. Edited by Gerhard Kittel. Translated by Geoffrey W. Bromiley. Eerdmans, 1967.

Guimond, John. *The Silencing of Babylon: A Spiritual Commentary on the Revelation of John.* Paulist, 1991.

Guthrie, Donald. "The Lamb in the Structure of the Book of Revelation." *Vox Evangelica* 12 (1981): 64–71.

Hamilton, James M., Jr. *God's Glory in Salvation through Judgment: A Biblical Theology.* Crossway, 2010.

Harrington, Daniel J. *Invitation to the Apocrypha.* Eerdmans, 1999.

Harris, M. J. "Tent, Tabernacle (σκηνή)." Pages 811–816 in *NIDNTT*. Vol. 3. Edited by Colin Brown. Zondervan, 1986.

Hasel, Gerhard F. *Old Testament Theology: Basic Issues in the Current Debate.* 3rd rev. ed. Eerdmans, 1972.

Hatina, Thomas R. "Exile." Pages 348–352 in *Dictionary of New Testament Background.* Edited by Craig A. Evans and Stanley E. Porter. InterVarsity, 2000.

Haugen, Philip S. "The Consummation of the Exodus: A Study of the Exodus Motif in the Revelation." S.T.M. thesis, Concordia Seminary, 1985.

Hays, Richard. *The Conversion of the Imagination: Paul as Interpreter of Israel's Scripture.* Eerdmans, 2005.

Hays, Richard. *Echoes of Scripture in the Letters of Paul.* Yale University Press, 1989.

Hill, Linzy H., Jr. "Reading Isaiah as a Theological Unity Based on an Exegetical Investigation of the Exodus Motif." PhD diss., Southwestern Baptist Theological Seminary, 1993.

Hillyer, Norman. "'The Lamb' in the Apocalypse." *EvQ* 39 (1967): 228–236.

Hoehner, Harold W. *Ephesians: An Exegetical Commentary.* Baker, 2002.

Hofmann, C. K. von. *Interpreting the Bible*. Translated by Christian Preus. Ausburg, 1959.

Hollander, John. *The Figure of Echo: A Mode of Allusion in Milton and After*. University of California Press, 1981.

Hoskins, Paul M. *Jesus as the Fulfillment of the Temple in the Gospel of John*. Paternoster Biblical Monographs. Wipf and Stock, 2006.

Hoskins, Paul M. *That Scripture Might Be Fulfilled: Typology and the Death of Christ*. Xulon, 2009.

Howard, David M., Jr. *Joshua*. NAC 5. Broadman & Holman, 2000.

Hübner, Hans. "ἀλήθεια." Pages 57–60 in *EDNT*. Vol. 1. Edited by Horst Balz and Gerhard Schneider. Eerdmans, 1990.

Hyde, Clark. "The Remembrance of the Exodus in the Psalms." *Worship* 62 (1988): 404–414.

Irenaeus. *Adversus haereses 4*. Vol. 2 of *Irénée de Lyon: Contre les heresies*. Translated and edited by A. Rousseau, B. Hemmerdinger, L. Doutreleau, and C. Mercier. SC 100. Cerf, 1965.

Isaac, E. "1 (Ethiopic Apocalypse of) Enoch." Pages 5–90 in *Apocalyptic Literature and Testaments*. Vol. 1 of *OTP*. Edited by James H. Charlesworth. Doubleday, 1983.

Jenkins, Ferrell. *The Old Testament in the Book of Revelation*. Baker, 1972.

Jensen, Irving L. *Joshua: Rest-Land Won*. Everyman's Bible Commentary. Moody, 1966.

Jeremias, J. "ἀμνός, ἀρην, ἀρνίον." Pages 338–341 in *TDNT*. Vol. 1. Edited by Gerhard Kittel. Translated by Geoffrey W. Bromiley. Eerdmans, 1967.

Johns, Loren L. *The Lamb Christology of the Apocalypse of John: An Investigation into Its Origins and Rhetorical Force*. WUNT 2nd series 167. Mohr Siebeck, 2003.

Johnson, Dennis E. *Triumph of the Lamb: A Commentary on Revelation*. P & R, 2001.

Josephus, Flavius. *Judean Antiquities 1–4*. Translated by Louis H. Feldman. Vol. 3 of *Flavius Josephus: Translation and Commentary*. Brill, 2000.

Judge, E. A. "The Mark of the Beast, Revelation 13:16." *TynBul* 42 (1991): 158–160.

Kaiser, Walter C., Jr. "The Promise Theme and the Theology of Rest." *BSac* 130 (1973): 135–150.

Kaiser, Walter C., Jr. "The Promised Land: A Biblical-Historical View." *BSac* 138 (1981): 302–311.

Kee, Howard Clark. "Appropriating the History of God's People: A Survey of Interpretations of the History of Israel in the Pseudepigrapha, Apocrypha and the New Testament." Pages 44–64 in *The Pseudepigrapha and Early Biblical Interpretation*. Edited by James H. Charlesworth and Craig A. Evans. JSPSup 14, SSEJC 2. Sheffield, 1993.

Keesmaat, Sylvia C. "Paul and His Story: Exodus and Tradition in Galatians." *HBT* 18 (1996): 133–168.

Kelly, Balmer H. "Revelation 7:9–17." *Interpretation* 40 (1986): 288–295.

Kilpatrick, Robert Kirk. "Against the Gods of Egypt: An Examination of the Narrative of the Ten Plagues in the Light of Exodus 12:12." ThD diss., Mid-America Baptist Theological Seminary, 1995.

Klappert, B. "βασιλεία." Pages 372–390 in *NIDNTT*. Vol. 2. Edited by Colin Brown. Zondervan, 1986.

Klein, Ralph W. *Israel in Exile: A Theological Interpretation*. OBT. Fortress, 1979.
Knight, George A. F. *The Song of Moses: A Theological Quarry*. Eerdmans, 1995.
Knight, Jonathan. *Revelation*. Sheffield, 1999.
Koester, Craig R. *Revelation and the End of All Things*. Eerdmans, 2001.
Koptak, Paul E. "Intertextuality." Pages 332–334 in *Dictionary for Theological Interpretation of the Bible*. Edited by Kevin J. Vanhoozer. Baker, 2005.
Kratz, Reinhard. "θάλασσα." Pages 127–128 in *EDNT*. Vol. 2. Edited by Horst Balz and Gerhard Schneider. Eerdmans, 1990.
Kreitzer, L. J. "Apocalyptic, Apocalypticism." Pages 55–68 in *Dictionary of the Later New Testament and Its Developments*. Edited by Ralph P. Martin and Peter H. Davids. InterVarsity, 1997.
Kruger, Paul A. "Hosea." Pages 707–708 in *New International Dictionary of Old Testament Theology and Exegesis*. Vol. 4. Edited by Willem A. VanGemeren. Zondervan, 1997.
Ladd, George Eldon. *A Commentary on the Revelation of John*. Eerdmans, 1972.
Ladd, George Eldon. *A Theology of the New Testament*. Rev. ed. Eerdmans, 1993.
Lampe, G. W. H. "The Reasonableness of Typology." Pages 9–38 in *Essays on Typology*. By G. W. H. Lampe and K. H. Woollcombe. SBT 22. Allenson, 1957.
Lawrence, John Benjamin. *New Heaven and a New Earth: A Contemporary Interpretation of the Book of Revelation*. American, 1960.
Lewis, Scott M. *What Are They Saying about New Testament Apocalyptic?* Paulist, 2004.
Lioy, Dan. *The Book of Revelation in Christological Focus*. SBL 58. Peter Lang, 2003.
Lodahl, Michael E. *Shekhinah/Spirit: Divine Presence in Jewish and Christian Religion*. Paulist, 1992.
Loewenstamm, Samuel E. *The Evolution of the Exodus Tradition*. Translated by Baruch J. Schwartz. Publication of the Perry Foundation for Biblical Research in the Hebrew University of Jerusalem. Magnes Press, Hebrew University, 1992.
Lucas, Ernest. *Daniel*. ApOTC. InterVarsity, 2002.
Mánek, Jindřich. "New Exodus in the Books of Luke." *NovT* 2 (1957): 8–23.
Mann, Thomas W. *Divine Presence and Guidance in Israelite Traditions: The Typology of Exaltation*. Johns Hopkins University Press, 1977.
Marshall, I. Howard. "An Assessment of Recent Developments." Pages 1–21 in *It Is Written: Scripture Citing Scripture; Essays in Honour of Barnabas Lindars*. Edited by D. A. Carson and H. G. M. Williamson. Cambridge University Press, 1988.
Marshall, I. Howard. "The Development of the Concept of Redemption in the New Testament." Pages 153–169 in *Reconciliation and Hope: New Testament Essays on Atonement and Eschatology, Presented to L. L. Morris on his 60th Birthday*. Edited by Robert Banks. Paternoster, 1974.
Martin, Ralph P. "Mark, Brand." Pages 572–573 in *NIDNTT*. Vol. 2. Edited by Colin Brown. Zondervan, 1986.
Mathewson, David. "Assessing Old Testament Allusions in the Book of Revelation." *EvQ* 75 (2003): 311–325.
Mathewson, David. *A New Heaven and a New Earth: The Meaning and Function of the Old Testament in Revelation 21:1–22:5*. JSNTSup 238. JSOT, 2003.

McKenzie, Steve. "Exodus Typology in Hosea." *Restoration Quarterly* 22 (1979): 100–108.

McKnight, Scot. "Israel." Pages 344–346 in *Dictionary for Theological Interpretation of the Bible*. Edited by Kevin J. Vanhoozer. Baker, 2005.

Melito of Sardis. *On Pascha and Fragments*. Translated and edited by Stuart George Hall. OECT. Clarendon, 1979.

Merrill, Eugene H. *Everlasting Dominion: A Theology of the Old Testament*. Broadman & Holman, 2006.

Merrill, Eugene H. *Kingdom of Priests: A History of Old Testament Israel*. Baker, 1996.

Metzger, Bruce M. *Breaking the Code: Understanding the Book of Revelation*. Abingdon, 1993.

Metzger, Bruce M. *The Canon of the New Testament: Its Origin, Significance, and Development*. Oxford University Press, 1987.

Meyer, Lester. *The Message of Exodus: A Theological Commentary*. Augsburg, 1983.

Michaels, J. Ramsey. *Interpreting the Book of Revelation*. Baker, 1992.

Michel, Otto. "Σφάζω, σφαγή." Pages 925–938 in *TDNT*. Vol. 7. Edited by Gerhard Kittel. Translated by Geoffrey W. Bromiley. Eerdmans, 1967.

Moberly, R. W. L. *At the Mountain of God: Story and Theology in Exodus 32–34*. JSOT, 1983.

Mol, Robert W. "Sources and Their Use in Revelation 12:1–17." MA thesis, Trinity Evangelical Divinity School, 1981.

Moo, Douglas J. "Nature in the New Creation: New Testament Eschatology and the Environment." *JETS* 49 (2006): 449–488.

Morris, Leon. *The Apostolic Preaching of the Cross*. 3rd rev. ed. Eerdmans, 1994.

Morris, Leon. *The Cross in the New Testament*. Eerdmans, 1965.

Morris, Leon. *The Revelation of St. John*. Eerdmans, 1980.

Motyer, J. A. *The Prophecy of Isaiah: An Introduction and Commentary*. InterVarsity, 1993.

Mounce, Robert H. *The Book of Revelation*. NICNT. Eerdmans, 1977.

Mounce, Robert H. "The Christology of the Apocalypse." *Foundations* 11 (1968): 42–51.

Moyise, Steve. "Intertextuality and the Study of the Old Testament in the New Testament." Pages 14–41 in *The Old Testament in the New Testament: Essays in Honour of J.L. North*. Edited by Steve Moyise. JSNTSup 189. Sheffield, 2000.

Moyise, Steve. *The Old Testament in the Book of Revelation*. JSNTSup 115. Sheffield, 1995.

Moyise, Steve. "The Use of the Old Testament in the Book of Revelation." PhD diss., University of Birmingham, 1994.

Muilenburg, J. *The Way of Israel: Biblical Faith and Ethics*. Harper, 1961.

Murphy, James. *A Critical and Exegetical Commentary on the Book of Exodus*. Halliday 1868. Repr., James Publications, 1979.

Newport, John P. *The Lion and the Lamb*. Broadman, 1986.

Newsom, Carol A. "The Past as Revelation: History in Apocalyptic Literature." *QR* 4.3 (1984): 40–53.

Nickelsburg, George W. E. *Jewish Literature between the Bible and the Mishnah*. SCM, 1981.

Nielsen, Kirsten. "Shepherd, Lamb, and Blood: Imagery in the Old Testament – Use and Reuse." *Studia Theologica* 46 (1992): 121–132.

Ninow, Friedbert. *Indicators of Typology within the Old Testament: The Exodus Motif.* Friedensauer Schriftenreihe; Reihe I, Theologie, Bd. 4. Peter Lang, 2001.

Nixon, R. E. *The Exodus in the New Testament.* Tyndale New Testament Lecture 1962. Tyndale, 1963.

Oecumenius. *Commentary on the Apocalypse.* Translated by John N. Suggit. FC 112. Catholic University of America Press, 2006.

Oesterley, W. O. E. *An Introduction to the Books of the Apocrypha.* MacMillan, 1935.

Origen. *Treatise on the Passover and Dialogue of Origen with Heraclides and His Fellow Bishops on the Father, the Son, and the Soul.* Translated and annotated by Robert J. Daly. ACW 54. Paulist, 1992.

Osborn, Thomas. *The Lion and the Lamb: A Drama of the Apocalypse.* Abingdon, 1922.

Osborne, Grant R. *Revelation.* BECNT. Baker, 2002.

Pao, David W. *Acts and the Isaianic New Exodus.* WUNT 2nd series 130. Mohr Siebeck, 2000.

Pate, C. Marvin, ed. *Four Views on the Book of Revelation.* Zondervan, 1998.

Pate, C. Marvin, J. Scott Duvall, J. Daniel Hays, E. Randolph Richards, W. Dennis Tucker, Jr., and Preben Vang. *The Story of Israel: A Biblical Theology.* InterVarsity, 2004.

Patrick, Dale A. "Epiphanic Imagery in Second Isaiah's Portrayal of a New Exodus." *HAR* 8 (1984): 125–141.

Pattemore, Stephen. *The People of God in the Apocalypse.* Cambridge University Press, 2004.

Patterson, Paige. *Revelation.* NAC 39. Broadman & Holman, 2012.

Paul, Ian. "The Use of the Old Testament in Revelation 12." Pages 256–276 in *The Old Testament in the New Testament; Essays in Honour of J. L. North.* Edited by Steve Moyise. JSNTSup 189. Sheffield, 2000.

Paulien, Jon. "Allusions, Exegetical Method, and the Interpretation of Rev 8:7–12." PhD diss., Andrews University, 1987.

Paulien, Jon. "Elusive Allusions in the Apocalypse: Two Decades of Research into John's Use of the Old Testament." Pages 61–68 in *The Intertextuality of the Epistles: Explorations of Theory and Practice.* Edited by Thomas L. Brodie, Dennis R. MacDonald, and Stanley E. Porter. New Testament Monographs 16. Sheffield Phoenix, 2006.

Paulien, Jon. "Elusive Allusions: The Problematic Use of the Old Testament in Revelation." *BR* 33 (1988): 37–53.

Piper, Otto A. "Unchanging Promises: Exodus in the New Testament." *Interpretation* 11 (1957): 3–22.

*Pirke de-Rabbi Elieser.* Translated and edited by Dagmar Börner-Klein. SJ 26. Walter de Gruyter, 2004.

Plastaras, James. *Creation and Covenant.* Bruce Publishing, 1968.

Plastaras, James. *The God of Exodus: The Theology of the Exodus Narratives.* Bruce Publishing, 1966.

Porter, Stanley E. "Further Comments on the Use of the Old Testament in the New Testament." Pages 98–110 in *The Intertextuality of the Epistles: Explorations of Theory and Practice*. Edited by Thomas L. Brodie, Dennis R. MacDonald, and Stanley E. Porter. New Testament Monographs 16. Sheffield Phoenix, 2006.

Porter, Stanley E. "The Use of the Old Testament in the New Testament: A Brief Comment on Method and Terminology." Pages 79–96 in *Early Christian Interpretation of the Scriptures of Israel: Investigations and Proposals*. Edited by Craig A. Evans and James A. Sanders. JSNTSup 148, SSEJC 5. Sheffield, 1997.

Prigent, Pierre. *Commentary on the Apocalypse of St. John*. Translated by Wendy Pradels. Rev. ed. Mohr Siebeck, 2001.

Primasius. *Commentarius in Apocalypsin*. Edited by A. W. Adams. Brepols, 1985.

Prosic, Tamara. *The Development and Symbolism of Passover until 70 CE*. T&T. Clark, 2004.

Rahlfs, Alfred, ed. *Septuaginta*. Württembergische Bibelanstalt/Deutsche Bibelgesellschaft, 1935.

Redford, Donald B. *The Ancient Gods Speak: A Guide to Egyptian Religion*. Oxford University Press, 2002.

Reeves, John C. *Trajectories in Near Eastern Apocalyptic: A Postrabbinic Jewish Apocalypse Reader*. SBL Resources for Biblical Study 45. SBL, 2005.

Resseguie, J. L. *Revelation Unsealed: A Narrative Critical Approach to John's Apocalypse*. BibInt 32. Brill, 1998.

Richard, Pablo. "Plagues in the Bible: Exodus and Apocalypse." Pages 45–54 in *The Return of the Plague*. Edited by José Oscar Beozzo and Virgil Elizondo. Concilium 5. SCM, 1997.

Richardson, Alan. *An Introduction to the Theology of the New Testament*. SCM, 1958.

Rissi, Mathias, *Time and History: A Study in the Revelation*. Translated by Gordon C. Windsor. John Knox, 1966.

Robinson, G. L. "Zechariah, Book of." Pages 3136–3140 in *The International Standard Bible Encyclopaedia*. Vol. 5. Edited by J. Orr. Rev. ed. Eerdmans, 1939.

Rosner, Brian S. "Salvation, History of." Pages 714–717 in *Dictionary for Theological Interpretation of the Bible*, Edited by Kevin J. Vanhoozer. Baker, 2005.

Ruiz, Jean-Pierre. *Ezekiel in the Apocalypse: The Transformation of Prophetic Language in Revelation 16,17–19,10*. European University Studies: Theology 23. Peter Lang, 1989.

Russell, D. S. *The Method & Message of Jewish Apocalyptic, 200 BC–AD 100*. SCM, 1964.

Sabourin, Leopold. *The Names and Titles of Jesus*. Macmillan, 1967.

Sahlin, Harald. "The New Exodus of Salvation according to St. Paul." Pages 81–95 in *The Root of the Vine: Essays in Biblical Theology*. Edited by Anton Fridrichsen. Dacre, 1953.

Sarna, Nahum M. *Exploring Exodus: The Origins of Biblical Israel*. Schocken Books, 1986. Reprint, Pantheon Books, 1996.

Schippers, R. "Seal." Pages 497–501 in *NIDNTT*. Vol. 3. Edited by Colin Brown. Zondervan, 1986.

Schnackenburg, Rudolf. *The Gospel According to John*. 3 vols. Translated by Kevin Smyth. Herder and Herder, 1968.

Schneider, Gerhard. "δίκαιος." Pages 324–325 in *EDNT*. Vol. 1. Edited by Horst Balz and Gerhard Schneider. Eerdmans, 1990.

Schneider, Johannes. "βάσανος, βασανίζω, βασανισμός, βασανιστής." Pages 561–564 in *TDNT*. Vol. 1. Edited by Gerhard Kittel. Translated by Geoffrey W. Bromiley. Eerdmans, 1967.

Schneider, Johannes, and Colin Brown. "Redemption." Pages 177–223 in *NIDNTT*. Vol. 3. Edited by Colin Brown. Zondervan, 1986.

Schüssler Fiorenza, Elisabeth. "The Phenomenon of Early Christian Apocalyptic: Some Reflections on Method." Pages 295–316 in *Apocalypticism in the Mediterranean World and the Near East: Proceedings of the International Colloquium on Apocalypticism, Uppsala, August 12–17, 1979*. Edited by David Hellholm, 295–316. 2nd ed. Mohr, 1989.

Scott, J. M. *Adoption as Sons of God: An Exegetical Investigation into the Background of UIOTHESIA in the Pauline Corpus*. Mohr-Seibeck, 1992.

Seebass, Horst. "ὅσιος." Pages 236–238 in *NIDNTT*. Vol. 2. Edited by Colin Brown. Zondervan, 1986.

Seitz, Christopher R. *Figured Out: Typology and Providence in Christian Scripture*. Westminster John Knox, 2001.

Shea, William H. "Literary and Theological Parallels between Revelation 14–15 and Exodus 19–24." *Journal of the Adventist Theological Society* 12 (2001): 164–179.

Shorter, Alan W. *The Egyptian Gods: A Handbook*. Kegan Paul, Trench, Trubner, 1937.

Smalley, Stephen S. "John's Revelation and John's Community." *BJRL* 69 (1988): 549–571.

Smalley, Stephen S. *The Revelation to John: A Commentary on the Greek Text of the Apocalypse*. InterVarsity, 2005.

Smith, Christopher R. "The Portrayal of the Church as the New Israel in the Names and Order of the Tribes in Revelation 7.5–8." *JSNT* 39 (1990): 111–118.

Smith, Christopher R. "The Tribes of Revelation 7 and the Literary Competence of John the Seer." *JETS* 38 (1995): 213–218.

Smith, R. L. *Micah—Malachi*. WBC 32. Word, 1984.

Smith, Robert Houston. "Exodus Typology in the Fourth Gospel." *JBL* 81 (1962): 329–342.

Smith, T. C. *Jesus in the Gospel of John*. Broadman, 1959.

Smith, T. C. *Reading the Signs: A Sensible Approach to Revelation and Other Apocalyptic Writings*. Smyth & Helwys, 1977.

Southern, Pat. *Domitian: Tragic Tyrant*. Indiana University Press, 1997.

Spatafora, Andrea. *From the "Temple of God" to God as the Temple: A Biblical Theological Study of the Temple in the Book of Revelation*. TGST 27. Editrice Pontificia Università Gregoriana, 1997.

Spilsbury, Paul. *The Throne, the Lamb & the Dragon: A Reader's Guide to the Book of Revelation*. InterVarsity, 2002.

Stalker, D. M. G. "Exodus." Pages 208–240 in *Peake's Commentary on the Bible*. Edited by Matthew Black and H. H. Rowley. Thomas Nelson, 1962.

Stek, John H. "Biblical Typology Today and Yesterday." *CTJ* 5 (1970): 133–162.

Stock, Augustine. *The Way in the Wilderness: Exodus, Wilderness, and Moses Themes in Old Testament and New*. Liturgical Press, 1969.

Stone, Michael E. "Apocalyptic Literature." Pages 383–443 in *Jewish Writings of the Second Temple Period*. Edited by Michael E. Stone. Fortress, 1984.

Strand, Kenneth Albert. *Interpreting the Book of Revelation: Hermeneutical Guidelines, With Brief Introduction to Literary Analysis*. Ann Arbor, 1976.

Sweet, John. *Revelation*. SCM Pelican Commentaries. SCM, 1979.

Swete, H. B. *The Apocalypse of St. John: The Greek Text with Introduction, Notes, and Indices*. Macmillan, 1906.

Taylor, Vincent. *The Atonement in New Testament Thinking*. 2nd ed. Epworth, 1945.

Tenney, Merrill C. *Interpreting Revelation: A Reasonable Guide to Understanding the Last Book in the Bible*. Hendrickson, 2001.

Terrien, Samuel. *The Elusive Presence: The Heart of Biblical Theology*. Harper & Row, 1978.

Thomas, Gordon J. "A Holy God among a Holy People in a Holy Place: The Enduring Eschatological Hope." Pages 53–69 in *"The Reader Must Understand": Eschatology in Bible and Theology*. Edited by K. E. Brower and M. W. Elliott. Apollos, 1997.

Thomas, Robert L. *Revelation 1–7: An Exegetical Commentary*. Edited by Kenneth Barker. Moody, 1992.

Thompson, Leonard L. *The Book of Revelation: Apocalypse and Empire*. Oxford University Press, 1990.

Tolar, William Bert. "Re-Evaluation of the Evidences that the Domitianic Persecutions Served as the Background for the Book of Revelation." ThD thesis, Southwestern Baptist Theological Seminary, 1966.

Trudinger, L. Paul. "Some Observations Concerning the Text of the Old Testament in the Book of Revelation." *JTS* 17 (1966): 82–88

Tyconius. *Commentarius in Apocalypsin*. Edited by A. W. Adams. Brepols, 1985.

Ulfgard, Håkan. *Feast and Future: Revelation 7:9–17 and the Feast of Tabernacles*. ConBNT 22. Almqvist & Wiksell, 1989.

Vanhoye, Albert. "L'utilisation du livre d'Ézéchiel dans l'Apocalypse." *Biblica* 43 (1962): 436–476.

Von Rad, Gerhard. *The Theology of Israel's Prophetic Traditions*. Vol. 2 of *Old Testament Theology*. Translated by D. M. G. Stalker. Harper & Row, 1965.

Von Rad, Gerhard. "Typological Interpretation of the Old Testament." Pages 17–39 in *Essays on Old Testament Hermeneutics*. Edited by Claus Westermann. John Knox, 1963.

Von Rad, Gerhard. "Typological Interpretation of the Old Testament." Translated by John Bright. *Interpretation* 15 (1961): 174–192.

Wallace, Daniel B. *Greek Grammar Beyond the Basics: An Exegetical Syntax of the New Testament*. Zondervan, 1996.

Waltke, Bruce K. *An Old Testament Theology: An Exegetical, Canonical, and Thematic Approach*. Zondervan, 2007.

Watson, Francis. *Paul and the Hermeneutics of Faith*. T&T Clark, 2004.

Watson, Wilfred G. E. *Classical Hebrew Poetry: A Guide to Its Techniques.* JSOTSS 26. JSOT, 1984.
Watterson, Barbara. *The Gods of Ancient Egypt.* Facts on File Publications, 1984.
Watts, Rikki E. "Exodus." Pages 478–487 in *New Dictionary of Biblical Theology.* Edited by D. Alexander and B. Rosner. InterVarsity, 2000.
Watts, Rikki E. *Isaiah's New Exodus and Mark.* WUNT 2nd series 88. Mohr Siebeck, 1997.
Weiler, Antonius Gerardus, and Marcus Lefébure, eds. *Exodus—A Lasting Paradigm.* T&T Clark, 1987.
Weinrich, William C., ed. *Revelation.* ACCS New Testament 12. InterVarsity Press, 2005.
Westermann, Claus. *Isaiah 40–66: A Commentary.* Translated by David M. G. Stalker. OTL. Westminster, 1969.
White, Douglas M. *Holy Ground: Expositions from Exodus.* Baker, 1962.
Winkle, Ross E. "Another Look at the List of Tribes in Revelation." *AUSS* 27 (1989): 53–67.
Witherington, Ben, III. *Revelation.* NCBC. Cambridge University Press, 2003.
Woollcombe, K. H. "The Biblical Origins and Patristic Development of Typology." Pages 39–80 in *Essays on Typology.* By G. W. H. Lampe and K. H. Woollcombe. SBT 22. Allenson, 1957.
Wright, N. T. "New Exodus, New Inheritance: The Narrative Structure of Romans 3–8." Pages 26–35 in *Romans and the People of God: Essays in Honor of Gordon D. Fee.* Edited by Sven Soderlund and N. T. Wright. Eerdmans, 1999.
Wright, N. T. *The New Testament and the People of God.* Vol. 1 of *Christian Origins and the Question of God.* Fortress, 1992.
Yates, Gary. "New Exodus and No Exodus in Jeremiah 26–45: Promise and Warning to the Exiles in Babylon." *TynBul* 57 (2006): 1–23.
Yates, Richard Shalom. "The Identity of the Tribulation Saints." *BSac* 163 (2006): 79–93.
Young, Edward J. *The Book of Isaiah: The English Text, with Introduction, Exposition, and Notes.* 3 vols. NICOT. Eerdmans, 1972.
Young, Frances M. *The Use of Sacrificial Ideas in Greek Christian Writers from the New Testament to John Chrysostom.* Patristic Monograph Series 5. Philadelphia Patristic Foundation, 1979.
Zimmerli, Walther. "Der 'Neue Exodus' in der Verkündigung der beiden grossen Exilspropheten." Pages 192–204 in *Gottes Offenbarung: Gesammelte Aufsätze zum Alten Testament.* Edited by Walther Zimmerli. Theologische Bücherei; Neudrucke und Berichte aus dem 20. Jahrhundert, Bd. 19. Altes Testament. Kaiser, 1969.

# Index

## Old Testament

### Genesis
| | |
|---|---|
| 1-2 | 56 |
| 1-3 | 14, 15 |
| 1-14 | 25 |
| 1:1 | 15 |
| 1:1-2:3 | 126 n. 4 |
| 1:5 | 15 |
| 1:16 | 15 |
| 1:28 | 49 |
| 2:5-6 | 15 |
| 2:17 | 15 |
| 3 | 170 |
| 3:1 | 15 |
| 3:6-7 | 15 |
| 3:8 | 28 n. 20, 170 |
| 3:8-10 | 15 |
| 3:12-13 | 15 |
| 3:13 | 15 |
| 3:15 | 126 |
| 3:16 | 15 |
| 3:17 | 15 |
| 3:19 | 15 |
| 3:23 | 15 |
| 3:24 | 15, 39 |
| 9:16 | 143 |
| 11:31 | 41 n. 71 |
| 12:1 | 36 |
| 12:1-3 | 26, 170 |
| 12:2 | 28 n. 17 |
| 12:5 | 41 n. 71 |
| 13:14-17 | 36 |
| 13:16 | 27, 170 |
| 15:5 | 170 |
| 15:6 | 11 n. 21 |
| 15:15 | 27 |
| 17:4-6 | 28 n. 17 |
| 17:8 | 41 n. 71 |
| 17:16 | 28 n. 17 |
| 18-19 | 81 |
| 18:18 | 28 n. 17 |
| 19:24 | 81 |
| 22 | 120 n. 113 |
| 22:2 | 70 n. 105 |
| 22:17 | 53, 55 |
| 22:9-12 | 11 n. 21 |
| 25:23 | 28 n. 17 |
| 32:12 | 53, 55 |
| 35:11 | 28 n. 17 |
| 37:9 | 127 |
| 41:42 | 111 n. 71 |
| 46:3 | 28 n. 17 |
| 47:27 | 55 |

### Exodus
| | |
|---|---|
| 1:7 | 55, 55 n. 43 |
| 1:7-8 | 27 |
| 1:5-22 | 27 |
| 1:8-22 | 81 |
| 1:9-12 | 69 |
| 1:12 | 32 |
| 1:15-16 | 69 |
| 1:15-2:10 | 129 |
| 1:17-21 | 32 |
| 2:1-10 | 69 |
| 2:5 | 32 |
| 2:15 | 32 |
| 2:23 | 32 |
| 2:23-24 | 81 |

| | | | |
|---|---|---|---|
| 2:23-25 | 32, 89 n. 35, 94 | 9:14 | 31 |
| 2:24 | 27, 135 n. 33 | 9:23 | 83, 83 n. 9 |
| 2:24-25 | 32 | 9:26 | 27 |
| 3 | 72, 143 | 10:1-2 | 72 |
| 3:1-5 | 37 | 10:3 | 27 |
| 3:6 | 145 | 10:13-15 | 90 |
| 3:7 | 27 | 10:14 | 85 |
| 3:7-8 | 31 | 10:21 | 84 |
| 3:8 | 29 | 10:21-23 | 90 |
| 3:10 | 27 | 10:23 | 27 |
| 3:12 | 31, 72 | 11:1 | 95 |
| 3:13-15 | 64 | 12 | 86 n. 26, 117, 120, 136 |
| 3:14 | 154 | 12:3-7 | 95 |
| 3:17 | 29 | 12:3-11 | 97 |
| 3:18 | 130 | 12:5 | 100, 100 n. 22, 122 |
| 4 | 70 | 12:7 | 122 |
| 4:8 | 48 n. 14 | 12:7-11 | 159 |
| 4:8-9 | 72 | 12:11 | 64, 86 |
| 4:10-12 | 64 | 12:12-13 | 27, 51, 97, 101 |
| 4:22 | 70 n. 105 | 12:13 | 76, 95, 101 n. 26, 117 n. 104, 159 |
| 4:22-23 | 27, 28 n. 17, 52 | 12:14 | 73 n. 119 |
| 4:23 | 135 | 12:21 | 97 |
| 5:1 | 27, 135 | 12:21-27 | 117 |
| 5:1-2 | 80 | 12:22-23 | 51, 101 n. 26 |
| 6:4 | 29, 41 n. 71 | 12:22-28 | 97 |
| 6:6 | 48 n. 14, 54 | 12:23 | 23 n. 3, 86, 116, 117 n. 104 |
| 6:6-8 | 80 | 12:29 | 27 |
| 6:7 | 27, 53 n. 36 | 12:33 | 64 |
| 6:8 | 29 | 12:39 | 64 |
| 7-12 | 80 | 12:46 | 74 |
| 7:3 | 72 | 13-14 | 136 |
| 7:4 | 27, 80 | 13:3 | 48 n. 14 |
| 7:5 | 31 | 13:3-5 | 29 |
| 7:11 | 85 n. 21 | 13:8 | 23 |
| 7:12 | 85 n. 21 | 13:9 | 112 n. 76 |
| 7:14-24 | 89 | 13:11 | 29 |
| 7:15-25 | 93 | 13:17-18 | 130 |
| 7:16 | 27, 135 | 13:17-21 | 72 |
| 7:19 | 83 | 13:21 | 163 |
| 7:21 | 84, 89 | 13:21-22 | 30, 65 n. 83, 72, 143 |
| 7:22 | 85 | 13:22 | 143 |
| 8:1 | 27 | 14-15 | 109 |
| 8:2-6 | 85 | 14:2 | 37 |
| 8:7 | 85, 153 | 14:5 | 64 |
| 8:19 | 30 n. 25 | 14:6 | 105 n. 45 |
| 8:20-23 | 27 | 14:9 | 37 |
| 8:22-23 | 27, 157 | 14:13-14 | 37 |
| 8:23 | 72, 80 n. 2 | 14:15-28 | 30 |
| 9 | 83 | 14:15-31 | 105 |
| 9:1 | 27 | 14:19-20 | 30, 65 n. 83, 136 |
| 9:4 | 27 | 14:21 | 87 |
| 9:6-7 | 27 | 14:21-22 | 37, 85 n. 22 |
| 9:9 | 83 | 14:23-28 | 132 |
| 9:13-17 | 27 | 14:27-29 | 87 |
| 9:13-35 | 82 | 14:29 | 37 |

# Index

| | | | |
|---|---|---|---|
| 15 | 33, 46, 62, 64, 105, 107, 136 | 19:16-18 | 87 |
| 15:1 | 63 | 19:16-19 | 83 n. 9 |
| 15:1-5 | 33 | 19:16-20 | 30, 49 n.15 |
| 15:1-18 | 62 n. 73, 106 | 19:18 | 72, 142, 142 n. 61 |
| 15:1-21 | 37 | 19:19 | 72 |
| 15:2 | 132 n. 23 | 20:1 | 24 |
| 15:3 | 108 | 20:1-17 | 28 n. 17, 144 |
| 15:3-6 | 63 | 20:2 | 31 n. 30, 45, 48 n. 14, 55, 63, 118, 133 |
| 15:6 | 107, 108 | | |
| 15:6-10 | 33 | 20:4-6 | 144 |
| 15:7 | 108 | 20:6 | 114 |
| 15:8 | 63, 105, 105 n. 45, 108 | 20:13 | 144 |
| 15:10 | 63, 108 | 20:15 | 144 |
| 15:11 | 63, 68, 107, 109, 109 n. 65 | 20:16 | 144 |
| 15:11-16 | 33 | 20:18-21 | 30, 145 |
| 15:11-18 | 109 | 22:21 | 23 |
| 15:12 | 132 | 23:20 | 12 n. 23, 163 |
| 15:13 | 34, 63, 76 n. 134, 98, 107, 122 | 23:20-23 | 136 |
| 15:14-15 | 34 n. 38 | 23:30-31 | 170 |
| 15:14-16 | 108 | 24:1-18 | 23 |
| 15:16 | 98, 122 | 24:3-8 | 27 |
| 15:16-17 | 29 n. 21 | 24:8 | 73, 73 n. 120 |
| 15:16-18 | 33 | 24:10 | 104, 104 n. 44 |
| 15:17 | 63 | 24:16 | 71 |
| 15:18 | 100 n. 21, 108 | 24:17 | 72 |
| 15:19 | 63 | 25-27 | 144 |
| 15:22 | 130 n. 17 | 25-30 | 137 |
| 15:22-27 | 84 n. 15, 136 | 25-31 | 51, 137 |
| 15:23-25 | 30, 49 | 25:8 | 134, 138 |
| 16 | 73, 136 | 25:10-22 | 138 |
| 16:2 | 130 n. 17 | 25:17 | 139 n. 48 |
| 16:4-35 | 30 | 25:21-22 | 134 |
| 16:16 | 31 n. 30 | 27:21 | 139 |
| 16:32 | 34, 35 n. 42, 35 n. 43, 35 n. 44, 35 n. 50 | 27:21-40:35 | 139 n. 49 |
| | | 28 | 140 |
| 16:32-35 | 40 n. 68 | 28:2 | 64 n. 81 |
| 16:35 | 36 | 28:11-21 | 155 n. 21 |
| 17:1-6 | 49, 62 n. 72 | 28:15 | 111 n. 71 |
| 17:1-7 | 133 n. 24, 136 | 28:17-20 | 142 |
| 17:3-7 | 72 | 28:36 | 111 n. 71 |
| 17:6 | 30 | 28:36-38 | 112 n. 76, 142 |
| 17:8-16 | 30 | 28:39-43 | 139 |
| 19:2 | 130 n. 17 | 29:11-37 | 99 |
| 19:4 | 131, 131 n. 22 | 29:45 | 172 |
| 19:3-6 | 97 | 29:45-46 | 28, 50, 55, 134, 145, 158, 159 |
| 19:3-8 | 23 | 29:46 | 170 |
| 19:4 | 35 n. 52 | 30:36 | 139 |
| 19:5 | 99 n. 20, 100 | 32 | 154 |
| 19:5-6 | 28 n. 17, 76, 99 n. 20, 141 | 32:1-5 | 31 |
| 19:6 | 28 n. 17, 36, 64 n. 81, 99, 99 n. 20, 100 n. 21, 122, 141, 142, 168, 170, 172 | 32:10 | 28 n. 17 |
| | | 32:10-13 | 29 |
| | | 32:15 | 139 |
| 19:10 | 133 n. 27 | 32:26-28 | 155 n. 19 |
| 19:14-15 | 133 n. 27, 142 | 32:27-28 | 31 |
| 19:16 | 72, 142 | 32:33 | 158 n. 28 |

| | | | |
|---|---|---|---|
| 32:35 | 31 | 11:1-32 | 30 |
| 33:1-3 | 29 | 13:2 | 41 n. 71 |
| 33:1-5 | 31 | 13:17 | 41 n. 71 |
| 33:7 | 139 | 13:27 | 29 |
| 33:7-11 | 27 n. 16 | 14:2 | 130 n. 17 |
| 33:9-11 | 134 | 14:8 | 29 |
| 33:13 | 28 n. 17 | 14:14 | 30 |
| 33:14-16 | 136 | 14:20-35 | 129 n. 16 |
| 33:15-16 | 32 | 14:22-23 | 36 |
| 33:16 | 159 | 14:34 | 36 |
| 33:18 | 145 | 15:41 | 31 n. 30, 48 n. 14 |
| 33:20 | 145, 146 | 16:13-14 | 29 |
| 33:23 | 146 | 16:31-33 | 132 |
| 34:8 | 145 | 20:8-11 | 30 |
| 34:29 | 146 n. 73 | 21:4-9 | 90 n. 40 |
| 34:29-31 | 71 | 21:24 | 41 n. 71 |
| 35-40 | 51, 137 | 21:35 | 41 n. 71 |
| 36:13 | 111 n. 71 | 23-24 | 46 |
| 36:21 | 111 n. 71 | 23:22 | 46 |
| 39:14 | 111 n. 71 | 24:8a | 46 |
| 40:26 | 139 | 26:3 | 36 |
| 40:34-35 | 51, 139, 140, 143 | 27:17 | 62 n. 71 |
| 40:34-38 | 136, 137 | 32:29 | 41 n. 71 |
| | | 35:25 | 54 |

Leviticus

| | | | |
|---|---|---|---|
| 4:26 | 99 n. 15 | Deuteronomy | |
| 11:49 | 31 n. 30 | 1-3 | 40 n. 68 |
| 14:34 | 41 n. 71 | 1:30 | 35 n. 48 |
| 16 | 139 | 1:30-31 | 35 n. 42, 35 n. 43, 40 n. 68 |
| 16:14-19 | 99 | 1:31 | 35 n. 52 |
| 16:18-19 | 99 | 1:33 | 30 |
| 16:30 | 99 | 1:40 | 130 n. 17 |
| 17:11 | 102 | 2:7 | 36, 130 n. 17 |
| 19:36 | 31 n. 30 | 4:34 | 72 n. 116 |
| 20:24 | 29 | 5:2-4 | 23 |
| 22:32-33 | 31 n. 30 | 5:6 | 24, 31 n. 30, 118, 133 |
| 23:33-43 | 135 | 6:3 | 29 |
| 23:40 | 53, 135 | 6:8 | 112 n. 76, 112 n. 79 |
| 23:42 | 135 | 6:12 | 31 n. 30 |
| 23:42-43 | 35 n. 42, 35 n. 43, 35 n. 52, 41 | 6:20-25 | 24 n. 3 |
| 23:43 | 35 n. 44, 53, 135 | 6:21 | 24 |
| 25:37 | 98 | 7:9 | 114 |
| 25:38 | 31 n. 30, 41 n. 71 | 8:1-10 | 35 n. 42 |
| 25:55 | 98 | 8:1-20 | 35 n. 43, 40 n. 68 |
| 26 | 104 n. 39 | 8:4 | 36 |
| 26:13 | 31 n. 30 | 8:14 | 31 n. 30, 35 n. 44 |
| 26:21 | 104 n. 39 | 8:15 | 35 n. 49 |
| 26:24 | 104 n. 39 | 8:15-16 | 35 n. 50 |
| | | 9:7 | 35 n. 43, 35 n. 44, 35 n. 52, 40 n. 68 |

Numbers

| | | | |
|---|---|---|---|
| 8:1-3 | 140 n. 52 | 9:9 | 71 |
| 9:5 | 130 n. 17 | 9:17 | 35 n. 42 |
| 9:12 | 74 | 10:5 | 139 |
| 9:15-22 | 30 | 10:18-19 | 23 |
| 10:36 | 114 | 11:2-6 | 35 n. 42, 35 n. 43, 40 n. 68 |

*Index* 195

| | | | | |
|---|---|---|---|---|
| 11:3 | 35 n. 45 | | 22:9 | 41 n. 71 |
| 11:4 | 35 n. 47 | | 22:13 | 41 n. 71 |
| 11:5 | 35 n. 51 | | 22:15 | 41 n. 71 |
| 11:9 | 29 | | 22:32 | 41 n. 71 |
| 11:19 | 112 n. 76 | | 24:2-13 | 38 |
| 13:5 | 31 n. 30, 48 n. 14 | | 24:5 | 35 n. 44, 35 n. 45, 35 n. 48 |
| 13:10 | 31 n. 30, 48 n. 14 | | 24:6 | 35 n. 44, 48 n. 14 |
| 15:15 | 23 | | 24:5-8 | 24 n. 3, 35 n. 42, 35 n. 43, 40 |
| 16:13-15 | 135 | | 24:6 | 31 n. 30 |
| 18:15 | 71 | | 24:7 | 35 n. 47, 35 n. 52 |
| 18:15-20 | 37 n. 54, 69 n. 101 | | 24:15 | 162 |
| 20:1 | 31 n. 30, 48 n. 14 | | 24:17 | 31 n. 30, 35 n. 43, 35 n. 44, 35 n. 45, 35 n. 48, 41 |
| 25:5-9 | 24 n. 3 | | 24:17-18 | 35 n. 42, 35 n. 52 |
| 26:8-9 | 40 | | | |
| 26:9 | 29 | | Judges | |
| 26:15 | 29 | | 5:4-5 | 27 |
| 27:3 | 29 | | 6:8 | 31 n. 30, 48 n. 14 |
| 28:15-68 | 46 | | | |
| 28:59 | 103 | | 1 Samuel | |
| 28:59-60 | 107 | | 4:8 | 81 |
| 29:2 | 35 n. 48 | | 12:6 | 31 n. 30 |
| 29:2-3 | 35 n. 45 | | 18:7 | 114 |
| 29:2-6 | 35 n. 42, 35 n. 43, 41 | | | |
| 29:5 | 35 n. 49, 35 n. 52, 36 | | 2 Samuel | |
| 30:1-10 | 47 | | 5:10 | 107 |
| 31:1-8 | 32 | | 7:23-24 | 28 n. 17 |
| 31:20 | 29 | | | |
| 31:30-32:44 | 106 | | 1 Kings | |
| 32:4 | 106, 107, 109 | | 6-8 | 137 |
| 32:11 | 131 n. 22 | | 7:23 | 105 n. 46 |
| 32:49 | 41 n. 71 | | 8:10-11 | 140 |
| 34:4-12 | 37 | | 8:11 | 138 |
| 34:7 | 43 | | 8:51-53 | 31 n. 30, 48 n. 14 |
| 34:10 | 69 n. 101 | | 19:11 | 72 |
| 34:10-12 | 37 n. 54 | | 20:41 | 112 n. 76 |
| | | | 21:8 | 111 n. 71 |
| Joshua | | | | |
| 1-5 | 38 n. 59 | | 2 Kings | |
| 1-12 | 36 | | 2 | 71 |
| 1:3-9 | 37 | | 17:7 | 31 n. 30, 48 n. 14 |
| 3-4 | 37 n. 56 | | 19:35 | 116 |
| 3:1 | 37 | | 25:23 | 111 n. 71 |
| 3:5 | 37 | | | |
| 3:14-17 | 37 | | 1 Chronicles | |
| 4:1-9 | 37 | | 16:31 | 108 |
| 5:6 | 29, 36, 130 n. 17 | | 17:21-22 | 28 n. 17 |
| 5:11-12 | 37 n. 56 | | 28:18 | 137 |
| 5:13 | 39 | | | |
| 5:13-15 | 37 n. 56 | | 2 Chronicles | |
| 6-12 | 38 n. 39 | | 4:2 | 105 n. 46 |
| 7 | 53 | | 5:13 | 140 |
| 11:16-23 | 38 | | 7:22 | 31 n. 30, 48 n. 14 |
| 13-21 | 38 n. 39 | | | |
| 14:1-19:51 | 41 n. 71 | | | |
| 22-23 | 38 n. 39 | | | |

| Ezra | |
|---|---|
| 12:18 | 128 n. 10 |

| Nehemiah | |
|---|---|
| 8:15 | 135 |
| 9:9 | 35 n. 48 |
| 9:9-21 | 35 n. 42, 35 n. 43, 40 |
| 9:10 | 35 n. 45 |
| 9:11 | 35 n. 46, 35 n. 47 |
| 9:12 | 35 n. 49 |
| 9:13 | 35 n. 52 |
| 9:15 | 35 n. 50 |
| 9:16-17 | 35 n. 51 |
| 9:19 | 35 n. 49 |
| 9:20 | 35 n. 50 |
| 9:21 | 35 n. 52 |
| 10:1 | 111 |

| Esther | |
|---|---|
| 3:10 | 111 n. 71 |
| 8:8-10 | 111 n. 71 |

| Job | |
|---|---|
| 3:21 | 9 |
| 11:7 | 107 |
| 14:17 | 111 |
| 22:17 | 107 |
| 42:3 | 107 |

| Psalms | |
|---|---|
| 2:9 | 129 |
| 6:3 | 109 n. 65 |
| 11:2 | 109 n. 66 |
| 15:1 | 109 n. 65 |
| 16:10 | 109 n. 66 |
| 18 | 144 n. 64 |
| 18:7-19 | 144 n. 64 |
| 23 | 62 n. 71, 134 |
| 27:11 | 62 n. 71 |
| 31:6 | 109 n. 66 |
| 34:20 | 74 |
| 44:7-14 | 47 n. 11 |
| 46:3 | 108 |
| 47:8 | 108 |
| 74:1-2 | 98 |
| 74:12-14 | 104 n. 41 |
| 74:12-17 | 47 n. 11 |
| 74:13-14 | 126 n. 4, 128 |
| 77:12-20 | 47 n. 11 |
| 78 | 47 n. 11, 62 n. 71 |
| 78:12 | 35 n. 45, 47 n. 10 |
| 78:12-20 | 35 n. 42, 35 n. 43, 41 |
| 78:13 | 35 n. 46, 47 n. 10 |
| 78:14 | 35 n. 49, 47 n. 10 |
| 78:15-16 | 35 n. 50, 47 n. 10 |
| 78:18 | 35 n. 51, 47 n. 10 |
| 78:20 | 35 n. 50, 47 n. 10 |
| 78:23-29 | 35 n. 42 |
| 78:24-29 | 35 n. 50, 47 n. 10 |
| 78:40-41 | 35 n. 51, 47 n. 10 |
| 78:40-54 | 35 n. 42, 35 n. 43, 40 |
| 78:43-51 | 35 n. 45, 47 n. 10, 72 n. 116 |
| 78:44-51 | 87 n. 28 |
| 78:52-53 | 35 n. 49, 47 n. 10 |
| 78:53 | 35 n. 47, 47 n. 10 |
| 80:8-11 | 47 n. 11 |
| 81 | 47 n. 11 |
| 81:10 | 24, 31 n. 30, 48 n. 14 |
| 84:10 | 114 |
| 85:2 | 109 n. 66 |
| 86:8 | 109 n. 64 |
| 86:8-10 | 106, 108 |
| 86:9 | 108, 108 n. 63, 109, 109 n. 68 |
| 88:16 | 101 |
| 89:10 | 128 |
| 96:10 | 108 |
| 98:2 | 109 |
| 103:15-17 | 11 n. 21 |
| 105 | 47 n. 11 |
| 105:26 | 35 n. 48 |
| 105:26-45 | 35 n. 42, 35 n. 43, 40 |
| 105:27-36 | 35 n. 45, 47 n. 10, 87 n. 28 |
| 105:36 | 35 n. 48, 47 n. 10 |
| 105:37 | 35 n. 44, 47 n. 10 |
| 105:39 | 35 n. 49, 47 n. 10 |
| 105:40-41 | 35 n. 50, 47 n. 10 |
| 105:43 | 35 n. 44, 47 n. 10 |
| 106 | 47, 47 n. 11 |
| 106:7 | 35 n. 45, 47 n. 10 |
| 106:7-27 | 35 n. 42, 35 n. 43, 40 |
| 106:8-12 | 47 |
| 106:9 | 35 n. 46, 35 n. 49, 47 n. 10, 130 n. 17 |
| 106:11 | 35 n. 47, 47 n. 10 |
| 106:13-27 | 35 n. 51, 47 n. 10 |
| 106:47 | 47 |
| 110:2-4 | 107 |
| 111:2 | 106 |
| 130:8 | 99 n. 15 |
| 135 | 47 n. 11 |
| 136 | 47 n. 11 |
| 136:10-16 | 35 n. 42, 35 n. 43 |
| 136:10-22 | 40 |
| 136:11 | 35 n. 44, 47 n. 10, 48 n. 14 |
| 136:13-14 | 35 n. 46 |
| 136:13-15 | 47 n. 10 |
| 136:15 | 35 n. 47 |
| 136:16 | 35 n. 49, 47 n. 10, 130 n. 17 |
| 139:14 | 106 |
| 142:10 | 62 n. 71 |

*Index*

| | | | |
|---|---|---|---|
| 144:17 | 109 n. 66 | 40 | 61 |
| 145:17 | 106, 107, 109 | 40-55 | 55, 55 n. 45, 56, 59, 59 n. 59, 60, 162, 163 n. 36, 164, 166, 166 n. 45 |

Song of Solomon

| | | | |
|---|---|---|---|
| 6:10 | 127 | 40-66 | 55 n. 45, 56 |
| | | 40:1-11 | 77 n. 136, 163-165 |

Isaiah

| | | | |
|---|---|---|---|
| | | 40:2 | 165 n. 40 |
| 1-39 | 55 n. 45 | 40:3 | 12 n. 23, 77, 77 n. 135, 77 n. 136, 130, 163-165 |
| 1:18 | 99 | | |
| 2-12 | 61 | 40:3-4 | 61 |
| 4:2 | 61 | 40:3-5 | 163-164 |
| 4:2-6 | 61 | 40:5 | 61 |
| 4:3-4 | 61 | 40:6-7 | 11 n. 21 |
| 4:5 | 61 | 40:12 | 165 |
| 4:5-6 | 134 | 40:14 | 164 |
| 5 | 56 | 40:25 | 109 n. 65 |
| 6:1 | 140 | 40:27 | 164 |
| 6:1-4 | 166 | 40:31 | 132 n. 22 |
| 6:4 | 140 | 41:17-20 | 62 |
| 6:5 | 146 | 41:18 | 62 n. 72, 130 |
| 9:1-7 | 61 | 41:20 | 63 n. 76 |
| 10:16-19 | 168 n. 52 | 42:5 | 62 |
| 10:24-27 | 55 n. 45 | 42:10-17 | 62 |
| 10:26 | 41 n. 72 | 42:13 | 63 |
| 11:1 | 61 | 42:14 | 164 |
| 11:10 | 61 | 42:15-16 | 63 |
| 11:11 | 61 | 42:16 | 63 |
| 11:11-12 | 61 | 42:17 | 63 |
| 11:12 | 61 | 43 | 63 |
| 11:12-16 | 55 n. 45 | 43:1-3 | 98 |
| 11:15-16 | 61, 167 | 43:2 | 62, 63 |
| 11:16 | 41 n. 72, 61 | 43:14 | 56 |
| 12 | 106 n. 53 | 43:16-17 | 63 |
| 12:1-3 | 55 n. 45 | 43:19 | 63 |
| 13:8-22 | 168 n. 52 | 43:19-20 | 130 |
| 14:13 | 167 | 44:2 | 62 |
| 19:2 | 168 n. 52 | 44:5 | 112 n. 76 |
| 19:5-8 | 93, 168 n. 52 | 45:18 | 62 |
| 24:1 | 56 | 45:20-25 | 63 n. 76 |
| 24:18-19 | 56 | 48:20-21 | 59 n. 58, 62 n. 72 |
| 25:8 | 135 n. 32 | 49 | 63 |
| 26:16-27:1 | 126 | 49:5-6 | 63 |
| 26:17 | 128 n. 10 | 49:6 | 63 |
| 27:1 | 126 n. 4, 132 | 49:8 | 63, 64 |
| 28:2 | 168 n. 52 | 49:8-11 | 63 |
| 29:6 | 168 n. 52 | 49:9 | 134 |
| 29:11 | 111 | 49:10 | 134, 134 n. 31, 135, 135 n. 32 |
| 30:27-30 | 168 n. 52 | 49:12 | 64 n. 78 |
| 32:15 | 130, 165 | 49:15 | 56 |
| 32:19 | 168 n. 52 | 50:2-3 | 168 n. 52 |
| 33:3-4 | 168 n. 52 | 51-52 | 64 |
| 34:2-10 | 168 n. 52 | 51:2 | 57 |
| 34:4-14 | 166 | 51:3 | 57, 64, 130 |
| 35:1 | 130, 165 | 51:9-10 | 56, 126 n. 4, 128 |
| 35:1-10 | 55 n. 45 | 51:9-11 | 64 |

| | | | |
|---|---|---|---|
| 51:11 | 64 | 29:14 | 171 |
| 51:15 | 62 | 30-31 | 50 |
| 51:19-20 | 168 n. 52 | 30:3 | 50 |
| 52 | 64 | 30:9 | 50 |
| 52:1 | 64 n. 81 | 30:21 | 50 |
| 52:1-2 | 60 | 30:22 | 50, 53 n. 36 |
| 52:3 | 98 | 31 | 48 n. 14, 73 n. 120 |
| 52:3-4 | 64 | 31:1 | 50 |
| 52:6 | 64 | 31:2 | 130 |
| 52:11 | 135 n. 33 | 31:4 | 50 |
| 52:11-12 | 60 | 31:5 | 50 |
| 52:12 | 65 | 31:7 | 50 |
| 53 | 121 n. 114, 121 n. 115, 122 n. 120 | 31:8 | 50 |
| 53:3 | 65 | 31:9 | 27 n. 14, 50 |
| 53:4-5 | 65 | 31:12 | 50 |
| 53:5 | 65 | 31:12-13 | 50 |
| 53:6 | 65, 164 | 31:31 | 50, 75 n. 127, 77 |
| 55:6-13 | 58 | 31:31-32 | 31 n. 30, 41 n. 72 |
| 53:7 | 65, 120, 121, 122 n. 122, 168 | 31:31-33 | 35 n. 42, 72 |
| 53:12 | 65 | 31:31-35 | 171 |
| 54:11-12 | 142 n. 59 | 31:32 | 35 n. 43, 35 n. 44, 35 n. 52 |
| 56-66 | 55 n. 45 | 31:32-33 | 50 |
| 60-66 | 166 n. 45 | 31:34 | 50 |
| 60:1-19 | 166 | 32:21 | 31 n. 30, 48 n. 14 |
| 60:19-20 | 127 | 32:28 | 50 |
| 63:13 | 130 n. 17 | 32:37-38 | 28 n. 20 |
| 65:15-20 | 166 | 34:13 | 48 n. 14 |
| 65:17-66:24 | 57 | 46:23 | 93 n. 48 |
| 65:18-25 | 57 | 51:6-9 | 135 n. 33 |
| 66:7 | 128 n. 10 | 51:14 | 93 n. 48 |
| 66:7-8 | 129 | 51:34 | 128 n. 11 |
| 66:15-16 | 168 n. 52 | 51:45 | 135 n. 33 |
| | | 52:3 | 171 |
| Jeremiah | | | |
| 2:6 | 35 n. 42, 35 n. 43, 35 n. 44, 35 n. 49, 48 n. 14, 130 n. 17 | Ezekiel | |
| | | 1 | 118 |
| 2:6-7 | 40 | 1:22 | 104 n. 44 |
| 5:14 | 107 | 1:26-28 | 104 n. 40 |
| 7:22 | 31 n. 30, 48 n. 14 | 1:28 | 146 n. 70 |
| 8:14 | 49 | 3:23 | 146 n. 70 |
| 9:15 | 49, 84 n. 16 | 8 | 116 |
| 10:6 | 109 n. 64 | 8:5-6 | 116 |
| 10:6-7 | 106, 108 | 8:6 | 116 |
| 10:7 | 108, 108 n. 63 | 8:17 | 116 |
| 11:3-8 | 41 | 9 | 51, 51 n. 27, 110, 116, 116 n. 99, 117, 118, 120 |
| 11:4 | 31 n. 30, 48 n. 14 | | |
| 11:7 | 31 n. 30, 48 n. 14 | 9:1-2 | 116 |
| 16:14-15 | 41, 50, 55 | 9:2 | 116 |
| 23:1-8 | 49 | 9:4 | 116, 117 n. 104 |
| 23:3 | 49 | 9:5-6 | 51 |
| 23:5 | 49 | 9:6 | 117 n. 104 |
| 23:7 | 49 | 9:7 | 116 |
| 23:7-8 | 41, 50, 171 | 9:8 | 146 n. 70 |
| 23:15 | 84 n. 16 | 10 | 118 |
| 29:10 | 171 | 10:2-4 | 140 |

## Index

| | | | |
|---|---|---|---|
| 11:13 | 146 n. 70 | 9:26 | 91, 92 n. 45 |
| 14:12-23 | 116 n. 99 | 10 | 140 n. 52, 146, 146 n. 71 |
| 16:59-62 | 72 | 10:7-9 | 146 |
| 20 | 51 n. 23 | 10:9 | 146 n. 70 |
| 20:5-26 | 50 | 10:12 | 146 |
| 20:6 | 35 n. 44 | 10:13 | 130 |
| 20:6-10 | 41 | 10:21 | 130 |
| 20:9 | 35 n. 44 | 12:1 | 91 n. 44, 130 |
| 20:10 | 35 n. 44 | | |
| 20:10-14 | 35 n. 43 | Hosea | |
| 20:10-16 | 40 | 1:2 | 52 n. 28 |
| 20:10-26 | 35 n. 42 | 1:7 | 52 |
| 20:11-12 | 35 n. 52 | 1:9 | 53 n. 36 |
| 20:13 | 130 n. 17 | 1:10 | 53 |
| 20:13-16 | 35 n. 51 | 2:1-12 | 52 |
| 20:21-26 | 35 n. 51 | 2:14-15 | 52, 130 |
| 20:32-44 | 51 | 2:15 | 53 |
| 20:34-36 | 35 n. 43 | 2:16 | 53 |
| 20:34-38 | 41 | 2:16-17 | 41 n. 72 |
| 20:34-44 | 35 n. 42 | 2:17 | 53 |
| 20:35 | 51 | 2:18 | 53 |
| 20:35-38 | 35 n. 51 | 2:18-19 | 53 |
| 20:37 | 35 n. 52 | 2:21 | 53 |
| 20:38 | 41, 51 | 2:23 | 53, 53 n. 36 |
| 20:42 | 51 | 8:13 | 52 |
| 20:44 | 51 | 9:3 | 52 |
| 26-28 | 118 n. 109 | 11:1 | 27 n. 14, 52, 70 |
| 29:3 | 128 | 11:5 | 52 |
| 32:2-3 | 128 | 12:9 | 31 n. 30, 48 n. 14, 53 |
| 34:6 | 51 | 12:10 | 41 n. 72 |
| 34:10-13 | 51 | 13:4 | 31 n. 30, 35 n. 48, 48 n. 14 |
| 34:11-16 | 51 | 13:4-5 | 35 n. 42, 35 n. 43, 41 n. 72 |
| 34:25 | 51, 130 | 13:5 | 35 n. 52 |
| 34:25-29 | 51 | | |
| 34:27 | 51 | Joel | |
| 34:30 | 51 | 1-2 | 41 n. 72, 93 |
| 37:1-14 | 118 | 1:4 | 85 |
| 37:25-28 | 51 | 2:25 | 85 |
| 37:27 | 134 | 2:30-31 | 83 |
| 40-42 | 51 | | |
| 43:1-5 | 51 | Amos | |
| 43:3 | 146 n. 70 | 2:10 | 31 n. 30, 35 n. 42, 35 n. 43, 35 n. 44, 40, 48 n. 14, 130 n. 17 |
| 43:19-27 | 99 | 3:1 | 31 n. 30, 48 n. 14 |
| 44:4 | 146 n. 70 | 3:13 | 107 |
| | | 4:9 | 93 n. 48 |
| Daniel | | 9:7 | 31 n. 30, 48 n. 14 |
| 2:46 | 146 n. 70 | | |
| 6:18 | 111 n. 71, 111 n. 74 | Micah | |
| 7 | 140 n. 52, 146 n. 71 | 4:1 | 54 n. 38 |
| 7:4 | 104 n. 40 | 4:1-10 | 53 |
| 7:10 | 114 | 4:5 | 54 n. 38 |
| 7:25 | 129 n. 16 | 4:10 | 54, 126, 128 n. 10 |
| 8-9 | 146 n. 71 | 6:4 | 31 n. 30, 48 n. 14, 54 |
| 8:17 | 146 n. 70 | 6:9-16 | 54 |
| 9:15 | 48 n. 14 | | |

| | | | | |
|---|---|---|---|---|
| 7:15 | 54 | | 2 Maccabees | |
| 7:18 | 109 n. 65 | | 2:8 | 67 |
| 7:19 | 54 n. 38 | | 2:18 | 67 |
| | | | 10:7 | 133 n. 26, 135 |
| Nahum | | | 14:4 | 133 n. 26 |
| 1:1-8 | 49 n.15 | | | |
| 1:2 | 49 n.15 | | Baruch | |
| 1:4 | 49 n.15 | | 1:19-20 | 66 |
| 1:5 | 49 n.15 | | 2:11 | 66 |
| 1:7 | 49 n.15 | | | |
| 1:8 | 49 n.15 | | Wisdom | |
| 3:15-17 | 93 n. 48 | | 3:1 | 128 n. 10 |
| | | | 10-19 | 88-91 |
| Zechariah | | | 11-19 | 67 |
| 2:10 | 134 | | 11:1-14 | 88 n. 32 |
| 10:6 | 55 | | 11:5 | 88 |
| 10:8 | 55 | | 11:6 | 88 |
| 10:8-11 | 54 | | 11:6-7 | 89 |
| 10:10 | 55 | | 11:7 | 89 |
| 13:6 | 112 n. 76 | | 11:9 | 128 n. 10 |
| 14 | 113 n. 83, 136 | | 11:16 | 88 |
| 14:13 | 91 n. 44 | | 16:1-19:17 | 88 n. 32 |
| 14:16 | 136 | | 16:5 | 90 n. 40 |
| | | | 16:8-10 | 90 |
| Malachi | | | 16:9 | 90 |
| 1:11 | 108 | | 16:9-10 | 89 |
| 3:1 | 12 n. 23 | | 16:10 | 90 n. 40 |
| | | | 16:16-17 | 89 |
| | | | 16:17 | 89 n. 37 |
| **Apocrypha** | | | 17:1-20 | 90 |
| | | | 17:3-10 | 89 |
| 2 Esdras (4 Ezra) | | | 17:14-19 | 89 |
| 1:7 | 92 | | | |
| 1:10 | 66, 92 | | | |
| 1:12-23 | 66 | | **New Testament** | |
| 1:13-23 | 92 | | | |
| 2:1 | 66, 92 | | Matthew | |
| 2:38-41 | 92 n. 47 | | 2:13-16 | 70 |
| 2:42-48 | 92 n. 47 | | 2:15 | 70 |
| 3:7 | 92 n. 47 | | 2:16 | 128, 129 |
| 3:17 | 92 | | 3:17 | 70 n. 105 |
| 4:35-37 | 92 n. 47 | | 4:1-2 | 70 |
| 6:17 | 92 n. 47 | | 4:2 | 71 |
| 7:39-42 | 92 n. 47 | | 5-7 | 71 n. 108 |
| 11:37 | 104 n. 40 | | 5:21-22 | 70 |
| 14:3-6 | 92 | | 5:27-28 | 70 |
| 14:28-30 | 66 | | 5:31-32 | 70 |
| 15:10-12 | 67 | | 5:33-34 | 70 |
| 15:40-42 | 92 | | 5:38-39 | 70 |
| 15:58 | 92 | | 5:43-44 | 70 |
| 16:18-22 | 91 n. 44 | | 8:6 | 128 n. 10 |
| | | | 10:5-6 | 114 |
| 1 Maccabees | | | 12:39-41 | 20 n. 54 |
| 4:9-10 | 67 | | 12:42 | 20 n. 54 |
| 13:51 | 133 n. 26 | | 17:5-6 | 143 |

# Index

| | | | |
|---|---|---|---|
| 17:6 | 146 n. 70 | 22:1-23 | 73 |
| 19:28 | 114 | 22:15-16 | 73 |
| 21:15 | 103 n. 37 | 22:19 | 73 n. 119 |
| 21:42 | 103 n. 37 | 22:20 | 50 n. 20, 77, 171 |
| 24 | 92 | 24:36 | 98 n. 9 |
| 24:6-7 | 93 n. 51 | | |
| 24:6-8 | 91 n. 44 | John | |
| 24:8 | 93 n. 51 | 1:14 | 27 n. 16, 73, 134, 147, 171 |
| 26:17-30 | 73 | 1:21 | 69 n. 101 |
| 26:28 | 50 n. 20 | 1:29 | 65, 74, 74 n. 122, 121, 122, 133, 168, 175 |
| 27 | 138 n. 46 | | |
| 27:45-54 | 143 | 1:36 | 121, 168 |
| 27:51 | 138 n. 46 | 1:45 | 69 n. 101 |
| 27:66 | 111 n. 74 | 1:47 | 114 |
| | | 2:11 | 72 |
| Mark | | 3:14 | 130 n. 17 |
| 1:2-3 | 12 n. 23, 77 | 3:14-15 | 20 n. 54 |
| 1:3 | 165 | 4:26 | 72 |
| 1:11 | 70 n. 105 | 4:48 | 72 |
| 1:12-13 | 70 | 4:54 | 72 |
| 8:27 | 164 n. 37 | 5:43-47 | 114 |
| 8:27-11:1 | 164 n. 37 | 6:4 | 73 n. 117 |
| 9:2 | 71 | 6:14 | 72 |
| 9:2-3 | 71 | 6:23 | 73 |
| 9:7 | 71 | 6:31 | 130 n. 17 |
| 9:7-8 | 143 | 6:41 | 73 |
| 9:33 | 164 n. 37 | 6:49 | 130 n. 17 |
| 9:34 | 164 n. 37 | 7:40 | 69 n. 101 |
| 10:17 | 164 n. 37 | 8:12 | 72 |
| 10:32 | 164 n. 37 | 8:21-24 | 74 n. 122 |
| 10:45 | 98 | 8:24 | 72 |
| 10:46 | 164 n. 37 | 8:28 | 72 |
| 10:52 | 164 n. 37 | 8:34 | 74 n. 122 |
| 12:11 | 103 n. 37 | 8:58 | 72 |
| 12:35-37 | 20 n. 54 | 9:16 | 72 |
| 13 | 92 | 9:30 | 103 n. 37 |
| 14:12-25 | 73 | 11:47 | 72 |
| 14:24 | 50 n. 20, 73 | 11:55 | 74 |
| | | 12:1 | 74 |
| Luke | | 12:13 | 133 n. 26 |
| 1:7 | 163 n. 36 | 12:46 | 72 |
| 1:68-79 | 114 | 13:1 | 74 |
| 1:76 | 163 n. 36 | 13:19 | 72 |
| 2:30 | 163 n. 36 | 14:6 | 72 |
| 3:4-6 | 163 n. 36, 165 | 16:33 | 110 |
| 3:22 | 70 n. 105 | 18:5 | 72 |
| 4:1-2 | 70 | 18:28 | 74 |
| 5:8 | 146 n. 70 | 18:39 | 74 |
| 9:31 | 71 | 19:14 | 74 |
| 9:34-36 | 143 | 19:32-35 | 72 |
| 9:51 | 71 | 19:33 | 74 |
| 11:29-32 | 20 n. 54 | 19:36 | 74 |
| 16:23 | 128 n. 10 | 20:19 | 98 n. 9 |
| 16:28 | 128 n. 10 | 20:26 | 98 n. 9 |
| 21 | 92 | | |

Acts
1:2    129
1:11   129
1:22   129
2      72
2:1-4  143
2:24   99 n. 15
2:27   109 n. 66
2:38   111 n. 73
3:19-22  69 n. 101
3:20-22  72
7      41, 138 n. 45
7:30   130 n. 17
7:30-44  41
7:34   35 n. 48
7:34-43  35 n. 42
7:35   35 n. 48
7:36   35 n. 43, 35 n. 44, 35 n. 45, 35 n. 46, 35 n. 49, 35 n. 52, 130 n. 17
7:37   35 n. 48, 72
7:39-42  35 n. 51
7:40   35 n. 44, 35 n. 48
7:42   35 n. 52
7:45   41
7:51-53  42
8:32   121, 121 n. 114, 122 n. 122, 168
10:47  111 n. 73
13:23-36  163 n. 36
13:35  109 n. 66
26:14  146 n. 70
26:14-23  114
28:28  163 n. 36

Romans
3:25   99 n. 15, 101
4:11   111
4:24-25  65
5:3    113 n. 82
5:3-5  113 n. 82
6      75
6-8    75 n. 126
8:12-39  113 n. 82
8:21   75
8:31-39  75
9-11   114
9:6-8  171
9:24-26  171

1 Corinthians
3:12-13  105 n. 49
4:8-13   113 n. 82
5:7      74, 121
6:11     99, 111 n. 73
10:1-2   35 n. 49, 42

10:1-11  35 n. 42
10:2     35 n. 46, 35 n. 48
10:3-4   35 n. 50
10:4     42
10:5     130 n. 17
10:5-10  35 n. 51
10:5-11  42, 75
10:6     75
11:24-25  73 n. 119
11:25    50 n. 20, 77
12:13    111 n. 73
15:3     99 n. 15

2 Corinthians
1:21   111 n. 73
1:22   111
3:3-6  72
3:3-18 75
3:6    50 n. 20

Galatians
1:3-4   65
3:23-26 75
4:1-7   75
4:21-31 171
4:24    75
4:25    75
4:28-31 75
5:1     75 n. 129
6:16    171

Ephesians
1:13-14  111
4:30     111
5:25-27  99

Philippians
2:9-11   108
2:10-11  142

Colossians
1:13-14  75

1 Thessalonians
1:4-7   113 n. 82

1 Timothy
2:19    112
3:16    129

Hebrews
3:1-6    76
3:16     35 n. 44, 35 n. 48
3:16-18  35 n. 42
3:16-4:11  76

|  |  |
|---|---|
| 3:17 | 35 n. 52, 130 n. 17 |
| 3:17-18 | 35 n. 51 |
| 3:19 | 42 |
| 4:1 | 42 |
| 4:6-9 | 76 |
| 4:14-5:11 | 76 |
| 7:1-28 | 76 |
| 8:6-13 | 171 |
| 9 | 138 n. 45 |
| 9:1-22 | 76 |
| 9:4 | 138 n. 47 |
| 9:13-14 | 99 |
| 9:14-15 | 72 |
| 9:15 | 98, 171 |
| 9:22 | 99 n. 15 |
| 9:25-10:12 | 76 |
| 10:4 | 102 |
| 10:15-16 | 72 |
| 10:16-23 | 76 |
| 12:4-11 | 113 n. 82 |
| 12:18-24 | 76 |

James
| 1:1 | 114 |
| 1:2-4 | 113 n. 82 |
| 1:10-11 | 11 n. 21 |
| 2:21 | 11 n. 21 |
| 2:23 | 11 n. 21 |

1 Peter
| 1:6-7 | 113 n. 82 |
| 1:13-2:10 | 122 |
| 1:17-19 | 76 |
| 1:18 | 76 n. 134 |
| 1:18-19 | 98, 122 n. 120 |
| 1:19 | 121, 122, 122 n. 120, 133, 168 |
| 2:5 | 122 |
| 2:9 | 76, 99 n. 20, 103 n. 37 |
| 2:9-20 | 114, 171 |
| 2:11 | 76 |
| 3:13-4:19 | 113 n. 82 |

2 Peter
| 2:8 | 128 n. 10 |

1 John
| 1:7 | 99, 99 n. 15 |
| 2:2 | 99 n. 15 |
| 3:5 | 99 n. 15 |

Jude
| 9 | 71 |

Revelation
| 1 | 118, 143, 146 n. 71 |
| 1-11 | 126 n. 1 |
| 1:1 | 1 n. 2, 114 n. 86 |
| 1:1-8 | 149 n. 1 |
| 1:4 | 154, 157 |
| 1:5 | 98, 99 n. 15, 99 n. 17, 153, 158, 162, 165 n. 40, 175 |
| 1:5-6 | 96, 118 n. 106, 141, 168 |
| 1:6 | 79, 100 n. 21, 158, 172 |
| 1:8 | 107, 154, 157, 157 n. 27 |
| 1:9 | 150 |
| 1:9-10 | 150 n. 1 |
| 1:9-3:22 | 149 |
| 1:10 | 143 |
| 1:10-17 | 4 |
| 1:12 | 140 n. 52 |
| 1:12-16 | 139 |
| 1:13 | 139, 146 |
| 1:14 | 105, 133 n. 25 |
| 1:15 | 92 n. 47 |
| 1:17 | 146 |
| 1:17-18 | 146 |
| 2-3 | 149, 152 |
| 2:3-5 | 161 |
| 2:7 | 106 |
| 2:9-10 | 161 |
| 2:13-17 | 161 |
| 2:17 | 133 |
| 2:18 | 105 |
| 2:19-26 | 161 |
| 2:20 | 114 n. 86 |
| 2:23 | 89 |
| 3:3 | 86 n. 24 |
| 3:3-5 | 161 |
| 3:4 | 133 n. 25 |
| 3:5 | 133 n. 25 |
| 3:7 | 107 n. 55 |
| 3:8-12 | 161 |
| 3:12 | 155, 155 n. 19 |
| 3:14 | 107 n. 55 |
| 3:18 | 133 n. 25 |
| 3:19-21 | 161 |
| 3:20 | 105 n. 48 |
| 3:21 | 106 |
| 4 | 118 |
| 4-5 | 96, 149, 154 |
| 4:1-2 | 150 n. 1 |
| 4:1-16:21 | 149 |
| 4:5 | 105, 143 |
| 4:5-6 | 105 n. 45 |
| 4:6 | 104, 104 n. 40, 105, 105 n. 45 |
| 4:8 | 107, 154, 157 |
| 4:9-10 | 97 |
| 5 | 95-100, 172 |
| 5:1-4 | 111 |
| 5:4 | 96 |

| | | | |
|---|---|---|---|
| 5:5 | 115, 121 | | 115, 118, 118 n. 106, 120, 133, 133 n. 25, 133 n. 27, 158 |
| 5:5-6 | 106, 118 n. 105 | | |
| 5:5-10 | 110 | 7:14-15 | 161 |
| 5:5-14 | 115 | 7:14-17 | 136 |
| 5:6 | 65 n. 85, 96, 96 n. 1, 97, 104 n. 40, 115, 117, 117 n. 105, 120, 121, 154 | 7:15 | 133 n. 27, 134, 137 |
| | | 7:15-17 | 134 |
| | | 7:16-17 | 120, 134, 134 n. 31 |
| 5:6-10 | 79, 173 | 7:17 | 96 n. 1, 120, 135 n. 32 |
| 5:6-14 | 96 | 8 | 125 |
| 5:7 | 97 | 8-9 | 149, 167, 173 |
| 5:8 | 96, 96 n. 1, 120 | 8:1 | 120 |
| 5:8-9 | 104 n. 40 | 8:1-5 | 86 n. 25 |
| 5:9 | 92 n. 47, 96, 97, 97 n. 8, 98, 99 n. 15, 101 n. 26, 108 n. 60, 120, 122 n. 120, 158 | 8:2 | 103 n. 34 |
| | | 8:3-4 | 103 n. 34 |
| | | 8:5 | 82 n. 7, 103 n. 34, 143 |
| 5:9-10 | 96, 100, 118 n. 106, 141, 175 | 8:5-8 | 105 |
| 5:10 | 79, 99, 100 n. 21, 118 n. 105, 120, 158, 168, 172 | 8:6 | 103 n. 34 |
| | | 8:6-9:21 | 80, 167 |
| | | 8:7 | 82, 89, 89 n. 37, 103 n. 34, 112, 118 n. 106 |
| 5:12 | 96 n. 1, 97 n. 8 | | |
| 5:12-13 | 120 | 8:7-11 | 112 |
| 5:13 | 96 n. 1, 117 n. 105 | 8:7-12 | 82 n. 7 |
| 6:1 | 96 n. 1, 120 | 8:7-9:21 | 4, 79 |
| 6:1-17 | 93 | 8:8 | 83, 104 n. 40, 112, 118 n. 106 |
| 6:6 | 104 n. 40 | 8:8-9 | 82-87, 89-91 |
| 6:8 | 82 n. 7 | 8:9 | 84 |
| 6:9 | 86 n. 25 | 8:10-11 | 84 |
| 6:9-11 | 92 n. 47 | 8:11 | 84, 89, 90 |
| 6:10 | 89 n. 35, 94, 107 n. 55, 118 n. 106, 118 n. 106 | 8:12 | 84, 90 n. 39 |
| | | 8:15 | 82 n. 7 |
| 6:11 | 114 n. 86, 133 n. 25 | 8:18 | 82 n. 7 |
| 6:12 | 118 n. 106 | 9 | 85 |
| 6:16 | 96 n. 1, 120 | 9-17 | 136 |
| 6:17 | 107 n. 55 | 9:1-11 | 90 |
| 7 | 51 n. 27, 101 n. 26, 112, 115, 117, 118, 133, 135, 136, 149, 158, 173, 174 | 9:2-5 | 85 |
| | | 9:4 | 90, 113, 113 n. 81, 157, 158 |
| | | 9:5-6 | 9 |
| 7:1 | 86, 86 n. 25, 105 n. 48, 112 | 9:13-21 | 85, 86 |
| 7:1-4 | 110 | 9:14 | 85 |
| 7:1-8 | 79, 110-113, 125, 133, 136 | 9:14-15 | 86, 86 n. 25 |
| 7:1-17 | 4 | 9:15-19 | 85 |
| 7:2 | 112 | 9:17 | 85 |
| 7:2-8 | 92 n. 47 | 9:20-21 | 85, 157 |
| 7:3 | 110, 112, 114, 116 | 10 | 143 |
| 7:4 | 120 | 10:1 | 105, 143 |
| 7:5-8 | 113, 114 | 10:5 | 105 n. 48 |
| 7:9 | 92 n. 47, 96 n. 1, 108 n. 60, 115, 133 n. 25 | 10:7 | 114 n. 86, 143 n. 63 |
| | | 10:8 | 105 n. 48 |
| 7:9-10 | 120, 172 | 10:11 | 108 n. 60 |
| 7:9-17 | 64 n. 79, 79, 113, 113 n. 83, 115, 118 n. 106, 132-136, 141 | 11 | 80, 138 n. 46 |
| | | 11:1-11 | 118 |
| 7:10 | 96 n. 1 | 11:2 | 108 n. 60, 129 n. 16 |
| 7:12 | 136 | 11:5 | 105 |
| 7:13 | 133 n. 25 | 11:6 | 80, 81, 118 n. 106 |
| 7:13-14 | 92 n. 47 | 11:7 | 81, 104 n. 41 |
| 7:14 | 96 n. 1, 99, 101 n. 26, 105, 110, | | |

# Index

| | | | |
|---|---|---|---|
| 11:8 | 81, 114 n. 86 | 14:1 | 96 n. 1, 105 n. 48, 118, 120, 133, 155 |
| 11:9 | 92 n. 47, 108 n. 60 | 14:1-5 | 105, 136 n. 38 |
| 11:11 | 105 n. 48 | 14:2-3 | 104 n. 40 |
| 11:15-19 | 79 | 14:3 | 118, 133 |
| 11:17 | 107, 154, 157 | 14:3-4 | 115 |
| 11:18 | 108 n. 60 | 14:4 | 113 n. 83, 120 |
| 11:19 | 82 n. 7, 87, 138, 141, 144 | 14:6 | 92 n. 47, 108 n. 60 |
| 12 | 79, 125-132, 141, 165, 174 | 14:7 | 104 |
| 12:1-2 | 103, 127 | 14:8 | 108 n. 60 |
| 12:1-6 | 127, 130, 131 | 14:9 | 155 |
| 12:1-17 | 4 | 14:9-10 | 120, 161 |
| 12:1-13:8 | 126 n. 1 | 14:9-11 | 114 |
| 12:3 | 103, 128 | 14:10 | 96 n. 1 |
| 12:3-4 | 128, 130 | 14:10-11 | 155 |
| 12:4 | 128 | 14:12 | 161 |
| 12:5 | 109, 129, 130 | 14:12-13 | 106 |
| 12:6 | 127, 129, 129 n. 16, 132, 159, 165, 165 n. 41 | 14:20 | 118 n. 106 |
| 12:7-12 | 127, 130, 132 | 15 | 103, 103 n. 34, 104 n. 39, 138, 140, 157, 165 n. 39, 173 |
| 12:8-9 | 130 | 15:1 | 80, 103 n. 34, 103 n. 36, 103 n. 37, 104 n. 39, 107, 125, 139 |
| 12:9 | 130, 131, 153, 162 | | |
| 12:10 | 131 | 15:1-4 | 103-110, 125, 138 |
| 12:10-11 | 120 | 15:1-8 | 4, 79 |
| 12:10-12 | 131 | 15:1-16:21 | 103 |
| 12:11 | 96 n. 1, 106, 110, 115, 118 n. 106, 158, 161 | 15:2 | 104, 105, 105 n. 46, 120, 136 n. 38 |
| 12:11-12 | 131 | 15:2-4 | 103 n. 34 |
| 12:12 | 104 n. 41, 132 | 15:3 | 96 n. 1, 103, 103 n. 37, 106, 107, 108, 109, 164 |
| 12:13-17 | 127, 129 | | |
| 12:14 | 129 n. 16, 131, 131 n. 22, 159 | 15:3-4 | 106, 106 n. 51, 120, 154, 154 n. 14 |
| 12:15-17 | 112 n. 79 | | |
| 12:16 | 132 | 15:4 | 108, 108 n. 60 |
| 12:17 | 106, 132 | 15:5 | 103 n. 36, 138, 139 |
| 12:18 | 104 n. 41, 105 n. 48 | 15:5-7 | 103 n. 34 |
| 13 | 105 n. 47 | 15:5-8 | 125, 138-140, 141 |
| 13:1 | 104 n. 41, 105 n. 47 | 15:5-16:21 | 109 |
| 13:3 | 154 | 15:6 | 80, 138, 139 |
| 13:4 | 68 n. 97, 153 n. 14, 154 | 15:7-8 | 140 |
| 13:4-8 | 161 | 15:8 | 80, 103 n. 34, 138 |
| 13:7 | 92 n. 47 | 16 | 82-87, 89-91, 103, 103 n. 34, 110, 125, 149, 165 n. 39, 167, 173 |
| 13:7-8 | 120 | | |
| 13:8 | 96 n. 1, 97 n. 8, 158 | 16:1 | 103 n. 34 |
| 13:11 | 96 n. 1, 105 n. 47, 154 | 16:1-21 | 4, 79, 80, 138, 167 |
| 13:11-14 | 120 | 16:2 | 82 n. 7, 89, 155, 157 |
| 13:11-18 | 112 n. 79 | 16:3 | 82 n. 7, 83, 89, 118 n. 106 |
| 13:12 | 154 | 16:3-7 | 89 |
| 13:12-14 | 154 | 16:4 | 83, 118 n. 106 |
| 13:13 | 154 | 16:4-6 | 89, 90 |
| 13:14 | 154, 154 n. 16 | 16:5 | 107 n. 55, 109, 154, 157 |
| 13:14-15 | 154, 155 n. 19 | 16:5-6 | 84, 118 n. 106 |
| 13:14-17 | 155 | 16:6 | 89, 118 n. 106, 157 |
| 13:15 | 151 | 16:7 | 107, 107 n. 55 |
| 13:16-17 | 114, 155 | 16:8-9 | 85 |
| 13:17 | 155, 159 | 16:9 | 80, 85, 157 |
| 14 | 112 | | |

| | | | |
|---|---|---|---|
| 16:10 | 82 n. 7, 157 | 21:3 | 15, 28 n. 20, 134, 147 n. 73, 158, 172 |
| 16:10-11 | 84, 89, 90 | 21:3-7 | 160 |
| 16:11 | 157 | 21:4 | 15, 172 |
| 16:12 | 83, 85, 86 n. 22, 164, 167 | 21:6 | 15, 133 |
| 16:12-16 | 85 | 21:7 | 15 |
| 16:13 | 153, 154 | 21:8 | 108 n. 60, 144, 159 |
| 16:13-14 | 85, 112 n. 79 | 21:8-25 | 4 |
| 16:14 | 86, 107, 153 n. 12 | 21:9 | 80, 96 n. 1, 120 |
| 16:15 | 86 | 21:9-10 | 150 n. 1 |
| 16:16 | 167 | 21:9-22:5 | 149 |
| 16:17-21 | 82 n. 7, 144 | 21:10 | 144 |
| 16:18 | 82 n. 7, 87 | 21:10-11 | 147 n. 73 |
| 16:19 | 108 n. 60 | 21:10-21 | 144 |
| 16:21 | 80, 82 n. 7, 87 | 21:11 | 104 n. 44 |
| 17 | 128 | 21:14 | 96 n. 1 |
| 17-18 | 118 n. 109 | 21:18 | 104 n. 44 |
| 17-19 | 149 | 21:18-20 | 142 n. 59 |
| 17:1-3 | 150 n. 1 | 21:18-21 | 142 |
| 17:1-21:8 | 149 | 21:21 | 104 n. 44 |
| 17:6 | 118 n. 106 | 21:22 | 96 n. 1, 107, 120, 147 |
| 17:8 | 154 | 21:22-26 | 158 |
| 17:10-14 | 161 | 21:23 | 15, 96 n. 1, 120 |
| 17:14 | 96 n. 1, 120 | 21:23-25 | 92 n. 47 |
| 18:3 | 108 n. 60 | 21:25 | 15 |
| 18:4 | 80, 135 n. 33 | 21:27 | 15, 96 n. 1, 108 n. 60, 159, 172 |
| 18:5 | 135 n. 33 | 22 | 112 |
| 18:24 | 118 n. 106 | 22:1 | 15, 96 n. 1, 104 n. 44, 120 |
| 19:1 | 92 n. 47 | 22:1-5 | 158 |
| 19:1-5 | 161 | 22:3 | 15, 96 n. 1, 114 n. 86, 120, 172 |
| 19:2 | 107 n. 55, 107 n. 55, 114 n. 86, 118 n. 106, 159 | 22:3-4 | 15, 146, 172 |
| 19:5 | 114 n. 86 | 22:3-5 | 160 |
| 19:6 | 107, 143 | 22:4 | 15, 142, 172 |
| 19:7 | 96 n. 1, 158 | 22:5 | 15, 100 n. 21, 120, 142, 155, 172 |
| 19:7-8 | 133 n. 27 | 22:6 | 114 n. 86 |
| 19:9 | 96 n. 1, 158 | 22:6-21 | 149 n. 1 |
| 19:10 | 114 n. 86 | 22:7 | 165 |
| 19:11 | 107 n. 55, 133 n. 25, 143 | 22:9 | 114 n. 86 |
| 19:13 | 118 n. 106 | 22:10 | 111 n. 74 |
| 19:14 | 133 n. 25 | 22:12 | 165 |
| 19:15 | 107, 108 n. 60 | 22:14 | 15, 99, 133 n. 27, 160, 172 |
| 19:20 | 153 | 22:15 | 108 n. 60, 144 n. 65, 159 |
| 20:2 | 130 | 22:17 | 133 |
| 20:2-3 | 111 n. 75 | 22:18 | 80 |
| 20:4 | 151, 155 | | |
| 20:4-6 | 160 | | |
| 20:6 | 100 n. 21, 120, 141, 168, 172 | **Additional Texts** | |
| 20:10 | 15, 172 | | |
| 20:11 | 133 n. 25 | 1 Enoch | |
| 20:13 | 104 n. 41 | 80:2-7 | 91 n. 44 |
| 20:15 | 158 | 89-90 | 121 n. 116 |
| 21 | 52 n. 27 | 96:2 | 131 n. 22 |
| 21-22 | 14, 15, 79, 149 | 99:4 | 91 n. 44 |
| 21:1 | 15, 104 n. 41 | 99:5 | 91 n. 44 |
| | | 99:8 | 91 n. 44 |

*Index*

2 Baruch
   27:10        92

3 Maccabees
   2:6         67
   2:29       111

Antiquities of the Jews
   2.312       102

Apocalypse of Abraham
   29:14-16   92
   30:2-31:1   92
   30:4-31:1   91 n. 44
   30:6       92

Assumption of Moses
   10:4-6     91 n. 44
   10:8       131 n. 22

Damascus Document (CD)
   VII, 5      67

Jubilees
   15:26      112 n. 76
   23:13      91 n. 44
   49:7-8     101

Pirqe Rabbi Eliezer
   29         101
   42         127

Psalms of Solomon
   2:29-30    128 n. 11

Rule of Community Scroll (1QS)
   II, 9       68
   II, 11-12   68
   IV, 23     68
   V, 1-3     68
   V, 21-23   68
   VII, 2     67

Sibylline Oracles
   3.330-336   91 n. 44
   3.530-544   91 n. 44
   3.672-701   91 n. 44
   4.173-178   91 n. 44
   5:377-378   92
   5:454      93

Testament of Benjamin
   3:8        121 n. 116

Testament of Joseph
   9:3        121 n. 116
   19:8      121 n. 116

War Scroll (1QM)
   I, 9-11    84
   XI, 9-10   68
   XII, 13    68
   XIII, 7-9  68
   XV, 1-2    68 n. 96

www.ingramcontent.com/pod-product-compliance
Lightning Source LLC
Chambersburg PA
CBHW072005110526
44592CB00012B/1208